W9-CGN-924

044 005 825 161

AFRICAN SUCCESSES

African Successes

*Four Public Managers of
Kenyan Rural Development*

David K. Leonard

UNIVERSITY OF CALIFORNIA PRESS
Berkeley   Los Angeles   Oxford

HC 865 .L46 1991
Leonard, David K.
African successes

AKH 9329-9/5

University of California Press
Berkeley and Los Angeles, California
University of California Press, Ltd.
Oxford, England
© 1991 by
The Regents of the University of California

Library of Congress Cataloging-in-Publication Data

Leonard, David K.
    African successes : four public managers of Kenyan rural
development / David K. Leonard.
        p.   cm.
    Includes bibliographical references and index.
    ISBN 0-520-07075-5 (cloth : alk. paper)
    ISBN 0-520-07076-3 (pbk: alk. paper)
    1. Kenya—Economic policy.   2. Rural development—Kenya.
3. Kenya—Politics and government—1963–1978.   4. Kenya—Politics
and government—1978–   5. Management—Kenya.   I. Title.
HC865.L46   1991
338.96762—dc20   90-11089
                                                               CIP

Printed in the United States of America
1 2 3 4 5 6 7 8 9

The paper used in this publication meets the minimum requirements of American
National Standard for Information Sciences—Permanence of Paper for Printed
Library Materials, ANSI Z39.48-1984 ∞

RECEIVED

MAY 1 8 1992

Kennedy School
Library

To

Al and Agnes Hay,
retired from Westtown School

Alfred Diamant,
once at Haverford College

and

Aristide Zolberg,
formerly of the University of Chicago

Their teaching shaped this book.

CONTENTS

LIST OF ILLUSTRATIONS

LIST OF TABLES

PREFACE

This book addresses themes of concern to several different audiences. At a first level this book is about management in conditions of adversity. It is well known that most public endeavors in Africa have not been well managed. Among these, rural development efforts have fared the worst of all.[1] But some have done quite well. Why were some African public servants able to succeed in their managerial tasks when so many others were failing? We will find answers in the biographies of four Kenyan administrators.

At a second level we are concerned here with why Kenya has done reasonably well in its rural development endeavors when most of Africa is doing abysmally. This and the preceding question will enable us to learn from success and to indicate how African states and managers might be able to regenerate the continent's developmental dynamic.

Third, we are interested in the nature and evolution of the Kenyan state. How does its government work? How are its decisions made and implemented, particularly those concerned with rural development? How are the economic, social, and political processes of its society mediated through the governmental structure? What have been the processes of institutional change? It is common to look at political systems through the lenses of their presidents, legislatures, or political parties. We look at them here through the lens of their bureaucracies. It is particularly useful to take this perspective in Kenya, for civil servants there play an unusually public role in policy-making.

These three highly complementary themes make this book of interest to a number of different audiences: generalists seeking to understand African government, development professionals hoping to promote economic and social progress, organization theorists, and managers.

These audiences in turn may be divided into those who are new to their area of inquiry and those who are far advanced in it. And finally, there are both those in Kenya and those abroad who are seeking answers to these questions.

Normally, it would be dangerous to try to write for so many different audiences. But in this case it seems more than feasible, because the multiple arguments are all grounded in a common body of evidence that has universal appeal—the life stories of four successful public servants. I believe that this human dimension gives extra life and insight to the social science that is developed in this book.

The major points of interest to each of these sets of readers are addressed without compromising their complexity. But to make sure that all of these audiences can follow the book's multiple arguments, I have continually asked myself if these points would be intelligible to someone new to development administration and to Africa. Other readers may find that there is extra material in the book that is designed to keep the interest and understanding of nonspecialist audiences, and they therefore will find passages that they may wish only to skim.

More seriously, this is a cross-cultural book. It is written for American, European, and African audiences alike. Leo Strauss used to argue that different cultural settings require the expression of different ideas in different forms.* I have tried hard to be culturally sensitive, and I ask my readers to understand some of my narrative decisions in that light.

Berkeley, California
January 1990

*Leo Strauss, *Persecution and the Art of Writing* (Westport, Conn.: Greenwood Press, 1952, 1973). Please see pp. 25, 30, and 36.

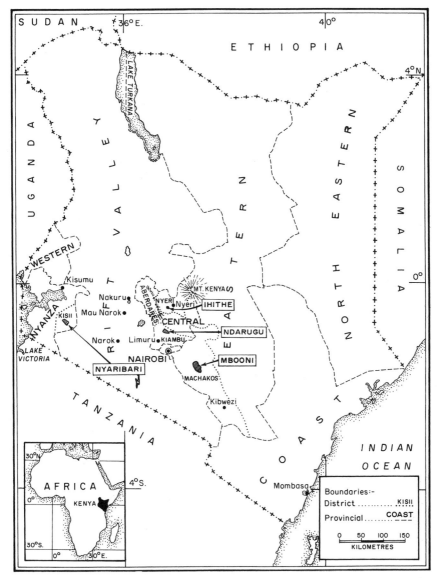

Map 1. The Birthplaces of the Administrators Studied. Ihithe: Ishmael Muriithi and Dan Mbogo; Mbooni: Harris Mule; Ndarugu: Charles Karanja; Nyaribari: Simeon Nyachae.

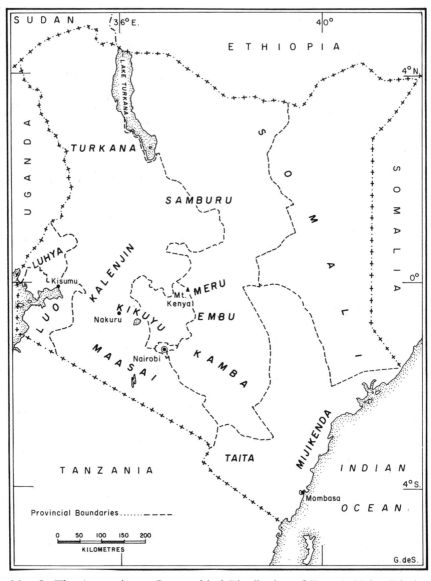

Map 2. The Approximate Geographical Distribution of Kenya's Major Ethnic Groups

ABBREVIATIONS
AND GLOSSARY

AI	Artificial insemination
AIC	African Inland Church
AIM	African Inland Mission
ASAL	Arid and Semi-Arid Lands program
CAIS	Central Artificial Insemination Station
CBK	Cooperative Bank of Kenya
CDC	Commonwealth Development Corporation
DC	District commissioner
DDC	District Development Committee
DDO	District development officer
DVO	District veterinary officer
EEC	European Economic Community
GEMA	Gikuyu, Embu, Meru Association
IADP	Integrated Agricultural Development Project
ILO	International Labor Organization
ILRAD	International Laboratory for Research on Animal Disease
IMF	International Monetary Fund
KADU	Kenyan African Democratic Union
KANU	Kenyan African National Union
KAU	Kenyan African Union
KCC	Kenya Cooperative Creameries
KDB	Kenya Dairy Board
KETEPA	Kenya Tea Packers, Ltd.

KPU	Kenya People's Union
KTDA	Kenya Tea Development Authority
K.shs.	Kenya shillings
MADO	Maasai Agricultural Development Organization
MIDP	Machakos Integrated Development Program
MIS	Management information system
M.P.	Member of Parliament
NCPB	National Cereals and Produce Board
OPEC	Organization of Petroleum Exporting Countries
PC	Provincial commissioner
PCEA	Presbyterian Church of East Africa
PS	Permanent secretary
RDF	Rural Development Fund
SRDP	Special Rural Development Program

harambee	self-help
majimbo	regionalism
matajiri	well-to-do

ABBREVIATED CHRONOLOGY OF
POLITICAL EVENTS IN KENYA

1895   Establishment of a British protectorate over Kenya.

1901   Completion of the Uganda Railway (through Kenya).

1922   The "Harry Thuku riots" mark the beginning of modern nationalist protest.

1924   Formation of the Kikuyu Central Association.

1944   Formation of the Kenyan African Union (KAU).

1952   Declaration of a state of emergency in response to the Mau Mau uprising.

1954   Lyttelton Constitution provides for limited participation of elected Africans in the Kenya government.

1960   Lancaster House Conference accepts principle of majority rule and ultimate independence for Kenya.

Formation of Kenyan African National Union (KANU) and Kenyan African Democratic Union (KADU).

1961   KADU forms a government with white liberals.

Kenyatta is released from detention.

1962   KADU and KANU form a coalition government.

1963   (June 1) Kenya becomes independent under the "Majimbo" constitution with Kenyatta as prime minister.

1964   Voluntary dissolution of KADU and emergence of a de facto one-party state.

(December 12) Kenya becomes a republic with a unitary constitution and with Kenyatta as president.

1966   Formation of the Kenya People's Union (KPU).

"Little General Election."

1969   Assassination of Tom Mboya.

Reestablishment of a de facto one-party state.

1975   Assassination of J. M. Kariuki.

1976   The movement to change the constitution.

1978   Death of President Kenyatta and succession of Daniel arap Moi to the presidency.

1982   Coup attempt by the air force.

1989   Minister of Finance Saitoti becomes vice-president after Joseph Karanja's brief tenure in the office.

LIST OF PRINCIPAL PERSONS
IN THE BOOK

(alphabetical by surname)

Pauline BOSIBORI: Wife of Musa Nyandusi; mother of Simeon Nyachae

Joseph IVITA: Cofounder of Catholic church in Kilungu Location, Machakos District; grandfather of Martha Ngina Mule

Ruth KATUKU: Wife of Philip Mule; mother of Harris Mule

Jackson KAMAU: Chairman of the KTDA and business associate of Charles Karanja

Charles Kibe KARANJA: General manager of the KTDA during the 1970s; son of Karanja wa Kiarii and Njeri (Nyagitiri) Karanja

Njeri (Nyagitiri) KARANJA: Mother of Charles Karanja

Philomena Ndanga KARANJA: Wife of Charles Karanja

KARANJA wa Kiarii: Prosperous farmer in Kiambu District; father of Charles Karanja

Geoffrey KARIITHI: Head of the civil service under President Kenyatta in the 1970s

Jomo KENYATTA: First president of Kenya

KIARII wa Wanjema: Grandfather of Charles Karanja

Mwai KIBAKI: Minister of finance under President Kenyatta; vice-president under President Moi

Mbiyu KOINANGE: Minister of state in the Office of the President and confidant of Kenyatta

Dan MBOGO: Assistant director of livestock development in charge of artificial insemination; brother of Ishmael Muriithi

Tom MBOYA: Trade unionist and leader in independence struggle; early secretary general of KANU; key cabinet minister under Kenyatta; assassinated in 1969

Daniel arap MOI: Second president of Kenya

Harris MULE: Chief economist and deputy permanent secretary for planning under President Kenyatta; permanent secretary for the Ministry of Finance under President Moi; son of Philip Mule and Ruth Katuku

Martha Ngina MULE: Wife of Harris Mule; granddaughter of Joseph Ivita

Philip MULE: Former president of the African Tribunal Court for Southern Machakos District; father of Harris Mule

Ishmael MURIITHI: Director of veterinary services under Presidents Kenyatta and Moi; son of Elijah Waicanguru and Lydia Wangeci

Martha Wangui Munene MURIITHI: Wife of Ishmael Muriithi

Philip NDEGWA: Principal secretary to the Ministry of Finance under President Kenyatta; governor of the Central Bank under President Moi

Charles NJONJO: Attorney general under Presidents Kenyatta and Moi

Druscilla Kerubo NYACHAE: Second wife of Simeon Nyachae

Esther Nyaboke NYACHAE: First wife of Simeon Nyachae

Grace Wamuyu NYACHAE: Fifth wife of Simeon Nyachae

Martha Mwango NYACHAE: Third wife of Simeon Nyachae; sister of Lawrence Sagini

Simeon NYACHAE: Provincial commissioner under President Kenyatta; chief secretary under President Moi; son of Musa Nyandusi and Pauline Bosibori

Sylvia NYACHAE: Fourth wife of Simeon Nyachae; sister of Jane Kiano, wife of Gikonyo Kiano, prominent Kikuyu cabinet minister throughout the Kenyatta years

Musa NYANDUSI: Former senior chief of Nyaribari Location, Kisii District; father of Simeon Nyachae

Oginga ODINGA: Luo leader of independence struggle in Nyanza Province; first vice-president of Kenya; founder of KPU

Lawrence SAGINI: First member of Parliament from Kisii District; brother of Martha Mwango Nyachae

Elijah WAICANGURU: Former elder (judge) of the African Tribunal court for Tetu Division, Nyeri District; father of Ishmael Muriithi and Dan Mbogo

Lydia WANGECI: Wife of Elijah Waicanguru; mother of Ishmael Muriithi and Dan Mbogo

SIMPLIFIED FAMILY TREES
OF THE ADMINISTRATORS STUDIED

KARANJA FAMILY

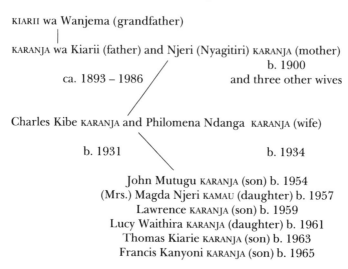

KIARII wa Wanjema (grandfather)

KARANJA wa Kiarii (father) and Njeri (Nyagitiri) KARANJA (mother)
b. 1900
ca. 1893 – 1986 and three other wives

Charles Kibe KARANJA and Philomena Ndanga KARANJA (wife)

b. 1931 b. 1934

John Mutugu KARANJA (son) b. 1954
(Mrs.) Magda Njeri KAMAU (daughter) b. 1957
Lawrence KARANJA (son) b. 1959
Lucy Waithira KARANJA (daughter) b. 1961
Thomas Kiarie KARANJA (son) b. 1963
Francis Kanyoni KARANJA (son) b. 1965

MULE FAMILY

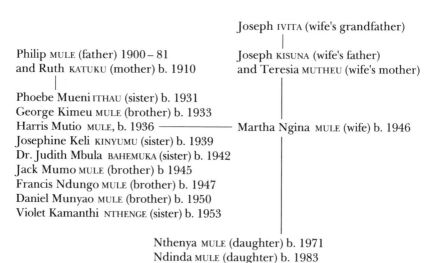

Joseph IVITA (wife's grandfather)

Philip MULE (father) 1900 – 81   Joseph KISUNA (wife's father)
and Ruth KATUKU (mother) b. 1910   and Teresia MUTHEU (wife's mother)

Phoebe Mueni ITHAU (sister) b. 1931
George Kimeu MULE (brother) b. 1933
Harris Mutio MULE, b. 1936 ——————— Martha Ngina MULE (wife) b. 1946
Josephine Keli KINYUMU (sister) b. 1939
Dr. Judith Mbula BAHEMUKA (sister) b. 1942
Jack Mumo MULE (brother) b 1945
Francis Ndungo MULE (brother) b. 1947
Daniel Munyao MULE (brother) b. 1950
Violet Kamanthi NTHENGE (sister) b. 1953

Nthenya MULE (daughter) b. 1971
Ndinda MULE (daughter) b. 1983

MURIITHI FAMILY

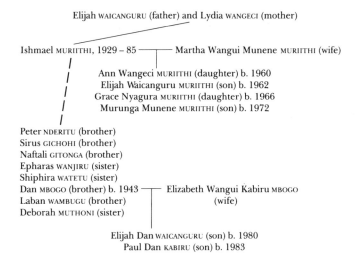

Elijah WAICANGURU (father) and Lydia WANGECI (mother)

Ishmael MURIITHI, 1929 – 85 ———— Martha Wangui Munene MURIITHI (wife)

Ann Wangeci MURIITHI (daughter) b. 1960
Elijah Waicanguru MURIITHI (son) b. 1962
Grace Nyagura MURIITHI (daughter) b. 1966
Murunga Munene MURIITHI (son) b. 1972

Peter NDERITU (brother)
Sirus GICHOHI (brother)
Naftali GITONGA (brother)
Epharas WANJIRU (sister)
Shiphira WATETU (sister)
Dan MBOGO (brother) b. 1943 ———— Elizabeth Wangui Kabiru MBOGO
Laban WAMBUGU (brother)   (wife)
Deborah MUTHONI (sister)

Elijah Dan WAICANGURU (son) b. 1980
Paul Dan KABIRU (son) b. 1983

NYACHAE FAMILY*

Musa NYANDUSI (father) and Pauline BOSIBORI (mother) b. ca. 1910
   ca. 1895 – 1970   and multiple other wives

James OIRURIA (brother) b. 1930
Simeon NYACHAE, b. 1932 — and Esther Nyaboke NYACHAE (first wife) b. 1937

Grace Rosemary NYACHAE (daughter) b. 1954
and several other children

and Druscilla Kerubo NYACHAE (second wife) – 1956

Mary NYACHAE (daughter) b. 1956

and Martha Mwango NYACHAE (third wife) b. 1940

Charles Ayako NYACHAE (son) b. 1958
Kenneth Bitange NYACHAE (son) b. 1959
and several other children

and Sylvia NYACHAE (divorced fourth wife)

several children

and Grace Wamuyu NYACHAE (fifth wife)

several children

*It is contrary to Gusii custom to enumerate one's children. Therefore, out of respect for the wishes of the Nyachae family, specific individuals are placed on this genealogical chart only if they are mentioned in or were interviewed for this study.

ACKNOWLEDGMENTS

I incurred many debts of gratitude as I wrote this book, the largest of which is to the men whose biographies are recounted here and to their families. Not only did they allow me to take days of their time but they endured with good humor the indignity of my cross-checking their accounts with others. Although I was not always able to write their histories in the way they might have preferred, I think they will share with me the satisfaction of seeing in print an account of their accomplishments. At the same time I want to make it clear that I did not discuss with them general matters of Kenyan politics. I am solely responsible for the facts and opinions expressed in this book, and this is especially true with regard to observations on Kenya's political system.

I want also to acknowledge the splendid help given me by the various research assistants who have worked on this project: Louise Fox, Lizz Kleemeier, Zeverino Mogaka, Catherine Akinyi Muketi, Kamene Mutambuki, Patrick Muzaale, Samwell Ngigi, Herzon Olouch, Martha Saavedra, and Fred Schaeffer. The book simply would not have been possible without their efforts.

I wish, too, to express my appreciation to the various agencies that funded this research: The United States National Science Foundation, the U.S. Fulbright program, and the Institute of International Studies of the University of California at Berkeley.

I greatly enjoyed as well the gracious hospitality of Donald and Ruth Thomas and Pheroze and Villoo Nowrojee during my field trips to Kenya. It would have been a much lonelier and less comfortable time without them.

I am grateful to those who took the time and care to read and comment on various parts of the draft manuscript: Christopher Aiken, Lou

Ann Bieging, John Cohen, Emeka Ezera, James Fearon, Barbara Grosh, Susan Hall, Bruce Johnston, Kenneth Jowitt, Todd LaPorte, Glenn Leggett, John McCarthy, Rwekaza Mukandala, Fenno Ogutu, Jesse Riebo, Emery Roe, Carl Rosberg, Stephen Peterson, Stevens Tucker, Norman Uphoff, and Makoba Wagona. Their suggestions were sharp and perceptive, and I am indebted to them.

Finally, I must express my appreciation to my wife, Leslie. She has shared my love of Africa and my belief in the importance of this project. As a result, she both joined me during my longest stays in Kenya and endured my absence when I had to do field work without her. She also has been understanding when my writing has fallen behind schedule. Few wives would have been willing to sacrifice so much so graciously.

CHAPTER ONE

Introduction:
Individuals, Institutions, and Interests

AN EXAMPLE OF SUCCESSFUL MANAGEMENT

In 1973 Charles Karanja beat the odds. As general manager of the Kenya Tea Development Authority (KTDA), he took on the World Bank, the multinational tea corporations, and Kenya's Ministry of Agriculture. What's more, he won. At that time the KTDA had already started to acquire a reputation as one of the world's greatest success stories in rural development.[1] Begun in the waning days of colonialism in the late 1950s, the KTDA had succeeded in integrating African small farmers into tea production. Previously, tea had been the exclusive preserve of large estates, and earlier attempts in Asia to involve smallholders in its growth had failed. In 1973 the KTDA was already launched on a trajectory of expansion and quality control that today enables it to produce half of Kenya's tea and to command 5 percent of the world market.[2] In the process it has led Kenya to rank as the world's top producer of quality tea,[3] and it has become probably the world's largest tea corporation.

When Charles Karanja took over as general manager of the KTDA in 1970, the Authority was involved almost exclusively in agricultural extension and the collection of green tea leaf. The international marketing and the critical processing (or manufacturing) of the tea were then done for the KTDA by several multinational tea firms. Karanja wanted these functions performed directly by the KTDA, thereby expanding Kenyan control of this sector of the economy and facilitating the placement of Africans as tea-factory managers. Without much difficulty he persuaded the Kenyans on his board of directors of the wisdom of his proposal. But the multinationals, the Commonwealth Develop-

1

ment Corporation (CDC), and the World Bank did not agree, arguing that these functions were extremely demanding technically and that hasty nationalization and Africanization might jeopardize the viability of the entire small-farmer tea initiative. As the CDC and the World Bank were the major financiers of KTDA's growth, they effectively had acquired the right to veto such major shifts in policy.

The dispute was carried to the Ministry of Agriculture. There, two of the big names in Kenyan politics and administration, Jeremiah Nyagah as minister and Joseph Kibe as permanent secretary, sided with the CDC and the Bank. Under the rules of the game the matter should have ended there.

But Karanja would not be stopped. He used his contacts among the president's personal advisers and took the chairman of his board with him for an interview with Jomo Kenyatta. There, Karanja told President Kenyatta that African tea growers were grateful to the president for having fought for their right to grow the crop and that the KTDA ought to have the right to process and market the tea as well. Karanja then remarked that if he failed to oversee successfully the KTDA's assumption of these functions he wished to be dismissed.

Kenyatta then turned to Nyagah, his minister of agriculture, said he had a high regard for Karanja, and gave his personal approval for the KTDA's assumption of the new functions. Kenyatta added that if Karanja failed in this new endeavor he would be sacked. This single interview gave high government backing to Karanja's ambitions, and so the CDC and the World Bank backed down.

The KTDA actually managed these new functions well; the policy was a success. How and why was Charles Karanja able to score a coup in this policy dispute? How did he manage the KTDA so that it handled successfully these technically demanding new functions when the World Bank's experts and the multinationals were predicting failure? These are specific versions of the larger, more general issues to be explored.

WHY THIS BOOK?

This study addresses three major sets of questions: (1) Why is it that some African managers are effective while others—a far larger number—fail, and what can we learn from their successes and failures? (2) What factors have enabled Kenya to promote agriculture relatively successfully when food deficits plague most of Africa? (3) How has the nature and evolution of the Kenyan state affected its rural-development policies and their implementation? These questions have great importance for Africa. Their answers require an understanding of the interaction of individuals, institutions, and interests.

Successful Managers

Africa is in a development crisis. Its national economies have not grown, standards of living have fallen, agricultural production has not kept up with population growth, and hunger stalks the land. The first concern of this inquiry is with effective Kenyan management in this adverse administrative context, an issue of central importance to the study of administrative behavior in all of Africa. International donor officials and academics alike have been pessimistic recently about the ability of African civil servants to administer public development programs. They point to the strong ties of social obligation that African elites have to the countryside and to the patterns of patronage, nepotism, and corruption that have resulted from them. They see a public service that rarely accomplishes its intended objectives and instead sometimes appears to exist primarily to extract surplus from the rest of society. The picture they paint of the continent's government organizations and their employees is depressingly bad. Those who take this contextual approach assert that African social forces create a distinctive type of administrative behavior that is not amenable to Western solutions.[4]*

The "contextual" case has to be qualified in several important respects. First, it implicitly discounts the importance of the larger environment of African development. International economic conditions have not been especially favorable to Africa since the 1950s and are particularly harsh now with the global debt crisis. Throughout the developing world many well-run enterprises, both public and private, have failed because of the crisis. If it is true that Africa has fared worse in the world economy than have most other nonindustrial societies, some of the problem lies in the series of droughts that have ravaged the continent.

Second, many of the problems of Africa's management are related directly to the stage of its economic development. A recent systematic review of the World Bank's experience found that the most important determinant of the success of a project was not the country where it was implemented but the type of project undertaken. Industrial and telecommunications projects, for example, tended to do well everywhere. Agricultural, livestock, and rural development ventures had consistent problems, however, and represent a much higher proportion of African portfolios than they do for other regions, because of the continent's low level of economic development. Much (but not all) of the higher rate of

---

*This leaves aside the issue of the utility of Western *theory* for understanding (as opposed to improving) African administration. In *Reaching the Peasant Farmer: Organization Theory and Practice in Kenya* (Chicago: University of Chicago Press, 1977) I demonstrated that, although the contextual constraints are real enough, African administration differs in the magnitude of certain dysfunctions, not their nature. Western organizational understandings based in social-exchange theory explain them quite well.

failure of African public managers is due to their tackling inherently more difficult tasks than are commonly undertaken in other regions.[5]

Finally, some of the "contextualists" imply (perhaps unintentionally) that Africa's difficulties in the public sector are largely due to *administrative* behavior. Instead, a large number of the problems can be traced back to policy decisions that have been taken by politicians.[6]

There is still a problem, however. These qualifications to the "contextual" school are themselves contextual. They too come close to seeing effective management as impossible in Africa; they simply differ as to the reasons. Yet *some* senior African public servants *are* effective program managers, at least for some programs.[7] The Kenyan administrators we will examine have somehow beaten the odds against them and offer the continent the prospect of doing something other than wallowing in misery. They provide important clues to what does make administration work in Kenya and Africa. The search here is for the keys to their success.

Rural Development Policies

The African picture is not uniformly dismal. A few countries have done moderately well despite the inclement international economic winds that have buffeted the continent. Kenya has been one of these few. Its agriculture has prospered and fueled an expanding economy.[8] If we examine a variety of indicators of Africa's economic and agricultural health, we find that Kenya consistently ranks near the top of the list. Surely Kenyans would like to have performed better still, but they have done well. (See table 1.1.)

Agriculture is to African states what heavy industry was to the Soviet Union in the 1930s and what high technology is to the United States today—the sector upon which the future prosperity of the country and the well-being of its population ultimately depend. If Korea today rightly concentrates policy attention on the health of its automotive industry, Africa correctly focuses on rural development. Why? First, because most of its people live in the rural areas. In Kenya 81 percent of the labor force is engaged in agriculture, and 80 percent of the population is rural.[9] If the quality of rural life is poor and if agriculture fails, most Kenyans will be miserable.

Second, agriculture is important because the economic future of Africa depends on it. Almost all of today's developed countries achieved industrialization by extracting resources from agriculture for investment in the rest of the economy. If the rural areas are so poor that they have no surplus production, then transferring some of their resources to other sectors will produce starvation and potential political unrest. The population will be too impoverished to offer a mass-consumer base

TABLE 1.1
Indicators of Kenya's Economic and Agricultural Performance

Indicator	Performance	Rank Order out of (N) African States
Rate of annual overall economic growth, 1965–80	6.4%	6 (35)
Rate of per capita annual economic growth, 1965–80	2.7%	8 (35)
Rate of annual overall economic growth, 1980–86	3.4%	7 (35)
Rate of per capita annual economic growth, 1980–86	−0.67%	10 (35)
Rate of annual overall agricultural growth, 1965–80	4.9%	3 (21)
Rate of annual agricultural growth per capita, 1965–80	1.25%	5 (21)
Rate of annual overall agricultural growth, 1980–86	2.8%	5 (37)
Rate of annual agricultural growth per capita, 1980–86	−1.25%	14 (37)
Cereal imports—metric tons per million people, 1974	708	2 (37) [lowest]
Cereal imports—metric tons per million people, 1986	8,915	7 (37) [lowest]

NOTE: Malawi is the only African country that has scored in the top third on all of these indicators. Kenya follows with 9 out of 10, and Cameroon with 7.
SOURCE: Calculated from figures provided in The World Bank, *World Development Report 1988* (Washington, D.C.: The World Bank, 1988), tables 1, 2, 7.

for domestic industry, and the rest of the economy will stagnate. Agriculture, therefore, is the base on which a healthy developing economy must be built.[10] The World Bank has urged Africa to give priority attention to agriculture, and the African states with the best rates of economic growth are the ones that have done so—Kenya, Botswana, Cameroon, Malawi, Mauritius, and Zimbabwe.[11]

If policies for rural development are important to Kenya, what have they been and what factors have determined their character? A good deal has been written about the broad outline of these policies and the fundamental socioeconomic and political forces that have shaped them.[12] In this book I hope to reconcile the many and apparently conflicting determinants these studies offer—sociopolitical, culture, ethnicity, class, institutional interests, international donors, and so forth.[13] For example, I will show that class and ethnicity frequently interact with each other, both reinforcing and subtly shifting the influence of each.[14] But a full synthesis requires an understanding of the state.

The Nature and Evolution of the Kenyan State

Social forces both shape and are shaped by the state. Institutions are created in response to social and economic forces at work at one time and then take on a causative force of their own, perpetuating patterns of decision long after the socioeconomic forces that started them have changed.[15] The examination of the formation and development of the state is essentially an analysis of such institutional evolution. One of the purposes of this book is to elucidate these subtle interactions and to show how they have created a favorable environment for agricultural development in Kenya.

Recent theoretical developments in political science have stressed the autonomy of the state as a causative force in society.[16] Some of this autonomy reflects the idiosyncracies of political leaders. But most of it comes from the lag effects of institutions. One of the most important manifestations of the state's institutional heritage is its administrative apparatus. Thus we must understand how the civil service works. The literature on comparative administration, now often neglected, has a great deal to add to our understanding of the character, evolution, and autonomy of the state.[17]

Administrative behavior is also important because policies, once made, are not automatically implemented or successful. A decision is only one step in the process whereby the state is used to alter the shape of society. Equally important are the processes by which that decision can be creatively implemented, altered, subverted, or ignored. Good policies can fail and poor ones be made workable. We know much less about implementation in Kenya than we do about the more visible arenas of politics and policy-making. To overcome this weakness we have to get inside the "black box" of government and probe its inner workings.

Kenya has an unusually powerful civil service[18]—just how powerful is open to dispute, but Kenyan citizens and their press give nearly as much attention to senior appointments in the public service as they do to those members of Parliament (M.P.s) named cabinet ministers. All political observers agree that Kenya's public policies cannot be explained without reference to the inner workings of the civil service.

Of course, the "bureaucracy" is a factor in public policy to some degree in all countries.[19] Max Weber considered history to involve a continuous struggle between political chiefs and their administrators over the resources of the state.[20] The literature of political science is rich with assertions and analyses of bureaucratic power. Despite this attention, the relative power of politician and civil servant is a hotly debated issue in almost every political system.[21] This study aspires to a careful statement of the considerable role that administrators have in making and implementing public policy in Kenya. It considers all the actors in the policy process, but does so through the lens of the bureaucracy, just as others have examined it through the lens of parties or legislatures. These administrative roles and the ways they are played have been deeply influenced by the processes of Kenya's formation as a state.

A MODEST THEORETICAL FRAMEWORK

The subtitle to this chapter bears the triad "individuals, institutions, and interests" because the book seeks to understand the influence of all three on Kenya's rural development policies. The study of politics is dominated by the impact of interests, whether they are represented by classes or by interest groups. This is as it should be, for interests are the most important forces at work in politics.

Such a focus, however, runs the risk of ignoring several other important, underlying processes. The first is that people choose the causes of their behavior. Social science faces an interesting anomaly: whether we look back individually or collectively, it appears that the course of human action has been heavily determined and that the range of truly viable options has been narrow. But it is extremely difficult to predict future behavior. If social actions are as closely determined as historical analysis seems to show, how can they be so hard to predict? Part of the answer lies in the fact that most social forces have to be perceived before they can be the causes of human behavior. A particular course of action may objectively be in the best interests of someone, but if he *thinks* that his interests lie in another direction, he will therefore take the latter course. Decision makers discern and weigh the relative significance of the causes of their decisions for themselves. Once an action has been taken, it is relatively simple to identify the perceived cause on which it was based, particularly if we are aided by the actors themselves. But it is very hard to pick out the cause of a future action. Thus it matters who the particular decision maker is—who it is who is perceiving and weighing the "causes" of his or her actions.

The second underlying process is that of interest aggregation. Most of the interests weighing heavily on the policy-making process are those of collectivities, not of discrete individuals. The shape of interests in society is therefore determined by the ways in which people group themselves for political action. Once again, perceptions are important: what are the attributes of a "we" or of a "they"? Whether "we" are coffee producers or peasants or Africans or Kikuyus or clansmen will profoundly mold the collectivity that we present to the body politic and the interests to which we ask it to respond. People first tend to pursue their interests in association with people with whom they have successfully sought them in the past, so that patterns of interest aggregation generally are institutionalized.

The third process is related therefore to the second: policy is shaped by the lag effect of institutions that interests create to serve themselves. Social behavior is shaped not only by the immediate configuration of interests and opportunities that surrounds the actors but also by a set of inherited institutions through which the messages of the present will be filtered.

Virtually everyone acts so as to maximize their interests, which simply means that they pursue that which interests them, including but not limited to their material well-being. To achieve those interests, they must interact with other people. To make that achievement efficient and stable, there must be some predictability to the patterns of interaction. When one shops for vegetables in the United States one expects a fixed price, but in Kenya bargaining is the expected pattern of interaction for the same transaction. When a university student lends an item of clothing to her roommate, she has a right to expect that she can later borrow clothes from her in turn. In both Kenya and the United States, those giving wedding presents anticipate that there will be reciprocal gifts at their marriage or that of their children. These latter two examples are social exchanges, in contrast to the preceding purely economic one of the marketplace. They illustrate that exchanges do not have to be explicit, simultaneous, or direct to be built on principles of reciprocity, as is made clear in the seminal work of Peter Blau.[22] What is more, the expectations or regularity on which these social exchanges are grounded derive from a community of values. Someone who failed to reciprocate would eventually be subject to criticism by mutual acquaintances and fall victim to social sanctions. Knowledge that there are sanctions behind a pattern of exchanges gives one increased confidence in its stability and increases the efficiency of the transactions.[23]

The anthropologist Radcliffe-Brown suggested that an institution is a standardized mode of behavior; the political philosopher John Rawls defined it as a generally acted-upon system of rules that, by defining positions, rights, and duties, gives form and structure to social activity.[24] Both definitions make it clear that an institution can be, but is not necessarily, an organization. Universities, armies, interest groups, families, codes of etiquette, and market systems are all institutions; in all of them participants have roles (positions), rights, and duties that help to standardize the patterns of activity and interpersonal exchange.

A mode of interaction or an organization's method of operating becomes more predictable (or standardized) as people come to value it for its own sake. I refer to the process whereby a pattern of behavior becomes embedded with value as institutionalization. Arthur Stinchcombe suggests that

> the key to institutionalizing a value is to concentrate power in the hands of those who believe in that value. It can be arranged that they should believe in it by surrounding powerful roles with rewards and punishments that make it in their interests to believe in that value.[25]

Social institutions certainly are not static; they will change as the structure of interests in society evolves and as the distribution of power shifts. Because they are imbued with value, however, they do not change quickly. People are not quick to alter their values, even when it is in their interests to do so. As the Nobel Laureate Herbert Simon has taught us, humans are "satisficers," not optimizers. He means that when individuals make decisions they tend to adopt the first acceptable (or satisfactory) alternative that they find, rather than going on to look for the best possible (or optimal) one.[26] Individuals and societies alike will allow themselves to slip into institutional arrangements that do not perfectly suit their interests and will allow them to persist for some time after they have become even less perfect—as long as the discrepancy is not too great. The present behavior of humans in society is therefore determined not only by the contemporary distribution of interests and power but also by the institutional heritage that is left over from previous such distributions.[27]

Nonetheless, institutions are not disembodied entities; they are the patterned behavior of individuals. When the membership of an institution shifts markedly we must pay careful attention to the ways the patterns are transmitted to the new participants. If the new members learn to value different behavior than the old ones endorsed, then the institution will be different. In seeking to understand the operation of Kenya's contemporary political and administrative institutions, it is important to look at the colonial heritage out of which they developed. But we do not want to look directly at the country's colonial institutions. Instead, we will concentrate on how Kenya's African elites, those who succeeded to leadership positions after independence, *experienced* those institutions and were thereby socialized into the state and its administration. Stinchcombe has suggested that

> institutions will tend to be preserved to the degree that power holders select their successors, to the degree that they control socialization for elite positions, to the degree that they control the conditions of incumbency of their successors, to the degree that they become heroes after whom potential leaders model themselves.[28]

As we shall see, the transition from colonialism to independence was flawed along virtually every one of these degrees or dimensions.

FOUR PUBLIC SERVANTS

As a way of exploring its multiple themes this study presents abbreviated biographies of four senior African public servants who have had an unusually great impact on Kenyan rural development. All four men were born in the 1930s. Their family histories encompass both the early and the later history of modern Kenya. Their parents belonged to the generation whose way of life was transformed by British colonialism; they, in contrast, represent the generation that supplanted colonialism.

Charles Kibe Karanja (pronounced *Key*-bay Ka-*ron*-ja) was general manager of the Kenya Tea Development Authority (KTDA) from 1970 to 1981. The KTDA is one of the world's greatest success stories in rural development. It is an international-class corporation in terms of its size and impact; Karanja guided it through its period of greatest growth and vertical expansion.

Ishmael Muriithi (pronounced Mur-*ee*-thee) became Kenya's director of veterinary services in 1966 after independence and remained in that post until 1984. During his tenure the character of smallholder dairy production underwent a transformation and growth as impressive as, if less well known than, that of tea. Muriithi's management of veterinary services was an essential precondition to that transformation. His accomplishment was made, however, in a very different way than was Karanja's in the KTDA.

As a subordinate part of our study of Muriithi we will also look briefly at the life and career of his younger brother, Dan Mbogo. Mbogo worked under Muriithi in the Veterinary Department as head of the Artificial Insemination Service, which was critical to the success of the dairy industry. Like his older brother, he too was a good manager.

Harris Mule (pronounced *Moo*-lay) rose through the ranks of the Planning Department and from 1980 through 1986 was permanent secretary to the Ministry of Finance, one of the three most important economic policy-making positions in the government. He had a major influence on the way Kenya has shaped its rural development efforts, and he shares the credit for the economic policies that make Kenya one of the most prosperous African states today.

Simeon Nyachae (pronounced nYah-*chai*) in 1964 became one of Kenya's powerful provincial commissioners, a post in which he was the instrument of the president in controlling regional political developments and in supervising the change in land ownership from British to African hands. In 1979 he became chief of the president's policy staff and in 1984 was made chief secretary, a post that combined the positions of head of the civil service and secretary to the cabinet. At the time of his retirement in 1987 he was the most important civil servant in Kenya. Many thought of him as the president's closest adviser on matters of public policy. Nyachae was responsible for implementing a significant decentralization of the Kenyan government in the 1980s and had a great impact on the country's agricultural marketing and pricing policies.

These men were public servants, which is to say they had careers as appointed officers of the government. They were not elected or appointed to fulfill any representative functions. All but Karanja were civil servants and therefore were tenured in the regular government service. Karanja held office in a government corporation at the pleasure of his board and of the president. In most governments such men are invisible and noncontroversial. Not so in Kenya.

A NOTE ON METHODOLOGY

We are still at the stage of seeking clues to the forces behind the intricacies of Kenyan policy-making and effective administrative behavior. Thus it is premature to apply large-sample and quantitative-measurement techniques to most aspects of this problem. Instead, we offer a qualitative, deviant case analysis. The general, negative pattern of management is well documented, but the deviant, positive one has tremendous practical and theoretical significance. Qualitative work is needed to isolate the probable causative factors that are at work; these can then be studied systematically in later research.

These four administrators had their strengths and their weaknesses; none of them was an unequivocal success. I selected them at the recommendation of many well-informed observers. There were other highly regarded public servants who might have been chosen, but their primary impact was not on agriculture, and I wanted to focus on people working on rural development, both because of its intrinsic importance to general development and because it is the policy domain I understand best. In the broad field of rural development these four men were the best who were accessible to me. As I researched their careers I became more aware of some of their failings and of the fact that some of them had a greater impact than others. But all of them were substantially better than the norm and had a positive effect on development.

Through the device of biography we will seek to understand these men holistically. By examining their early education, their professional development, and their ties to their families, villages, and businesses, we can sort out what has made them exceptional and what has shaped their managerial successes and occasional failures. In this way we will be taking into consideration the social and political forces on which the "contextualists" insist, but seeing them as factors that *interact* with whole human beings, not treating them as immovable constraints. The men on whom we will focus have generally managed somehow to *use* their environments productively rather than be trapped by them. We want to understand how and why.

The material for the biographical part of this study was collected in over three hundred interviews with more than two hundred different people, as is detailed in Appendix C. The biographical method provided a remarkably frank access to the subjects of this study and those who knew them and their work. A great deal was learned about the policy process that almost certainly would not have come out in any other way. The biographies are built on several extensive interviews with the subjects and their families, friends, associates, and village neighbors, giving a wide variety of perspectives.* Most interviews lasted at least an hour; many were substantially longer; one took a whole day. Fewer than five people declined to be interviewed for this project, and a similar number were evasive in their responses to my long, open-ended questioning. This is a remarkably high level of cooperation, particularly given that many of the interviewees were extremely busy, ranging in status from villagers to cabinet ministers.

I have sought to follow the usual rules of historical scholarship in the following presentation, taking care to corroborate important facts, to give preference to primary over secondary sources, and to allow for bias in the accounts. It was more difficult to follow these rules rigorously for the pre-1960 materials than for the later ones. Fortunately, biases and faulty details in the early episodes are unlikely to have harmed the validity of the study's basic thrust, which relies much more on the reliability of the postindependence accounts. I have kept careful record of the specific interviews on which the multitude of undocumented statements in this book are based. However, because of my promises of confidentiality, this complete referencing and the interview transcripts cannot be released until the year 2000. Those interested in the documentation for specific statements are encouraged to consult me after that date.

The biographical data are supplemented with a number of other types of material. First is the considerable literature on Kenyan politics and society, without which this study would have been much poorer. Second are the insights I developed while living in Kenya for seven years between 1969 and 1986, through my two years as a management adviser in the Ministries of Agriculture and Livestock Development in 1980 to 1982, and through my earlier research at the grass roots of Kenyan development administration.[29] The third type of materials used are vari-

---

*I was not able to conduct biographical interviews with Ishmael Muriithi, for he died just before I began work on the study. I decided to proceed with his biography nonetheless, as I had worked earlier for him as an adviser in the Ministry of Livestock Development and knew something about him and his work personally. I also had the benefit of some brief notes about him and his career that he had prepared in anticipation of this study.

ous quantitative indicators of the relative influence of Kenyan politicians and administrators, which I collected in the mid-1970s.

A PREVIEW OF THE BOOK

Chapter 2 examines Kenya's colonial institutions as they were experienced by the parents of the four men we are studying. This analysis is critical to our understanding of the processes of state formation as they evolved after independence.

In chapter 3 we turn to the childhood and education of the four administrators. This provides an intimate view of the socialization that they brought to their roles in the Kenyan government.

We come to independent Kenya in chapter 4. The ways in which the Africanization of the civil service and the economy affected the four subjects of this study is provided against a background analysis of the Kenyan political and economic system and its emerging social class structure as it developed under President Kenyatta.

The power of the Kenyan civil service is probed in chapter 5, and Simeon Nyachae's early career in the politically sensitive Provincial Administration is described. We give particular attention to the transfer of land from European settlers to African smallholders, the most important aspect of rural development in the 1960s and a process in which the provincial administration and Nyachae played a major role.

The Kenya Tea Development Authority and its general manager, Charles Karanja, are the focus of chapter 6. The KTDA's horizontal and vertical expansion in the 1970s is one of the world's great success stories of rural development. We seek to understand the policy-making and managerial dimensions of this achievement.

The dramatic expansion of Kenya's smallholder dairy industry after independence presents an interesting contrast to that of the KTDA. Although the accomplishments in dairy are almost as great as they are for tea, they are much less well known. One of the reasons is that whereas the KTDA provided a single, integrating direction to tea development, the dairy industry was served by a number of separate agencies. It is important to understand just how this unintegrated development initiative was able to succeed; this is the subject of chapter 7. The Veterinary Department under Ishmael Muriithi and its Artificial Insemination Service under Dan Mbogo were critical to this achievement.

In 1978 Jomo Kenyatta died and Daniel arap Moi succeeded him as president. In 1982 the air force attempted a coup d'etat. Both events produced significant changes in the Kenyan political system. These changes and their impact on the management of rural development are addressed in chapter 8.

Throughout the 1970s the Kenyan government wrestled with ways to deal with rural development, food-crop production, regional inequality, and the state's overly centralized bureaucratic structure. Harris Mule's career in Planning involved a series of frustrated attempts to deal with these issues. Then in the 1980s he and Simeon Nyachae joined forces to make significant progress on them as they sought to implement President Moi's District Focus policy. Chapters 9 and 10 sketch the high drama of these policy-making initiatives.

On one dimension Kenyan administration and politics is deeply influenced by networks of personal relationships and patron-client ties. The latter is played out through both public appointments and contributions to community self-help schemes. On another dimension policy making is driven by the interests generated by the transfer of businesses and large farms to African hands in the aftermath of independence. These economic advantages have created a new African class of the well-to-do, which is now striving to transmit its advantages to its children. Chapter 11 analyzes the intersection of these two dimensions, illustrating the larger processes with the sometimes nonconformist behavior of the four senior administrators.

Chapter 12 draws on the evidence of the preceding chapters to suggest aspects of managerial behavior that are particularly important to organizational success in Kenya. Political support and professionalism are found to be especially critical.

Chapter 13 reflects on the interaction of politics and administration as they shape institutional development, the evolution of the African state, and agricultural growth.

This book will demonstrate that a good civil service and a congenial political climate have *interacted* to produce relatively successful rural development in Kenya. I stress the important role played by civil servants and suggest that Kenya would have done still better if it had more men and women like the ones portrayed here. But they did not do, and could not have done, what they did without political support. Sometimes they stimulated that support or greatly extended its effect on policy, but they were never the sole actors. Thus politicians too receive considerable attention in the following chapters.

Similarly, neither Kenya nor these men had unequivocal success. They also experienced failures, which help to illuminate their achievements. They could have done better. And in other, different, circumstances or with different actors they could have done worse. Individuals, institutions, and interests are all important and can compensate for one another to some degree, but ultimately they interact to create public policy.

CHAPTER TWO

The Foundation

EVERYTHING HAS A HISTORY

No human social activity can be fully understood without knowing its historical context. Social behavior is shaped not only by the immediate configuration of interests and opportunities that surrounds it but also by a set of inherited institutions through which the messages of the present will be filtered.

At its independence in 1963 Kenya had two important sets of institutions shaping its public policy making. The first were those that regulated people's behavior in face-to-face groups: the social conventions that define how one is related to those about one, how one should interact with them, and what one's obligations are toward them. In Kenya these social institutions primarily involve kinship and ethnic groups and are labeled "traditional," not because they are ill adapted to "modern" conditions and not because they are unchanging, but simply because they have their roots in social systems that precede British colonialism and the modern state.

The second set of institutions were those that British colonialism had imposed in creating the new state of Kenya. They represented not only the formal mechanisms of government decision making but also the habits of political influence, the established patterns of administrative control, and the structure of the economy. Although with the end of British suzerainty independent Kenya had the opportunity to reform these institutions, they represented a half century of ingrained experience and were the starting point from which change had to take place. What were they and what was the experience of Kenya's Africans with them?

Emphasis here is on the way Africans experienced these institutions, not the ways they may have operated in the European parts of the colony. After independence it was African expectations and values about these institutions which would largely influence how they subsequently evolved, not their "objective" character.

In order to understand the interaction of colonial institutions and "traditional" African ones, we start at the turn of the century. Not only was this the time when Britain seized control of the territory, it also was when the parents of the four administrators we are studying were born. This period created the foundations both of the state and of their family experiences.

DISRUPTION

The family of Charles Karanja, the tea manager, has vivid memories of the early impact of the British presence on upland Kenya. On that fateful day in 1897 the sun was well up at the cluster of thatched huts that housed Kiarii, his twenty wives, and their children.* Nonetheless it was still cool, for Ndarugu in upper Kiambu (see map 1) is a mile high, and the strong tropical sun must do more than just break the chilling morning mists for the day to feel warm. Kiarii was a wealthy man, so that his homestead made up a small village at Kang'ori in the Ndarugu area. But these were not prosperous times. The great rinderpest epidemic of the 1890s had only recently completed its awful work of killing nine of every ten cattle in east Africa, wreaking a similar devastation on those people, such as the Maasai, who depend wholly on livestock for their livelihood. Kiarii was of the Kikuyu, a settled agricultural people. But even they were weakened, as they had lost valuable supplemental sources of animal protein and had to cope with dying Maasai questing for food.

This natural disaster had been exacerbated by a human one. The British had chosen this very period to begin their work of establishing a colonial presence in what is now Kenya and Uganda and had created a major provisioning post for their expeditions among the Kiambu Kikuyu near Nairobi. The local peoples had no previous experience with such a sizable market, and they had sold off all their food reserves to the succession of caravans.[1] Thus when the Kikuyus' food stocks ran out,

---

*Most of the dates given for events in the lives of Kenyan Africans prior to 1940 are estimates only, for written records and a European type of calendar were rarely kept before then. With the help of Professor G. Muriuki of the University of Nairobi it was possible to establish that the incident recounted here occurred in 1897 or shortly thereafter.

they were unable to find more from their usual backup source of relatives and neighbors. These were difficult times indeed.

As family tradition has it, Karanja, Charles Karanja's father (see plate 4), then a four-year-old and one of Kiarii's many sons, was playing around the three stones of his mother's cooking fire when suddenly it happened. The young warriors of another Kikuyu clan at Mangu came shouting out of the forest, brandishing their spears and firing their arrows. Their object was to steal the diminished herd of sheep, goats, and a few cattle that Kiarii had left, and to do so they charged through the scattering, frightened villagers. One of Kiarii's sons, still a child, tried to stand against the marauders and was swiftly killed, together with the mother who tried to protect him. Karanja, small as he was, somehow fell in their way and would have died as well had his mother not begged for his life. Then, just as suddenly, the raiders and the livestock were gone.

As the frightened family regrouped, an older son of the murdered wife grabbed his spear and ran off after the invaders. Coming upon them on the trail, he pretended to be one of the band, which was not hard to do, as they all were Kikuyu and dressed and spoke alike. Then, on a bend in the trail, when he found himself alone with one of their number, he killed him from behind and sprinted back off into the woods.

Despite, or perhaps because of, his son's bravado, Kiarii thought it unsafe to keep his family alone at this fertile place. So he moved them to Nganga to join forces with an elder brother (whose own son was to become Chief Mukui). Unfortunately for Kiarii, however, the times were too desperate and the homestead he had temporarily abandoned too attractive, for their place was then taken by another family, which was too strong to dislodge.

The wily Kiarii went to the very clan that had first raided his family and asked for their help in driving out the interlopers. "We want to increase more so we may have even more for you to take in the future," he said. Remarkably, they did help.

Thus, as the century began, Karanja had already felt the first of the series of violent disruptions from the British colonial presence that was to totally transform his life and that of his countrymen. Although, like his father, Kiarii, he would be resourceful in the face of these forces for change, he would be their victim, not their master.

In a manner unusual in the world's history of colonial occupations, however, Karanja not only would live through the radical alteration of the way of life of his people, but also would see the departure of the conquerors and the assumption by his son Charles Kibe Karanja of a leading role in the tea industry and the shaping of an independent Kenya that followed.

THE AGRICULTURAL ECONOMY

The turn of the century evokes a different set of traditions in the family of Harris Mule, the planner and economist. In 1897 Ivita, a Kamba teenager living in the Kilungu highlands of Machakos, heard that there was an iron snake making its way slowly across the plains from the coast. The Kamba were well known for their adventuresome trade between the Indian Ocean and points further inland, and so Ivita was within local tradition when he decided he would go to see this snake for himself. With nothing but a couple of water gourds to sustain him, he made the 250-km (150 mi.) journey on foot through what is now the Tsavo National Park, avoided its infamous man-eating lions, and arrived in Voi to see a British railroad being built by imported Indian laborers.[2] The railway would not reach its destination on the shores of Lake Victoria until 1901, but Ivita recognized the forces of change that it represented and began to align his life in accordance with them. A half century later his granddaughter would marry Harris Mule.

The rail line that Ivita walked so far to see was to alter profoundly the economic, racial, and hence political character of East Africa. As is often the case with historical causation, it was not built with that purpose primarily in mind. In the late nineteenth century Great Britain's economic interests were fundamentally rooted in international trade and in the sea routes necessary to exploit it. East Africa was peripheral to both; it neither bought nor sold much of significance in the world market, and the opening of the Suez Canal had made its ports irrelevant to the Asian shipping routes. Suez did alter Britain's strategic interests, however, making the control of Egypt imperative. The military theories prevailing at the time gave considerable importance to the security of the tributaries of a country's principal rivers. Hence Britain was quite interested in the upper Nile, risking the Fashoda crisis with France in 1898 in order to take control of the Sudan. In a similar vein the English thought it imperative to control Uganda, since the Nile originates there at Lake Victoria. What initially was called the Uganda Railway was built from the Indian Ocean port of Mombasa, through what now is Kenya, to the shores of Lake Victoria in order to render the headwaters of the Nile militarily secure.[3]

Having built the Uganda Railway because of its *global* economic interests, Britain was nonetheless determined to pay for it with revenues from *East African* business.[4] This would be no mean feat, as East Africa's principal (if minor) contribution to international trade had been the recently suppressed slave trade.

At this time land was an abundant commodity in East Africa, and everyone had access to as much as they could use. It was labor that was scarce, particularly female labor, for most agricultural work in East Africa is done by women. Agriculture was oriented entirely to subsistence needs, and its output was traded only for subsistence goods that were not produced locally. Salt and ironwork were the only products of specialized labor that were traded over long distances. A man could become wealthy and lay claim to large amounts of land but only by having many wives, whom he obtained by paying bride price out of the surpluses he accumulated from skillful management of his existing land and cattle and from trade.[5]

Given the predominately subsistence nature of these economies, there were no readily attachable market commodities that the British could tax or trade to meet their financial outlays. In the case of Uganda, a colonial state was built on the foundation of the already existing, strong African kingdoms of the lake region. Cotton grown by small farmers then was vigorously promoted and was transported to the world market on the new railway.[6]

Kenya was more problematic. Its kingdoms were small and even then existed only in enclaves on its eastern and western boundaries. The vast majority of its peoples were governed by gerontocracies: small, kinship-based democracies of elders, grouped in loose informal federations along linguistic lines.[7] The British were unable to visualize these political systems as states.[8] In any case, as nonhierarchical systems, they did not provide the ready administrative framework that the hierarchical British Empire could use to force economically self-sufficient peoples into new market relations. Furthermore, the railway passed through long stretches of semi-arid lands, which at the time were underpopulated and offered few export possibilities because the inhabitants' herds of cattle had been all but wiped out by the great rinderpest epidemic.

The British probably could have met their revenue requirements by involving Kenya's Africans in the world market as producers in the Ugandan pattern,* although it might have taken longer to accomplish because of the aftermath of the rinderpest and the absence of a ready hierarchical administrative apparatus. They did promote African export trade in hides and wattle bark (which is used for tanning). Using the ample, well-watered land they had in Kiambu, Kiarii and his son Karanja participated in wattle production and prospered from it. After independence, Karanja's son Charles would manage the dramatic involvement of Kenyan African smallholders in world tea production. In

---

*This is the view of Hugh Fearn in *An African Economy: A Study of the Economic Development of the Nyanza Province of Kenya, 1903–1953* (London: Oxford University Press, 1961). In fact, African export production exceeded the small value of European exports until the early 1920s.

this period, however, the colonial authorities decided to restrict African participation in the production of such other export commodities, and the value of indigenous contributions to international trade actually declined after 1925.[9]

Instead, the governor, Sir Charles Eliot, opted in 1903 to promote large-scale farming by European settlers. These white farmers and ranchers primarily occupied lands that were underutilized at the turn of the century. But the lands were far from unclaimed and represented 18 percent of Kenya's good farm acreage.[10] The African population of East Africa was at a historic low ebb at the time because of famine, disease, and the decimation of its cattle by rinderpest.[11] The expropriation of these lands by European settlers and their designation as exclusive white preserves (the "White Highlands" of literary fame) confined a number of Kenya's African peoples within their minimum territorial requirements and guaranteed that there would be severe population pressure on the land as the indigenous people regained their health and prosperity.[12]

Thus was created the "bimodal" pattern of agriculture that characterized colonial Kenya,[13] one in which there was not one "average" or modal type of farm but two: the small African farm that frequently was too small and too deprived of capital and market opportunities to be fully productive or self-sufficient; and the large, inappropriately capital-intensive, European farm, whose land was underutilized and which drew its labor from the African families whose farms were too small to support them and their ambitions.

Because the European farms were distant from the international markets on which they depended, and because the infrastructure that existed to support their efforts was weak, white agriculture (particularly mixed farming) was actually a marginal economic enterprise until World War II, when it was needed to provision the British war effort.[14] A great deal of Kenyan colonial economic policy was designed to shore up these struggling European farms. Initially, their greatest problem was labor. The markets in which they sold were not especially lucrative, and they enjoyed no technical advantages over small African farms. Hence the white farmers had a great deal of difficulty getting labor at prices they could afford.

The colonial government helped them in a number of ways. First, it imposed taxes on all Africans and insisted that they be paid in cash. Second, it systematically narrowed to wage labor the ways in which Africans could earn this cash, prohibiting them from growing the most lucrative of the market crops. Third, it used its administrative apparatus to forcibly recruit labor. By the mid-1920s as many as half of the able-bodied Kikuyu and Luo men were working for whites.[15] Fourth, it tacitly permitted European farmers to collusively set wage levels at a uniformly low level. Africans thus found themselves faced with an artificial need for cash and no way to earn it other than by working on European farms at wages kept low by oligopolistic agreements.[16] As African populations began to recover from the traumas of the rinderpest and other late-nineteenth-century disasters, these pressures were particularly severe for those, such as the Kikuyu, whose traditional opportunities for expansion had been shut off by European settlement.[17]

Waicanguru, the father of the veterinarian Ishmael Muriithi, exemplified this pattern of labor in a dual economy. He was born in 1901 in what is now the Ihithe Sub-Location of Nyeri District, high up against the forest of the Aberdare mountains.* (See map 1.) He was poor, as his father had died when he was very young, and he was raised by his mother. The only way he could get money was to work for the Europeans, and so in 1914, having only just entered his teens, he began work on the European farms 60 km (40 mi.) away around Nakuru. He would work for a three-month season, go home for a time, and then go back again. By 1921 he was an adult, old enough to work year round, and became the supervisor on the farm of Colonel Peter Were. The latter took an interest in him and happened to be a teacher, a double piece of unusual luck for Waicanguru, for Were began to teach him how to read and write in the evenings after supper. Waicanguru's fingers were muscular and stiff from the heavy farm work and he couldn't hold a pencil; Were tied his thumb and first two fingers around the pencil. In 1925 Waicanguru returned home for two years of mission education at Wandumbi. He did go back to work on other farms in Nakuru twice more, first for three months in 1927 and then for a year in 1930 as a foreman and teacher. But by this point he had been able to accumulate enough education and experience to launch himself on a prominent career at home, and he did not have to be a migrant again. Most laborers were not so talented and lucky, and they instead became "squatters" on the farms where they worked. When the Europeans were no longer experiencing a labor shortage and forced these "squatters" off their lands in the late 1930s and 1940s, the Kikuyu Mau Mau rebellion was set off.[18]

THE MISSIONS

Waicanguru had heard missionaries of the Church of Scotland preaching in Nyeri during his times off from work in Nakuru, and he became

---

*In Kenya the hierarchy of political-administrative geographical divisions runs as follows: nation; province; district; division; location; sub-location; village (an administrative term for a set of homes that usually are actually physically dispersed); and homestead.

a "full Christian" in 1926, the first in his sub-location to do so. In joining what is now the Presbyterian Church of East Africa (PCEA), he took the name Elijah. He had paid the customary dowry for his future wife, Lydia Wangeci, in 1923, having met her at traditional dances. (See plate 6.) After they were engaged through this payment of livestock to her father, Waicanguru asked her to go to mission school as well. She did so only because he asked it of her, but once there she loved it and studied for a year and a half, learning to read in her native Kikuyu. Lydia Wangeci thus became one of an extremely small number of women of her generation who was literate. She also joined the church, and the two of them received a Christian marriage in June 1926. Their first child was born November 18, 1929, and was baptized Ishmael Muriithi (the veterinarian). The first name is biblical, following strict mission tradition; the second is that of Waicanguru's father, following the equally strict Kikuyu tradition.* Altogether they would have nine children, all but one of whom would become a professional.

The PCEA was central to the lives of Elijah Waicanguru and Lydia Wangeci, and they were prominent among the small numbers of church members of the time.† He became a deacon in 1926 and a member of the national church synod in 1944; she held positions in the PCEA Women's Guild. The strength of her Christian commitment is illustrated by the female circumcision conflicts of 1929–1931. The Kikuyu traditionally circumcised both boys and girls as they entered puberty. The practice can be dangerous for girls, and the Presbyterian missionaries therefore decided in 1906 that it was unchristian and inconsistent with church membership. Other missions eventually came to take the same position, and in the late 1920s many of them decided that girls should be expelled from mission schools if they submitted to circumcision. This coupling of a material sanction with a challenge to tradition set off tremendous conflict in Kikuyu society and led to the creation of many non-mission, independent African schools.[19] One of the central functions of the Women's Guild in the 1930s was to shield girls from circumcision, a role that Lydia Wangeci played at the cost of her relations with her own family.

*Kikuyu naming traditions are among the strictest in Kenya. The second son is named for his maternal grandfather, the first daughter for her paternal grandmother, and so on. Kikuyus are encouraged to have enough children to "perpetuate the grandparents," thereby exemplifying the African theology of immortality through the offspring. Joseph G. Donders, *Non-Bourgeois Theology: An African Experience of Jesus* (Maryknoll, New York: Orbis Books, 1985), pp. 11–12, 19–20. Other Kenyan peoples give names according to circumstances of the birth or characteristics of the child.

†The Presbyterian Church had fewer than 1,000 Kenya African members in 1914 and 10,000 in 1938. Roland Oliver, *The Missionary Factor in East Africa* (Longmans, 1965), p. 236.

A Christian mission played an even more central role in the life of Philip Mule, father of Harris Mule (the planner). Philip, a Kamba, was born about 1900 in the Mbooni Location of the Machakos highlands. (See map 1.) His mother died in childbirth, and his father passed away when Philip was three or four years old. Following traditional patterns of social obligation, Philip was then placed in the care of his uncle Mwaniki, who, since his mother had been unable to name him, called him Mule, meaning "one who has been forgotten." In 1908 young Mule was building a path with his uncle when he was seen by Rev. George William Rhoades of the African Inland Mission. The AIM represented a consortium of U.S. and Canadian churches, particularly the Southern Baptists, and in 1908 it opened its fourth Kenyan mission in the Kamba highlands at Mbooni, where the climate was more comfortable and the mosquito-borne malaria less prevalent. Rhoades had particularly strong feelings about education and was looking for young people he could teach to read the Bible and convert.[20] Mule must have seemed neglected to Rhoades, who demanded that Mwaniki give him over to the mission to be clothed and educated. At first Mwaniki refused and was given a kick by Rhoades; he then surrendered the boy, who was dispensable and a burden in any case. Rhoades gave Mule to Samuel Ndava, a Kamba catechist, who educated and cared for him. Philip Mule thus was raised on the mission and received about six years of primary education, an unusually large amount for an African at that time. He became a member of this fundamentalist church and worked first as a cook and then as a teacher for the mission. (See plate 5.) Mule thus exemplifies a common Kenyan pattern whereby the early converts to Christianity were drawn from the disadvantaged and became members of the colonial elite because of the access to education that their membership provided.[21]

Meanwhile, Ivita, who had walked from another part of the Kamba highlands to see the railway's being built and into whose family Harris Mule later married, had gone to work near Nairobi for Father Hoerber, a Holy Ghost missionary. While in his employ Ivita and two other Kambas from Kilungu were baptized into the Catholic church. When it came time for them to marry, Father Hoerber insisted that they take Catholic wives, but they didn't want to marry the Kikuyus who were available, and Kamba Catholics were not at hand. Thus in 1918 Hoerber sent them home as catechists, telling them to convert to Catholicism the women they intended to marry. In this way the three men introduced Catholicism to Kilungu and prepared the ground for Father Hoerber to follow them there in 1920. These same three men were among those who spent five days carrying on foot the materials for building the first church. The eucalyptus that today dominate the Kilungu landscape had only just been brought from Nairobi by Ivita's group. The boundaries between the denominations, which motivated this entire episode, were much more important to the missionaries than they were to their converts, for Ivita's convent-educated granddaughter would marry the son of the Protestant fundamentalist Philip Mule, and one of the latter's daughters was a Catholic nun for a time.

Mission education was almost a necessary condition for African elite status in colonial Kenya, and it certainly gave all of its recipients a large head start in life's race. Three of the four administrators we are studying had parents who were both educated, whereas only 9 percent of that generation had been to school.[22] But mission education was not a sufficient condition to become a local elite. Joseph Kisuna, Harris Mule's father-in-law and the husband of Joseph Ivita's daughter, had Catholic primary schooling. He nonetheless spent his life as a house servant to Europeans while his wife remained poor and at home farming their two-acre plot and caring for their six children. After having met his urban living expenses he would send home small remittances from his salary for school fees and the like. His life was typical of the large number of colonial and present generations of migrant laborers. All lived the strained existence of "one family and two households."[23]

Musa Nyandusi, the father of Chief Secretary Simeon Nyachae, followed still another path into the missions and local prominence. Nyandusi was born just before the turn of the century, within a few years of the other three fathers in this study. His early years appear to have been untouched by colonialism. The British crushed local resistance and established a presence in Kisii District, where he lived, only in 1907.[24] (See map 1.) No mission entered this area of southwestern Kenya until 1911, and the only one abandoned its station at the outbreak of World War I. The reality of a new state's existence broke upon Nyandusi only when he was conscripted into the Carrier Corps, to serve the British as a porter and servant in the Great War against the Germans in Tanganyika (now Tanzania). Nyandusi was one of the lucky draftees. Although there was very little actual fighting in the East African theater, 46,618 African members of the Carrier Corps were officially recorded as having died, mostly of disease. Most of their families were never traced, and no insurance or compensation was ever paid to them.[25] Nyandusi, on the other hand, not only survived the war but learned to read numbers and to speak some English and Swahili (the lingua franca of East Africa).

On his return to Kisii after the war Musa Nyandusi availed himself of the educational opportunities at the new Seventh-Day Adventist mission at Nyanchwa, where he was taught by an American. He also was later sent by the mission for a time to Uganda to carry his education further. During this postwar period he both taught school and served as the principal Gusii preacher for the Seventh-Day Adventists. (The people of Kisii are the Gusii.) When the position of chief of Nyaribari Location fell vacant in 1926, the missionaries used their influence with the British administration to have Nyandusi appointed to the post, which he held until 1964.[26]

Once under the patronage of the British government rather than the Seventh-Day Adventist mission, Nyandusi opted to follow the traditional practice of wealthy African men and became a polygamist. In about 1930 he took Pauline Bosibori as his fourth wife. (See plate 7.) Her grandfather had been a local *sansora*, a man who settles interclan disputes, and her childhood was a comfortable one. At the time that her father was paid the dowry of six head of cattle for her, she had only just entered her teens and had not yet met Nyandusi, then in his thirties. She had been selected for her beauty and remembers Nyandusi as tall, big, and very strong. Her firstborn was James Oiruria, who would later become chief of Kisii town; her only other child was Simeon Nyachae, born on February 6, 1932.

Pauline Bosibori reports that in about 1937 she had a powerful dream in which she was lifted up and placed in a house at the local mission at Nyabururu. She was told in the dream that it was a hostel for girl students and that there was another one for boys. Bosibori took this dream as a divine vision and asked her husband if she could go to school. He replied that he knew nothing of Nyabururu, as it was Catholic. She persisted, however, went to the mission, and asked if they would baptize her if she studied there. They answered that she could say Catholic prayers but that she couldn't be baptized, because she had a polygamous marriage. So she then went to the Seventh-Day Adventist mission and received the same answer. She decided to fight for baptism nonetheless and entered the latter's school, taking her boys with her to the mission. She learned to read the Bible in both Kisii and Swahili, but at the end her baptism was still blocked. Although her appeals were consistently turned down in East Africa, she sent her case to the Seventh-Day Adventist Union headquarters in the United States. There it was argued that since no one else in her family was Christian, perhaps her dream was a vision from God calling on her to show the way for them, despite her polygamous marriage. She finally was baptized by the head of the Union when he visited in Kenya in 1944, as the church in East Africa would not perform the sacrament for her. Bosibori remained a strong Seventh-Day Adventist throughout her life, occasionally preaching, refusing ever to drink tea, coffee, or alcohol, and demanding that her grandchildren keep Saturday holy when they were in Kisii. However, she never became convinced that the God of Abraham and Jacob was opposed to polygamy. Prophetic dreams have been noted among other

Gusii women.[27] Perhaps they are a device whereby women sometimes can unconsciously insist on their way in a strongly patriarchal society in which the views of a husband cannot be directly questioned. In any case, the saga involved in fulfilling Bosibori's dream leaves no doubt that she was an extremely determined individual.

COLONIAL AFRICAN ADMINISTRATION

Prior to British colonialism the extent of hierarchical rule among most Kenyan peoples was extremely limited. Most of the territory's large number of competing ethnic groups had no single political organization but were simply cultural and linguistic entities or were loose alliances against other invading peoples.* The basic unit of governance tended to be the extended family, headed by the oldest living ancestor (father or grandfather). In a polygamous society these basic, patriarchal units could be quite large, constituting a village, such as the Kiambu one of Kiarii, Charles Karanja's grandfather. Typically superimposed on the family were clans, which were defined by relationship to a common ancestor and usually were loosely governed by the assembled elders (gerontocracies). In these systems loyalty to one's relatives and loyalty to the polity were the same thing.[28]

These entities were either too small or too democratic or both to serve as administrative units within the highly hierarchical British Empire. The English needed a manageable number of "leaders" whom they could hold responsible for the behavior of "their" people. In other words, they needed kings or chiefs, and where they did not find them they created them.[29]

In some places the British at first seemed unwitting in their creation of chiefs. For example, the colonial administration had little idea how the Mbere people of Embu District in eastern Kenya were governed when it asked them to send their chief to negotiate with it. The Mbere actually were a gerontocracy, and the elders thought it unwise to delegate one of their number. Instead, they sent as ambassador a young man who had some experience in dealing with outsiders. The British took him to be the chief, however, and treated him accordingly. By virtue of

---

*I prefer the term "ethnic group" to "tribe." By and large, in Africa the word tribe is applied to a group that shares a single language, whether or not it had a common political organization before colonialism, although even this identity is not perfect. In Europe the same sort of group is generally called a "nationality." What other than cultural stereotyping leads us to call Spain's Basques a nationality and Nigeria's Yoruba a tribe when the latter is numerically larger and both had separate governmental institutions before they were incorporated into their present states? The term "ethnic group" is more accurate and less loaded.

his monopoly over the channels of communication between the Mbere and the colonial administration, he was able to turn this mistake into a reality, for the British were prepared to use force to support the "legitimate" authority of chiefs who assisted them. In this way Chief Kuguraria and others like him ruled for half a century.[30]

One of these men was Musa Nyandusi, the father of Chief Secretary Simeon Nyachae. By the time Nyandusi became assistant chief of Nyaribari Location in Kisii District in 1926, the British were no longer under any illusion that the office was a traditional one. Although consideration was given to Nyandusi's membership in the strong Abanyamasicho clan, named for one of the sons of Nyaribari, it was not a primary qualification for appointment. More important were his literacy, the quality of his public speaking, his interest in economic and educational development, and the mission's recommendation. Musa Nyandusi became one of the most prominent of Kenya's colonial African chiefs, was made senior chief for Kisii in the early 1950s, and received five medals from the British for his service.[31] His position was the highest to which an African could aspire within the colonial system.

Above all else, the chiefs were responsible for the maintenance of law and order. They commanded the tribal (now administration) police and mediated disputes. Although the African tribunal courts were created for rendering judgment under traditional law, the British granted great scope to the chiefs for making binding orders, and it would be the rare, educated African who would know the limits to this authority under English law and how to go about challenging it.[32]

When Nyandusi became assistant chief in 1926 he immediately used these powers to hound the adherents of the Mumbo religious movement, whose aim was to drive the British out of the district. "Musa realized that the Gusii, who had been twice butchered by the British, in 1904 and 1908, had to be protected from the activities of disgruntled individuals whose movement would only lead to further bloodshed."[33]

Nyandusi had been made only an assistant chief because the British wanted to consolidate his Nyaribari Location into Kitutu Location and put it under its chief, Onsongo. Nyandusi wrote a letter of protest to the authorities and then led a campaign of noncooperation with Onsongo. Nyaribari's separate identity was finally accepted, and Nyandusi was elevated to the office of full chief in 1930.[34]

Robert and Barbara LeVine did anthropological field work among the Gusii in 1955 and wrote of Nyandusi:

> Except for some elders, the chief tolerates no contradiction or criticism at the weekly assembly meetings of the location. Most people are extremely deferential to him, but those who have defied him in some way find themselves ordered to court for tax delinquency or even told to leave the district

if they wish to avoid dire punishment. . . . The autocracy of the chief is resented by some but opposed by no one. Most people regard his power as vast, being backed up by the even greater power of the district commissioner. They respect his authority and appeal to it when they need to rather than protest against it.[35]

Chiefs were expected to be authoritarian figures, who would make quick, final decisions and keep order by commanding respect and even fear. They were not notable for their respect for the niceties of law or due process; they were known instead for their decisiveness, courage, presence, and ability to hold a crowd. Musa Nyandusi had these characteristics.

That people expected this type of behavior from chiefs and did not protest against it suggests that the role had a kind of legitimacy, but it does not mean that it was popular. As Arthur Stinchcombe suggests, the boundaries of a role's legitimate authority derive from the limits within which it will be supported by other centers of power in society. The consent of the governed is only one of the possible sources of such power.[36] In the colonial period legitimate authority was defined not by Africans, who had little power, but by Europeans and Great Britain. As Africans came to understand the rather broad boundaries within which the Crown was prepared to defend the authority of its representatives, they refined their conceptions of the role of the chief accordingly. They did not necessarily like the office or the way it was frequently used, but they had clear expectations of how its occupants would behave, nonetheless. When independence finally came and African power did become meaningful, the colonially developed expectations about the role behavior of chiefs helped shape the manner in which citizens, chiefs, and political authorities redefined the legitimate content of the office. Thus the role had greater continuity than one would have thought at first, given its frequent unpopularity and the grudging consent often given to it in the colonial period.

The resolution of land disputes was central to the chief's role. One of these incidents illustrates some of Nyandusi's qualities. The boundaries of the agricultural Gusii people touch on those of the pastoral Maasai, and conflicts between them over land are a part of their traditional relationship. The British, ever interested in law and order, wanted to resolve the problem and reduce the fighting. Nyandusi was prominent in demarcating the boundary and called public meetings to persuade his people to accept them and not fight the Maasai. When conflicts broke out nonetheless, he would literally stand between the combatants in order to get them to calm down. Such physical courage was characteristic of Nyandusi, a former wrestler known for his strength and quickness.

Chiefs were also responsible for the hut tax, which every family was required to pay and which was important to forcing Africans into the Europeans' cash economy. Nyandusi was aggressive and impressed the British with his effectiveness in tax collection. This revenue function made the chiefs unpopular, but it also contributed greatly to their power. The colonial government never expected one hundred percent effectiveness in tax collection, so chiefs had informal discretion in deciding whose tax obligation would be forgiven. It could be economically disadvantageous to lose the chief's favor.[37]

Musa Nyandusi's prominence derived not from his maintenance of law and order, however, for that was an area in which many other chiefs were equally effective. He also was aggressive in trying to modernize his location in the European model. He promoted education so vigorously that even today his Nyaribari Location enjoys an advantage over the rest of Kisii in this domain. He organized his people to build a large number of primary schools, put tremendous pressure on his subjects to let their children go to school, and personally donated the land for the first government secondary school in Kisii. Because of his efforts the Location also led the area in athletics and soccer.

Nyandusi was quick to accept the Europeans' economic innovations as well. He forced his people to build many primary (or feeder) roads, opening the area up to the market. At first the white settlers were successful in getting the government to prohibit Africans from growing coffee, the most lucrative market crop of the day. When the ban was dropped in the 1930s for those areas that were relatively remote from European farms, Nyandusi may have been the first African in Kenya to plant the crop. This helped to show the way for Kisii to become one of Kenya's prime smallholder areas for coffee.

Nyandusi understood the nature of the economic system the British were creating and saw clearly that Africans would have to work within it if they were to advance. The energy he applied to that vision has led the historian William Ochieng to defend him as one of the progressive colonial chiefs and to remark that he was "loved and respected" by his own people.[38]

Neither Nyandusi nor the colonial administration saw any conflict between his position and the advancement of his private wealth. The British were eager to encourage African participation in their market economy and pressed the chiefs in their employ to set an example for their subjects. Far from being subject to a conflict-of-interest code, chiefs were implicitly encouraged to use their positions to amass wealth and to demonstrate thereby that it paid to cooperate with the Europeans. Nyandusi became one of the wealthiest Africans in Nyanza Province. In addition to substantial landholdings, he owned shops and several maize-grinding mills (the first of which he opened in 1926). The outward signs of his wealth were his many wives, over one hundred children, a motorbike bought in 1933, and the area's first African-owned car in 1939.[39]

Having observed Nyandusi, the LeVines wrote:

> The power of the chief is of benefit to himself as well as to others. . . . The Gusii consider it appropriate for a chief to be wealthier than other persons, and if not outstandingly wealthy when appointed to office, he takes steps to acquire wealth as soon as possible afterward.[40]

Remember that this office was British created, not a traditional one.

Because of the multiplicity of his services to the colonial state, Nyandusi became quite influential within it. If there was a problem in another Location in Kisii, he would be sent to restore order. His opposition to candidates for chieftainships in the district was frequently definitive, and he was able to have his two immediate successors appointed from his clan.

Probably only Nyandusi's prominence enabled him to survive his "indiscreet" relationships with the cause of African nationalism. When Jomo Kenyatta toured western Kenya in the 1940s to broaden the base for the cause of greater African rights, he stayed at the home of Nyandusi. As the conflict with the British intensified and the Mau Mau uprising began among the Kikuyu, Nyandusi continued his relationship with Kenyatta. Although Nyandusi's power and wealth derived from his service to the British Crown, he shared with many other chiefs a deep resentment of European discrimination against Africans. Their advancement and that of their constituents would be still greater in a state in which the monopoly of whites over political power was broken. Thus many colonial chiefs covertly supported at least some African nationalist politicians. On October 15, 1952, Kenyatta was campaigning in Kisii for self-rule when he received a tip that the colonial administration was seeking to arrest him. Nyandusi hid him for the night and helped him escape to Nairobi. Kenyatta was arrested five days later. The British were furious when they discovered what Nyandusi had done, but he begged that he was only meeting traditional African obligations of hospitality to a visitor.

Despite such covert assistance to the African nationalist cause by some of the chiefs, none of them was able to survive the transition to independence. In the public's eye the colonial chiefs were too closely identified with the British, and they were swept out of office in 1964 by the new minister of home affairs, Oginga Odinga.[41] The intense tightening of the repressive apparatus of the state which the British instituted in response to the Mau Mau uprising in the early 1950s created deep resentment against those who administered it. Nyandusi had reached the age of mandatory retirement in 1964, and his departure therefore was routine rather than forced. Certainly, however, there were those who associated him with the subjugation of the old regime and who thought ill of him for it.[42]

Nonetheless, the chief's role that Musa Nyandusi and his peers carved out has survived them in independent Kenya. Contemporary chiefs adhere to an only slightly softened version of the role,[43] and Kenyan administrators who have assumed formerly British positions have been deeply influenced by the chief's model. Their concept of effective administration often is authoritarian, decisive, loosely bound by the law, and untroubled by conflicts of interest. It is important to see that such behavior is not at all a rejection of the socialization that the British administration provided but is instead in conformity to the roles the colonial government created *for Africans*.[44]

Another aspect of the colonial state in which Musa Nyandusi participated was local government. As the African response to colonialism changed in the 1920s from rebellion against the new state to demands for fuller participation in it, the British created local government bodies to try to channel the pressures. The Local Native Councils (LNCs) promulgated in 1924 had the power to levy taxes and to make bylaws concerning agriculture and education, but they were only advisory to the English district commissioners. Furthermore, LNC members were appointed by the colonial administration from among the chiefs and others judged friendly to the regime. Nominally, the LNCs were paralleled by the elected councils set up in the White Highlands to give Europeans a voice in their district affairs. But whereas the latter institutions were designed to give real power to democratically elected whites, the LNCs were instruments of co-optation and control.

Nyandusi became a member and the vice-chairman of his district's LNC when he became an assistant chief in 1926, but the proceedings were dominated by the British district commissioner, who was its chair. Significant elected representation was added to the councils in 1948, when they were renamed African District Councils (ADCs). Nyandusi retained both of his posts on the body, however, and it remained subject to control by the colonial administration. He finally became chair of the Kisii ADC in 1960 when independence was clearly imminent. He continued in that office until 1965, after which he remained chair of the Finance Committee until his death in 1970.

The African experience with local government was never with fully representative institutions and always involved supervision and control by field officers of the central government. The traditionally English elected and independent local government bodies that existed in the White Highlands might as well have been in another country as far as African experience was concerned.[45]

In 1931 Elijah Waicanguru (father of the veterinarian Muriithi) also joined the colonial administration, becoming the headman for Ihithe Sub-Location in Nyeri District. He was appointed one of the three elders (judges) on the African Tribunal Court for Tetu Division in 1935 and resigned as headman. He remained a tribunal elder until his retirement from the civil service in 1957. The tribunal courts were also a creation of the colonial state. They operated in order to adjudicate disputes under customary law, but had wider geographical jurisdiction and were more governed by English law and administrative supervision than purely traditional judicial processes would have been. In fact the British district commissioner served as the court of appeal for the tribunals. The proceedings in the tribunal courts were entirely oral and were conducted without the benefit of a written record. Thus the elders had to have an excellent memory for the details of the case and an ability for shrewd cross-examination of witnesses. In his eighties Waicanguru still had a superb memory and was an intense listener, leaning forward on his cane, watching closely, and speaking sparingly. Even at this advanced age, his sons deferred to his powers of recall on matters of family history.

Elijah Waicanguru too became a man of substance. He was able to buy a Chevrolet pickup truck in 1946, which even forty years later would be a sign of wealth in the rural areas. He didn't enter commerce, but his landholdings in Nyeri became significant, and he was innovative in his farm management. He and Chief Muhoya founded the first Kenyan African dairy cooperative, which opened at Githerere in Nyeri in 1949. He helped keep it operating during the years of the Mau Mau emergency by driving his own pickup for it. He was greatly interested in improved dairy stock and bought his own Friesian bull in 1956. It is little surprise that two of his sons became veterinarians.

Similarly, Philip Mule (father of the planner) left his employ as a mission-school teacher and joined the colonial government as a cashier clerk in the Kiteta Location of Machakos District in 1930. Before leaving his teaching, however, he married Ruth Katuku, one of his students, on September 20, 1930. She had started school in 1923 at age ten because there seemed to be nothing else to do. (Normally she would have been participating in traditional dances, but the missionaries had influenced the local government to ban them.) From school she joined the AIM church. She was bright, did extremely well in her studies, and reached Standard 4. She also was a bold young woman, as can be seen in her willingness to look into the "eyes" of the camera in her wedding photo. (See plate 8.) When her husband went off to Kiteta to take up his government position, she remained behind on their farm in Mbooni, which she continued to do throughout his official career. This was a common pattern; Lydia Wangeci and Elijah Waicanguru established two households as well when he became a tribunal elder in Nyeri town.

From his clerkship Mule was appointed first an elder and then president of the African Tribunal Court for Southern Machakos District, located at Tawa. (See plate 9.) In later years Philip Mule was extremely proud to have finished his 25-year career in the courts without ever having been imprisoned for corruption, which was not true for many of his colleagues. The temptation for the president of a tribunal court was great, for his judgments were rarely overturned and he had a lot of discretion. But Mule felt strongly that one should not take money one has not earned.

In spite of his principles, Mule became a man of substance; the combination of his salary, his rural residence, and his wide contacts gave him a competitive advantage. His wife had three permanent employees to help her on their farm—a housemaid, a foreman, and a supervisor of the casual laborers. Mule bought land near the court at Tawa, on which he grew fruit and kept livestock. He gradually sold this off to the government and the mission as they expanded. He built his first shop in 1948 and subsequently came to own three. This entry into commerce drove him out of the AIM, despite his status in it as a lay preacher. The sale of cigarettes and beer was crucial to the profitability of these early rural shops, but both were anathema to the fundamentalist AIM, and he was expelled. Despite this sacrifice of principle to profit, Mule was not an especially keen businessman; he seized whatever opportunities he could find to escape the discipline of personally managing his shops. Perhaps he felt stifled by the AIM in any case, as would his son Harris, and welcomed its objection to the imperatives of his trade. Certainly Philip Mule's modest success in commerce and his relative prosperity demonstrate how easy it was to make money in the middle years of colonialism for those who had a government salary and were ready to seize market opportunities.

In the years after Mule's retirement the shops failed, probably because competition became more intense with the fuller incorporation of rural Africans into the market economy, and perhaps partly because of his generosity. Philip Mule was always ready to help someone in need. He paid for the education not only of his brothers' children (a common practice for prosperous Africans) but of more distant relatives as well. He also helped to build an AIM church in Tawa in 1938 and a school in

Mbooni, giving of his own substance and organizing campaigns for the contributions of others.

Philip Mule's generosity was exceptionally great, but it also exemplifies certain strongly held values in African society. The life of a small farmer is an extremely risky one. Not only is one subject to the vagaries of weather and pests, but sickness at a time of peak agricultural labor can have devastating consequences. There are limits to the extent to which a family can provide for these risks all by itself in a subsistence economy: although grain can be stored, it is perishable; although animals can be acquired, they may die in a drought. The best protection comes from having a very wide and broadly dispersed network of friends and relatives with whom one regularly exchanges favors. If a crucial family member falls sick, someone in the network will help with the farm work. If the rains fail on one's own land, perhaps a distant relative's farm has had a good year. Helping one another is not just neighborliness in subsistence society—it is a crucial survival strategy in the face of large risks. Social exchanges are just as important as economic ones, and people invest heavily in the quality of their personal relationships. Wealth can be a transitory phenomenon given the fickleness of nature, and subsistence societies encourage the advantaged to buy community status and power by helping those in need.[46]

THE EMERGING AFRICAN SOCIAL STRUCTURE

The wealth and status accumulated by Musa Nyandusi, Elijah Waicanguru, Philip Mule, and those like them were something new in African society. (Contrast plate 15 with plates 12 and 14.) It was not the fact of wealth itself that was new; as is illustrated by Kiarii and Karanja, "traditional" African society had its share of rich men and the resultant inequalities. Instead, it was the fact that the wealth was coming from new sources. Colonialism had brought a dramatic expansion in the possibilities of commerce and for the first time made possible substantial sales of agricultural commodities; some, such as coffee and dairy products, sold for very high prices. Colonialism also introduced wages into the African economy, and salaries gave civil servants and teachers a huge relative advantage over their neighbors—a drought-free, steady, and easily tradeable income. Although wages, commerce, and agriculture were separate sources of income, they did not produce separate corresponding social formations; instead, those who had advantages in one sector tended to convert them into similar ones in other sectors as well. The new African elite stratum was simultaneously grounded in several parts of the economy.[47]

The new elites also were culturally differentiated from the rest of their societies. Previously, men of wealth and status had represented the epitome of a unified set of social values. The new stratum was distinguished by Christianity and literacy and held values that were at least partly and sometimes fundamentally distinct from those of most of their relatives. This was evident, for example, in the opposition of Elijah Waicanguru and his wife Lydia Wangeci to Kikuyu female-circumcision rites of initiation.

Most observers now see in this group the beginnings of an African petty-bourgeois class.[48] These men and their families still felt very much a part of their societies and were generally accepted as leaders within them. That the other, higher-class positions in colonial society carried substantially greater wealth and power and were monopolized by Europeans (and, to a lesser extent, Asians) dampened people's consciousness of inter-African class differences. Over time the value differences associated with this developing petty-bourgeois class actually have become less clear, as Christianity and education have become more widespread. But its social distinctness continues and remains rooted in the overlapping advantages of wage employment, cash-crop agriculture, and small commerce.

The final novelty of this elite, which reinforces our acceptance of it as an emergent new class, was its ability to pass on its privilege to its children. Traditionally, a wealthy man would acquire many wives, have large numbers of children, and thereby quickly disperse his riches into multiple small inheritances. Indeed, for those such as Musa Nyandusi, who followed in the polygamous tradition and most of whose wives were illiterate, this pattern of dissipation of wealth was followed, and most of their children have fallen back into the mass of the peasantry. Those who were monogamous and who expended a special effort to pass on their educational advantages to their offspring were able to propel them to positions at least as privileged as their own. All of Philip and Ruth Mule's nine children and eight of nine of Elijah and Lydia Waicanguru's either became or married professionals. This success rate may be unusually high, but a casual, informal survey of Kenya's senior civil servants will reveal that a surprisingly large minority have parents of similar background. Surveys of university students in East Africa have shown, for example, that the children of schoolteachers are overrepresented by twenty times their proportion in the population.[49] Independence brought tremendous upward mobility for some, but the chances of rising were not evenly distributed. Rather than seeing the mobility as a random or intelligence-based leap out of the mass, it is more accurate to see much of it as the opening up of a compressed accordion, with those families that were on the top by the middle of the colonial period generally remaining there, though at a higher level.

MONOPOLY AND CONTROL

A look at the formal face of Kenya's institutional heritage reveals twin features of monopoly and control. Unprofitable white settlers distorted the colony's polity and economy. Although the settlers appropriated huge farms at concessionary prices, most of them had to struggle to make their enterprises viable, until they were saved by the explosion in demand for primary products brought on by World War II. As these were Englishmen, and some were even members of the British House of Lords, they expected and demanded representation and a government responsive to their needs. Although the settlers' Legislative Council never gained internal self-rule in the Rhodesian model, it was able to dominate in many policy spheres and to skew both the economy and government services to meet the needs of whites. Thus the pattern of a bimodal economy, in which favoritism was shown to large farms at the expense of small ones, was created in the colonial period. The expectation that large-farm owners would have political influence and would be pampered by the state was institutionalized in this era. As Africans had neither benefited from nor participated in the exercise of this power, it was an open question whether this set of values could survive independence. The British were determined that they should, and as it happened, they succeeded. The mechanisms by which these values were reinstitutionalized after Africans achieved power will be analyzed in chapter 4.

The white settlers thought of themselves as an outpost of capitalism, but they were not averse to socialist measures to protect their profits. During the tribulations of the 1930s the government introduced subsidized credit for white farms and created a number of marketing monopolies. Some, such as the Kenya Cooperative Creameries, were large-farmer owned; others, such as the Coffee and Wheat Boards, were explicit state structures. All of them held legal monopolies, were governed by settler-dominated boards, and existed to serve large-farm interests.

As Africans began to be permitted to grow the more lucrative market crops in the 1930s, they found themselves participating through these monopolistic state structures. Where, as with coffee and milk, an intermediary was needed between the large-scale-oriented settler institutions and the small African producers, the state created monopolies for African producer cooperatives. Thus Africans rarely experienced the modern agricultural market as a domain of private competitive enterprise; instead, it was almost always the province of a state socialism for the well-to-do.[50] Kenya's contemporary leaders inherited their distrust of competition and private commerce in agricultural commodities from their colonial predecessors.

Whereas the white settlers governed these monopolies, African producers were subject to their control. In the colonial era peasants were believed to be economically irrational, unresponsive to the normal incentives of profits. Thus it was thought that African farmers had to be administratively controlled if they were to participate effectively in world agricultural markets. As new crops were introduced, African producers were often coerced as to what, when, and how they would plant, were subject to supervision by the state's agricultural agents, and had to sell through state-sanctioned monopolies, which regulated the quality of their product and deducted taxes, debts, and overhead before payment was made. As the colonial chiefs were frequently the instruments and supervisors of this coercive apparatus, they understood well a system in which it was the state, not the market or the producer, who determined what was best for the farmer.

Obviously, these institutions governing agricultural production and exchange were not designed with African interests in mind. They nonetheless enjoyed some advantage in the struggle to design a new set of institutions after independence because of two interacting social processes. Exchange functions most efficiently when it is predictable. It takes time and effort to understand how a new system of exchange works and to develop and enforce new rules for its operation. Thus economic growth is greater in systems in which economic institutions are stable and enjoy broad support than in those troubled by rapid change and conflict.[51] A significant alteration of the institutions that regulate and operate an economy will lead to at least a short-term decline in the total production of value, because it will generate conflict, and exchange processes will no longer be routine. The change may still be worth it; it may lead to even greater growth in the long run, or it may redirect value to a newly powerful group, which will be better off even if the economy as a whole is not. The point is, not that change is inappropriate, but that it will be experienced as costly by the system as a whole in the short run, thus giving considerable inertia to existing arrangements.

The second social process interacts with and reinforces the first. We noted in chapter 1 that humans are "satisficers," not optimizers; they seek a satisfactory solution to their problems, not the best one possible. By the end of the colonial period Africans were deeply discontented with the discrimination that they were suffering within their own country, but in seeking to change the system they tended to adopt the first acceptable new arrangements that they found, not to search and struggle until they found the optimal ones for their interests. This social process, like the first, provided a definite (but not insurmountable) advantage to Kenya's existing, colonial institutions.

CONCLUSIONS

These governmental, economic, and social institutions were the ones that Kenya inherited at independence and that were most influential in determining its approach to rural development and governance. Although they were not all the institutions that Kenya had, they were the ones to which the colonial African elites had been most thoroughly socialized; and it was the children of this group who disproportionately assumed the reins of power at the transition.

These colonial African elites had experienced the transition from subsistence agriculture to a system increasingly oriented to the market and had personally profited from the sale of export crops. They had witnessed the forcible change of Kenya from societies in which land was abundant and which were characterized by a unimodal distribution of small farms to a bimodal system with large farms, labor markets, and land scarcity. The institutions servicing this new agriculture were not those of a free market but those of monopoly and control. They had seen the replacement of their relatively democratic gerontocracies by a hierarchical and unresponsive state, which used chiefs as instruments of arbitrary control and local government as mechanisms of co-optation. They had experienced the converting power of the Christian missions and had adopted many new values from them. But they had also found in the education the missions provided the vehicle for upward mobility in colonial society and the tool for eventually challenging it.

By the end of the colonial era they were members of an emergent petty-bourgeois class and had become increasingly differentiated from the peasant class of subsistence farmers and ordinary laborers by the overlapping advantages of export-crop production, small commerce, and government employment. They were beginning to challenge the European and Asian commercial and agricultural bourgeoisies for dominance over Kenyan society. But they were not really separated from the peasantry from which they came. Their neighbors and most of their relatives were peasants, to whom they were still tied by traditional social exchange obligations. Only their grandchildren would feel free to neglect these village demands.

CHAPTER THREE

Growing Up and Out of Colonialism

Nyandusi, Mule, Waicanguru, and Karanja could only accommodate to colonialism; their children were to supplant it. The older generation lent what support they could as their offspring scaled the steep pyramid of the colonial educational system and came out on top where, after independence, they could challenge the British for the management of the new state. The lives of the four future administrators we are studying were similar in this phase, but the ways they responded to the school system in this period presaged later differences in their careers.

CHARLES KIBE KARANJA

Karanja, the father of the tea administrator, had held out against the new forces of colonialism as long as he could. As the son of Kiarii, he was a man of wealth and status in traditional society, with 160 acres of prime land and five wives. Christianity and wage employment offered him no advantages; they only threatened the system in which he was already an elite. He did seek to expand the benefit of his assets and grew wattle for the export market. This very market involvement, however, ultimately led him to realize that he had underestimated the force of the changes taking place around him. It became clear that his family would have to adapt if it was to retain its privileged position. In 1939 he went to Thika to sell a truckload of wattle bark and felt that he was cheated in the sale because he could not read. After discussing the matter with Kiarii, his father, he decided that despite the dangers of Christianity that infected the schools, one of his children would have to learn how to read, so as to represent the family's financial interests. Among his sons,

Kibe was obedient, had a good memory, and was interested, and so he was the one chosen.

Kibe wa Karanja was born in Karatu village of Ndarugu Location in Kiambu District in about 1931, the second child of Karanja's second wife, Njeri (more usually known by her nickname, Nyagitiri). As an adult, he would become general manager of the Kenya Tea Development Authority and be known as Charles Karanja.

Kibe was a very active child. At four he often followed his father to the field when he went to plant potatoes and tried unsuccessfully to imitate his digging with a panga (a machete). Nyagitiri trained her children when young to work, setting out two sticks and asking them to dig between them. As is common among the Kikuyu, friends used to compliment Nyagitiri on the child Kibe's brightness.

Kibe began his studies in September 1939 at the Ndarugu Out School of the Gospel Missionary Society, which later merged into the PCEA. To attend, he had to have special clothes, for the family of Karanja did not accept European dress. The head teacher took Karanja and young Kibe to a local shop, where they bought the shirt and shorts which constituted the school uniform.

When Karanja had decided to send Kibe to school, he gave the eight-year-old firm instructions that he must always obey his father and not become a Christian. The mission influence pervaded the schools in this era, however, and after only two years Kibe already was having doubts about traditional religious practices. In 1941, when Karanja slaughtered a goat for a Kikuyu ceremony, Kibe refused to eat it. Karanja in anger sent the boy off to tend the family's herd of goats while the other celebrants were eating. One hundred goats were beyond the capability of a ten-year-old, however, and unbeknownst to Kibe, some got away from him. Only when he was bringing the herd home at the end of the day did he see the wayward ones eating a neighbor's crops. He knew that he would be in trouble, and rather than face his father's wrath, he decided to run away.

He set out for a pyrethrum plantation where one of his father's relatives was a supervisor. It was two days' walk away, ten miles into the Aberdare Forest, and Kibe had to ask directions on the way, having never been there before. The first night he found himself at the forest's edge and asked someone to give him food and shelter. He knew there were wild animals in the forest and was afraid to go into it alone. He waited until another party passed along the path and then followed behind out of sight. Once there he got work through his relative for a wage of three shillings a month. After three weeks, however, Karanja got word of where he was and sent Kibe's older brother to fetch him home, promising that the boy would not be beaten. Kibe never did get any pay for his three weeks' work.

Back at home, Kibe refused to go back to Ndarugu School, being shy of returning to something he had left. So Karanja arranged for him to go to Mutunguru Kikuyu Independent School, where a cousin was headmaster. The independent schools had been set up to escape the missionary objections to female circumcision, and doubtless Karanja welcomed the idea of getting education for his son without more Christian contamination.

The school was farther away from home, however, and Kibe had to do the milking before he went. One day he was late and for his tardiness was given five strokes of the cane (switch). Coming home that day, he and a friend agreed to meet the following morning and get to school early. They arranged that the one who first passed a certain point on the way to school would leave a branch to let the other know that he should hurry to catch up with him. But the friend forgot to leave the branch, and Kibe walked slowly, thinking that he must be early. When he got to school he saw that he was late and knew that he would be caned. So instead he went to play. He played hooky for a week until the teacher complained to Karanja.

Kibe knew that his father would beat him, so this time he ran away to work on a coffee plantation 25 km (15 mi.) away. Once again he managed to stay only three weeks before he was brought home, but this time he returned with 2.15 shillings in earnings. He refused to return to school and instead stayed home to tend the sheep and goats and to master a new Kikuyu dance, the Muthuu. The dance was very popular among boys of that generation, involving bells tied to the legs and the twirling of imitation swords. Sometimes the boys would be paid to perform it as a praise dance for someone. Forty years later Kibe would still leap to his feet at the mention of the Muthuu to demonstrate its rhythm and basic steps.

In 1942 Karanja asked Kibe if he'd like to return to school, and he finally agreed. He was sent back to the mission school at Ndarugu where he had first begun. Kibe had settled down and become serious about his studies at this point, and the teacher had difficulty in deciding which class to place him in. In those days Africans received two years of pre-primary school before they took the regulation Standards 1 and 2, after which they had to pass the first of a series of competitive exams before going further. The teacher decided to try Kibe in Standard 2, where he quickly rose to the head of the class. At the end of the year he took the exam that passed him out of the school.

For Standard 3 Kibe went to Ng'enda Primary School, which was too far away for him to live at home. The first term he stayed in a bungalow with other boys, and they cooked for themselves. The second term he stayed with a teacher, for whom he worked. For the third he lived with a friend nearby, whose mother cooked for them. Children were not "cared for" in boarding schools in this era.

At the end of Standard 3 Kibe took the Common Entrance Exam, on which he did extremely well, and was picked by interview to go to the Presbyterian Thogoto Primary School at Kikuyu. No more than ten of the class at Ng'enda were ever selected to go on, and Kibe's new school was the most prestigious in central Kenya. At every one of the frequent examination points, the educational pyramid narrowed considerably and the competition was intense.

When Kibe entered Thogoto at age thirteen in 1944, he found no one whom he knew, and students from as far away as Nyeri and Nakuru were there. In fact, he and Ishmael Muriithi (the veterinarian) did Standard 6 together in 1946. The annual fees, including board and uniforms, were eighty shillings ($16.15). Karanja was proud that, as a rich man, he was always able to pay the school fees for his children. (Many of his other offspring subsequently opted for education.) Many African youngsters have to drop out of school because of the inability of their families to pay their school fees; until relatively recently, others have been unable even to begin. The brightest poor students often get scholarships or are helped by their relatives with their fees. But if they have the kind of rocky beginning to their education that Kibe had, even the gifted youths can fall by the wayside if money is scarce for their families. Children whose parents are better off and clearly understand the importance of education to upward mobility in Kenyan society have a definite advantage in an otherwise meritocratic climb to the top.

There were seventy-two in the entering class and Kibe's class standing was forty-ninth in the first term and fiftieth in the second. At this point he realized that only fifty students were going to be permitted to continue to Standard 5. He was on the borderline, and he thought that if he were dropped, his father would decline to send him to another school. He was already working hard and didn't know how to improve. So he befriended the boy who was first in the class. He followed him absolutely everywhere he went, often without the other's realizing it. When he slept, Kibe slept; when he played, Kibe played; and most important, whenever he studied, Kibe studied. Kibe's class standing rose to twenty-sixth. From this experience he realized that he hadn't been studying as hard as he could, and in Standard 5 he spent most of his time reading. He finished that year in the top six in the class, and Standard 6 in the top ten. There were only a few whom he could never beat in school, among them Margaret Wambui, daughter of Jomo Kenyatta.

Kibe was circumcised during the school holidays in August 1946, but he declined to participate in the traditional initiation education and the ceremony of "rebirth," for he felt he was a Christian. Karanja accepted this affront to his beliefs because Kibe was the only boy from the area who had been able to reach such prestigious heights in the educational system. When Kibe was baptized into the church he took the name Charles and became officially known as Charles Kibe Karanja. In this way his given name was subtly transformed into a middle initial, and he has since been known as Charles Karanja, confusing him somewhat with his father among the Kikuyu. The same happened to Harris Mutio Mule. Ishmael Muriithi and Simeon Nyachae dealt with the dilemmas of English naming conventions by assuming their given names as their surnames.

Charles Kibe Karanja took the Kenya African Primary Examination (KAPE) in November 1946 and passed well with nine points. He had applied to go to the elite Alliance High School, however, and when he was turned down there, he was offered admission at an agricultural training school instead. He declined the place, for his father said that agricultural instructors and teachers never become rich.

Instead, he looked for a school in which he could repeat Standard 6 and the exam and was accepted at St. Mary's Primary School, Lioki. While he was there a protest developed over the food they were being given—maize without the accompanying beans to which the Kikuyu are accustomed. Other boys called a meeting to discuss a strike, at which Kibe spoke forcefully in favor of the action. He and his cohorts went home in protest, but after two weeks Kibe's father sent him back to see what had happened. He found that all the others had already returned and been disciplined. Furthermore, someone had told the headmaster of his protest speech. He received eight strokes of the cane and as a result decided never again to join a strike.

This time he passed very well, with fifteen points, but he had decided not to risk application to the Protestant Alliance High School again. Thus he was one of five boys in his class of fifty at St. Mary's who was selected to go to the nearly as prestigious Catholic equivalent, Mangu High School. This pair of school choices inclined Charles Karanja away from the Presbyterians and toward the Roman Catholic church, which he joined at Mangu in 1949. Even his father, Karanja wa Kiarii, in his very old age was eventually baptized into the faith. Charles Karanja, the only one of the four administrators whose parents were not Christian, was also the only one who attended church frequently as an adult. It is unusual for well-educated Africans to be regular church attenders, even for those such as Ishmael Muriithi (the veterinarian) who took their membership seriously.[1]

When Charles Karanja entered Mangu High School, near Thika, in

January 1948, his class consisted of but twenty-five boys, the whole school of only a hundred. Most of them were destined for elite positions in Kenyan society. (See plate 10.) Mwai Kibaki, who later became vice-president of Kenya, was in the class ahead of him, a class that ultimately produced ten medical doctors as well. A tight network of friendships, cutting across district and ethnic boundaries, was formed during these years. (This phenomenon was somewhat less characteristic of the later generations of educational elites, who passed through a broader, less selective funnel and who therefore more often attended schools near home with others of their ethnic group.) These networks of "old school boys" were frequently quite important to Kenyan policy-making.

At Mangu Charles was the best debater in his class, ran for Kiambu in an athletics meet in Nyeri in 1951, and played on the second string of the football team. The game was played without shoes, and he complained that this hurt his toes. He conformed strictly to the school rules and went through four years without ever being punished, which was very unusual. As a consequence he was made first a prefect and then deputy head prefect in his final year. Prefects were appointed by the school administration and were an important part of the way in which these schools sought to socialize future elites in the exercise of authority.[2] Charles was an effective and hard disciplinarian.

The pattern of selective national exams continued at Mangu, with one after two years and the Ordinary Level School Certificate at the end of four. (See fig. 3.1.) All the remaining members of his class passed the latter, but Charles was one of only eight who was in the First Division. Nonetheless, he could not go to the elite Makerere College in Uganda. He had received only a Pass on the English-language portion of the exam. This was ironic, for he was among the top in the subject at Mangu, and his essays were often read in class. He had misinterpreted a key essay question on the exam and because of that error lost his chance to pursue a career in the social sciences or humanities.

He went instead to the Kampala (Uganda) Engineering School for a five-year diploma course in civil engineering in 1952. (No degree programs of any kind were available for Africans in East Africa until 1954.) This too was a prestigious course; there were those who were accepted at Makerere who opted for the Engineering School instead. At one point all of the African engineers in the Kenyan Ministry of Works had been through it. The course was a rigorous, practical one, teaching applied rather than pure science. The students studied surveying and the construction of buildings, roads, and water supplies, doing a great deal of practical work in the process. Charles finished somewhere in the upper half of his class.

He held a number of school offices while at Kampala. He was elected

Fig. 3.1 The Kenyan colonial education system for Africans

Primary	Preprimary	A	
		B	
	Standard	1	
		2	
		3	
			Common Entrance Exam
Upper Primary or Intermediate		4	
		5	
		6	
			Kenya African Primary Exam
Secondary	Form	I	
		II	
		III	
		IV	
			School Certificate (Ordinary
College (Technical School) University	Form	V (1)	Level) (Cambridge)
		VI (2)	
			Advanced Level School
		1 (3)	Certificate
		2 (4)	
		3 (5)	
			(University degree or technical school diploma)

KEY: ══════ major, state-administered, filtering exams

────── minor, school-administered, filtering points

NOTE: The Kenyan African educational system was in flux in the colonial period, and the requirements and names of various stages shifted at some points. The above is a modal picture of the system.

class representative to the school's Student Club in his first year, was reelected each subsequent year, and was unanimously selected as president in his final year. At one point he served as catering officer for the students and at others was president of the Debating Society and of the Catholic student group. Charles's love of office and speaking were such that he and many of his classmates expected him to run for Parliament one day, something that in fact never came to pass.

Mau Mau from Kiambu

This aptitude for politics did not lead Charles Karanja to involvement in the struggles sweeping his homeland during his school years. The simmering revolt of the Kikuyus against their restricted access to land and colonialism's white domination finally led to the declaration of a state of emergency by the colonial government in 1952. Central Province was effectively placed under military occupation, and Kikuyus were repatriated to their homes from jobs in the urban areas and the "White Highlands." Many fled into the forests to fight a guerrilla war, and thousands of others were put in detention for their suspected involvement. Kikuyus themselves were bitterly divided between those who supported the Mau Mau (now known as the freedom fighters) and the Home Guards. The latter assisted the British to suppress the uprising because of the Mau Mau's brutality and rejection of both Christian and traditional religious values.[3]

Karanja wa Kiarii and his family, however, remained uninvolved in the struggle. No member of the family either took the Mau Mau oath or identified with the Home Guards. Many of the wealthy Kikuyu were able to escape without ever being forced by either side to commit themselves. Some of Karanja wa Kiarii's land was taken over for a "strategic hamlet" type of village, into which the Kikuyus were herded to keep them from the guerrillas. But he was subsequently compensated for this loss during the process of land registration and consolidation that the British forced on the Kikuyu as part of the pacification effort.

Charles Karanja himself was never asked to take the oath. There seems to have been a tacit decision on the part of the Mau Mau not to involve the Kikuyu student elite, so as to speed them on their way to the education that would eventually pose a different type of challenge to the British. And because of that disengagement the government did not disrupt the progress of Kikuyus in school. Charles Karanja was even able to discuss politics in Uganda to an extent that would have been dangerous in Kenya. He was harassed somewhat while at home for the holidays, but not overly much. He is unusually dark for a Kikuyu and so generally wasn't taken for one as long as he kept quiet. He was detained in a Mau Mau screening camp for two weeks when he finished at Kampala, but was released when he persuaded the Home Guard elders that he had never taken the oath. In his own words, "As a tribe we suffered, but I didn't personally."

After graduation Charles Karanja married Philomena Ndanga on December 22, 1956. Her father was a court elder, like Elijah Waicanguru and Philip Mule, and her grandfather had been a chief. Karanja had met her at a Catholic church near his home in 1949. She went to Loreto Convent, Limuru, for her secondary education. She qualified as a primary-school teacher in 1953 and started teaching early in 1954. In October of that year she bore Charles a son. In accordance with Kikuyu custom, Charles's father paid a dowry to her parents of a thousand shillings, two heifer calves, and five lambs. It was mutually agreed that the actual marriage had to be postponed until after Charles Karanja's graduation at the end of November 1956.

With marriage and graduation Charles assumed a position as engineering assistant in Nakuru with the Ministry of Works, which had given him a full bursary (scholarship) at Kampala. His education was extended further in 1961 when the Kenya government decided to provide scholarships for Africans with his qualifications to go oversees for an engineering degree. He was sent to the University of Toronto in Canada, without his wife and family, which by then consisted of four children. The combination of homesickness for his family and excitement at Kenya's impending independence led him to abort his degree program after one year and to return home in August 1962. This decision effectively ended Charles Karanja's chances of ever reaching the highest engineering positions in the Kenya government.

Karanja's school years exhibited his willfulness, ambition, and love for public roles. They also brought him to an acceptance of authority and gave him practice in its exercise. His mistaken reading of a single essay question on the English portion of the Secondary School Certificate exam, by precluding his study of the social sciences, consigned him to a technical career.

SIMEON NYACHAE

Chief Secretary Simeon Nyachae's early years were spent with his mother. He was later to remark, "In a polygamous home the women tend to take hold of the children [especially when they are young], leaving the father nowhere." As Nyachae grew up he became unusually close to his father, but in the years before his schooling he belonged to his mother. Pauline Bosibori had but two children, and James Oiruria was only two years older than Nyachae. The two brothers were very close. Nyachae was brighter, more aggressive, and more talkative (like his mother), so that he tended to dominate Oiruria. But whatever conflicts they had were quickly compromised in their friendship. These earliest years included ones on the mission station while their mother was learning to read.

When Nyachae was about eight years old his father employed a teacher for several of his boys at his home. After a year or so, in 1941, Musa Nyandusi sent Nyachae and Oiruria to begin their formal education at Nyanchwa Primary School, which was run by the Seventh-Day

Adventists. During these years the boys lived at home, and Pauline Bosibori watched over their education. She would punish them with a switch if they missed classes, and she drilled them on their arithmetic. The boys would cry if they got a sum wrong and laugh if it was right. Because they had a literate mother, Oiruria and Nyachae got more help at home with their education than was usual for those of their generation. Simeon Nyachae was the timekeeper at Nyanchwa, the one who hand rings the bell that signals the start and end of classes. There would be twenty to thirty children in a class at Nyanchwa. All writing was done with chalk on wood-frame slates. The first several years of primary education were in the local vernacular, after which teaching in Swahili (East Africa's Bantu lingua franca) was begun. Instruction in English began in intermediate school. All the national examination hurdles through which Kenyan children pass were (and still are) taken in Swahili or English. A gift for languages therefore is a prerequisite to education in Kenya.

In 1947 the two brothers and two of Nyandusi's other sons graduated to intermediate school and were sent to Kereri. It was too far away for the boys to stay at home, so Nyandusi arranged a place for them with Stephen Obure, an African Native Council employee whose son much later became a member of Parliament from Kisii. Nyachae left his brother behind at Kereri in 1949 and joined the Kisii government African High School, which was built on land donated by his father. This secondary school was not as cosmopolitan as those attended by Karanja, Mule, and Muriithi, for only 20 percent of its students came from outside Kisii District. Chief Nyandusi would visit the school regularly to check on his son's progress, until Nyachae terminated his secondary education in 1953.

During his school years Nyachae excelled in athletics. He was first in Nyanza Province in the hurdles and the long jump, and his record in the latter stood for thirteen years. He ran the 100- and 440-yard dashes as well, but he did not play football (soccer). When he was young he had hit his head on a goalpost playing the game, and his father forbade his further participation in the sport.

Most of Musa Nyandusi's sons did poorly in school. This was common for the children of chiefs, unlike the other African elites. The chiefs were more likely to be polygamous and to have illiterate wives. Their many children also suffered from being too visibly close to wealth and power, and so they often would be bossy, flash money around, and fail to apply themselves seriously to their studies. Given the extreme competitiveness of education in that generation, this lack of attention was fatal to their progress. Simeon Nyachae was different; he was bright, more serious about his studies, and less affected by his father's status.

Nyandusi's first son, Ayako, had also done well in school, and the chief had hoped that he would succeed him in office, although the post was not hereditary. Ayako died in 1951, however, and Musa Nyandusi increasingly came to focus on Nyachae. He would take him in his car to meetings, send him round to collect the money from his several flour mills, and delegate him to report on coffee Cooperative Society meetings.

Although Nyachae did well in school, he was more of an all-rounder than a scholar. It appeared to his teachers that his maturity was ahead of his academic development. Thus some of them concurred with Musa Nyandusi when he withdrew Nyachae from the system in 1953 when he was a year shy of the secondary Ordinary Level School Certificate exam. Nyandusi felt that a higher education was unnecessary for the chief's career that he wanted for his son. (See fig. 3.1.)

In 1954 Nyachae began work as a district clerk, stationed in Nyaribari Location where his father was chief. In effect he was being apprenticed. During the time that he worked there he was sent for some basic administrative courses at Maseno Government Training Institute.

In 1954 the elders also helped him select a wife, Esther Nyaboke, who came from a prominent family in a neighboring clan, was sixteen years old, and had gone as far as Standard 4 in primary school. Later that year she bore him a daughter. She was ultimately to bear him several more children, including sons.* But in the first years of the marriage the elders were concerned that the couple had not had a son. The elders and Musa Nyandusi put considerable pressure on Nyachae to take a second wife, which he did in 1955. This wife, Druscilla Kerubo, died three months after she gave birth to a daughter, who was then reared in her early years by her grandmother, Pauline Bosibori.

In 1957 Nyachae took as his wife Martha Mwango, who like Esther was sixteen at the time and had left school after Standard 4. She came from another prominent family and was the half-sister of Lawrence Sagini, who was a close friend and adviser to Nyachae and later became Kisii's first member of Parliament. Sagini's influence was important in gaining consent for the marriage, for Martha was to have the lower status of being a second wife. Between 1958 and 1975 Martha gave Nyachae several more children.

Both of these wives remained in Kisii when Nyachae moved to a national-level career in 1960. He himself feels that his polygamy was a mistake, that a father cannot give adequate attention to a family of this

---

*Gusii custom dictates that one's children should never be counted, which makes it inappropriate to give their names or birth dates in a public document. Out of respect for this custom, the details of Nyachae's family are kept vague here.

nature, and that there is a danger that his children will be emotionally lost to him. The marriages of these years reflected the image his father and the elders held of the type of wives that were appropriate to a chief. He himself would never say so, but these women clearly were not ideally suited to help him in the national arena in which he was to operate subsequently. Polygamy at least enabled him to marry more advantageously later without severing his responsibilities to his early wives through divorce.

By 1957 it was evident to both Nyachae and Musa Nyandusi that they had made a mistake in renouncing his higher education. Ghana won its independence from Great Britain in that year, and it was clear that able Africans could aspire to considerably higher offices than that of chief. His mother, Pauline Bosibori, dreamed that Nyachae would not become a chief, and he himself was quite upset when his friend and brother-in-law, Sagini, won a scholarship to pursue his B.A. in the United States.

With the help of the district commissioner and Robert LeVine, an American anthropologist, Nyachae found a place at South Devon Technical College at Torquay in the United Kingdom, where he could pursue a one-year Diploma in Public and Social Administration. To get him there Musa Nyandusi shrewdly insisted on raising assistance for his expenses through the African District Council (of which he was vice-chair) so that Nyachae and the Gusii would both feel that he had an obligation to serve them in administration.

Torquay was a relatively small and provincial college of three thousand in those days, and its public-administration program was designed for those who would serve in local governments and the middle levels of welfare administration. Those who were expected to hold the highest administrative posts in Great Britain and the colonies would have studied instead at Oxford or Cambridge. The particular program in which Nyachae participated was designed for students from the colonies; a group photo from the period shows Nyachae with students from Sarawak, Zambia, Borneo, and Malawi. (See plate 11.) The curriculum covered the geography of developing countries, community economics, social policy, law, government, and administration. The things that struck Nyachae about the program were the comparisons of administrative systems that it offered and the openness to criticism of British government. Visits to farms, local council debates, and central ministries were frequent.[4] His "digs" were with a local family. The amount, quality, and breadth of Nyachae's education were limited, compared with the other three managers and with most of those who achieved the most senior administrative (as opposed to political) positions in independent Kenya.

Upon his return to Kenya, Nyachae became a district assistant in the Provincial Administration. This position was the African equivalent of the district officer, the office that an Englishman first held on entry to this elite cadre, which was responsible for the general administration of the colony. Through Nyandusi's influence Nyachae's first posting was to Kisii. There his main duties were assisting the cooperative movement, supervising the traditional courts, and facilitating the expansion of education. More schools were needed as the political struggle for independence burst out of the strictures of the Emergency. But the missions, which were still the primary vehicle for education, had difficulty in getting land. Nyachae spent a great deal of time working with the District Education Board to get land set aside for the purpose. He also supervised Kisii's four tribunal courts, making sure that their application of customary law did not contradict the Penal or Civil Procedure Codes. As a district assistant, he had the powers of a third-class magistrate and could overturn certain classes of cases. Others could be referred to the district commissioner in his capacity as a first-class magistrate. The colonial Provincial Administration combined aspects of the executive, legislative, and judicial functions in its governance of Africans. In Kisii, though adjustments to fines were common, it was rare for the Provincial Administration to have to overturn a tribunal court decision.

Nyachae wanted to move out from under his father's wing and finally succeeded in getting transferred out of Kisii in 1960. He was posted to Ukwala in Siaya District, a Luo area. There was tension between the Luos and the Gusii at the time, and Nyachae did not feel comfortable administering the Luo; he resigned immediately. He became instead the labor and welfare officer and the first African in management of the East African Breweries. Musa Nyandusi's shrewdness in asking council assistance for Nyachae's studies in the U.K. became evident at this point. A delegation of eight Kisii chiefs, including Nyandusi, was sent to Nairobi, and Nyachae was summoned to the office of the chief native commissioner. Under great pressure Nyachae finally consented to rejoin the Provincial Administration, but only on condition that he not be sent back to Ukwala.

The Political Struggle for Independence

In November 1961 Nyachae was posted to Kangundo Division in Machakos District, where he served first as a district assistant and then as the district officer for the division. This was one of the more difficult Provincial Administration postings in Kenya at the time because it was a center of agitation against British rule.

The earliest forms of resistance to colonialism had been directed *against* the state itself. However, beginning with what are known as the Harry Thuku riots of 1922,[5] protest turned to a demand for increased rights for Africans *within* the state. Jomo Kenyatta, a nationalist Kikuyu, was the leader of this struggle from the late 1920s, even during his extended stays in England.[6] As the people most disrupted and changed by colonialism, the Kikuyu played a leading role in the accelerating progress of African nationalism, and it was among them that the Mau Mau uprising occurred. From the 1930s, however, Kenyatta had used the vehicle, first, of the Kikuyu Central Association, and second, of his Kenya African Union (KAU) to spread the nationalist gospel among the country's other peoples. Although Kenyatta denied to his death that either he or the KAU had any involvement in Mau Mau, he and five other officers of the KAU were detained when the State of Emergency was declared. Among those so imprisoned without trial or sentence was Paul Ngei, a Kamba who would serve in the independent country's cabinet into the 1980s. Kangundo, to which Nyachae was posted, was his home.

During the time of the Emergency, African politics were heavily restricted, especially in Central Province. Country wide African political parties were banned, for example, and the district-level parties that were permitted contributed to the fragmented, ethnic politics that were to trouble Kenya after independence.[7] Men such as Tom Mboya used the labor movement and other vehicles to keep the struggle for African political rights alive with a momentum that accelerated through the 1950s despite (or perhaps because of) the Emergency.[8] African demand for the vote and the end of colonialism became genuinely nationwide, and political participation was truly a mass movement. By the end of the decade it was evident that universal suffrage, majority rule, African governance, and independence were on the horizon. As a result of sustained pressure by the "legal" African nationalist parties, Jomo Kenyatta and the rest of the KAU executive were released from detention in August 1961. An African coalition government was formed in 1962 under the authority of the colonial governor.[9]* With full internal self-government coming in 1963, the air was filled with excited anticipation on the part of Africans and with dread anxiety from Europeans and those who had supported their colonial endeavor.

Kangundo was Paul Ngei's constituency as well as his home, and he did nothing to ease the task of the colonial administration during this difficult time of transition. People were expecting to be given land for free and therefore were refusing to cooperate in settlement schemes in which they would be expected to pay. Kenyatta had not yet given his "no free things" speech, and Ngei was encouraging people not to buy. The colonial chiefs were deeply unpopular and subject to constant harassment. A great deal of the antagonism was directed at the senior chief,

*The African ministers governed under the authority of the colonial governor. Full internal self-government was granted in 1963.

Uku, who was taking a hard line in his insistence on order. Having a senior chief for a father himself, Nyachae was sympathetic to the chiefs and gave them public backing. But he also recognized the forces of change at work and tried to turn the uncompromising ones such as Uku from their self-destructive course. Even at this early stage in his career Nyachae seemed to have his characteristic ability to sort out the essential from the peripheral objectives and to be unbending in his pursuit of the former and flexible about the latter.

In these times it was imperative to be in close touch with the people, particularly as Nyachae was frustrated by Ngei's unwillingness to listen to reason. "A leader is bound to be able to listen carefully to what other people are saying and [Nyachae] was of that caliber. He would think carefully before deciding." Public meetings (*barazas*) did not work as a means of communication. As Nyachae recalls:

> It is extremely misleading to go to a public meeting and see people clapping. It doesn't mean that they are convinced. . . . We traveled in the countryside and slept in tents to let them understand me and vice versa. . . . We had the best understanding when we walked. Though we have more administrators now, they do not understand the ordinary people the way we did. The most effective communication is to visit in their homes.

He remained in Kangundo Division for only six months, too short a period to have a real impact on it, but he considered the experience to be a seminal one in his career. From it he understood what field administration really means and that independence would bring problems as well as prospects.

Nyachae's next assignment was to the Kenya Institute of Administration, where he took the district officer's course. There he took the law exam and qualified as a first-class magistrate, a role which at the time was combined with that of district commissioner. That course and the one on colonial administration to which he was sent in 1963 at Cambridge University were also designed to socialize the new recruits into their roles as their colonial predecessors had understood them. In addition to training in the law and administrative practice, there was instruction in small arms, horseback riding, and table manners. These courses symbolized the kind of administrative and social role they were expected to play in Kenyan society. The socialization process was clearly rushed, and one would have expected its impact to be diminished as a result. For example, Nyachae was able to stay for only six of the nine required months at Cambridge because the Kenyan government needed him. But the instruction had its effect nonetheless. The law-and-order component of the role remained the primary concern of the Africans inducted into the Provincial Administration in this period, and they re-

sisted attempts by a later generation of expatriate administrative train-
ers to shift the courses decisively toward the primacy of a developmental
role by stressing economics, sociology, and planning.[10] Although many
of them were strong supporters of economic and social development,
they firmly believed that it could be achieved only if law and order were
maintained, and they considered the latter their first priority.

How were the British administrators able to socialize their successors
into a law-and-order orientation when they failed to transmit many of
the other values they held dear? First of all, this was the role to which
they actually gave primacy, whatever their intentions. Actions speak
louder than words, and the Provincial Administration had just emerged
from a period of intense effort to suppress the Mau Mau rebellion. Second, the law-and-order role not only was the one their first superiors
expected them to play, it also was the one they had been able to observe
from afar as they were growing up. It was a role in which many of their
parents had assisted, and the public expected them to play it when they
put on the Provincial Administration uniform. Third, the role met the
requirements of the newly independent African state. Despite the sincere rhetoric of development which African politicians used, they were
most concerned with the survival of the regime itself in the face of deep
interethnic conflicts and dangerously inflated expectations.[11] They perceived the new state as needing security even more than it needed prosperity, and they rewarded careers accordingly. Thus the traditional role
expectations of the Provincial Administration were reinforced from all
directions.

Between the Kenya Institute of Administration and the Cambridge
courses Nyachae also served briefly in Makweni Division of Machakos
District. During this period Nyachae had a serious accident in his Land
Rover, which left him with recurrent back troubles. When Nyachae returned to the Provincial Administration from Cambridge, England, in
March 1964, he was to face the challenge of governing an independent,
not a colonial, Kenya.

Nyachae's entire upbringing aimed him toward the Provincial Administration and its law-and-order orientation. His father's example and
wishes so inclined him, and his early withdrawal from secondary school
precluded more professional options.

ISHMAEL MURIITHI

Ishmael Muriithi, the veterinarian, was born on November 18, 1929, at
Kindara village of Ihithe Sub-Location, Thigingi Location, in Nyeri District. (See plate 12.) In December he was baptized into the Presbyterian
church. His childhood was an uneventful and typical one. He played,

assisted in the care of his younger brothers and sisters, and helped to tend the livestock. From an early age he enjoyed looking after the farm's animals, worried about them when they were sick, and was so quick and good at milking that none of the cows he worked ever got mastitis.

He started school at what was then the relatively young age of eight, spent a year first at Ihithe Primary School and then went on to Wandumbi in the same sub-location. He was very serious about his studies; he never objected to doing his homework, was always on time for school, and took coaching from his father.

Muriithi did well on the Common Entrance Examination and was accepted at the PCEA Thogoto Primary School at Kikuyu in Kiambu District in 1943. (See fig. 3.1.) A younger brother who would later join him in veterinary work, Dan Mbogo, was born in the same year. There was a famine in the province at the time, and there was some concern that he might not be able to get enough to eat at Thogoto, but Muriithi insisted on going anyway. His father, Elijah Waicanguru, was already a man of substance and had no trouble meeting the school fees for his children's educational careers. Nonetheless, Muriithi always used well the money he was given, not splurging it, as did many other sons of the well-to-do. He also did not allow the status of being in such an elite school go to his head. At home on the holidays he helped with harvesting, weeding, cutting the firewood, milking, terracing, and so on. In later years he would be unusual in insisting on the same farm-work discipline for his own children. During the Christmas holidays he joined the carollers singing from house to house in the village. He also led a choir that performed throughout the district.

Muriithi's first sitting of the Kenya African Primary Examination was not up to his ambitions, and he repeated the year at Thogoto, joining the class of Charles Karanja. His father wanted to send him to another school, but the headmaster argued that the boy was working hard and had just had bad luck. Among his teachers at Thogoto was James Gichuru, who was later to be central in the formation of the Kenya African National Union (KANU) and a cabinet minister. Muriithi did much better on the 1946 exam; his certificate shows four passes and four credits, including the crucial ones in English and mathematics.

He entered Alliance High, the elite Protestant school, in 1947. Six years earlier Alliance had become the first Kenyan school to offer four years of secondary education to Africans.[12] (Makerere was in Uganda.) Muriithi was an "all-rounder" at Alliance. He played on the first eleven for football (soccer) and developed a lifelong love for tennis. He also was recognized for his leadership abilities; he became a prefect in 1949 and was made senior prefect of Wilberforce House in 1950. The prefects were responsible for the organization and discipline of the schoolboys, and he made his house something to reckon with in school activities. In the weekly meetings of senior prefects, "his was not the sort of mind who dithered. He formed his opinions quickly, expressed his views forcefully and stood by them." He was also a very down-to-earth person. Each house had its own garden, and forty years later a classmate could still "see him wearing his pink working shirt and his jembe [hoe] on his shoulder going to and from the shamba."

Alliance High School was a very special place in those years, offering, together with Mangu, the highest education available to Africans in Kenya at the time. A contemporary remarks:

> To even go there was a very major achievement. . . . It was a wonderful life—we had water regularly, uniforms, highly trained English teachers, . . . sporting facilities, . . . and the opportunity to play the piano. . . . We enjoyed special privileges such as a special coach on the train [when we went home to Nyeri for the holidays].

The "Old Boys" who went to Alliance in these years were disproportionately represented in the administrative leadership of Kenya after independence. Their mutual respect for one another's accomplishments and their network of friendships and acquaintanceships often facilitated the business of government. Muriithi was greatly helped in later years, for example, by the fact that he spent 1947 and 1948 at Alliance with Geoffrey Kariithi, who later held the powerful post of head of the civil service under President Kenyatta.

Under the legendary leadership of Carey Francis, Alliance was modeled on the ideals of service by Christian gentlemen which underlay the English public (i.e., prep) school. Discipline was extremely strict, and the style of leadership authoritarian. Francis identified deeply with his students and with African progress, but he held views on matters such as politics and salary differentials between Africans and Europeans that his charges deeply resented at times. Thus the gap between the students and their schoolmasters was greater than in the English public schools after which Alliance was modeled.[13] A classmate of Muriithi's observed:

> Alliance was a mixture of conflicting relationships. . . . There we were the cream and here were people who had given up great opportunities back home [in England] to come to Kenya to educate the black people. But there was a social gap, not hostility but an enormous gap [all the same]. They would invite us to their homes from time to time, but you never developed totally free rapport.
>
> They had in their own minds stereotyped professions for which they were preparing us—teaching, medicine, [the] civil service, [the] ministry, agriculture, and veterinary [medicine]. It never occurred to them that

some of us could decide to go and do law or join a private firm. . . . That set of values was being ingrained in us. . . . A lot of emphasis [was placed] on *public* service. The motto of Alliance is "Strong to Serve."

Carey Francis visited Muriithi's home in Nyeri, as he did with many of "his boys."[14] He and Elijah Waicanguru had a particular respect for each other, which Muriithi used to his advantage later. When Muriithi finished Makerere in 1956, his father, Chief Muhoya, and the Nyeri district commissioner put pressure on him to join the Provincial Administration. Muriithi used Carey Francis's advice to defend his commitment to the veterinary profession.

Muriithi showed a strong preference for the sciences in his schoolwork. He was much interested in nature and enjoyed the practical work of the labs. He was even a natural at dissecting frogs, which repelled many of the others, as, traditionally, frogs are not even touched. But English was a different matter. He hated writing essays. He did not want to elaborate on something once he'd said it, occasioning constant arguments between him and his English master. A classmate remarked, "If I found something [today in his office] files of over two pages, I'd be surprised if it was his [writing]."

In 1950 at the end of his stay at Alliance, Muriithi got a First Division pass on the Cambridge School Certificate Examination, which was set from Britain. Despite, or maybe because of, the predictions that he would fail in English, his seven credits included one in English. Thus he was one of an even more elite group who entered Uganda's Makerere College in 1951, in his case to pursue a Diploma in Veterinary Medicine, which he received in 1956.

The first years of the course were held in Kampala, and the final two in Kenya at Kabete, on the site of the University of Nairobi's present veterinary faculty and next door to the headquarters of the Veterinary Department. These years corresponded with the Kikuyu Mau Mau uprising and the State of Emergency.

Muriithi's father, Elijah Waicanguru, was a colonial civil servant, a member of the Home Guards who assisted in putting down the rebellion, and enjoyed government protection from the insurgents. But no Kikuyu escaped from the Emergency untouched or emotionally unscarred. Waicanguru was based at the courts in Nyeri town and thus was somewhat removed from the forest and the greatest action. Lydia Wangeci, Muriithi's mother, stayed on the family homestead at Ihithe, however, and was very near to the Aberdare Mountains, where the insurgents hid. At one point she had fifty people staying with her in the house, as the government forced the populace back from the forest edge into fortified villages, which were sealed at night. Peter Nderitu, the second child in the family, who was working in Nakuru, had to return to Nyeri because of the general repatriation of Kikuyus from the urban areas in the State of Emergency.

The chief of the Location was killed by the insurgents in 1952 when he tried to disrupt a Mau Mau oathing ceremony.[15] The family lost only four sheep to the insurgents during the whole period of the rebellion, but by 1953 they were concerned for their security, and Waicanguru had Muriithi's younger brother Dan Mbogo transfer from primary school in Ihithe to Nyeri town, where he could be with him. The contradictions and complicated allegiances of the period are revealed by the ten-year-old boy's decision to use the opportunity to smuggle medicines regularly from a dresser at Nyeri Hospital through the guarded checkpoints to a Mau Mau courier. As the son of a government judge, he was never suspected or searched, and his parents never knew of his activities.

At one point the government considered having the Kikuyu students expelled from Makerere because of fears that they might be involved with Mau Mau. Elijah Waicanguru and Senior Chief Muhoya interceded on their behalf with the district commissioner for Nyeri, arguing that it was impossible that they were involved, as under Kikuyu custom only an adult could take an oath. Given Mbogo's assistance to the insurgents and the many ways in which the Mau Mau broke with Kikuyu custom, this was hardly a definitive argument, but in any case no mass expulsions took place. Instead, two police officers were sent to Makerere to uncover those involved with the rebellion. Kikuyus were subjected to grueling interviews, and several of them lost their scholarships and had to go home. Others developed ulcers from the tension. Open dissent was dangerous, and so opposition at Makerere tended to take petty, symbolic forms. Muriithi grew a beard during these years, so that "he looked fierce, like a terrorist." He also joined Mwai Kibaki (later vice-president) in refusing to stand for the singing of "God Save the Queen."

The age of the four administrators was such that it was difficult for them to join directly in nationalist activity without sacrificing their careers. This was particularly true for the Kikuyus among them, for under the Emergency political activity became legal only after 1957. Perhaps they could have done more than they did; Mwai Kibaki was their contemporary and launched his political career in late 1960. But they did see themselves as participating in the struggle for independence. They saw their education and careers as preparing them for the management of the new state and enabling them to challenge the British on another part of the battlefield in the larger struggle. Perhaps this view was self-serving, but it was sincere and was encouraged by many of their elders and peers. It gave a larger purpose to their ambitions and created an ambivalence and tension in their relationships with their English instructors.

In 1954 as Muriithi was traveling to Nyeri on the special train coach for African students, he met Martha Wangui Munene, who had just begun at Alliance Girls High School. They met again at home on another school holiday and started writing to each other. Muriithi began pressing her to marry him after he finished his diploma in 1956, but he was eight years older and she had finished her School Certificate only in that year. She insisted that she not be married until she was trained. She went to Siriba Teacher Training College for a diploma, which she completed in late 1958. They were married on December 12, 1959, after she had taught for a year in Embu.

Muriithi began work as a veterinary officer in Kigumo Division, Murang'a District, in 1957, shortly after he finished Makerere. Following in his father's footsteps, he was deeply interested in the dairy industry for the high-rainfall highland areas (which are known as the "high potential" zones). The white settlers had introduced artificial insemination for their cattle in the late 1930s, and Muriithi brought the practice to Kigumo as a way of upgrading the quality of the traditional African Zebu cattle and increasing milk production. After a short time he was transferred to Githunguri Division in Kiambu. There too he concentrated on the incipient African dairy industry and began artificial insemination.

At one point the colonial governor made an official inspection of African agriculture in Kiambu. Muriithi was responsible for part of the tour. The English provincial commissioner wanted the governor to visit the farm of Harry Thuku, an early African nationalist who had become a supporter of the colonial order after his several years in detention. Muriithi refused, on the grounds that he wanted the governor to see real farmers. He proposed a more typical farmer who was making exceptional progress, but the provincial commissioner opposed this choice on the grounds that the man was known as a Mau Mau sympathizer. In any case, when Muriithi joined the governor's party, he took it to the dissident farmer. Ishmael Muriithi had a stubborn determination to promote an African livestock industry and he ignored colonial political sensitivities in doing so.

In August 1960 Muriithi was surprised to learn that he was to go to Scotland to study for a full degree in veterinary medicine at Edinburgh. (See plate 13.) At first he thought the news was a joke, for the school year was about to start. But a joke it was not. The British veterinarians in Kenya did not consider the Makerere diploma the equivalent of their own degrees. Other Makerere veterinarians were sent to the United States or India for upgrading, but Muriithi was selected for the honor of receiving the rigorous training through which they themselves had passed. At the time this honor appeared questionable, for Muriithi was made to spend four of the normal five years at Edinburgh, whereas those who went to the United States received greater credit for their Makerere work and took only an additional two years to get their degrees. It is clear, however, that the Edinburgh imprimatur was later critical to his selection by his British superiors to succeed them as director of the Veterinary Department.

On September 4, 1960, Ishmael and Martha's first child, Ann Wangeci, was born, and two weeks later Muriithi left for Scotland. No money was provided for Martha to go with her husband; she finished the year in the teaching job that she had secured in Githunguri and then went to live with Ishmael's parents in Nyeri. The following year she managed to win a Commonwealth scholarship for herself to take a primary-school teaching course at Mary House in Edinburgh and joined Ishmael in September 1961, leaving her daughter with Elijah and Lydia Waicanguru in Kenya. Though the scholarship was only for a year, she managed to stay on until May 1963, giving birth on October 1, 1962, to Elijah Waicanguru.

Muriithi was disappointed that he was given very little credit for the work that he had done at Makerere and was somewhat resentful of it throughout his life. He was made to begin the first term with the entering British students, but by the end of October he had been able to test out of all the first-year courses except for physics and began the second-year syllabus, shortening the five-year program to four. Included were internships with private practices in Wales and Scotland. In the end he graduated in May 1964 with a prize and was often considered the top student in his class.

Martha had returned to Kenya a year earlier, driven out by the coldest winter in eighty years and by housing difficulties. Their landlord was a Polish refugee who was willing to let to foreign students but who complained about the noise that little Elijah was making while he was teething. They tried to get another flat but were unable to do so "because we were Africans. When they heard your voice or saw your face they would say no."

His school years gave Muriithi the valuable Edinburgh imprimatur and training in decision making. They also registered his love for the sciences, his ill ease with writing, and his willingness to get his hands dirty in his work.

Dan Mbogo

The experience of Muriithi's brother Dan Mbogo at a later day and in a different part of the world represents an interesting counterpoint. Dan performed solidly in school, but not brilliantly, as had his eldest brother.

His primary education was in local schools, where he had to repeat Standards 1 and 4. From there he went to the second-echelon Kigumo Secondary School, from which he got a good Division II pass (in contrast to his brother's First) on the Ordinary Level fourth-year exam, doing especially well in the sciences.

Mbogo could have gone on for the two additional secondary years necessary for the Advanced Certificate had it not been for the misfortune of a school riot. His class created a disturbance two days before the end of school, and someone falsely accused him of having participated. As a consequence, the school to which he had hoped to go to study science refused to accept him. In fact, he was the school librarian and had been checking the books and turning over his office to his successor on that day. But by the time the charges against him had been refuted, it was too late to undo the damage for that year. Another school offered to take him if he did liberal arts, but he refused.

Instead, he joined the Veterinary Department in Nyeri as an untrained junior animal husbandry assistant. Although he loved veterinary work, he resigned by the end of the year and joined the post office; he had heard a false rumor that his brother was going to be made district veterinary officer for Nyeri, and he felt that he could not work under him.

Kenya was then freshly independent, and the country was alive with competing foreign study opportunities, for which Mbogo began to interview. He did not want to go to Britain or the United States, "because they were our colonizers." He was offered a scholarship to Israel in agricultural engineering but declined it because he would have had to pay for the plane ticket himself and thought it was too expensive. Then he was offered a chance to go to Bulgaria in forestry, which he accepted, although he had no interest in the subject.

He arrived in Bulgaria in October 1964 and immediately and without difficulty changed to veterinary medicine. He spent the first year at the Institute of Foreign Students, where they were grouped according to their area of academic interest and taught Bulgarian, with emphasis on the appropriate vocabulary. Bulgarian girls were assigned to help teach them, which Mbogo took as a sign that the Bulgarians were not trying to keep their women from the African students. In that first year he and a friend volunteered to go to a harvest work camp in the north of the country. The Bulgarian volunteers were billeted with families, but the two foreigners were given a special room, which they took to be discrimination. Then an old man invited them to dinner. In the course of the evening it became evident that he thought that they had refused to stay with Bulgarian families. When he found that they had not been invited, he asked them to stay with him, which they did. Every holiday after that they went to stay with old Nicholai in Kuruchavene, near the Danube. They knew where the key to the house was kept, and Mbogo regarded Nicholai as a father to him.

Mbogo then went to the Higher Institute of Veterinary Medicine at the University of Sophia, from which he graduated in December 1970, second in his group of twenty-five. He had nothing but praise for the faculty, whom he found always ready to help the foreigners with free extra lessons.

> I experienced no racism in Bulgaria. I traveled over the whole country, missing only one town. What people called racism there was due to ignorance, not racism, for an ordinary Bulgarian knows little of Africa. When people found I spoke Bulgarian they would be very friendly, take me to their houses, even get me somewhere to sleep with people who I had never seen before. There were some problems in big towns [but that is true of big towns everywhere.] There was no problem dating Bulgarian girls. Of course [one sometimes had] conflict with another man over a girl [as is normal]. . . . If I went into a bar to buy a drink, after a while someone would come over to see if I spoke Bulgarian. I never had to buy more than my first drink. . . . [In homes] we would drink wine out of a common jar and eat off the same plate, as was the Bulgarian custom.

Mbogo returned from this positive experience in Bulgaria to find difficulty in getting Kenya to accept his degree. Many of the early students who had gone to Eastern Europe had had very weak academic backgrounds, and this discredited the credentials of those who came later. Fortunately Muriithi, who was by then director of veterinary services, had passed through Sophia while Mbogo was there, had visited the Higher Institute, and had received thorough reports on the quality of the Kenyans who were in the program, which should have been enough to justify Mbogo's employment. Nonetheless, Muriithi would not have even the slightest suspicion that he was doing something special for his brother. A procedure for validating all their credentials was established. Those who had non-Commonwealth degrees were sent to the diagnosis section to be observed.

> I was taken to Geoff Holm, who was the trouble. He looked very unfriendly. He showed me an office with a microscope and he [and] his technologist, Ashford . . . [gave] me twenty-six slides to analyze. Then they marked them and I still don't know what I got. After three [more] days someone [finally] came and showed me where I could get some coffee. I finally discovered three other men who were in the same state as I [was] and I went and joined them in their office. We were not given specific duties. We drafted diagnostic reports for Holm to sign. Every time I went to Holm for a question he gave me a book, until I had nine. Then I read them, took them back, gave him one in Bulgarian, and told him to read it.

Ashford would refuse to go and get samples and would make us go and get them, although he was but a technologist. One day I went and brought the whole offal and put it on a tray on his desk.

After a year of this guerrilla war, Mbogo was licensed by the Kenya Veterinary Board for work with the government and received a regular post with the Central Artificial Insemination Station.

Those who attended non-English universities had a much harder time gaining acceptance from the British on their return to Kenya. Eastern European degrees were at the bottom of the pecking order, followed by those from India and then America.

HARRIS MUTIO MULE

The boy who would eventually be known as Harris Mule, the planner, was born on December 7, 1936, in Mbooni Location, Machakos District. He was the second son of Ruth Katuku and Philip Mule, the third of the nine children they would eventually have. Ruth Katuku gave birth at home under the care of a traditional midwife, as did everyone else at the time. The house was a "permanent" one, which only the elite could afford at that time but which are common in the highlands of Kenya today. (See plate 14.) Built by his father in 1930 and still standing today, it has several rooms, the walls are made of mud and wattle covered with a layer of cement, and the roof is galvanized iron, from which the family can collect drinking water and save the women the hard work of carrying it up from afar.

There was a small problem with the baby at the birth, and the midwife sent for the assistance of an American missionary, who came the short distance on foot with his wife. After taking care of the problem, he remarked that the baby "is a cock," that is, a boy and strong. (The cock is a traditional symbol of strength, which is why it later became the symbol of the Kenya African National Union, the party that brought the nation to independence.) At first Ruth Katuku called the baby Ngumbau, which means "strong." His sister, who was six at the time, remembers that he was strong enough to struggle out of her arms, so that she wasn't allowed to care for him. But there were three years between the boy's birth and that of his elder brother, and two years separated the births of the other children. So he also was named Mutio, which means "one who is delayed," and came to prefer that name.

At what was then the young age of seven, Mutio (Harris Mule) began his studies a mile away at the Mbooni African Inland Church School. The floor was dirt, six students sat to a desk, and writing was done with chalk on slates, but "in those days our school was the best." Mutio quickly identified with school and did well at it. As a lower-primary-school child, he would load up a washbasin with stones and push it around the yard, playing that it was a car. He said that when he came back from Makerere (the highest educational institution to which Africans could then aspire) he would have a big car and give the family gifts (which the stones represented). His progress, however, was not all smooth. He didn't do well in one of the sets of lower-primary-school exams, and the teachers were concerned, because they regarded him as very bright. Mutio told them that he was coming to school late because he had to look after the cattle for his father, which was a lie. When his parents were called in, he finally admitted that he did not like mathematics and so was playing on a swing in the bush each morning until the class in that subject was over. It came out that the problem was that he did not understand "carrying" in addition. His teacher told him that if he did not like math he would not have to do it and that he was to bring six of two types of fruit to school. The teacher then used the fruit to show him how to do the carrying. From then on Mutio liked math.

Philip Mule took a great deal of interest in his children's education; he would discuss them with their teachers, check their notebooks, and inquire after their class rank. He was also very much concerned that they learn the moral value of work, even when he was well enough off that the family had others working on the farm. Philip considered work a virtue and no task beneath him. He would even cook sometimes, which was "women's work," for he had worked as a cook early in his life. He expected the children to rise early in the morning, say their prayers, and put in a full day of effort, working up to eight or nine at night. They dug many of the bench terraces on the farm (which were used both to prevent erosion and to conserve water). The boys shared the responsibility for the cattle.

For seven years Mutio spent his school vacations helping to care for the family's some two hundred cattle across the Athi River in the Crown (public) Lands of Yatta. This was fifty miles away, and Mutio would have to walk two days through dry bush to get there. Once there, he would help his father's men tend the cattle, reassembling them when they were scattered by the lions, walking them ten miles each way for water each third day, sleeping with them in a kraal (corral) made of thorn branches, and eating a simple diet of ugali (maize porridge) and milk. In the midst of this period, at age eleven in 1947, Mutio was circumcised, although he never went through the traditional puberty rites, as the church opposed them. Later in his education Mutio graduated to running one of his father's shops.

Mutio went through five years at the local Mbooni AIC School, after which he took the Common Entrance Exam. He placed first in his school and earned a place in one of Machakos District's four intermediate schools. He was sent to Masii, where he had to board with another family because the school was fifteen miles from his home. At the end of Masii he took the Kenya African Primary Exam, again placed first, and earned a place at Government African School in Machakos, the only secondary school in the district.

He entered Form I at Machakos in 1950 when he was only thirteen, the youngest boy in his class. He was saved from the usual harassment that younger boys received from the upperclassmen, however, by his older brother's presence in an upper form. Mutio never was a prefect nor particularly active in sports in school, probably largely owing to his relative youth. But there may have been other reasons for his not being seen as "leadership material" by the headmaster—reasons that can be inferred from the following incident. At Machakos, Mutio was required to assume a "Christian" name—that is, a European one. Much to the annoyance of the very religious headmaster, Mutio chose the name Harris, a nonbiblical one. The choice was deliberate, for by this time the boy was in rebellion against the fundamentalist morality of the African Inland Church. He began smoking and drinking at age twelve and went through life without ever being baptized, a sacrament that the AIC administers only to adults.

At the end of Form II Harris Mule (as he has since been known) took the Kenyan African Preliminary Exam but did poorly in math and nature study and did not qualify for Form III. Fortunately for him, the school made an exception and let him continue. He made up for his near miss by scoring near the top of his class on the Kenya African Secondary School Exam at the end of Form IV.

In the normal order of things Harris should then have gone to Alliance High School, where he would have followed in the footsteps of Ishmael Muriithi and eastern Kenya's other Protestant elites. But these were not normal times. A State of Emergency had been declared in the colony because of the Mau Mau rebellion, and the British were anxious to prevent any alliance between the Kikuyu and the linguistically related ethnic groups that neighbored them. Thus the 1954 Form V class of Kamba boys was sent to Kakamega High School in western Kenya. There they were celebrated anomalies and were well treated in the area. After two years there Harris passed the Cambridge Overseas School Certificate Exam with a Division I and earned the right to go to a university.

Harris chose to go to the new Royal Technical College (now the University of Nairobi) rather than the more prestigious Makerere. He knew that if he went to Makerere he would be compelled to study English, geography, or history, as those were the subjects on which he had excelled on the Cambridge exam. These subjects would lead him into a career in education, and he did not like teaching. He wanted to study economics, "as it was associated with money," and since the Royal Technical College did not offer liberal arts degrees, he would be permitted to take it.

The Royal Technical College was an exciting place for Harris when he joined its first class of 200 in 1956. It was the first multiracial school in Kenya, with about 130 Africans, 60 Asians, and 3 Europeans. It also was a breath of freedom after the iron discipline of secondary boarding school; one could speak one's own mind and go to sleep and get up whenever one wanted. The facilities seemed very good to him: each person had a cubicle to himself, good food, and twenty shillings (about $3) pocket money a month. He also found the teachers to be very good. All were British except for one Indian and the Kikuyu Dr. Gikonyo Kiano (another later cabinet minister). The head of the Economics Department was William Rodgers, who took a very personal interest in his students. Rodgers thought that his students were brighter and better prepared than the educational authorities did. Despite having studied the same number of years as British students entering university, they were considered to be behind in their educational development and in need of another two years before taking their Advanced Level exam, the English university-entrance test. Rodgers encouraged half of his students (about 15) to try the London A Level exam at the end of the first year, and 7 of them passed. Harris Mule was among them.

Rodgers's success, however, was a mistake. The college was not yet ready to offer economics classes at the full university level, and the seven victors were left with no place to study. He managed to get places for two at Makerere, one in England, and two in the United States. Harris too was offered a place at Makerere, but he decided to wait out a year and to try to continue at the college.

So Harris Mule took a job and experienced what he says was the biggest adjustment he ever had to make. He held several jobs, as they were easy to come by with the qualifications he had. But the customary salary at the time for those who had passed the A Level was K.shs. 486 ($70) a month and the standard of living he had experienced at the college would have cost about K.shs. 1,000. The returns to education in east Africa are extremely high. One's salary increases by at least 50 percent for every two years of additional education. Because Harris had not finished his degree, he found himself on the labor market with income expectations one step higher than that which he had yet achieved.

As it was, the Royal College delayed the start of its degree program in economics still further. Harris thus applied for and got Fulbright and Smith Mundt Fellowships from the United States embassy and entered the University of Denver in September 1959. The people of his home area also contributed about $150 to his four-year stay. He entered the University of Denver as a sophomore and received his B.Sc. in economics in 1962. He went on to receive an M.A. in economics in 1963, supported by a University of Denver fellowship.

Mule was struck by the higher standard of living in the United States, the high wages, and the relatively low costs. He also experienced a substantial increase in his own income, for his Fulbright allowances were four times what his Kenyan wages had been. More fundamental, he reports, was the difference in freedom, especially freedom of expression and of association, for African nationalism was still a subversive ideology for the British Empire.

A different kind of freedom startled Mule during his very first weekend at Denver at a school-sponsored dance, itself a departure from what he would have expected of a Methodist college, given his upbringing in the fundamentalist AIC where dancing is forbidden. At the dance Mule found the college chaplain playing a clarinet in the band. Though he had broken with the church himself, Mule was scandalized to find the chaplain condoning dancing and confronted him afterward. He became quite close to the chaplain, the Reverend William Rhodes, and attended his optional chapel services faithfully. Rhodes recruited Mule as a teaching assistant for the required philosophy and religion course, for he knew the Bible thoroughly—although it took him a long time to get over his literalist interpretation of the scriptures. Mule also used to preach occasionally at the black Zionist Baptist Church, for he enjoyed the spontaneous, extemporaneous preaching style.

Mule's sole involvement in the American civil rights movement was attendance at a large student conference in Athens, Ohio, in December 1960, where Martin Luther King, Jr., spoke, and he heard talk of African independence. He was buoyed up by the student idealism of the time and was disappointed to find it missing at Harvard when he returned to the United States in 1966.

Although not a civil rights activist, Mule could not help being affected by the racial problems of the United States. He found the warmth and friendliness of midwestern Americans a pleasant contrast to the Kenyan British.

But those who were prejudiced were very nasty, for American prejudice was worse than colonial discrimination and oppression. As a small black minority in the United States you had to live with discrimination constantly, whereas in a colonial setup it is more intermittent. When I went to Texas with an American Indian, his white wife, his Indian cousin, a Mexican American, and an [African] Swazi, we had a good time in the Indian Reservation and in Albuquerque but in Farmington, Texas, we could not find a place to eat or drink. The people in the restaurant panicked at our coming; the women ran out. We had to go to the airport, where we demanded to be served [on the grounds that] it was under the Federal Aviation Administration and subject to federal regulations. It still took the intervention of some FBI agents for us to be fed.

He was unintentionally the first black to get a haircut from the university barbershop at Denver. He was in the process of being refused service when the chaplain came by and forced them to cut his hair. Unfortunately (he reported), they did a very bad job!

There were a few other blacks at Denver, both American and African, and Mule was close to them. Among them was Francis Mashakalia, who later followed Mule up the hierarchy of Kenyan Planning. The Africans around the state of Colorado got together for a party in 1961 to honor Ghana's independence. Afterward, at 2:00 A.M., they drove some of the celebrants back to Boulder and stopped at a coin-operated pump to buy some gas. Unbeknownst to them, it had been burgled by some black Americans earlier, and they were followed and arrested when they got to Boulder. It was 6:00 A.M. before the error was discovered and they were released. Enraged, they went and woke up the mayor of Boulder to protest, waving their Fulbright cards, which asked for respect and help. The worried mayor gave them breakfast and wrote a letter of apology to the university.

The Economics Department at the University of Denver had only four faculty and was not as quantitatively oriented as most modern American departments. Mule was most influenced by John Foster, an institutional economist from whom he took four courses. Mule's quantitative skills came instead from his minor in statistics. Because of his friendship with a mathematics professor, he served two years as a teaching assistant in the introductory mathematics course and learned the basics of the subject through the grinding work of grading it. Looking at his transcript from these years, one would not necessarily guess that he would later become such an accomplished economic policymaker. Although he did well in most of his economics classes, his grades in the quantitative courses ranged in the Bs and Cs. Looking back at that transcript, Mule and some of the American economists who knew his later accomplishments concluded that perhaps institutional rather than mathematical economics is a better preparation for policy-making. The focus on quantification in economics makes one into a technician, letting one forget that production takes place in a cultural and institutional context.

Mule returned to Kenya in June 1963 and was offered positions as a labor officer or a district officer, the latter being the same job then held by Nyachae. He declined, for he had always wanted to be a government economist. Instead he took a post as a statistician in the Ministry of Agriculture and from there became a planning officer in 1965. His upward mobility would have been more rapid if he had become a district officer, but he had pursued an interest in economics for a long time and wanted to continue with it.

After he had worked for the Government of Kenya for a few years Mule returned to the United States in 1966–67 to attend Harvard University as a Mason Fellow. He was disappointed. He found Harvard students rich, self-centered, and cynical, unlike the warm, idealistic youth he had known in Denver. The economics disappointed him as well. He studied with several economists of note, but most of them left him cold. They made the subject dry and technical and robbed it of its institutional richness. Only the young radical economist Samuel Bowles impressed him, both for his careful, objective professionalism in the classroom and for his extracurricular commitment to redistributive policies. Mule's performance struck most of his professors as indifferent too; his grades were all in the B range, something that some of them found ironic later on when his performance as a policymaker so impressed them.

Harris Mule's educational career, then, showed an early and consistent focus on economics. Although not a brilliant quantitative technician, he mastered the principles needed for effective policy-making. He rebelled at the formal aspects of the religion that surrounded his upbringing, but he seems to have been profoundly affected by its deeper values.

CONCLUSIONS

The educational pyramid these men climbed was extremely steep, littered with examinations and small rates of promotion to the next level. Those who went all the way through it, as did Karanja, Mule, and Muriithi, were the leaders of a genuine meritocracy. Those such as Mbogo and Nyachae who did not go quite so far through the regular Kenyan system were nonetheless still members of a relatively small educated company. They were innocent of the degree to which their parents' relative wealth and education had advantaged them in this upward struggle. The fact that so many of their siblings did relatively well too indicates that more than just brains and chance were at work. They were correct, though, in believing that they could not have gotten as far as they did without intelligence and hard work. They had won against a colonial educational system in which the odds were heavily stacked against them, giving all of Africa's educated elites a great sense of self-confidence and the right to lead.

Karanja, Mule, Muriithi, Mbogo, and, to a lesser extent, Nyachae all emerged from the colonial period with educations that left them deeply committed professionals. Nyachae fought an administrative career while he was in school, and his allegiance to administration therefore emerged more from his experience than from his training. This made his conception of his professional role distinctly Kenyan and not international. Only Muriithi, by having been in the top of his class at Edinburgh, can be said to have had a distinguished background in his field. But the training that all of them received was solid, thorough, and practical, the type of instruction that often sinks in deeper and has a more profound effect on values than a more theoretical education does.

, All five men reviewed here studied overseas, though the time involved was much less for Karanja and Nyachae. A relationship appears to exist between the length of time abroad and the degree of identification with their professions that these men showed in their later lives. But the correlation is probably spurious. Karanja was dedicated to his work in a way that was equivalent to professionalism. If he did not spend his whole career in engineering, it was largely because his qualification was seen as second-class in Kenya. His work as a manager clearly reflected an engineer's approach. Other Kenyans also spent time in foreign universities without developing the same kind of professional commitment that these men showed. The truth is that the professional nature of the education was probably more important than its place, the foreign exposure counting most in the extent to which these men looked to international peers for their professional standards.

The strong values these men held about their administrative roles appear to have come from several, rather subtle sources. Much of the explicit value socialization to which they were exposed they rejected. In terms of Stinchcombe's four conditions for institutional continuity,[16] the British did control the conditions for socialization into elite positions and initially were able to select their administrative (but not their political) successors. But independence meant that they were not able to determine their subsequent advancement, and even under colonialism racism prevented them from being "heroes" on whom Africans would pattern their careers, undermining some of the effectiveness of the value education they controlled. Too much of it was provided by whites, who, even when well meaning, were socially foreign and irrelevant as role models. For example, Mule, Muriithi, and Nyachae also were raised in strongly Christian homes but were quite lax about their involvement in the church as adults; Mule rebelled strongly against his religious upbringing and refused to be baptized. At the surface level this socialization did not "take"; at a deeper level it appears to have shaped their more fundamental moral values about charity, honesty, integrity, and so forth. One of Mule's sisters, who became a Catholic nun, felt that despite his rebellion Harris's personal moral standards were the most deeply religious of all the siblings. Both Harris Mule's and Ishmael Muriithi's fathers had found success out of commitment to these values, and their example clearly shaped their sons.

Similarly, the strong values of public service that were taught at Alliance High School did not take as well as they did in the English public schools. But they had an effect nonetheless. In order to affirm their own distinct, personal identities, these men rejected the form of much of what they were taught but (perhaps subconsciously) kept its substance. Their routes to the top had been through institutions where these values were imparted, and they could not both proclaim their merit for having succeeded in them and completely reject all that they stood for.

Some of the effective socialization the British provided they did not fully intend. An orientation to law and order, authoritarianism, and the use of public office for personal benefit were all embodied in the institution of the African chief, which the British created. The first two values were also central components of the relationships that European administrators had with Africans throughout the colonial period. Strong role expectations were thereby created. These were sustained despite the postindependence efforts of donor experts in development administration to change them, both because they were deeply ingrained and because they served the political needs of the new, insecure African government.

Subtle value socialization was embodied in the professional education these men received as well. These values were rarely taught explicitly, and they probably would have been rejected if they had been. Instead, they were premises that were shared by the international community of professionals with whom these men came to identify and were assumptions that underlay the technical problems these men were trained to solve. Thus civil engineers are trained to maximize the quality of their product while seeking efficiency in their use of labor and materials. They also tend to think of labor as an adjunct of machines, thus subverting a human relations approach to management. All these values will be evident in the later work of Charles Karanja, the tea manager. Economics is premised on the primacy of the public interest and trains its practitioners to maximize it. in the form of Gross National Product, at the expense of special interests. We will see that Harris Mule, the planner, gave national economic interests priority over sectional ones and saw his distributive concerns in terms of "equity," an attribute of the national economy. Veterinary medicine gives great importance to disease prevention, which is a collective good, and thereby stresses the quality and integrity of disease reporting and quarantines. Ishmael Muriithi will find himself at odds with his political superiors over these issues. A profession is defined both by the technical skills it embodies and by the standards it expects of its members. Both techniques and standards are grounded in values—assumptions about the kinds of problems it is important to solve and the ethics that should be observed in doing so. When one is trained into and identifies with an international community of professionals, one is adopting a strong implicit set of values.

Superficially, this chapter has described educational experiences similar to those of virtually everyone reading it. On a deeper, more profound level, however, the experience discussed here concerns the struggle for national independence and racial dignity. Most of the East Africans described here understood that their upward mobility through the education system was not just a matter of their own personal advancement; essentially it was also a contest to prove that Africans were as capable as Europeans and could and would replace them. Almost all of them reported having to deal with incidents of explicit racial discrimination, including many they encountered during their studies abroad. This dimension of their education gave them a special energy and excitement in the long struggle against a system that was heavily stacked against their achieving success. They were truly growing up and out of colonialism.

They had received more than a formal education in the process: they had become part of an informal network of old schoolmates who were also in the meritocracy and who would govern Kenya. The schools through which they had passed had also socialized them to hard work, discipline, and authoritarian leadership. These values influenced their subsequent administrative styles.

1. The civil service core of Kenya's economic decision making in 1986: (from left) Harris Mule, Permanent Secretary to the Ministry of Finance; John W. Gi-thuku, Permanent Secretary to the Ministry of Planning and National Development; Simeon Nyachae, Chief Secretary; and Philip Ndegwa, Governor of the Central Bank of Kenya. By permission of *The Daily Nation* (Nairobi).

2. Ishmael Muriithi, Director of Livestock Development in the late 1970s.

3. Charles Kibe Karanja in 1970 when he became General Manager of KTDA.

4. Philip Mule, father of Harris Mule, in 1930. Note the elaborately European dress.

5. Elijah Waicanguru, retired Tribunal Court Elder, and Lydia Wangeci, parents of Ishmael Muriithi.

6. Karanja wa Kiarii, father of Charles Karanja.

7. The parents of Simeon Nyachae, Chief Musa Nyandusi and his wife Pauline Bosibori, in the late 1940s.

8. Philip Mule (left) and Ruth Katuku (center), parents of Harris Mule, at their wedding in 1930.

9. Philip Mule (at table, facing camera) presiding at a session of the African Tribunal Court for Southern Machakos in the early 1950s.

10. Schoolboys at Mangu High School in 1951: (from left) Francis Nderitu, later Chief Engineer, Ministry of Works; Riphat Mwangi, subsequently a Forester; Charles Karanja; and Frances Munge, later a senior official in the government's Directorate of Personnel Management.

11. Simeon Nyachae (second from right) at South Devon Technical College in the U.K. in 1957, with fellow students from Sarawak, Zambia, Borneo, and Malawi.

12. The home of Lydia Wangeci and Elijah Waicanguru at Ihithe in Nyeri District. This house was built after Ishmael Muriithi's birth but in time for Dan Mbogo to be born here.

13. Ishmael Muriithi (left) with fellow veterinary students from Zanzibar and Nigeria at Edinburgh University (Scotland).

14. The Mule family home in Mbooni, built in 1930, into which Harris Mule was born. The corrugated iron (mabati) roof and cemented walls would have marked it as the house of an extremely prosperous man at the time it was built.

15. Peasant farms across the road from Simeon Nyachae's house in Kisii. Note the small, patchwork fields and the homesteads with a mixture of thatch and corrugated iron (mabati) roofs. Farming in most of Kiambu and Nyeri (the birthplaces of Karanja and Muriithi) is of similar density.

16. Simeon Nyachae's large wheat farm at Mau Narok in Nakuru District. Compare with plate 15.

17. Philip Mule presenting a stool to Harris Mule at the latter's wedding in 1970.

18. The view from Harris Mule's Mbooni farm in the Machakos hills. Note the mixture of thatched and corrugated iron (mabati) roofed houses. The farms are a bit more widely spaced and the land much drier than in the areas around the birthplaces of the other three administrators. (See the photograph of Kisii in plate 15.)

19. Harris Mule's terraced coffee farm at Mbooni.

20. Simeon Nyachae as Provincial Commissioner of Central Province addressing a *baraza* [public meeting] in 1978. Note the uniform of the Provincial Administration that Nyachae and his District Commissioners behind him are wearing. By permission of *The Daily Nation* (Nairobi).

21. Charles Karanja (center) at the opening of a tea factory with the Minister of Agriculture, Jeremiah Nyagah (left).

22. Ishmael Muriithi (right) with President Kenyatta (center) and President Yakubu Gowan of Nigeria (in white) at the Nairobi Agricultural Show in the early 1970s.

23. The Ndanga Hotel in Ruiru, which Charles Karanja built and named after his wife, Philomena Ndanga.

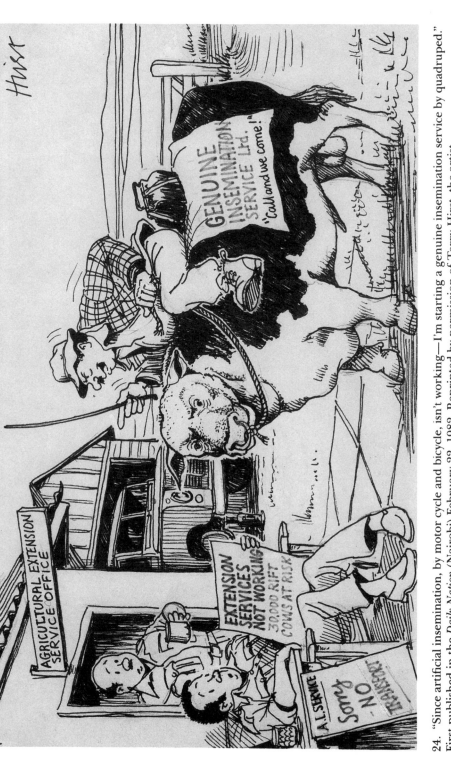

24. "Since artificial insemination, by motor cycle and bicycle, isn't working—I'm starting a genuine insemination service by quadruped." First published in the *Daily Nation* (Nairobi) February 22, 1982. Reprinted by permission of Terry Hirst, the artist.

25. Harris Mule (left) as Permanent Secretary to the Ministry of Finance shaking hands with President Moi and welcoming Vice-President Mwai Kibaki (at Moi's right) in the early 1980s.

26. The neotraditional circular house Simeon Nyachae put where his father said he should build.

27. Charles Karanja and Philomena Ndanga (his wife) with their children (from left) Lucy, Thomas, and Lawrence at their home at Kiratu in 1964.

28. The Karanja family home on their coffee estate in Ruiru, lower Kiambu District in 1986.

29. The Presbyterian Church at Hubuini (in Ihithe) in Nyeri, which Ishmael Muriithi helped build through 1976 and 1979 harambee fund-raising events.

30. Martha Ngina Mule, Ndinda, Nthenya, and Harris in 1986.

CHAPTER FOUR

Independence and the
Emerging Class Structure

THE POLITICAL BACKGROUND TO THE REPUBLIC

The use of British troops to put down the Mau Mau uprising shifted effective control of Kenya's constitutional development from the white settlers to the Colonial Office in London. At the end of the 1950s Britain had decided to grant independence to its African colonies and in a series of complicated constitutional negotiations started Kenya down that path.

Although Jomo Kenyatta had been imprisoned throughout this period, he remained the symbol of African nationalism, and there was tremendous pressure for his release. Kenyatta emerged from detention in 1961 to face a volatile and threatening political predicament. It is a tribute to his political skill that he mastered it. In the process he profoundly shaped Kenya's future. The class and ethnic dimensions of the situation in which he found himself will be dealt with in this chapter, the institutional issues in the next.

The Colonial Class Structure

Classes are treated here as groups that arise from economic interests that are in systematic conflict with other interests and that are sufficiently conscious of those interests to see themselves as distinct social and political entities.[1]

Class analysis is not synonymous with the study of interest groups, though the two are closely related. First, the term "class" presupposes the existence of another group in direct conflict with it, whereas "interest group" does not necessarily carry such a connotation.[2] Second, classes are much larger entities than interest groups and have a social dimension. Classes represent a bundle of interests, not all of which will be shared by every one of their members. Interest-group studies predict only that people will defend their personal interests. Class analysis, in contrast, predicts that individuals, because of their social ties with other members of their class, may take on political stances that defend interests they do not personally share. For example, a top Kenyan civil servant who owned no businesses but who advocated probusiness policies would be acting out of his class but not his personal interests. One of the questions to which we will be sensitive in this study is when the behavior of administrators is better predicted by class than by personal interests.

Since the forms of production, the patterns of political conflict, and the nature of social affiliations vary from society to society, class categories cannot be universal but have to be developed specifically for each system studied. The largest single class in Kenya was and is that of the workers and peasants. Workers are, simply, those who derive income from their wage labor. Peasants are small farmers using household labor to produce for subsistence and limited markets.[3] In Western societies these have been separate classes, but in Kenya they make up a single class, for several reasons.

Colonial wage employment was generally insufficient to support a laborer's family and often even himself. The worker therefore was dependent upon the agricultural production of his wife, tying him integrally to the peasant sector. As Mahmoud Mamdani has argued, the very act of employing Africans involved an extraction of value from the peasantry for the benefit of European employers, because the employee had to be subsidized by his family. The African was driven to work in these conditions by the colonial imposition of cash taxes and the oligopolistic European control over the labor market (which kept wages depressed).[4]

It is possible that many (though no longer most) wage laborers in Kenya are still subsidized by their peasant families. People continue to work in these conditions because wage employment remains the only way to accumulate cash savings when the worker has no liquid capital to invest (in farming or elsewhere).

Given these economic conditions, it is hardly surprising that it was (and to a considerable extent still is) very difficult to distinguish the life history of a worker from that of a peasant. By and large, Kenyan workers come from the peasantry, raise their families on peasant plots, and retire to the peasantry at a relatively young age.[5] They certainly do not think of themselves as a separate group. It is important for public policy that Kenyan peasants have not organized themselves politically to counter worker demands for cheap food and high wages.

This is not to say that workers and peasants will remain one class indefinitely. Today there is an indirect economic basis for conflict between peasants and workers. The prices received by the peasants largely determine the food costs of the workers, and the wages received by the workers are a part of the cost of manufactured goods consumed by the peasants. Thus the economic basis for their unity is declining, but sociological and conscious separation has not yet been achieved. A separate "proletariat" is just beginning to emerge in Kenya.

In the colonial period four other groups stood in contradiction to this worker-peasant class. The conflicts generated by three of the four groups were quite visible and produced correspondingly high class consciousness. These classes were the European industrial capitalists, the European capitalist farmers, and the Asian commercial bourgeoisie. The two European groups were in conflict with their employees over the proportion of value produced that was to be paid out in wages, and with one another over the relative prices and privileges of their manufactured goods and raw materials. The industrialists were based primarily in Britain and exported manufactured products to the colonies. They were represented in Kenya largely by their agents and the British Colonial Office. Large-scale commercial agriculture, however, was represented by local white settlers. Some of the clash between settler politics and the British Colonial Office grew out of the conflict between these differently located groups.

The relationship of Africans to the Asians (Indians and Pakistanis), who dominated commerce, was antagonistic because of struggles over the prices of goods bought and sold by the peasantry. We have followed Mahmoud Mamdani and Issa Shivji in calling this class the commercial bourgeoisie, though most of its members might more accurately be called petty-bourgeois.[6] The potential for class conflict that exists in commerce between the bourgeoisie and petty bourgeoisie—wholesaler and retailer—was not realized among the Asians in Kenya, because of the unity imposed on them by the antagonism of the Europeans and because the other struggles over the distribution of value were so much more significant. With cohesion imposed by external forces and consciousness of internal conflicts consequently low, leadership in the Asian communities remained in the hands of the wealthier, more bourgeois elements, and even Asian workers supported their leaders' political stance as a commercial bourgeoisie. This phenomenon is a good example of an interaction between economic and social structures. Though it prevented an alliance of African workers or traders with their Asian counterparts, it nonetheless infused the conflicts between the racial groups with a class content.

The final class in the colonial equation was an emergent one, the African petty bourgeoisie. The name is a misnomer, as its economic base is somewhat different from its Western European counterpart; it will be used, however, for it has wide currency and there are interesting parallels with other groups called petty-bourgeois. This class had three different economic bases: petty-capitalist (usually export) agriculture, small trade, and clerical or government employment, with no necessary economic connection between them and hence no material reason why they must produce a single class. The links between these bases were provided by the particular sociological patterns of mobility and investment in Kenya. The ties between trade and petty-capitalist agriculture were particularly strong.

"Petty capitalist" designates those farmers who have transcended a purely peasant status by acquiring above-average amounts of land and by employing labor. They cannot be called full capitalist farmers, for their enterprises are relatively small and they usually engage in agricultural labor themselves, rather than solely managing the labor of others. But neither are they simply peasants, for they are in potentially antagonistic relations with their peasant neighbors. By using the new possibilities of a cash economy to expand their production beyond the limits of their families' labor, they intensify the struggle for land, and by employing others, they create the possibility of conflict over the just division of the fruits of production. In those areas where land was scarce, the acquisition of land by this group added to landlessness and heightened the resulting bitterness. A nascent consciousness of class conflict between these petty-capitalist farmers, on the one hand, and workers and peasants, many of them landless, on the other, was already evident in Kikuyu politics in the late 1940s.[7]

This petty-capitalist agriculture had been created by the gradual opening of market opportunities to Africans, particularly export ones. This trend was generally resisted by the white settlers, but it received significant impetus from the need for agricultural produce to support the British effort in World War II. The decision to incorporate "progressive" African farmers into the cash economy was then adopted as a strategy for combating the Mau Mau uprising.

The links between this petty-capitalist agriculture and small trading were and are very strong. The small African trader often has acquired his initial capital in peasant farming and usually is simultaneously a petty-capitalist farmer.[8] Of course he is in a potentially antagonistic economic relationship with his neighbors in both capacities.

The ties between junior civil servants, teachers, and clerical workers and other parts of the African petty bourgeoisie were weaker than those linking the petty-capitalist farmers and traders, although they were still significant. First, many were able to move into commercial agriculture and trade from a base in rural government employment, as was the case with Musa Nyandusi, Philip Mule, and Elijah Waicanguru.[9] Unlike the workers, who used the labor of their wives on the land, the clerks and teachers tended to take on employees (sometimes their relatives). Junior civil servants also usually looked forward to retiring to petty-capitalist farming, as their pensions were insufficient. The second link with the other economic bases of the petty bourgeoisie is that by the end of the colonial period many of the African civil servants and clerks were coming from families in commercial agriculture or trade, which is how their parents had been able to pay their school fees.

The leadership of the petty bourgeoisie in the independence movements of Africa is well known and well documented. The colonial regimes sometimes pointed out that the nationalist parties were led by an elite class that could not truly represent peasant interests. Nationalists replied that African societies were classless.[10] This was and is false. But contradictions between the worker-peasant and the African petty bourgeoisie were minor compared with those with the other classes in colonial society. Consciousness of this petty bourgeoisie as a separate class varied from place to place and time to time. This is why it is identified here as an emergent class. Often it was thought of only as an elite stratum within traditional society. Hence the African petty bourgeoisie was able to take command of the nationalist movement as the legitimate representative of the masses. The problem facing Jomo Kenyatta at independence, however, was that in his own Kikuyu constituency worker and peasant consciousness of the petty bourgeoisie as a separate class was most fully developed, and it was there that its leadership had been challenged by the radicals who led the Mau Mau uprising.[11] In class terms the Kikuyu politicians had the least unified constituency of any ethnic group in Kenya.

Ethnic Tensions

Kenya's many ethnic groups are generally characterized by distinct languages and thus have the same tendency as Europe's nationalities to unite politically and socially. As is seen in table 4.1, the Kikuyu are the largest of Kenya's ethnic groups and together with the closely related Embu and Meru make up 26 percent of the population. The other large groups are the Luo and Luhya in the west, the Kamba to the east of the Kikuyu, and the Kalenjin groups around the Rift Valley. (See map 2.) Most of these groups did not have unified governmental organizations traditionally, but they did have a strong consciousness of common ancestry.

Prior to the imposition of British rule, these ethnic groups both traded and fought with one another, just like the rest of the world's nations. The conflicts tended to be more pronounced with those immediately neighboring groups that were culturally and linguistically most

TABLE 4.1
Kenya's Population by Ethnic Group

Ethnic Group	Percentage of Population	
Kikuyu	20.1	⎫
Meru	5.1	⎬ 26.3
Embu	1.1	⎭
Kamba	10.9	
Luo	13.9	
Luhya	13.3	
Kipsigis	4.3	⎫
Nandi	2.4	⎬ 10.9
Other Kalenjin	4.2	⎭
Other African (e.g., Maasai)	20.7	
Europeans	0.4	
Asians	1.3	
Others	0.8	
Total	100.0	
Base (1969)	10,942,705	

SOURCE: Republic of Kenya, Statistics Division, Ministry of Finance and Economic Planning, *Kenya Population Census, 1969*, vol. 1 (Nairobi, 1970), p. 69.

distinct—the Kikuyus with the Maasai in central Kenya, the Luo with the Luhyas, and the Luhyas with the Kalenjin in the west. Colonialism both reinforced these conflicts and introduced new ones. The introduction of European agricultural settlement had made land a scarce commodity and intensified the competition around it. During the colonial period itself these tensions had united African ethnic groups against the Europeans. As independence approached so did the prospect of transferring European lands to new owners. Thus many of the old conflicts over access to territory were renewed—the Kikuyu against the less numerous Maasai and Kalenjin for the east of the Rift Valley "White Highlands" and the Luhya against the Kalenjin for the west.

New tensions also had developed over access to wage employment. The three largest groups—the Kikuyu, the Luo, and the Luhya—were also the disproportionate leaders in education and urban jobs and found themselves in entirely new competitive relationships. Because new migrants to the cities naturally looked to their relatives for help in finding housing and jobs and because social life takes place most easily in one's mother tongue, this competition readily assumed ethnic overtones.

The British consciously fostered conflicts among the colony's other ethnic groups, following the old slogan of "divide and rule." In the 1920s they deprived Asians of rights in the name of protecting Africans. During the crucial period in the 1950s when mass political mobilization was taking place, the colonial government confined African political organizations to single districts, forcing most nationalist politicians to build from an ethnic base. (Tom Mboya, a Luo, escaped this trap by building a multiethnic following out of the labor movement in Nairobi, but he was the exception.)[12]

Finally, the white settlers saw their own economic interests as most threatened by the large and better-educated African groups, particularly the Kikuyu and to a lesser extent the Luo. Thus they helped to split the nationalist movement by fostering the formation of the Kenyan African Democratic Union (KADU) to protect the territorial interests of the minority groups. In this way the whites helped many of the precolonial lines of conflict to resurface at independence. The new wine of land hunger was poured into the old bottles of ethnic difference and given new bite. At a later point the competition for urban jobs and businesses would be mixed into another set of these bottles and produce another set of conflicts, this time between the Kikuyu, the Luo, and the Luhya. Economic and ethnic differences were intermingled to produce tensions whose shape and force could not be explained by either alone.

This then was the dangerous political situation that Jomo Kenyatta faced when he emerged from detention. Kenyan politics had become fractionated along ethnic lines, with his own Kikuyu united with the Luo in the Kenyan African National Union (KANU) and in tight competition with KADU for control of the government. Almost all the leading politicians had built their organizations on ethnic bases, so it would not have been easy for Kenyatta to command support in a way that cut across these lines. Furthermore, the intra-African class conflicts that did exist in Kenya at the time were simmering just below the surface among the Kikuyu but were weakly developed among the other ethnic groups. If Kenyatta had played to the disadvantaged, as radicals such as Oginga Odinga and Bildad Kaggia wanted him to, he would have secured the enthusiasm of the Kikuyu poor, antagonized the Kikuyu petty bourgeoisie, and split his own political base, but without being able to make significant inroads into the ethnic bases of the politicians with whom he was competing. If Kenyatta had gone this route, he probably would have ended his career out of power.

Kenyatta instead chose to protect his own political base by taking a conservative line of intra-African class harmony and keeping the Kikuyu united by directing substantial benefits toward them without regard to need. Kenyatta argued that the bitter conflicts between Loyalists and Mau Mau should simply be forgotten (with the former retaining the advantages in land they had gained). He said that there would be "no free things" distributed to the landless. The radicals ultimately rebelled against this neglect of their concerns, formed the Kenya People's Union (KPU), and were crushed in the "Little General Election" of 1966. The political shrewdness of Kenyatta's strategy was thus confirmed. In the process he reinforced a political system in which class conflicts were subordinated to ethnic ones while still fueling much of their heat.[13]

The result was a political system that was largely constructed out of patron-client networks. This had particularly unfortunate consequences for the interests of peasant farmers and the organizations that serve them. Since peasant needs are central to rural development, let us pause to explore the policy implications of patronage more fully.

The character of risk in agricultural systems in preindustrial society leads peasants to invest heavily in personal relationships as a hedge against adversity. Not only may close ties with social equals, such as relatives and neighbors, provide help when one experiences calamities such as drought or illness, bonds to one's social or economic superiors can result in personalized assistance as well. For these latter, unequal types of relationships, the recipient promises support in return for the help that he or she receives. This social dynamic lies at the root of the patron-client relationships that pervade poor countries and dominate most of their political processes.[14]

Patron-client politics mobilizes political resources along the lines of clientage networks (which need not be ascriptive but which in Kenya do in fact tend to follow kinship lines at the local level). By necessity these networks group together people of dissimilar interests; a patron must be advantaged in some area in order to have something to trade for the support of his clients. The resulting political processes are substantially different from those that result from associational groupings, which bring together those who share a common interest.[15] Associational politics leads to the direct representation of the common interests of large or powerful groups in society. If Kenyatta had followed the urging of the KANU radicals to emphasize the needs of Kenya's poor, particularly its peasants, he would have been building such an associational form of political organization. In contrast, patron-client politics masks the interests of the multitude, who are the clients, for they are represented in the system by advantaged patrons, whose personal interests are significantly different from those of their followers.

Associational politics tends to result in the creation of "public goods" for the most powerful groups—policies that will serve the common interests of the groups' memberships. Patron-client politics tends to focus on the creation of "private goods," discrete products and services that can be disaggregated and distributed to individuals through clientage networks.[16] To the extent that patron-client systems produce any "public goods," such goods will tend to be those that will benefit the elite group of patrons and add to the personal wealth on which they can draw to maintain their clientage networks. Sometimes political systems are mixed; some groups will be incorporated through patron-client networks and others will be represented by associations. Such mixed systems generally work to the still greater disadvantage of small farmers. In systems like these, commercial and industrial interests, large farmers, and even sometimes urban workers have associations to press their interests, while the expression of peasant interests is dampened by patron-client networks. Kenya is such a mixed system. As a consequence, political demand for agricultural policies and programs meeting the common needs of small producers (public goods) is weakened, and emphasis has been placed instead on services that can be distributed to discrete groups of clients in return for their support (private goods).

AFRICANIZATION OF THE CIVIL SERVICE

The theme underlying Jomo Kenyatta's policies as president was Africanization. In this way he could provide the flow of benefits both to buy the unity of the Kikuyu and to provide patronage resources to keep the other ethnic leaders in his coalition. The first drive was to indigenize the civil service; the second, to take over settler agriculture; the third, to replace the Asian commercial bourgeoisie and the European managers of multinational firms; and the fourth, to compete eventually with international capital through new investment and the purchase of firms. All of the men whose biographies we are examining were influenced by at least one of these Africanization efforts, and two of them benefited from all of them. These policies altered the structure of Kenya's political economy and also affected the shape of its rural development.

The Africanization of the upper levels of the civil service took place extremely rapidly. It was essentially completed by 1965, save for professional and technical positions, which took a few years longer. The speed was remarkable, as there were very few Africans in the senior civil service in the late 1950s. Those with plausible qualifications were promoted with great rapidity and quickly found themselves at the top.

Recruitment and promotion of Africans in the lower and middle ranks of the senior civil service were based on qualifications and performance. Capture of the very top positions, however, tended to depend on having the confidence of the president or someone close to him, particularly for the generalist positions. Throughout the British Empire, the latter were (and are) held by members of a special cadre. In Kenya it is the Provincial Administration. The English Administrative Class and the Indian Administrative Service are its equivalents. The first slice of the careers of our four men illustrates these points.

Africanization and the Four Administrators

Simeon Nyachae (the future chief secretary) had held positions as district assistant and then as district officer in charge of a division during the late colonial period. For British officers these were entry-level positions, and many years of service would be required before one was put in charge of a district. In August 1963 Nyachae was sent to Cambridge University for the training course that all the English took before joining the Provincial Administration. He was recalled before it was completed, however, and upon his arrival at the Nairobi airport in March 1964 was made district commissioner of Nyandarua. This was a critical and difficult district, but Oginga Odinga, who was then minister of home affairs, was anxious to fill all the Provincial Administration posts with Africans.

In October 1964 Nyachae was called to Nairobi for special duties as deputy director of the December celebrations for Kenya's becoming a republic. In this position he worked under the then minister of constitutional affairs, Tom Mboya. The appointment may have been influenced by Mboya's alliance with Lawrence Sagini, Nyachae's brother-in-law. The post gave high visibility to Nyachae's considerable administrative talents. It also created an incident. Nyachae was in charge of the seating arrangements and decided that Kenyatta should sit alone on a high dais, with the chief justice coming up to him to give him the presidential oath of office. But Charles Rubia felt that as mayor of Nairobi and first citizen of the city he should sit on the dais with the president. Rubia felt extremely strongly about the matter and took it to Mboya. Mboya said that the decision was Nyachae's to make but warned Nyachae that if he were sacked because of it Mboya would be unable to protect him. Nyachae said he would take the risk.

At the celebrations, when Kenyatta's car arrived Rubia called for his own and left in protest at his not sitting with the president. As Kenyatta came up the stand, he called Nyachae over and asked what was going on. To Nyachae's brief explanation, Kenyatta simply said, "Well done." Immediately afterward the president made him senior district commissioner in charge of the Nairobi Extra-Provincial District and in January promoted him to be provincial commissioner in charge of the vast and sensitive Rift Valley. By virtue of coupling his administrative ability with an understanding of the president's unspoken wishes and the courage to act on it, Nyachae became Kenya's youngest provincial commissioner. He had vaulted into one of the positions that Kenyatta regarded as most important politically.

Charles Karanja (the future tea manager) was posted to Nakuru in 1957 by the Ministry of Works, which had paid his expenses at the Kampala Engineering School. He was appointed an African engineering assistant, which involved working under the guidance and supervision of more experienced engineers. He disliked the term "African" in his title, and the Kenyan Engineering Association, of which he was the first president, disputed it. He worked on the design of water supplies and constructed one dam and a pipeline.

In 1958 when the ministry decided to train more engineers for roads, he applied for the six-month course and was taken over the objections of his supervisor, who said he was too valuable to lose. At its completion he was assigned to the Embu District Council as the district engineer. He remained there from September 1958 to January 1960 and was in charge of road construction and maintenance, with a staff of two hundred. He was lucky, because when he arrived in Embu the council decided to embark on paving (tarmacking) the town roads. This gave him a chance to prove himself, and "they are still the way I did them."

The Kiambu District Council advertised for its own engineer in late 1959, and after some hesitation Karanja applied. Another candidate had the inside track with the council. But Peter Derrick, their new district commissioner, had been the DC in Embu and persuaded the council that Karanja was the best engineer available, so after confirming that he was indeed from Kiambu, the council appointed him.

Again Karanja was lucky. The Kiambu council had money and was building offices and houses and taking over responsibility for roads from the Provincial Administration. It also received a large grant from the central government to pave an eleven-mile stretch of road. All of these projects were completed under Karanja's direction. "The tarmac road stands to this day with little maintenance." He commanded a work force of about four hundred.

Karanja was among those who welcomed Jomo Kenyatta to his Gatundu home in Kiambu when he was released from detention in July 1961. He later helped to organize the reception the Kiambu council gave Kenyatta, and he bought, on behalf of the council, the fountain pen it presented to him.

Karanja was next sent to Canada for a university degree but gave it up after a year to return to his family and Kenya. He went back to his old job as Kiambu engineer in August 1962. He was privately approached to stand for Parliament in the Gatundu constituency and seriously considered it, as it was thought that Kenyatta would stand in Nairobi. When Kenyatta decided to run from his home, Karanja deferred to him and spoke publicly in his support. Politically, he really had little other choice.

When Kenyatta became prime minister, Karanja proposed that the Kiambu council obtain funds for paving the road to his home in Gatundu. Kenyatta would have the Kiambu Works Department take care of minor jobs on the house built for him by the colonial government just before his release from detention. The house was a replacement for Kenyatta's original house, which had been demolished by the same government during the State of Emergency, and Kenyatta was dissatisfied with some of its features. Karanja saw to it personally that the requested amendments were well done. Kenyatta noticed and was impressed by his performance.

Karanja was ambitious, however, and he saw that he could go no further in Kiambu or in public works engineering. He held the top engineering post in Kiambu, and to get ahead in the Ministry of Works he would have needed the B.Sc. that he forsook when he left Canada. There also was no way for him to enter politics as long as Kenyatta was alive and held his home's seat in Parliament. He decided to find another job to expand his experience and capital and then to go into business for himself.

Hence in 1964 he responded to an advertisement for an executive assistant in the Special Crops Development Authority (which was to become the Kenya Tea Development Authority, KTDA). Karanja had been encouraged to apply by Jackson Kamau, to whom he had been introduced by his old primary-school mate, Ishmael Muriithi. Kamau, who was from Kiambu, was one of the two Central Province representatives on the KTDA board. The general manager of the Authority at the time was W. B. G. Raynor, who had served as district commissioner in Kiambu during Karanja's tenure there. With Raynor's familiarity with his ability, Karanja captured the post and became the first African in the Authority's management.

Karanja's rise through the ranks of the KTDA to the post of general manager in 1970 is discussed in chapter 6. Most of Karanja's rapid upward mobility can be attributed to his hard work and the quality of his performance. The last step to general manager was aided, however, by the contacts he had made earlier with Kenyatta and the reputation for effectiveness that he had established in politically powerful Kiambu.

Ishmael Muriithi was made district veterinary officer in Eldoret when he returned from Edinburgh in May 1964. In December a position as deputy director of Veterinary Services was advertised, and the director, Anthony Dorman, advised Muriithi: "You wouldn't do yourself any harm if you filed for" the post.

There were two other strong African applicants, but Muriithi had a number of advantages. First, he was the only African veterinarian in Kenya with United Kingdom qualifications. The decision made in 1960 to send him to Scotland while his peers went to the United States and India definitely worked in his favor, even though it kept him away from Kenya longer. Second, Muriithi had placed at the top of his class at Edinburgh. He was regarded as "quick and bright," a "competent, serious scientist," and a "well-prepared professional" by those in a position to influence the selection. Third, he was already "noted for his extremely high ethical standards" and as "having a good feel for administration." Fourth, he was a close friend of Geoffrey Kariithi's, an old Alliance High School classmate and the new permanent secretary of the Ministry of Agriculture (in which the Veterinary Services were situated).

The appointment decision was made by the Public Service Commission, though it must have been influenced by the advice of those in the Ministry of Agriculture most competent to judge the professional calibre of the applicants. One of Muriithi's competitors lobbied hard for the post; Muriithi did not; he was too new to know how. He was appointed on his merits.

Once Muriithi was made deputy director in mid-1965 it quickly became evident that he was being groomed by Dorman to succeed him as director. He was appointed director of Veterinary Services in 1966, the post he held until he retired in 1984. His only connection with the president would have been an indirect one through Geoffrey Kariithi, who was later to become the extremely influential head of the civil service.

Harris Mule (the planner) returned to Kenya from the United States in June 1963. Neither his university nor his academic performance was particularly distinguished. He was immediately offered a position in the Provincial Administration but refused it. He was determined to be a government economist. If he had taken the post, he might have become a permanent secretary much more rapidly, but his influence on Kenya government policy would have been considerably less. By the end of the month he was appointed to the Planning Department and made a statistician in the Ministry of Agriculture. In 1965 he moved to the Ministry of Economic Planning as a planning officer. In this period those in a position to influence his career felt that Mule "worked hard, wrote a lot, but was quiet and took little initiative." His peers commented on the fact that he took work home, had an amazing memory for facts and people, and knew what was important in his work. But he was extremely deferential to his seniors and was not regarded as having leadership qualities. His superiors had little occasion to see the public-speaking abilities he had developed while preaching in Denver.

Mule was sent to Harvard for the 1966–67 academic year, where he performed indifferently. On his return, he was made a senior planning officer in charge of Agriculture, Settlement, and Cooperatives. He became principal economist in charge of Agriculture and Rural Development in 1969. He moved quickly to the post of chief economist in 1970 because of the support of his minister, Tom Mboya. In 1972 he was made deputy permanent secretary in charge of statistics and planning in the Ministry of Finance and Economic Planning, a position that enjoys the rank and salary of a permanent secretary.

Throughout this period, Mule showed a remarkable ability for learning on the job. He recognized quality in the ministry's advisers and listened carefully to them. His analytic ability to see a problem and its consequences grew considerably, as did his self-confidence in presenting his views. His honesty and integrity became evident. But he did not make the final leap to full permanent secretary until 1978, after Kenyatta's death. He himself was happy where he was and did not lobby for advancement. He also was not helped by his carelessness about his personal appearance, nor by the fact that his intelligence and sagacity did not register in first impressions. Still, less impressive men than he had become permanent secretaries, and others wanted him promoted. One informed source felt that Mule had been blocked by Kikuyus close to Kenyatta. A permanent secretaryship in the area of economic policy is a position of considerable influence and requires the confidence of the president. Under Kenyatta, Kikuyus were more likely to gain that trust than others were.

Did "Tribalism" Overlay Africanization in the Civil Service?

Kenyans have often been concerned that appointments and promotions in the civil service were going disproportionately to the ethnic group(s) of those in power. During the period of rapid Africanization in the 1960s, allegations frequently were made in Parliament and elsewhere of favoritism to Kikuyus.[17] Was this talk a manifestation of civil service reality? Or did it simply reflect the way Kenyans are prone to see their own political system? The answer appears to be some of both, but with the truth surprisingly lying somewhat closer to the latter.

Was any group disproportionately represented in the higher civil service? Yes, but at least in the 1960s this seems largely to have been a function of variations in educational opportunity, which arose out of differential exposure to the colonial economy and mission proselytizing. As can be seen from table 4.2, the Kikuyu were overrepresented relative to their proportion in the population, and this advantage increased as the decade went along. It is unlikely, however, that this was due to any discrimination or favoritism on the part of the new African government. The ethnic proportions of senior staff in the Ministry of Agriculture is particularly instructive in this regard. *All* Kenyan Africans with the requisite educational qualifications for such positions were hired during this period. Thus the ethnic percentages in Agriculture simply reflect

TABLE 4.2
The Ethnic Distribution of African Elites
(Asians and Europeans excluded from all calculations)

	Ethnic Group						
Percentage of:	Kikuyu, Embu, Meru	Luo	Luhya	Kamba	Kalenjin	Others	Base Number (100%)
Population in 1969[a]	27.0	14.3	13.6	11.2	11.2	22.7	10.7 mill.
Nongovernment Professionals in 1964[b]	30.0	25.0	25.0	5.0	1.0	14.0	183
Civil Service Elite in 1964[b]	30.0	23.0	20.0	9.0	5.0	13.0	123
Agricultural Senior Staff in 1968[c]	37.6	17.0	22.2	11.1	6.6	5.5	423
Civil Service Elite in 1968 in Planning, Co-ops, Labour, Education, and Housing[d]	40.1	15.0	19.7	4.7	4.7	15.8	127
Policy-making Civil Servants in 1969[e]	38.4	12.5	12.5	17.0	10.7	8.9	112
Policy-making Civil Servants in 1972[e]	59.0	10.0	8.0	5.0	8.0	10.0	101

[a] Republic of Kenya, *Kenya Population Census, 1969*, vol. 1 (Nairobi: Government Printer, 1970), p. 69.
[b] Gordon Wilson, "The African Elite," in *The Transformation of East Africa*, ed. Stanley Diamond and Fred Burke (New York: Basic Books, 1964), pp. 445, 448. The data are based on surveys done for *Who's Who in East Africa, 1963–64* (Nairobi: Marco Surveys, 1964).
[c] All established (i.e., senior) staff. Author's data, taken from Kenya Government official personnel records. Ethnic group determined by name analysis.
[d] The most senior staff. Author's data, taken from Kenya Government official personnel records. Ethnic group determined by name analysis.
[e] John R. Nellis, "The Ethnic Composition of Leading Kenyan Government Positions," Research Report, no. 24 (Uppsala: Scandinavian Institute of African Studies, 1974), pp. 12–13. Names of uncertain ethnicity are excluded from the calculations.

the character of the applicant pool, which was determined by educational decisions made during the colonial period. The proportions of Kikuyus and other ethnic groups found in Agriculture (row 4) are similar to those found at higher decision-making levels in the late 1960s (rows 5 and 6). The fact that the ratio of Kikuyus to others was increasing throughout the decade (compare rows 2 and 3 with 4 through 6) would have been nothing more than a readjustment from the job discrimination against Kikuyus during the Mau Mau/Emergency period.

But were Kikuyus, once recruited into the senior civil service, promoted more rapidly than others? Data from civil service establishment records in the late 1960s are presented in Appendix A and used to examine this question. The answer is no; there is no evidence of Kikuyu advantage in the aggregate data. Contrary to popular impressions, Kikuyus (or others) were not more likely to be promoted when they were working under members of their own ethnic group who were in a position to help them and might be predisposed to do so. The statistical material presented in Appendix A provides no evidence of supervisorial favoritism along ethnic lines.

Were senior civil service promotions then really blind to ethnic identity? I think that the answer is yes, until one reaches the very highest positions. The Public Service Commission was designed to assure the application of merit criteria in government employment, and it worked hard to achieve that result. It had multiethnic membership, and its chairman and executive secretary were not Kikuyu. There was a good deal of favoritism in the discretionary junior government jobs that the commission did not control, but it took special effort to achieve a promotion other than on merit criteria at the senior levels.

This is not to say that merit was never overlooked; insiders testify to the fact that it was. Because it was difficult to do so, however, it tended to be done only for those positions that required the confidence of the president and where the president's implicit or explicit influence could be used to achieve the result. Table 4.2 shows that by 1972 a considerable jump had occurred in the proportion of Kikuyus holding positions that could influence policy. Sometimes several non-Kikuyu would be promoted to positions that were not critical to public policy, in order to put a Kikuyu in line for a position that was. The locus of real power in a ministry also could vary between the offices of cabinet minister, permanent secretary, or chief of technical services, depending on which post was held by a Kikuyu.

Something other than just ethnicity appears to have been at work here, however. The president wanted to assure that the critical positions in his administration were held by people in whom he had personal confidence. Few presidents would do otherwise. And not all of those

Kenyatta relied upon were Kikuyu. Simeon Nyachae held the ear of the president against many senior Kikuyu. One illustrative incident should suffice to make the point.

In the mid-1970s, when Nyachae was provincial commissioner in Central Province, a Kikuyu deputy secretary in the Office of the President reshuffled the district commissioners in the province without consulting him. When Nyachae drove to Nairobi to protest, he was swept aside with the double assertion that the decision had already been taken and that as a non-Kikuyu he was not in a position to question decisions about Central Province. Nyachae was enraged and drove straight to Nakuru, where the president was staying at the moment. He told Kenyatta that if this particular man stayed in the Office of the President, then Nyachae would resign. In less than two minutes Kenyatta had decided to remove the offender and only later reassigned him to another post that was out of the line of policy. This incident was not exceptional. Nyachae's influence with the president frequently prevailed over senior Kikuyu politicians and administrators on provincial matters. The reason is simple. Nyachae had established in the Republic celebrations incident that his primary allegiance was to the president, and this gave Kenyatta a confidence in him that went well beyond mere ethnic identity. Nyachae says:

> One thing I have always maintained is loyalty. I borrowed [the principle] from my father. Understand the boss fully—his wishes, his temperament, his way of doing things. Before you reply think of it in his way. [He will] come to accept that you wish well and then . . . take your advice.

Few Kenyan civil servants see their duties in this same way. The majority put (or are suspected of putting) service to their home areas on a par with loyalty to their president. Presidents therefore disproportionately pick people from their own ethnic group to serve them, on the theory that the premises guiding their decisions will then be less in conflict, with the result that the president's needs will be better met. In so doing Kenyan presidents may be mistaken or reflecting a policy bias to service their own areas, but they probably are guided more by a concern for loyalty than by simple favoritism. Where they do find fidelity among those outside their ethnic group they generally use and reward it.

In any case, by the early 1970s almost all of the Kenyan public service had been Africanized. The departure of the British from technical positions was somewhat deceptive, however, for many of them were replaced with foreign advisers, albeit not in positions of authority. Tensions remain to the present time about the number and influence of these advisers. One of the critical factors in the success of the four administrators was their skill in handling these Africanization issues.

AFRICANIZING LAND OWNERSHIP

Land has been central to most political conflicts in Kenya's modern history. The pressures brought on by the European appropriation of the "White Highlands" led to the Mau Mau uprising. Among the Kikuyu, the landless were more likely to be Mau Mau, and petty-capitalist farmers to be Loyalists. The initial response of the British was the Swynnerton Plan of 1954. They undertook land registration and consolidation of African smallholdings, against the security of which they made agricultural credit available. Extension and marketing services were expanded to facilitate commercial agriculture. The previous restrictions on African cultivation of export crops, coffee in particular, were dropped, and production was instead encouraged. The idea was to secure the allegiance of the Loyalists by rewarding them with land and security of tenure and to build petty-capitalist agriculture as a new source of wealth and rural employment. The new policy explicitly accepted landlessness, and the new African "yeomen" were to be the bulwark against rebellion. In the ensuing ten years the recorded value of marketed production from smallholdings nearly tripled. The bulk of this development effort was concentrated upon the Kikuyu in Central Province. The African petty-capitalist agriculture, which had tentatively spoken its first lines in the 1930s, took center stage and assumed a prominent role in Kenya's economic play by 1960.[18]

Nonetheless, as independence approached, even the British recognized that African demands for more land could not be met simply by strengthening the economy of the "native reserves." The transfer of land to African hands began before independence, indeed even before KADU first formed a government. The prospect of majority rule under a black government was terrifying to most Kenyan whites; and when the British government made clear its intention to permit it, the bottom dropped out of the large-farm market, with more settlers wanting to sell than there were prospective buyers. Simultaneously, the African demand for land that underlay the Mau Mau uprising burst into the open again with a frenzied expectation on the part of many that independence would bring free land for those without it. It was in the interests of both the European settlers and the British government to accommodate the African land hunger while also shoring up the prices of large farms and letting those whites who wanted to leave do so.

A small Land Transfer Program for 7,800 African families was created in 1961, with financing from British government and World Bank sources. All the parties involved believed that the large-farm sector was critical to the health of the Kenyan economy, that as much of it as possible should be saved in the transfer, and that the smallholdings that were established should be large enough to continue producing the same crops for the market as the settler farms had done. The scheme was labeled a "Yeoman and Peasant" one, in continuity with the 1950s policy of creating an advantaged group of African "yeomen" to provide economic development and political stability. Six thousand "peasant" holdings were to be designed to provide K.shs. 2,000 a year net income above subsistence, while a further 1,800 holdings were to be created with K.shs. 5,000 incomes. Even the incomes projected for the smaller holdings were several times the average Kikuyu family cash intake from agriculture of K.shs. 354 at the time.[19]

Later in 1961, as KADU's condition for forming a government, the size of the transfer program was doubled, and the minimum target income was set at K.shs. 500. In 1962 KANU joined a coalition government, and the "Million Acre" settlement scheme was born, with explicit provision of land for Mau Mau freedom fighters to induce them to come out of the forest. But both the minimum target income and the explicit provision to use 15 percent of the land for African large farms remained.

The "high density," lower-income farms were seen as a necessary welfare measure to sap the political intensity of Kikuyu land hunger. The "low density," larger farms with high incomes were viewed as the core of the economic development initiative. The World Bank in this period refused to lend funds for any farms with projected incomes below K.shs. 2,000, adding to the pressures to maintain a prominent "low density" component to the program.[20]

The causes of the program then were a combination of political and economic "necessity." But to say so is to illustrate the proposition that policymakers choose the causes of their actions. Those involved in making the decision were genuinely convinced that the large mixed farms were essential to the economic health of Kenya and that peasant agriculture could not provide the marketable surplus needed for growth. They were wrong on both counts. By and large, the settlement schemes included neither European ranches, which were in semi-arid areas considered unsuitable for crops, nor corporate estates, which produced tea, coffee, and sisal with labor-intensive methods. The land transfers concentrated instead on the European mixed farms, which combined crop and livestock production and supported most of the white settlers. It was a myth that these farms were the backbone of the colonial economy, a myth sustained by the appearance of profitability that the protection and subsidized services they received generated. Leys, extending the argument of Britain's 1965 Stamp Mission, concludes that if one subtracts the value of this assistance, most of which was paid for directly or indirectly by Africans, the contribution of the European mixed farms to the economy was negligible or even negative.[21]

It was also a myth that peasant farms could not sustain economic growth. The low-density settlements, which were supposed to provide development, performed very poorly, and the high-density ones, which were seen as a political sop, gave a higher rate of return to investment and were more useful to the economy on a number of dimensions.[22] Since that time the orthodoxy among economists has come to be that development will be better served by a unimodal distribution of land in relatively egalitarian, small farms than by a bimodal one combining large commercial farms with tiny, marginal ones on which the bulk of rural families are sustained.[23] In 1971 an International Labor Organization mission urged that Kenya subdivide the larger mixed farms into small ones.[24] Chapters 6 and 7, on the development of the smallholder tea and dairy industries, conclusively demonstrate the ability of this sector to be an engine of development. By 1974 the government was taking the position that large farms were necessary only for wheat, hybrid seed production, and breeding herds.[25]

But such was not the understanding in the early 1960s. The European large farmers had created a legitimating myth of their indispensability, which led them to try to reproduce themselves by creating African large farmers as they departed. Once the African political and administrative leadership had started large farming itself, it chose to reaffirm its economic importance, even in the face of mounting contrary evidence. It is true that the conception of the role of large commercial farming was significantly narrowed, but the claim of even a small role for it legitimized a disproportionate continuance. Settlement schemes continued to accommodate the landless into the 1980s and covered double the million acres originally envisioned. But well over half the land transferred through settlements and private sales went into African large farms.[26] It was not a chance occurrence. The Land Control Act was passed to give district-level boards the power to veto land transactions, and by the early 1970s foreign land purchases had virtually ceased.[27] Great lengths were taken to assure potential African large farmers a competitive place in the land market. In fact, for a time all sales of European farms had to be approved by President Kenyatta himself.

This pattern of transfer did generate conflict. Those with little or no land raised demands for subdivision to a fever pitch, and the radicals in KANU wanted to place a cap on land purchases.[28] This issue was one of the core concerns that caused them to leave the party and to form the opposition Kenya People's Union in 1966. Their manifesto declared that the government was "promoting vigorously the development of a small privileged class of Africans; the rich are getting richer and the poor poorer." [29]

Kenyatta fought back as if struggling for his political survival. In a sense perhaps he was. He needed to have a united Kikuyu as the foundation of his political support and a flow of patronage to induce others to build upon it. To contain the danger of a class-based politics among the Kikuyu he had to provide land to those without it and to assure the petty-capitalists that he would protect their property. Settlement provided for the poor in his constituency. But once the British had started the low-density schemes, he could not argue for land ceilings without threatening the advantaged among the Kikuyu. Furthermore, the prospect of favored access to large farms enticed the leaders of other ethnic groups to support him, while their internal class conflicts were too weak to sustain a political division if land for the poor were offered instead. Thus Kenyatta opted for the conservative road to political survival, possibly with an eye to his own prosperity as well. He judged his electorate well, for the KPU was greatly reduced in the "Little General Election" of 1966, and he felt able to ban it and reestablish a de facto one-party state in 1969.

The fact that land reform was downgraded by the government, however, does not mean that it was abandoned by the workers and peasants. Although formal settlements have diminished since the early 1970s, an informal land reform has continued apace through the operations of the private market. Africans with little or no land have pooled their savings in cooperative societies and companies, bought out remaining European large farms, and divided them into small plots (sometimes illegally). Between 1963 and 1983, 24,000 land-buying firms were formed. [30] It is said that the Uasin Guishu District, which once had nothing but large farms, now has nothing but small ones, and a similar state has overtaken southern Laikipia District. In both cases the "informal land reform" of private sales has been prominent in the process. That the poor have undertaken these transfers with their own resources validates the economic attractiveness of small-scale agriculture in Kenya.

Class Formation and the Matajiri

The continued acquisition of land by the poor must not obscure the fact that the "land reform" of the 1960s perpetuated a bimodal agricultural economy. Kenya remains divided between small-farm and large-farm economies. Even if they are more modest in scale today, ranches, estates, and large farms still control one-third of all agricultural land and now are largely owned by a firmly entrenched African elite. [31] Those who purchased these large farms were either influential politicians or managers and professionals in the civil service and European-owned businesses. The same unity of employment, agricultural, and commercial interests that defines the African petty bourgeoisie characterizes this new group as well. On this basis we can speak of a third African social class emerging in Kenya today, to add to the petty bourgeoisie and the workers and peasants. We will follow the popular Swahili usage and term this group the *matajiri* (literally, the rich, or well-to-do). The stake that this class has in agriculture distinguishes it from ruling groups in most other African countries and has proved to be quite important to Kenya's rural development policies.

The matajiri class has its origin in the structure of public and private employment, which was taken over intact when it was Africanized. It is still possible to identify "European" and "African" positions in terms of salaries, perquisites, career prospects, power, and administrative behavior.[32] For the first five years or so after independence the importance of this bifurcation was masked by rapid promotions across the boundaries. The system then stabilized, however, and recruitment into the "European" and "African" sections is now separate and largely self-contained. In any hierarchical organization the potential exists for a division along the lines of authority between junior and senior staff. In the civil service one finds multiple signs of this split, ranging from conflict patterns and friendship groupings to the use of Swahili in the junior ranks and English in the senior.[33] This same division appears in the distinction between clerical and managerial employees in the private sector. This division is increasingly becoming one between petty-bourgeois and matajiri classes.

It might be objected that these two strata cannot be separate classes because they have the same social origins. In chapter 2 it was shown that Kenya's educated leadership has come disproportionately from petty-bourgeois parents. Nonetheless, many senior civil servants do come from poor farmer or worker beginnings. The junior civil servants' background would be more humble and also would show substantial upward mobility. If economic class were dependent on one's parents, there could be no matajiri class in Kenya, and the size of the petty bourgeoisie would be smaller than most have argued it is. American and European social research has assumed that an upwardly mobile individual retains a significant identity with his class of origin and thus does not participate fully in the social-class solidarity of his new economic group. Doubtless this is true, but more emphasis should be placed on the fact of participation than on its qualified nature.[34] The socialization experiences involved in the process of moving up in society that were presented in the preceding chapter must not be discounted. A social identification process that is the opposite of the European model is at work as well, one in which the parents of an upwardly mobile young man identify with his social class, not vice versa. Parents cajole their son, not to remember his peasant origins, but to remember his peasant relatives. He is likely to be encouraged, not dissuaded, to acquire new privileges so that his kinship group can participate in his prestige and benefit from his patronage.[35] Obviously, a member of the matajiri class who has village links will behave differently from one who does not, and so his class identity will not be pure. That it is impure should not obscure the existence of this class. The signs of its effect will be found when we see administrators who belong to it pursuing policies that serve the collective interests of this class but do not advance their personal ones.

This emergent matajiri group moved out from its beginnings in the higher reaches of politics and management to buy large farms in the former "White Highlands." Only they had the necessary regular incomes or the connections or both to satisfy the lending agencies. Thus we have not only an emerging African class with interests in large commercial agriculture, but one that also sits at the very center of public policy-making and administration. One of the functions of this study is to examine the implications of that fact for Kenyan rural development. First, however, let us see how these larger forces played themselves out in the careers of the four administrators.

Administrators and Land

Simeon Nyachae already had twenty acres in Kisii, managed by his wives Esther and Martha, when the land scramble began. (See plate 15.) In 1966 two cabinet ministers, Lawrence Sagini and Jackson Angaine, helped him identify a 100-acre farm on the Sotik Settlement Scheme, on the border of Kisii District. He set up his mother there and managed it in absentia, as did most of the other large African agriculturalists. At one time the farm had forty-five employees, but by 1986 it was down to seven permanent workers, owing to problems with his manager. In 1969 Nyachae acquired a very large farm at Mau Narok, a reasonable drive from his provincial headquarters. President Kenyatta personally helped to arrange both the purchase and the loan. Today Nyachae holds a group of three farms at Mau Narok and is a large wheat producer. (See plate 16.) He also owns a ranch in Meru jointly with two of his former Provincial Administration colleagues. (Incidentally, these men belong to three different ethnic groups.) These enterprises are all managed for him by trained personnel seconded by the government Agricultural Development Corporation. Part of the ADC's mandate is to assist Africans with running their farms, and Nyachae pays fully for these services. But as there are not enough good ADC managers to go around for all who want them, influence sometimes plays a part in acquiring one.

Charles Karanja began with a 13-acre plot near his birth place, 10 of which he put under coffee. Just before he joined the KTDA in 1964 he bought a 150-acre farm near Limuru in upper Kiambu from a departing settler. He lived there until 1974 and commuted twenty miles to work. He ran it initially as a dairy, but eventually he planted 120 acres of tea there. His immediate neighbors were Njenga Karume, Jackson Kamau, and Kenneth Matiba, all of whom were politically important Kikuyus; Kamau became the chairman of his board at the KTDA.

In 1974 Karanja bought a 300-acre coffee estate in Ruiru, in lower Kiambu, and moved there because the cold at Limuru was giving him bronchitis. By the 1980s he had interests in seven farms altogether—two more in the Limuru area of 300 acres each, two in the Nandi hills of 500 and 900 acres, and one in Nakuru of 600 acres. The Ruiru property is under coffee, and the Nakuru one is a dairy; the other five are all planted to tea. The Nandi estates are owned by three partners, but Karanja and his wife oversee the management of all of them.

Ishmael Muriithi had much more modest investments in agriculture. His father gave him 5 acres at home in Nyeri, and Muriithi built a house there. But his father still grazes his cattle on the land and uses the rental income from the house. He bought a small farm of about 25 acres with a pleasant stone house on it near the Veterinary Department headquarters at Kabete in 1966. He bought another 12 acres to add to it in 1969 and rented another 15. So the farm size is only medium. It is located close to Nairobi, however, and as the family lived on it, his wife, Martha, was able to manage it intensively and produce a reasonable income. In 1986 it had over twenty-five cows, two sheds of pigs, and four sheds of chickens and was being worked by eight permanent employees.

Muriithi also acquired several other small farms in the settlement schemes—in Kitale, Nakuru, Nyahururu, and Laikipia Districts and on the coast. He regarded land as an investment and had a peasant's instincts against ever letting it go. He does not appear, however, to have made much money from these farms. He and Martha found that they couldn't manage them well from a distance, and the local employees that they put in charge have not done a good job. They are a good example of the low productivity of what Kenyans call "telephone farmers."

Harris Mule's assets are by far the smallest of the four men. He had no land at all until he married Martha Ngina in 1970, relatively late in his life. She was a government secretary in a neighboring office building, and their relationship developed out of an acquaintanceship between fellow Kamba. She is ten years younger than he, and when they were courting she looked younger still. He would have difficulty getting her into an adult movie, and the first priest they went to for their marriage thought he was an older man taking advantage of an inexperienced girl.

(See plate 17.) Martha came from a poor family. She had been offered a scholarship to go to university in the United States when she finished secondary school in 1965, but she decided to get a job instead. Her younger sisters would be able to go to school only when she started contributing to the family's finances. At her request, Harris never paid dowry (bride-price) to her family because she wanted to be able to continue to support them after her marriage.

When a Kamba gets married his father is supposed to give him land. Philip Mule announced to Harris that he would buy him a big piece nearby so that he "wouldn't be squeezed at home." He then asked Harris for a loan for the down payment and took a loan from him for every payment that subsequently came due. So in truth Harris bought the 23-acre farm in Mbooni himself. He began to farm it in 1972, managing it on the weekends from Nairobi. He first broke even on it in 1984, but he improved it substantially in that period. Terracing was added, 20 acres of coffee were planted, and he had up to twenty-six grade steers at one time. (See plates 18 and 19.) In 1986 he had three employees on the farm but still had not built the house there for himself that tradition requires.

Mule finally acquired a fully commercial farm only in 1984—200 acres near Kibwezi at the southern tip of Machakos. The area is dry, but in 1985 Mule began to irrigate 11 acres from the Athi River and employed half the services of an Asian farm manager. The rain-fed land produced maize for sale to the National Cereals and Produce Board. Vegetables for export to Europe were grown on the irrigated portion. The farm machinery was rented from the Tractor Hire Service, a form of government assistance that was difficult to get.

Thus all four of the administrators have combined their salaried advantages with the ownership of large commercial farms, clearly qualifying them as members of the matajiri class. Both their civil service incomes and the influence their positions gave them with the banks would have helped them with these purchases. Nyachae and Karanja are among the richest Africans in Kenya, but even Mule, who lives modestly and has little interest in money, eventually acquired a modest large farm. In the following chapters we will look at the effect this class interest has had on the agricultural policy decisions with which the four have been associated.

AFRICANIZING COMMERCE AND INDUSTRY

The third stage of Africanization was directed at Asian commerce. Colin Leys has described the way in which the state promoted this process through the close control of commercial opportunity. Businesses are strictly licensed, local monopolies are often granted, and special access to contracts and credit may be arranged.[36]

The Asian commercial bourgeoisie has and will continue to decline in significance. The first stages in Africanization of trade were directed against the smallest Asian operators (most often in the rural areas). African traders and petty-capitalist farmers filled these vacancies fairly easily. The later stages involved retail and wholesale operations, which demand reasonable amounts of capital and a high level of skill. Most African traders have been unable to meet these requirements, and the opportunities have been taken most often by those who are still in or who have recently left higher salaried positions.

There is considerable potential for bourgeois and petty-bourgeois conflict in the wholesale/retail and the large-retail/small-retail dichotomies. These contradictions were contained within the Asian commercial bourgeoisie, in good part because they were swamped by the importance of other class conflicts, reinforced by race. The transfer of Asian commerce to African hands is still incomplete, and so it is too early to see if these contradictions will become manifest among their African successors. They probably will, because the lines of conflict correspond to those of higher versus lower salaries, and large versus intermediate farmers.

The final stage of Africanization was and will be the attempts of the matajiri to gain ownership and control of the industrial and financial sectors now dominated by the multinationals. Since both commerce and industry are peripheral to the rural development focus of this book, these transfer processes will only be sketched. The state bought a majority share in some industrial enterprises and banks but seems cautious about the speed with which it is moving or the control it is exercising. A few Kenyans, both as individuals and as groups, have made major entrepreneurial investments and have bought industries. Colin Leys originally doubted that they could escape dependency. Others, such as Swainson and Mushi, have been more optimistic.[37] A few classically bourgeois independent businessmen have emerged already, and more are likely, but the size and international character of contemporary capitalist enterprises makes it unlikely that for a considerable time their numbers will be sufficient to free the Kenyan economy as a whole from dependence.

Two of the four subjects of this study, Karanja and Nyachae, developed a stake in commerce and industry. Mule and Muriithi did not and stuck to their farming. Mule's only nonagricultural asset was the house in which he lived in Nairobi. Muriithi lived on his Kabete farm and owned a house down the street, which he rented out.

Charles Karanja actually entered commerce before he went into agriculture. In 1958 at the end of his first year of work he had saved enough money to build a small shop with accompanying rental apartments in Nakuru. In 1967, before he became general manager of the KTDA, he began a transport business, moving charcoal from up-country to Nairobi. He stayed on contract with the KTDA and regularly took a gratuity of 25 percent of salary, in lieu of a pension, to finance his investments. He had six trucks, would give the drivers enough money for their expenses, and would collect a preset figure from them at the end of the trip. The drivers had an incentive to make more for themselves if they could. By 1970 this business was producing more income for him than was his salary at the KTDA. As the competition intensified in the early 1970s, however, he withdrew from transport in order to concentrate his money on his farms, and his time on his duties at the KTDA.

In the early 1970s Karanja bought Ngorongo Tea Factory with several other prominent Kenyan Africans; in the later part of the decade he helped start Combrok, a tea brokerage firm. At the end of the decade he briefly had an interest in Maxim's, which did tea warehousing, but it went bankrupt when it failed to secure KTDA business. After he left the KTDA, Karanja founded a tea-exporting firm, Agrocom, but it failed. Combrok, Maxim's, and Agrocom were all the first African-owned firms in their respective parts of the multinational-dominated tea business. Karanja also expanded his real estate holdings after he left the KTDA. He built two luxury rental houses, turned a large house into the Karangi Hotel in the Parklands area of Nairobi, and built the modern Ndanga Hotel at Ruiru in Kiambu. (See plate 23.)

Simeon Nyachae's business interests are also wide-ranging; only a sampling of them are given here. He began early, establishing a small bakery in Kisii with his father's help in 1954. Raphael Kaplinsky's survey of the records of the Registrar of Companies in the mid-1970s found Nyachae listed as a shareholder in nine companies: A to Z Electroservice; Allied Rubber Industries; Kibleso Saw Mills; Molspi, Ltd.; Nakuru Flour Mills; Nakuru Medical Stores; Nakuru Tyre Sales; Odeon Theatres, Ltd.; and Sansora, Ltd. In 1987 he owned most of the same firms and had expanded the list to at least a dozen. He built the modern Sansora Bakery in Kisii town in 1978 and established the Sansora Wire and Nail Works there in 1982. He also has an interest in a small Nairobi bank.[38] Nyachae and his wife Grace manage the various Sansora companies themselves. His role in most of the other companies is more indirect, frequently being limited to financial participation. In the Flour Mills and Molspi, a molasses and spirits distributorship, he was a part owner with Daniel arap Moi.

Several of the other businesses involved partnerships with Asians. In the mid-1960s when Nyachae was PC for Rift Valley, Jagdish Patel, an Asian who was in the Provincial Accounts office, invited him to join in the purchase of some enterprises. Strong pressures for the Africanization of commerce had already developed, and Asians frequently took African partners so as to escape these demands. Senior government officials such as Nyachae were generally favored for these joint ventures because their names helped to clear the way in getting government approvals and licenses, even if no direct influence was ever exerted. Nyachae became a favorite for many of these partnerships because he kept his commitments once he had made them (even if they became unprofitable) and because he never tried to force a coinvestor out of a firm that had started to make money.

Nyachae never acquired any property or businesses in Central Province, despite his long stay there as provincial commissioner. He believed that to do so would create conflict because of the intense Kikuyu interest in both land and commerce.

INTERESTS: THE INTERACTION OF CLASS AND ETHNICITY

As a consequence of Kenyatta's public policies, Kenyan African society gradually changed from a two-class to a three-class structure in the 1970s. To workers-and-peasants and the petty bourgeoisie were added the matajiri (well-to-do). The distinctive feature of this structure is that all three classes are based in more than one sector of the economy, through overlapping ownerships and stages in their work lives. Kenyatta's decision to maintain both large farms and private business and to give the new African political and administrative elite privileged opportunities to buy into them created the matajiri. The matajiri were unlike most other African upper classes because of their substantial economic stake in agriculture. These interests had a profound effect on the subsequent shape of Kenyan public policy.

Great though its impact is, this class system is still only emerging and lacks the clear features of a clearly developed one for several reasons. First, the boundary line between the matajiri and the petty bourgeoisie is still not absolutely clear, falling at somewhat inconsistent points in the civil service, agriculture, and business sectors. Second, while the matajiri class favors itself over the petty bourgeoisie, there is little direct exploitation, and the two are allied in gaining advantage from the workers and peasants. Third, there is substantial interclass mobility, with worker-peasants moving into petty-bourgeois roles and some of the petty bourgeoisie still gaining access to the matajiri, especially through their children. Fourth, all three classes are tied to one another through ethnic and kinship-based patron-client links.

The existence of the three classes is an objective fact at the economic level of analysis and is fairly clear in terms of social interaction. Political class consciousness has been weak or confused in Kenya, however, because of the importance of the aforementioned patron-client networks. This yielded a complicated political structure in the 1960s and 1970s. The Kikuyu political elite (first a petty-bourgeois one, then graduated to a matajiri one) used its control of the state to provide differential benefits to its poorer ethnic brethren in order to avert the class struggle that would deprive it of its electoral base and threaten a revolutionary transformation of society. This discriminatory pattern of resource allocation strengthened the colonially encouraged propensity of Kenyans to see their politics in ethnic terms.[39] Matajiri and petty-bourgeois politicians therefore could retain worker and peasant allegiance in their constituencies by portraying grievances that arose out of class struggle as the results of "tribalism." The mass of Kenyan workers and peasants had weak political class consciousness and were at the mercy of their leaders/patrons.[40]

The petty bourgeoisie also suffered from ethnic obfuscation, and many of its interests came to be embodied in an anti-Kikuyu ideology. This ideology even penetrated to outlying Kikuyu areas, where it took the form of accusing the Kiambu Kikuyu (near Nairobi) of having monopolized the fruits of independence.[41] The theme was that the Kikuyu (or Kiambu Kikuyu) had taken over most large farms, big businesses, and senior positions in government and industry. The other tribes (or other parts of the Kikuyu) should be given access to the benefits of independence, with the large farms being broken up and small business interests being advanced over those of the bigger ones, the banks, and the multinationals. This populism attracted substantial worker and peasant support, but it is best to think of it as a petty-bourgeois ideology. It advocated the interests of that class in small business and promoted petty-capitalist over large-scale agriculture. (Note that in this era the opposition proposals to limit landholdings stopped at the size of petty-capitalist farms.)[42] It certainly was not a truly socialist program. This petty-bourgeois ideology was largely embodied in the populist program of J. M. Kariuki, who was assassinated in 1975, and explains the attraction of this Kikuyu politician to anti-Kikuyu political forces.

The accusations of "tribalism," which have come to dominate Kenyan politics, reflected both perception and reality in the 1960s and early 1970s. At the level of policy, programs were promoted that were particularly suited to the socioeconomic conditions of the Kikuyu and to the ecological conditions in the areas in which they lived. In this way the differential flow of benefits to Kikuyu workers and peasants, which was necessary to prevent their pursuing class-based politics, was maintained. But within the administrative apparatus the degree of favoritism was more constrained. Our quantitative analysis of civil service promotions in this period does not reveal any ethnic bias, until we reach the very highest, policy-making posts, where presidential favor was needed. The civil service had a set of inherited institutional mechanisms for checking patronage, and these were strong enough to prevail in this period. Thus there were constraints on the extent of ethnic favoritism. However, the public perceived "tribalism" to be rampant. Within the structure of a favorable set of public policies, the advantages that the Kikuyu enjoyed were increased by the head start in education and market involvement they had acquired in the colonial period. The public's attribution of these structural advantages to favoritism may be due to the fact that leaders needed to impress their political clients and consequently portrayed almost all benefits as resulting from their patronage.

In the following chapters we will see how this matajiri-dominated system, challenged by petty-bourgeois discontent and continued peasant demands for land, affected Kenya's government structure, income distribution, and rural development.

CHAPTER FIVE

Nyachae and Administrative Power in the Kenyatta State

THE INSTITUTIONAL LEGACY

Kenya's operative institutional inheritance continued the colonial pattern of central control and a strong Provincial Administration. After a brief experiment with strong, independent local government of the type that the white settlers had enjoyed, the country returned to the tradition of weak local government under Provincial Administration tutelage, which Africans had experienced in the colonial period. The powerful pull of new interests had created substantial pressures for a new institutional framework in Kenya, but as the conflicts deepened, the new political leadership retreated to the security of the old structures. As Aristide Zolberg has remarked of the continent as a whole, the new political leadership was overcome by insecurity, afraid that it would be unable to keep the new country and government intact. As a consequence, the agenda of control supplanted all others.[1] There was change, but more continuity than the new pattern of governing interests alone would have led one to expect.

To consolidate his political base and govern effectively, Jomo Kenyatta had to deal with the institutional instruments of rule that were bequeathed to him. Despite his immense popularity as the symbol of African nationalist resistance to colonialism, Kenyatta emerged from detention unable to control even the Kenyan African National Union (KANU), the political party that he headed. The Kenyan African Union (KAU), which he helped to found, had been banned during the Emergency, and many of its leaders were detained with him. Its successor, KANU, was created in his absence and was not his organization, having been formed by various people with whom he had had only weak ties.

The radical Oginga Odinga led one wing of KANU from his Luo base in Nyanza Province. The Luo moderate, Tom Mboya, controlled Nairobi and the labor movement. The Kikuyu wing of the party was dominated by more conservative figures, such as James Gichuru and Gikonyo Kiano. None of these men had been Kenyatta's allies before.

When Kenyatta assumed the prime ministership at independence in 1963, the state had been structured to frustrate his control as well. The minority ethnic groups in the Kenyan African Democratic Union (KADU), which had entered the government in 1961, had joined with the British to create a federal constitution that was designed to protect their interests by devolving substantial authority on regional legislatures, giving control of land to the counties (districts), and creating a bicameral national legislature.[2] This document was known as the Majimbo constitution, from the Swahili word for regions. This structure did build on the modest amount of decentralization in Kenya's colonial legacy, which had provided for weak African native councils and strong white county councils. But the decision to devolve onto the regions the Provincial Administration and Police was a major break with the traditions of a unitary state and of the overall guidance of central control. The discontinuity was all the more marked given the pivotal role played by the Provincial Administration in suppressing the Mau Mau uprising.

KANU had majorities in less than half of the seven regional assemblies, and in any case the party was too weak organizationally for Kenyatta to have used it as his informal instrument of control. He decided to crush decentralization, to restore the strong unitary state, and to use the Provincial Administration as his instrument of control.

He stretched the constitution, delayed the decentralization of finances, and ordered the Provincial Administration to remain under central direction, all moves of questionable legality. The Africans who had been newly elevated to positions of authority in the Provincial Administration (and who, like Simeon Nyachae, had been socialized into a strongly centralist orientation when they entered the colonial service) complied. Faced with Kenyatta's determination to retain central control of the "fruits of Uhuru (independence)," the KADU members of Parliament (M.P.s) yielded to the appeals of patronage and crossed the floor of the House to create a de facto one-party state in 1964. The constitution was amended, the unitary state was restored, and Kenya became a republic under President Kenyatta in December 1964 after only eighteen months of majimbo (regionalism).[3]

The dissolution of KADU did not end the intense political infighting set off by the Africanization of the economy. But it did change its form. When the more conservative KADU M.P.s became a part of the KANU majority, they significantly altered the balance of power within KANU against the radicals. Odinga, who led the radical wing, was removed as vice-president, and eventually the former KADU Daniel arap Moi assumed the office. Backed into a corner and with their concerns for a much more egalitarian form of development ignored, the radical M.P.s broke from KANU in 1966 and formed the Kenya People's Union (KPU). The electoral wisdom of Kenyatta's conservative strategy was confirmed by the special election he forced on the M.P.s who had crossed the floor against him. In the "Little General Election" of 1966 the number of KPU M.P.s decreased from twenty-nine to nine, and the party's strength was largely reduced to Nyanza Province and the Luos.[4]

The next blow to the KPU came with the 1968 local government elections. The government instructed the Provincial Administration, which was responsible for supervising the contests, to "closely scrutinize" the nomination petitions of the KPU candidates for errors. It complied, and all the KPU candidates were disqualified on supposed "technical grounds"; the KANU contestants were returned unopposed.[5]

After the KPU was marginalized, political infighting within KANU intensified, with increasing concern over who would be heir apparent to the aging Kenyatta. It was imperative to the Kikuyu matajiri political leaders around Kenyatta that they retain control of the state. Only in this way could they both secure the advantages of the wealthy and provide enough resources to Kikuyu workers and peasants to keep them united behind the matajiri M.P.s. Because resources were limited, a fully egalitarian approach to the distribution of benefits on either social-class or regional-ethnic grounds could lead to enough dissatisfaction among the Kikuyu to break apart their transclass alliance.

Conflict centered first on Tom Mboya, who had led the fight against his radical fellow Luo, Oginga Odinga. Mboya was an extremely skilled political organizer and seemed to have a good chance of mobilizing the parliamentary and KANU branch votes necessary to winning the presidency if Kenyatta were to die. As he was a member of Kenya's second largest ethnic group, an Mboya presidency would have seriously threatened the Kikuyus' favored hold on the state's resources. He was assassinated by a small-time Kikuyu politician in 1969. The trial failed to pursue the assassin's motives or to question whether he was acting for anyone else.[6]

The violent protests of the Luo against the combined elimination from contention of Mboya and Odinga encouraged Kenyatta to ban the KPU, leaving Kenya a de facto one-party state again at the end of 1969. To his credit, however, the president recognized that if he gave the discontented no place to vent their anger, they would eventually turn on him. He therefore introduced relatively open KANU primaries and brought electoral competition within the confines of the party. The result was that unpopular M.P.s could be removed by their constituents, but since the president controlled the party, no effective challenge could be made to him or to the government itself. He had brilliantly created a safety valve without diminishing the security of his regime.

A further centralization of control was achieved with the passage of the Local Government Transfer of Functions Bill in October 1969. Citing financial mismanagement and the need for greater efficiency, the government removed primary education, health, and secondary-road maintenance from the county (district) councils and put them under national control. These functions had been the core of the county councils' responsibilities.[7] The councilors were generally petty-bourgeois and were much more difficult for Kenyatta to control than were the national M.P.s. The Transfer of Functions Bill permitted the electorate to vote councilors in and out of office but left the councils with no meaningful influence on the direction or pace of development. The centralization that characterized the Kenyatta regime was complete.

The next threat came from a more dangerous direction. J. M. Kariuki, a wealthy Kikuyu M.P., began challenging the government and campaigning for the succession on a populist platform that criticized Kenyatta's inner circle of Kiambu advisers and called for a redistribution of benefits to up-country Kikuyu and non-Kikuyu alike. Kariuki's criticism of Kikuyu matajiri self-aggrandizement struck a responsive chord with both the petty bourgeoisie and the workers-peasants and gave him a multiethnic following. He epitomized Kenyatta's nightmare; he would divide the Kikuyu on class lines and thus dramatically weaken their political strength. Kariuki was assassinated in 1975 and the subsequent parliamentary inquiry implicated several very senior government officials in his disappearance and murder.[8]

The death of Kariuki created great bitterness, but it removed the last serious challenge to the political dominance of the Kiambu Kikuyu matajiri. Daniel arap Moi was left in the vice-presidency. There was a brief Kiambu challenge to his presumed right to succeed Kenyatta, but most of the Kikuyu leadership saw him as having too weak an ethnic political base to threaten their needs.[9] There have continued to be radical challenges to the regime, most recently by the Mwakenya group and those associated with the Kikuyu author Ngugi wa Thiongo, but so far the state has had little difficulty containing them.

NYACHAE AND THE PROVINCIAL ADMINISTRATION

The Provincial Administration, and not KANU, became the iron frame upon which Kenyatta built his political control of the country. He relied on it to provide him with political intelligence, to regulate political competition in his interests, and to see to it that government largess was distributed in a way that would add to his regime's prestige and strength. At each level of government—province, district, and division—the Provincial Administration supervised and coordinated the field representatives of all the central ministries. Kenyatta's provincial commissioners (PCs) were his effective proconsuls, supervising and controlling regional developments in much the same way as their colonial predecessors had done. (See plate 20.) In the field they were the agent of the executive and the personal representatives of the president, symbolizing government authority.[10] Kenyatta selected his PCs carefully and frequently took their advice over that of his cabinet ministers, particularly on matters of local politics and development. Wherever there were politically explosive conflicts or benefits to be authoritatively distributed, a PC was likely to be involved. Land is a rural-development example.

Administration of Land

In addition to benefiting personally from the large transfers of land from European to African hands, Simeon Nyachae had an administrative role in the process. Having been recalled from England in March 1964 and made district commissioner (DC) of Nyandarua, Nyachae was thrown into the midst of the land reform frenzy. The Provincial Administration had no direct responsibility for administering the settlement schemes. Nonetheless, it does oversee and coordinate all central government fieldwork, and its law-and-order duties had always included the adjudication of disputes, including those over land. The role of Chief Musa Nyandusi, Nyachae's father, in settling land conflicts on the Kisii border was described in chapter 2. As the hierarchical controllers of the chiefs, the Provincial Administrators have always been involved in the politically charged process of land transfer. By providing compulsory arbitration it is usually able to avoid lengthy court cases. The results sometimes are arbitrary or twisted by political influence. Indeed, the Provincial Administration provides the interface between politics and bureaucracy. But at least decisions are made quickly in an informal process that is widely understood and accessible. Many argue that productive resources therefore are not tied up in extended litigation, and development is accelerated.

As district commissioner (DC) in a white farming district that was immediately adjacent to a Kikuyu one, Nyachae found himself receiving landless people from all parts of Central Province as well as being responsible for the rehabilitation of Mau Mau freedom fighters just out of the forest. Through mass meetings he had to persuade these claimants that their needs would be met and that they should continue to live with the whites many of them hated while the process of resettlement took place. They started in the south of the district and apportioned land north across the district. The DC chaired the District Settlement Selection Committee and would frequently be engaged in allocations until nine or ten at night. Nyachae was already showing the ability to endure long hours that would mark his career. The former Mau Mau with whom Nyachae had to deal were a difficult group, determined to get the land for which they had fought and ill inclined to accept authority. He developed the habit of listening patiently before he made a decision, but once he had given his opinion he would not be swayed from it.

Land remained at the core of his work when he became provincial commissioner in Rift Valley in 1965. The province contained the bulk of the former "White Highlands" and therefore had most of the settlement schemes. Not all of the new lands opened up, however, were European. The Maasai, a pastoralist people, owned a large tract of land in Narok District that was suitable for wheat production. In 1966 the Ministry of Agriculture created the Maasai Agricultural Development Organization (MADO) to farm these lands and pay the profits to the Maasai. A series of problems requiring intervention by the Provincial Administration resulted.

First, the land belonged to whole Maasai communities, not to individuals, and it had been used on a pastoral basis. Technically, the land was held in trust by the district's council with the vague injunction that it was "for the benefit of the local residents." In conjunction with the council the Provincial Administration had to determine who had traditional occupancy rights to the land and make them the beneficiaries of the scheme.

Second, MADO and the Tractor Hire Service, which it used, did not prove very efficient. The operating costs were high, and there were delays in payments. Private contractors were offering much more competitive terms to the Maasai for the leases. The Maasai had not been consulted in the initiation of the project, and they became suspicious that it was a plot whereby the government would take over their land for the Kikuyu. MADO, which had been formed to prevent exploitation of the Maasai, was being accused of it and was fostering the conflict it was designed to avoid. Nyachae had to preside over its termination in 1968, even though many of the private contractors continued to use the subsidized services of the Tractor Hire Service.

Third, problems then developed between the predominately Kikuyu contractors and the Maasai over the terms of the leases. "Nyachae got involved to protect the Maasai. He would call the parties in one by one and go through the detailed accounts and by logic would show how they were being unfair." His ability to provide this detailed arbitration must have been helped by the knowledge he had gained from doing large-

scale farming himself. His approach to conflict resolution is characterized by meticulous attention to detail and tireless effort.

In due course the new arrangements stabilized. Afterward Nyachae
regarded as one of his great accomplishments in these years that "we
can now get cereals out of Maasailand, when you know that none was
there before." Not all observers are as sure as he is that the Maasai benefited fully from the new arrangement, but the effort certainly did lead
to expanded food-grain production.[11]

A substantial portion of the Rift Valley land transfers have taken
place in private sales between departing whites and Africans grouped
into companies, intending to subdivide the farm once it is acquired.
There was always conflict when more than one land-buying company
wanted the same farm, and it could escalate quickly if different ethnic
groups were involved. An example is an incident at Kipkelion near
Lumbwa in Kericho District. A European settler named Archer John
had made arrangements to sell his farm to the local Kalenjin. At the
same time, a company of Kikuyu and Gisii told its membership, from
which it had collected a large sum, that it had arranged to buy the farm.
Its members then occupied the land; the local Kalenjin were enraged
and violence was imminent. Nyachae was called by a Kalenjin colleague,
intervened personally with a show of police force, and resettled the Kikuyu and Gisii on another farm. "Fraud and trespass were involved. So
I had to stick to the law. If you allow it to happen to a white, it can
happen to a black." But he also put in long hours of talking the issue
through until he got a resolution.

In these and large numbers of other controversies and crises Nyachae
felt that it was important that he be directly involved. His success with
personal intervention in these years probably contributed to weaknesses
that he had with delegation when he later moved to the national level.
He was quick to break administrative bottlenecks, meeting with people
by day and writing memos to department heads in Nairobi in the evening. He would arrive at a meeting with a clear purpose and well
briefed, having consulted his local officers and read the relevant files
beforehand. He became a firm believer in the importance of persuasion
and tried not to force a project on people who were not yet convinced
of its benefit. He was good at communicating with and persuading gath-
erings of traditional elders. His style is frank and often appears over-
bearing and wordy in other settings. But it was expected in this one,
being much like that of the chiefs to whom the local leaders were accustomed. Members of the Provincial Administration are prone to pom-
posity and empty talk because of the many ceremonial functions that
they perform, but Nyachae was less guilty of these "sins" than most PCs.

To manage all these crises personally was no small task, as the Rift

Valley Province is immense and stretches between Kenya's northern and southern borders. Nyachae was constantly in the air in small police planes. Many of these trips were made in the company of Daniel arap Moi, vice-president and minister of home affairs, who had been chair of the Rift Valley Regional Assembly under the Majimbo constitution. Nyachae had several close calls with malfunctioning planes and short airstrips. Once his plane caught in an antelope hole on landing and flipped right over. Nyachae has a bullish courage; he kept on traveling.

In 1970 Nyachae was moved from the Rift Valley in a general reshuffle and made provincial commissioner (PC) to the Kikuyu Central Province. A great part of the reason for sending him there must have been the need for a neutral party to mediate in intra-Kikuyu political disputes. But some believe that Kenyatta wanted him out of the Rift Valley because he was too close to the Kalenjin Moi and was not sufficiently favorable to the Kikuyu who were competing with that group for access to land. Whatever the reason, the transfer restored Nyachae to a position where Kenyatta could have unreserved confidence in his judgment.

Later, when Nyachae was PC of Central Province, Kenyatta asked him to intervene personally in a Kiambu land dispute. The leaders of a land-buying company had not given genuine receipts to all of those who had contributed to a purchase and denied shares in the new farm to many members. Nyachae convened a meeting in which he personally went through people's receipts and other evidence of payment to determine who was to receive a portion of the land and straightened out the mess.

Political Representation and Control

As provincial commissioner of Central Province Nyachae became even more deeply involved in the control and mediation of politically sensitive disputes than he had been in the Rift Valley. On such matters he was generally cautious and tactful, briefing the president and getting his instructions before acting. A politician who was targeted as difficult by the Provincial Administration would be made to know that he was swimming against the current. Opponents of the regime were not given permits to hold meetings when they wished. A cabinet minister who was obstructing development in his constituency and who was vocally critical of Nyachae lost the next election. Aspiring politicians would go to the PC to ask his advice on whether they should stand for Parliament.

As the personal representative of the president, Nyachae could be quick to anger and quite decisive. At a public rally in Mukurweni an M.P. got up and said that this was the only Central Province division that did not have at least an assistant minister in the government. "Nyachae jumped on him, grabbed him by the collar and told him to sit down. For he was criticizing the government's decision. [Nyachae shouted,] 'This is a prerogative of the president. No one here appoints ministers. There are other forums for this.' The people even clapped."

The involvement of the Provincial Administration in self-help activities was also politically sensitive. When Kenyatta emerged from detention, he had cautioned Kenyans not to expect the government to take care of them. He urged them to launch development activities themselves instead and used the Swahili word *harambee* (meaning "let's pull together") to describe the self-help initiatives he wanted. His government quickly came to take the position that it would help first those who helped themselves, so that harambee (self-help) activities evolved into a prerequisite to government funding for a project.[12] As the Kikuyu were among the groups most actively involved in self-help, this policy helped to legitimate many of the disproportionate benefits that they received. Almost the sole route to electoral success for a prospective politician was to initiate, contribute to, raise money for, and gain a promise of government support for schools, health clinics, and other projects.

A signal that government approved of a particular harambee development project thus became highly charged politically. Sponsors would invite PCs to be the guest of honor at a fund-raising meeting as a way of indicating that the government was likely to support it in the long run. A guest of honor would have to make a contribution himself and raise funds from his friends and associates. But if he were a PC, such a sign would increase the contributions of others, since later government support for the project was then likely in the long run.

Since Nyachae was well-to-do himself and since he was eager to encourage developmental activity in the province, he accepted many guest-of-honor invitations. In doing so he would follow the recommendations of his district commissioners, making sure that the project was needed and viable and that no internal friction was involved among the officeholders. Typically, a lot of maneuvering would go on among a project's organizers as to its siting. Nyachae was known to be particularly good at resolving these disputes. He could develop a consensus in a short meeting when his DC had spent days on the matter without fruition. His good sense, humor, persuasiveness, and ability to give a ruling that felt definitive to participants produced results.

Provincial commissioners were the personal representatives of the president and the official agent of the executive at the local level. When the president visited an area, the PC, not the local cabinet member, would be his host. When the president was in the province the PC would be expected to be there to attend him, even if he were just in transit. This could be an onerous task. When Kenyatta was to pass through Central Province on his way to a vacation on the coast, Nyachae would have to leave his headquarters at 3:00 A.M. in order to be at the roadside when the presidential convoy went through.

Personally representing Kenyatta was sometimes an unpleasant task. The funeral of J. M. Kariuki was one such occasion. Feelings against the government and even Kenyatta were running extremely high after Kariuki's assassination. Only Mwai Kibaki among the cabinet members had the courage to attend the funeral, and several officials apparently declined the president's request to represent him. Nyachae accepted as a matter of duty. The press reported:

> PC Nyachae tried to read a message from President Kenyatta to the funeral and was booed and shouted down. Sensing the charged atmosphere of the gathering, Nyachae decided instead to pay a personal tribute to the fallen Kariuki. He chose . . . to speak of the solidarity of the people of Central Province. He spoke as one with the people at the burial scene, not as an administrator. "We in the Central Province and his constituents would have given any amount of money rather than lose Mr. Kariuki," the PC said. "He was not a politician in Nyandarua alone but the whole of Kenya." [13]

One of Nyachae's colleagues felt that his address at the funeral was "an act of courage," reporting, "he remained cool and calculating despite the shouts and threats, and he made them hear the Government of Kenya message. On that one occasion everything he had was tested. He turned it from booing to some of them clapping." Another colleague felt that the courage involved in the incident was more than facing down the crowd. Nyachae had associated himself with Kariuki when it was reasonably clear that many in the government had wanted him out of the way.

The authority exercised by provincial commissioners was highly personalistic under Kenyatta, only lightly constrained by formal procedure and the law. Their relationship with the president was personal as well. We saw in the preceding chapter that Kenyatta himself helped Nyachae secure his Sansora farm at Mau Narok. On another occasion the president assisted him in securing a commercial loan. Even family matters were laid before the president. In 1964 Nyachae had married a Kikuyu woman who was the sister of cabinet minister Gikonyo Kiano's wife. He eventually divorced her in 1971, at which time he married Grace Wamuyu, a Kikuyu government secretary. There is some evidence that the president was kept informed of certain aspects of this unfolding family drama. From these incidents we see that Kenyatta's relationships with his senior officials were diffuse and personal, not the kind of careful segmentation of the official and the personal that one might expect in the European and American administrative traditions. In this regard

Kenyatta was following the leadership conventions of African elders and chiefs.

THE BALANCE OF ADMINISTRATIVE AND POLITICAL POWER

Kenyatta's distrust of his own party, and Kenya's heritage of strong administrative leadership, conspired to produce a system of policy-making in which civil servants have a highly visible and powerful role. As Cherry Gertzel remarked,

> the decision to use the Provincial Administration as the agent of the executive meant that there were two groups of men in the country each of which believed [it] could legitimately claim to lead the people. On the one hand, [of course, were the Members of Parliament. On the other,] the Administrative Officers saw themselves, on behalf of the President, as leaders of the people, a role the President had explicitly assigned them. And they believed themselves much more able to assume that responsibility than the politicians.[14]

Kenyatta used a revealing metaphor to defend this conception of administrative power. He argued that

> the role of the civil servant is that of the professional. He is employed by the Government to get things done. There are not many of us, I hope, who would presume to tell a doctor how and where to operate on a sick person. We should apply the same restraint in our dealings with other professionals.[15]

This metaphor implies a tremendous delegation of authority to administrators. And this is precisely what occurred during Kenyatta's presidency.[16]

Just how, then, were decisions made in this era? How much discretion did civil servants enjoy and which ones exercised it? What roles remained for cabinet ministers? Appendix B provides a careful quantitative analysis of data that can help answer these questions. Although the analysis itself is complex, the answers it provides are simple enough.

Following the Commonwealth tradition, a Kenyan ministry is headed by a member of Parliament, selected by the president to thereby become a minister and member of the cabinet. (See fig. 5.1.) Formally, a minister is responsible for all policies and programs in his ministry. The cabinet meets regularly and makes decisions, but not all ministers play a significant policy role within it. Some of the ministers are both close to the president and deeply interested in matters of high policy. They have considerable influence. Many, however, see their ministries simply as sinecures from which they can draw jobs and other resources for them-

Fig. 5.1   The structure of a typical ministry headquarters

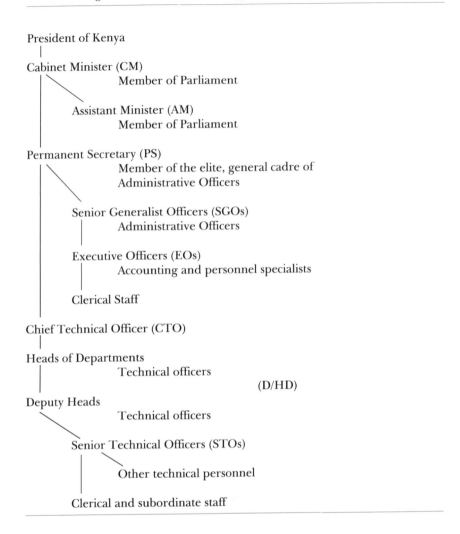

selves and their constituencies, leaving the determination of government policy to the president, his closest advisers, and civil servants. This breach of typical Commonwealth practice derives partly from the fact that many cabinet ministers (CMs) are included in the government because the president wishes to have their support, but not because he has any confidence in their decisions. More important, however, many of these ministers find little reward in policy-making because Kenyan politics is based more on patron-client networks, which distribute discrete benefits, than it is on the interests of associational groupings, which can be served by collective policies. Thus the system works in such a way that most ministers exercise more influence on matters of patronage and the regional distribution of benefits than they do on general matters of policy in their ministries. Even there their influence, although noticeable, is modest.

Nominally the next office in the hierarchy is that of assistant minister (AM). This role has no inherent policy significance. In Great Britain the office's title was that of parliamentary secretary, and the occupant was expected to represent the ministry in the legislature when the minister was unable to do so. In Kenya the role is used much more as a political plum, with the holder receiving a better salary, more prestige, some staff support, and access to a small amount of patronage. In Kenya over half the M.P.s are either ministers or assistant ministers. They are defined as members of the government and are required to vote with it on any matters of confidence, thereby assuring the government of an automatic majority in the legislature.

A ministry's permanent secretary (PS) reports directly to his minister and will be the ministry's de facto head if the CM does not have the interest or ability to exercise policy control. Permanent secretaries (PSs) are members of the elite generalist cadre of Administrative Officers, who also staff the Provincial Administration. Most PSs have served as district commissioners (DCs) or district officers (DOs) earlier in their careers. The post of provincial commissioner (PC) ranks as the equivalent of a PS, however, and very few PCs ever become PSs. Nyachae was among the very few to have held both positions.

The appointment of PSs attracts considerable public attention in Kenya, and they are presumed to exercise considerable influence. All civil servants in a ministry are supposed to communicate with their cabinet minister only through their PS and are subject to his authority. The analysis presented in Appendix B suggests that the real influence that goes with this authority is modest. First of all, like other civil servants, PSs are able to exercise influence only if they have the support of the president. In the Kenyatta years that generally meant that they were Kikuyus. They and other powerful administrators were more extensions of the president's power than influential in their own right. Thus what appears to be administrative power in Kenya is much more the dominance of the presidency over the cabinet and legislature.

Second, PSs appear able to influence the broad policies that their ministries adopt but to have very little effect on the way in which they are administered. They can have an impact on the setting of the formulae that are used to distribute benefits, if they have the president's support and if they have sympathetic technical officers working with them. But the evidence suggests that they have little influence beyond these broad policies, and even what they have is achieved in interaction with those above and below them in the hierarchy. Their policy role is one of transmitting presidential support to like-minded technical officers. They may be able to get little perks for their home areas, but their subordinates appear to deliver them by diverting projects from close neighbors, not by altering the broader ethnic or regional distribution of benefits. Permanent secretaries rotate too frequently between ministries and have too little command of the technical intricacies of their organizations to be able to have a deep impact. The exceptions to this general rule are PSs such as Harris Mule, who have come to their positions by rising through the technical ranks in their ministries—not those who are Administrative Officers and come from the Provincial Administration.

Next in line is the chief technical officer (CTO) of the ministry (whose specific title usually reflects the organization's professional task, e.g., chief engineer or chief medical officer). Under him are the department heads (DHs) and their deputies (DDHs), in most ministries technical officers straight down the line. The technical staff run a ministry's programs and projects, while the generalist Administrative Officers are the personnel and financial administrators and assist in policy formation. To the extent that we can speak of administrators as having real power in the ministries, it lies among the technical officers. Once again, this is a derivative form of influence; it depends on the support of the president. Again, during the Kenyatta years this generally meant being Kikuyu. In cases where broad policies are being set, this presidential backing appears most effective when it is mediated by a PS of the same ethnic group. Once we get to implementation, the relation of the technocrats (CTO, DHs, and DDHs) to the president does not seem to need an Administrative Officer as an intermediary.

In saying that the influence of the technical leadership is dependent on the president, we are speaking, of course, of positive influence. Such officers need presidential backing to accomplish something they favor. But if they are uninterested or opposed to some goal of the president's, that objective will be less well achieved than otherwise. Though dependent in their positive influence on policy and implementation, technocrats do have some independent negative influence.

The importance of the influence that the technical leadership has on public policy should not be overstated. It shares the same matajiri (well-to-do) class status of those above it and therefore can be expected to pursue economic policies that appeal to the common interests of both groups. In terms of class analysis, a role in decisions for technicians is more likely to make a difference in the style and effectiveness of policy than in its substance. The tensions between these hierarchical levels are most likely to be visible on matters relating to the regional distribution of benefits. Nonetheless, these are highly charged issues in Kenya.

This understanding of the technical leadership's having more influence than their Administrative Officer superiors is a new insight into the workings of Commonwealth systems. Once stated, however, it becomes clear why three of our four successful administrators have been technocrats.

THE WEBERIAN THEORY OF ADMINISTRATIVE POWER APPLIED TO KENYA

If we analyze in theoretical terms the balance of political and administrative power, we will understand better just why it arose and will be able to grasp what is happening in comparable situations. Max Weber's work on the struggle between political leaders and their administrative staff for control of the resources of the state is the obvious place to turn for such theory. (Although this issue was of central concern to Weber, his analytic insights about it are not as widely understood as are many other parts of his work. One has to probe his unfinished writings systematically in order to tease out his full model.)*

Max Weber observed that although politicians and administrators need one another, there is a continuous tension underlying their relationship, as each group seeks to advance the primacy of its own policy agenda and to use the other to achieve it. Sometimes this conflict is open; more often it is latent. The political/administrative relationship thus parallels that of capital and labor in private industry, but instead of the struggle's being narrowly concerned with the distribution of income (profits), in government it involves the very nature of the outputs of the state organization. The balance of control between the central state's political leadership and its administrative apparatus has shifted both across and within historical epochs.

Paralleling Marx's concern with the "ownership of the means of production," Weber suggests that the outcome of this internal struggle for control of the state is largely determined by "control of the indispensable means of administration." Weber's model of power relationships thus is resource based, but unlike Marx, the resources he considers go

---

*The following summary statement of Weber's analytic model is freely adapted from my exegesis of his work. For documentation of its derivation from Weber, see David K. Leonard, "The Weberian Theory of Administration: Differentiation and Control," Proceedings of the University of East Africa Social Science Council Conference (Nairobi: University of Nairobi, 1969).

Fig. 5.2 The Weberian model of the struggle for administrative control

---

The balance of control between the political leadership of the central state and its administrative staff is determined by the following:

A. the degree to which positions on each side are occupied by members of a group which maintains a unified bargaining position in dealing with the other side; and

B. the extent to which each side controls the various indispensable means of administration. The latter is made up of four major elements and nine subcomponents:

1. legitimations:	(a) political support
	(b) norms governing the scope of authority
2. expertise:	(a) qualified personnel
	(i) competence
	(ii) status
	(b) information
3. material resources:	(a) mode of remuneration
	(b) surplus of resources
	(c) discretion in rewards
4. physical force.	

---

well beyond the material. His conception encompasses the ways in which political support is accumulated, the values governing its use, and the professional skills of administrators as well as the more traditional fiscal and military resources.

In addition to the simple distribution of resources, Weber calls our attention to the internal dynamics of the groups of politicians and administrators that may affect the give and take between them. He is particularly concerned with the extent to which each of the two parties to this struggle is able to remain internally united in its bargaining with the other.

The Weberian model is summarized in figure 5.2. We can best understand the details of its working by applying it to the Kenyan case. In the process we will simultaneously enhance our understanding of the dynamics and limitations of administrative power there.

In Kenya the central political leadership of this schema would be the conventional president and his cabinet ministers. On class issues both the political leadership and the senior administrators are united internally and with each other in the matajiri. Conflict here is not between leadership and administrators but of both groups with nonestablishment politicians.

Issues that have implications for the regional division of resources, however, are much more divisive of political and administrative leadership. Both cabinet (political leadership) and administrative positions are held by members of all the major ethnic groups, so that potentially both sides are internally divided and subject to crosscutting cleavages. Nonetheless, until the death of Kenyatta the political leadership enjoyed much greater effective unity than did the bureaucracy. Kenyatta had such political skill and enjoyed such initial popularity as the "father of independence" that he dominated the political scene. The cabinet ministers who were thought to be close to him became known as his "inner cabinet," and they were all Kikuyu, usually from Kiambu. This informal "inner cabinet" generally operated in a cohesive manner and would have been united on the regional and ethnic distribution of benefits. In contrast, the administrative staff of every ministry is fragmented on these issues. The various elite technical cadres do enjoy a degree of professional unity, derived from their similar educational backgrounds and the understanding that they are to be posted to positions only within their realm of technical competence. The elite, generalist cadre of Administrative Officers (which included the PSs) quickly lost any meaningful corporate identity, however, as its ranks were rapidly filled with personnel from a wide variety of backgrounds. The range of their postings became very diverse, and their duties included direct involvement with politics.

The next step is to analyze the relative control of political leadership and administrators over the "means of administration" in the Kenyatta years. A first resource needed for governance is legitimacy, and the "inner cabinet" enjoyed a strong advantage because of the personal popularity of Kenyatta. Until the assassination of Mboya in 1969 people would not criticize Kenyatta even in private conversation. After that his personal ability to command support declined, dramatically so after the assassination of J. M. Kariuki in 1975. Even before then Kenyatta had needed the support of his non-Kikuyu cabinet ministers to some degree; he never had a monopoly of support.

Civil servants bring popular political support to the government in Kenya. Kenyans believe in administrative power and consequently see an ethnically "representative bureaucracy" as important. The ethnic distribution of permanent-secretaryships is followed as closely as is that of cabinet ministers in the press. This gives the PSs some small control of the means of administration, which can be used to protect themselves in exercises of positional influence. Unfortunately for the PSs, however, they control none of the other resources of administrative power and therefore have little effect by themselves. Technical officers, such as the chief economist or the director of veterinary services, have other power advantages, but they lack visibility and hence have little in the way of public support.

Another aspect of legitimacy is the norms governing the scope of authority. In this regard the presidency has a large advantage in Kenya, as it does in most of Africa. The colonial period created the expectation that executive authority is unlimited, and the years since independence have reinforced this norm. No one is likely to challenge any particular exercise of presidential discretion as beyond his authority, so one of the classic mechanisms of bureaucratic defense is missing. The extremely broad scope of presidential authority in Africa makes it much more personal, much less institutionally defined, and much more centralized than it is in most other systems of government.[17]

The second major means needed for administration is expertise. A scarcity in the supply of competent personnel is always to the advantage of the civil service. The drive to remove colonial officers and localize the civil service after independence created a tremendous demand for high-level African personnel, which gave a bargaining resource to those who were qualified.

But qualifications are not simply a means of acquiring or signaling competence. They also are a source of status. Thus the type of qualifications involved is of significance here. Some qualifications, particularly degrees and professional certificates, are *manifest*: they are self-evident, and whether or not they exist is beyond the direct control of the political leadership. Other qualifications—such as skill, potential, and leadership ability—are not wholly self-evident but are *acknowledged* by the employer. Since such qualifications are at least partly dependent upon the leadership's recognition of them, they are less likely to be used by staff as bargaining resources than are manifest ones. In the first instance, the administrator possesses his own status and bestows it on the tasks the leadership wants performed. In the second case, the leader bestows the status on the staff member, giving him or her the benefit of additional social standing. Of course most administrative senior positions involve a mixture of manifest and acknowledged qualifications, and leaders occasionally refuse to admit the relevance of even the most widely accepted formal qualifications. Nonetheless, the distinction is at the heart of the influence of professional groups.

Generalist administrators usually are no less skilled or expert in their work than technical ones, but the lack of visibility for their qualifications weakens their position. This is one reason why the chief technical officers and others with professional degrees were more influential than the talented personnel in the general cadre of Administrative Officers. Only when generalists have a protected corporate identity based on a highly competitive, formalized entry process, a closed career system, and a presumption of some special competence are they likely to rival the manifest qualifications of the technical groups. These conditions do prevail in Britain and India and are the basis for the perception of power that is accorded to this cadre throughout the Commonwealth. But they do not exist in Africa today, and therefore the independent influence of permanent secretaries and other Administrative Officers has been greatly weakened. (Another factor giving professional personnel greater influence was the fact that the available supply was much less than that of generalists in the years immediately after independence, slowing the localization of technical posts and further strengthening those in them.)

Another aspect of expertise is information. Decisions are formed out of the interaction of values and information, and the person who controls the needed information has the opportunity to structure the decision. The greater the extent to which experts encode their information and analysis in a special language or restrict access to their knowledge in other ways, the greater their potential for control of the resource of information. The highly technical professions have a special advantage in this regard. It is far from absolute, however; the information must be *monopolized* to be a critical instrument of influence. On regional allocation issues no such monopoly exists in Kenya. Every major ethnic group has experts in each ministry who can provide alternative channels of information and analysis. Thus a potential advantage for the bureaucracy is neutralized, as it is in most political systems. An information monopoly is likely to exist only in those policy domains where a profession is truly united against other groups in society.

The third major means of administration is material. Weber was mainly concerned with the method by which administrators are paid for their services. He was convinced that the payment of salaries from a national treasury gives a decisive advantage to the political leadership at the center. Subsequent research by S. N. Eisenstadt suggests that Weber may have overestimated the impact of this element, for even salaried officials are able to gain tenure in office and secure rights to their pay.[18] A *surplus* of centrally controlled material resources is probably more important, so that administrators and others can be rewarded for compliance with the wishes of the leadership. President Kenyatta was in a particularly good position in this regard. The economy was buoyant, healthy pay raises were possible, and Africanization made it possible to reward richly the faithful with promotions and the purchase of farms and businesses on government-subsidized terms. In a time in which African matajiri incomes were stagnant, bureaucratic compliance might not have been as easily achieved.

Another aspect of the material resources factor is *discretion* in the bestowal of rewards. In a very strictly controlled civil service system, advancement is largely determined by seniority, and no amount of salary increases or expansion in promotion opportunities can be used to reward the compliant at the expense of the uncooperative. Seniority systems probably never were as strong in Kenya as they are in some countries, but the postindependence drive for localization of the administration gave tremendous discretion to those with hierarchical authority. Upward mobility was so rapid in the early Kenyatta years that anyone who advanced at only the normal rate was being severely penalized. This advantage for the leadership was critical. It was balanced for most of the senior civil service by the requirement to prove "merit" to the Public Service Commission, which was particularly alert to signs of ethnic favoritism. But for the top decision-making positions considerable presidential discretion was permitted.

The final means of administration is the physical force necessary to retain control of the state and enforce its laws. At independence in 1963, the army was heavily Kamba and, to a lesser extent, Kalenjin. This gave politicians from these groups an added advantage in bargaining for governmental positions. Paul Ngei, the political boss of the Kamba, was advanced in the posts he held, despite a series of scandals. But the Kamba and Kalenjin were never able to translate their strength in the army into bureaucratic power for several reasons. First, they were behind the other major ethnic groups in educational advancement and so held fewer positions in the higher civil service. Thus they were not directly involved in as many decision areas as they might have been otherwise. Second, the British government committed its troops to put down the Kenya army mutiny of 1964, was thought to have promised to protect Kenyatta from any other coups d'etat, and had detachments constantly in Kenya "on training exercises."* Third, the president had a good intelligence system for detecting possible coups—witness the prosecutions, retirements, and resignations in the summer of 1971. Finally, recruitment of Kikuyu into the army was pressed hard during Kenyatta's presidency, so that they were believed to be at least at parity with the Kamba by the early 1970s. The Kikuyu units also were kept close to the capital, and the Kamba units were posted far afield. These attacks on Kamba control of the army would have been dangerous without the apparent support of the British, but in the long run they turned the army from a liability into an asset for Kikuyu political leaders. In the interim period of the 1960s the British military guarantee and the shortage of

---

*I can produce no hard evidence of such a commitment by the U.K., but many informed Kenyans believed it existed and such a belief would have been sufficient by itself to prevent a coup attempt.

Kamba and Kalenjin senior civil administrators to act as a link with the army neutralized the Kenyan military in the struggle for control of the state's resources.

CONCLUSIONS

To summarize: President Kenyatta and his Kikuyu "inner cabinet" enjoyed a strong net balance of advantages over the bureaucracy in Kenya's first decade and a half of independence. The president's "inner cabinet" was effective as a closely unified group facing a fragmented set of ministerial and administrative opponents. It also had a relatively firm control of the "means of administration." With respect to legitimacy, Kenyatta had a clear, though diminishing lead in the aggregation of political support. He also benefited from colonial norms that gave almost unlimited discretion to the chief executive and made for centralized "personal rule." With regard to expertise, qualified personnel were in short supply. Technical administrators whose qualifications are manifest rather than acknowledged held a particular advantage here. But they were not able to exercise a monopoly over the flow of technical information, for ethnic competition within the administrative ranks provided for upward flows to the major ethnic partisans at the ministerial level. With respect to the material means of administration, the presidency had a decisive advantage. A great surplus of resources were available to reward compliant African administrators, and hierarchical superiors effectively enjoyed considerable latitude in the granting of promotions. Finally, the resource of physical force was neutralized, for the Kamba-dominated army was checked by the British and had weak links within the civilian bureaucracy.

With the balance of power so clearly favoring the president, our finding that administrators had little independent positional influence is surprising but readily understood. The rewards for compliance and the dangers and difficulties of open opposition were too great for administrators to pursue their own policy objectives. The evidence in Appendix B makes it clear that the higher civil service was a dependent elite, able to advance its allocational interests only when it had political support. This is not to say, however, that the ethnic distribution of senior positions was unimportant. Non-Kikuyu administrators were unable to help their own regions, but Kikuyu expert officials were able to gain substantial extra resources for their areas. Although bureaucrats were a dependent elite, they were major actors in the decision-making arena. To put it somewhat differently, Kikuyu technical authorities, operating at the detailed level of decision making, were able to advance significantly the effective pro-Kikuyu policy objectives of the government, with which they agreed. Non-Kikuyu experts could not change these policies, but they could lessen their impact by insisting that they were above "tribalism" and were following objective, professional dictates. In this drama, the general cadre of Administrative Officers had little independent influence, despite its visibility; its members could not clothe their personal preferences in any expertise. Only the PS had some influence, which was largely restricted to favoring one general set of decision rules over another.

The Kenyatta years produced an "administrative state." Bureaucrats rather than politicians made most of the day-to-day decisions, and their impact on allocational issues was greater than that of the average cabinet minister. But their power was derivative and interactive: derivative, because it flowed from a president who had greater confidence in civil servants than he had in most politicians and who used the former to control the latter; interactive, because it did not exist without the president's support but it could extend his effectiveness. A skilled technocrat who shared the president's aims would accomplish a great deal more for him. One who disagreed might be able to frustrate the implicit wishes of the president if he were to dress his actions in professionalism, even if independent action was difficult without Kenyatta's support.

Kenyatta's "administrative state" represented a continuity with colonial practice, particularly as it had been experienced by Africans. The major emphasis was on control, expressed in an authoritarian manner and with few real legal constraints. Local government was quickly subordinated to central authority. Authority was highly centralized in the president and was diffuse and personal. All of these attributes were foreshadowed by the roles that the British had created for their chiefs and local native councils. These practices represented a path of institutional least resistance. The common experience of colonial rule, not similar social structures, is the reason they became prevalent in Africa so quickly.

What does distinguish Kenya from other African states is the speed with which administrators came to predominate over politicians. This difference was due to inhibitions the Mau Mau–induced State of Emergency put on the development of political parties and the estrangement of Kenyatta from the party organizations that were created. Many other African countries have come to resemble Kenya's "administrative state" in this regard too as political competition and party organizations have atrophied.

CHAPTER SIX

Karanja and the
Kenya Tea Development Authority

The four administrators on whom this book focuses were unusually successful. The preceding chapters have provided the general background to governance in Kenya and the location of the four administrators within it. We now turn to their special contributions to the country's rural development and learn what made them exceptional.

SUCCESS AND INSTITUTIONAL INHERITANCE

When Charles Karanja joined the Kenya Tea Development Authority (KTDA) in 1964, it was small and young but firmly established. Its structure had been deeply influenced by the historical moment of its creation. Although the organization was to take on *additional* features in the future, it kept most of its initial structural characteristics. These were a major factor in its accomplishments.

The KTDA is a success by almost any criteria of assessment. In 1959 the 1,000 hectares of tea grown by some 5,000 smallholders produced only one-fifteenth as much as Kenya's multinational tea estates. In 1980 the KTDA was servicing 130,000 growers with 50,000 hectares (110,000 acres), sold half of the country's tea exports, and had come to represent 5 percent of the international market. In the process the KTDA probably has become the world's largest tea corporation.

The KTDA also excelled in quality. In 1959 Kenyan teas commanded prices 14 percent below the average London price; by 1971 they brought the world's highest prices, at 6 percent above the average. This leadership in quality has been maintained ever since.

The organization has been immensely profitable for Kenya and its growers. The World Bank estimated that the KTDA achieved a 28 per-

125

cent return for the economy on its investments, and the incomes of its
smallholders are three times those of the Kenyan average.[1]

Finally, KTDA underwent considerable vertical expansion. It grew
from its base in helping smallholders to grow tea into the areas of manufacturing, international wholesale marketing, and retailing, in the process supplanting multinational corporations. These final areas called for
new structures and are the particular accomplishment of Charles Karanja. Before examining them, however, let us look at the organizational
forms that the KTDA inherited at independence.

Smallholder tea production was first introduced in two small areas of
Kenya by the colonial Department of Agriculture in the early 1950s. It
was a subsidized experiment, an aspect of the general attempt to put
down African rebellion by economic incorporation. As part of the experiment a tea factory was built at Ragati in Nyeri in 1957 and was run
by the department, but the management of the other factories used was
undertaken by multinational tea firms, as was the marketing of the produce. The Department of Agriculture confined itself to the problems of
getting the tea planted, providing extension to maintain its quality, and
transporting it to the factories. These functions all have economies of
scale that make them efficient on large estates but inefficient for smallholdings to provide for themselves. By "collectivizing" these functions
for smallholders the department was making their scale economic and
competitive. No one was sanguine about the success of the experiment;
tea is a very demanding crop technically, and other attempts at smallholder tea production in South Asia had failed. The World Bank declined its first opportunity to be involved in the early 1960s, being convinced the endeavor would fail.[2]

Out of this pilot project came the Special Crops Development Authority, which was established in 1960 and was renamed the KTDA in
1964. The pilot had been heavily subsidized, but the KTDA and its
growers were expected to pay most of their own way. Every aspect of
production was to be financed out of growers' sales, even including agricultural extension. The one exception was the necessary extensive development of feeder roads, which the government agreed to undertake.
Tea was spared the taxes that coffee growers had to pay in return for
their extension and road services. True, most crops pay no direct taxes,
but on balance tea probably fared well, particularly given the fact that it
produced high incomes for relatively well-to-do peasants and petty-
bourgeois small farmers. This trade of more comprehensive responsibility in return for no taxes also added to the KTDA's autonomy by making it self-sufficient in most of the resources it required.

The organizational approach adopted by the KTDA was a typical late
colonial one, stressing control as it sought to incorporate African peas-

ants into the market and make them petty-bourgeois. Farmers had to commit themselves to planting eventually a minimum of one acre of tea. Since the average farm size in the areas where it was being promoted ranged from two to three acres, and since tea produces no income for the first three years after it is planted, this requirement inclined the program toward the more advantaged, who had more land or other sources of income. Despite the fact that the late colonial policy of explicitly promoting a division of the rural areas into an entrepreneurial land-owning class and a landless laboring one was not adopted in independent Kenya, the idea of a one-acre minimum remained an official KTDA goal. The organization maintained that plantings below this minimum would not be worth the time and care of the farmer and would be unsuccessful. The benefits to the advantaged that the original policy entailed were congenial to the matajiri leadership, but the implication that the smallest producers would become landless by being denied access to the most profitable crops was politically troublesome. Thus the one-acre ideal was encouraged, with some advantage to the better-off producers, but the controls necessary to assure its achievement were not subsequently enforced.

Even though many have credited the profit incentives built into the KTDA system for its success, the KTDA's organizational design reflects the lack of faith that colonial officers had in the workings of the market.[3] They feared that the many services that are necessary for commercial tea production to succeed would not come together simply through market pressure. Thus they created a single, vertically integrated organization to provide all the planting materials, extension, transport, processing, and marketing. They also believed that African peasants were not sufficiently responsive to the market to make "economically rational" decisions and that they needed to be controlled by the state if development was to be achieved.* The KTDA therefore was constructed with

---

*It is possible that there was some historical basis for the perception that African peasants were insensitive to the market. Given the facts that (1) land was not scarce, (2) the economic survival of peasants was not dependent on the market, and (3) the price signals being given by the commercially underdeveloped colonial economies were quite weak, it is plausible that peasants were unresponsive to the fine price changes to which colonial officials thought they should be reacting. Whatever the early pattern, however, it has become clear that African peasants are responsive to market forces today. See Carl Eicher and Doyle Baker, *Research on Agricultural Development in Sub-Saharan Africa: A Critical Survey*, MSU International Development Paper, no. 1 (East Lansing: Department of Agricultural Economics, Michigan State University, 1982), pp. 28–30; Goran Hyden, *Beyond Ujamaa in Tanzania: Underdevelopment and an Uncaptured Peasantry* (Berkeley and Los Angeles: University of California Press, 1980); Sara Berry, "Agrarian Crisis in Africa? A Review and Interpretation," paper presented to the Joint African Studies Committee (New York: Social Science Research Council and American Council of Learned Societies, 1983), pp. 24–25.

monopoly and monopsony powers and multiple controls over grower behavior. The stumps needed for planting could be obtained only from the KTDA. Fertilizer was provided in kind to make sure that farmers used it, and its cost was deducted from the proceeds of the tea sales. Picked leaf could be sold only to the KTDA, and considerable efforts were made to prevent the development of sun-dried (i.e., homemade) tea, so growers would be unable to avoid paying the development costs the Authority was deducting from its producer prices. The extension agents were required to inspect and grade as well as advise the growers, so as to make sure that they were keeping up to the required quality standards, and lower-quality tea could be refused (instead of being paid a lower price).[4] The internal structure of the KTDA was similarly tightly organized and disciplined.

These controls were balanced, however, by something that was not typical of colonialism and instead reflected the period of transition to independence—elected grower representation. The pilot project undertaken in the early 1950s did not have grower participation. But when the Special Crops Development Authority (KTDA's predecessor) was formed in 1960, most government subsidies were dropped. In the highly charged political atmosphere of imminent independence, the growers responded by forming the Central Province Tea Growers Association. By creating elected tea committees at the local level the SCDA/KTDA was able to bring this protest within the organization, where it could be controlled. The growers' representatives on the national board were appointed by the minister of agriculture until 1966, after which they were elected by the provincial tea boards. The minister, however, retained the right to appoint the other members and thus control the board. Naphtali Wachira, who was from Nyeri and the president of the Growers Association, was appointed to the board but left it in 1963 when given a job within the KTDA. The other Central Province appointed (and then elected) representative on the board, Jackson Kamau of Kiambu, had declined to participate in the association and became chairman of the KTDA in 1966. Even though grower representation was forced upon the KTDA by the spirit of the times and was then controlled and co-opted, it helped protect the organization against external political encroachment and was instrumental to its success. The board's limited independence was reinforced by the fact that its concerns resonated with those of many individual cabinet members and M.P.s, causing the KTDA and the government to be sensitive to its views once it was in existence.[5]

The smallholder coffee industry, which also was established in the 1950s, has controlled participation as well, both through the Coffee Board and the cooperative movement. The board was established in the colonial era to represent the interests of white growers. Smallholders now join with estate owners in the election of some board members, with the government selecting others. There also is government supervision of the elected cooperative societies. The oversight is sufficiently tight that Kenyan farmers see no difference in the degree of say that they have in the coffee and tea industries, even though the cooperatives nominally give them more power than their representatives do on the KTDA board.[6] Still, institutions supporting smallholder agriculture initiated before and after this period generally have not provided for any meaningful participation. Both the colonial and postcolonial states accepted grower democracy only when it was forced upon them. We see here an instance of Stinchcombe's theorem that organizational form is best explained by the historical moment of creation.[7]

KARANJA'S RISE THROUGH THE RANKS

Charles Karanja joined the KTDA as its executive assistant in 1964. He was put in charge of transport, housing, staff recruitment, and the like, all areas in which he had gained strong experience in Kiambu and Embu as works officer. He did well and was promoted to executive officer in 1965. In this new capacity his responsibilities expanded to include the administration of leaf collection.

Leaf collection was one of the two foci of the KTDA's day-to-day functioning as it was then constituted. The Authority grew tea stumps from seed in its nurseries and sold them to the growers. The extension staff then supervised the care and picking of the tea. (KTDA insisted that its growers provide the highest quality tea by following the labor-intensive practice of always picking a bud and two leaves together. Some economists have recently questioned whether this practice maximizes profits, but the Authority has had a nationalist pride in the international recognition of the quality of its product.) All of this was the preserve of a senior agriculturalist who headed what was called the Technical Division.

The grower then had to carry his tea to a buying center, where it was inspected, weighed, and recorded. From there it was picked up and transported to factories for manufacturing. At this time the processing and marketing of the tea was handled for the KTDA by the multinational tea companies. The leaf-collection-and-delivery stage was administratively demanding for several reasons: (1) Tea had to be processed within twenty-four hours of picking to be of high quality, and it could easily be damaged in transporting. (2) All of the KTDA's financial transactions with growers revolved around the collection stage in the operations. (3) A large fleet of lorries (trucks) had to be kept functional and on time on unpaved rural roads in rainy conditions. (4) A large non-professional work force had to be kept working to tight time schedules under dispersed conditions where supervision was difficult. All of this came under Karanja's jurisdiction.

The leaf-collection operations accounted for most of the KTDA's variable costs, and Karanja became persuaded that he could lower them. He was asked to look into transportation problems, but, largely on his own, he sought additional areas where improvements were possible. His first suggestion concerned the method of transporting the plucked tea. The KTDA was using steel-wire baskets to provide air circulation around the tea and keep it from being damaged by overheating. These were costing K.shs. 45 each and were lasting only thirteen months. Karanja proposed the use of soft, sisal gunnysacks instead and had a new truck body designed so that they could be hung rather than stacked. The idea was to increase air circulation around the tea still more, as the KTDA had to transport the green leaf much farther than the estates did. The sisal bags had a life of over two years and cost only K.shs. 8 each, as sisal is locally grown.

His second proposed innovation was to reduce the KTDA staffing at the buying centers from two to one and on the trucks from three to two by combining tasks. Third, he suggested altering the standard work hours of the leaf-collection and trucking staff so as to significantly reduce overtime. Needless to say, these two innovations were resisted by the staff, for they increased the work and reduced the take-home pay.

Fourth, he developed a formula for deciding whether or not a leaf-collection (buying) center was handling an adequate volume and proposed that the underutilized centers be grouped into twos or threes, with a single leaf-collection officer rotating days between them. The same formula was used to determine when it would be appropriate to set up a new buying center. This innovation was not popular with the growers, who wanted collection centers close to their homes and open every day, to reduce their walking distances. Since the costs of having too many centers were born collectively, and the inconvenience of going farther was born individually, the voices of growers wanting more centers open more days were always louder.

These and further proposals were received with skepticism by the KTDA board when Karanja presented his paper arguing for them. Several of his ideas represented breaks with standard industry practice. He was new to tea, and some of the board members themselves owned estates. A long period of careful examination and trial testing of the innovations ensued. Karanja's argument was clinched in 1968, however, when the board hired an English consulting firm to study the same problems and it recommended acceptance of his proposals.[8]

These changes were simply refinements in the basic methods of operation that the KTDA had already established. Nonetheless, they did enable it to improve the efficiency of its operations and lower its costs. These savings were passed on to the growers in the form of improved prices, the incentives that do account for the KTDA's success.

A ruthless commitment to efficiency characterizes all of Karanja's career. Its results are reflected in a steady drop in the KTDA's operating costs, as is seen in table 6.1. Today the study that he carried out on leaf collection would be called operations research, which features in the curriculum for engineering degrees. Karanja had had no such formal training, for he never completed his studies in Canada. Nonetheless, some of the principles that underlie operations research were imparted in his diploma program in Kampala and were reinforced by his early job experiences. Engineering involves attention to detail and an approach to problem solving that is both systematic and based on particular circumstances. The efficient use of resources is one of its central preoccupations. Karanja's approach to his managerial work in the KTDA thus was influenced by his professional background.

Added to his engineer's instincts was a political commitment to the interests of growers. He believed that it was important that they benefit from independence, and he was troubled that even the least-paid wage earners at the Authority were making more than the tea smallholders. His sensitivity to the prices that producers were receiving was subse-

TABLE 6.1
Average Annual Operating Costs of the KTDA

Year	Cost per Ton in Constant (1976) K.shs.	Year	Cost per Ton in Constant (1976) K.shs.
1963	3,868.9	1974	341.6
1964	4,203.6	1975	372.0
1965	2,877.6	1976	334.5
1966	2,224.3	1977	238.5
1967	1,821.0	1978	237.9
1968	863.3	1979	256.7
1969	1,060.8	1980	360.3
1970	578.2	1981	383.4
1971	666.1	1982	379.8
1972	482.7	1983	287.9
1973	367.8	1984	287.7

SOURCE: Barbara Grosh, "Performance of Agricultural Public Enterprises in Kenya: Lessons from the First Two Decades of Independence," *Eastern Africa Economic Review* 3, no. 1 (1987), p. 63.

quently strengthened by his own interests as a new tea farmer in upper Kiambu. Similarly, his impulse for cost cutting was reinforced by his experience as a businessman.

Initially, Karanja's path to the general managership was blocked, and he was trapped in leaf collection. Shortly after he joined the KTDA, the Authority hired F. I. H. Moreithi, a Kikuyu economist from Nyeri, as its assistant general manager designate. Moreithi was made general manager in September 1968, and Karanja was named assistant general manager. They were very different men, and their relationship became stormy. Moreithi was a policy analyst, quiet, polite, and politically naive; Karanja was an administrator, talkative, aggressive, ambitious, and shrewd in politics.[9]

The board decided to plant three acres of tea for President Kenyatta in order to involve him in the affairs of the Authority. Kenyatta later brought it to six acres and then to eighteen, but he made no payment for the stumps. So Moreithi raised the matter with Mbiyu Koinange, the minister of state in the Office of the President, and got a very negative reaction. Subsequently, Kenyatta informed Karanja that he had decided to deliver his tea direct to the factory without going through the Authority's leaf collectors. This meant that the KTDA would not be able to deduct its service charges from his payments. If this practice became widespread, it would jeopardize the KTDA. Karanja sought and received Kenyatta's assurances that no one else would be extended this privilege. But Moreithi was deeply concerned with the precedent and objected informally through government channels. Again he got a strong negative reaction. Meanwhile, the chair of the board, Jackson Kamau, was seeking to involve himself in the details of the KTDA's operations to a greater extent than had been traditional for those occupying that position in Kenyan agricultural authorities. This was symbolized by his desire for an office in the headquarters (which he never did get). Moreithi thus was under a good deal of pressure from Kamau and felt blocked on many decisions.

In the midst of this, Karanja became upset with the work of his planning officer and wanted him dismissed. Moreithi declined to do so. Rumors circulated that Karanja wanted Moreithi's job, and the relations between the two men deteriorated still further. In May 1970 Karanja submitted his resignation, stating that he did not want to threaten Moreithi and reasoning that he could do better for himself in business.

Higher government officials intervened, and Karanja's departure was not accepted. Philip Ndegwa, then permanent secretary to the Ministry of Agriculture, called him, asked him to withdraw his resignation, and told him to report directly to the chairman of the KTDA, not the general manager. In Kenya one does not decline the presumed wishes of the president about the position one is to occupy, even if Karanja had been inclined to do so.

Moreithi interpreted Karanja's resignation as a ploy, not as a genuine offer. In any case, it had resulted in his authority's being seriously compromised. Moreithi submitted his own resignation and it was accepted. In addition to having a tense relationship with Kamau and to offending the Office of the President, he had a conflict with Mwai Kibaki, the senior cabinet minister from his home district of Nyeri. By contrast Karanja had built up impeccable political connections with the Kiambu political elite and the group around Kenyatta. He and Kamau also lived on neighboring large farms and would shortly be partners in business.

Karanja became general manager in October 1970, and Moreithi left Kenya to work for the Food and Agricultural Organization and subsequently the World Bank. Some of Moreithi's supporters in this conflict later became convinced that he lacked the toughness and political skill necessary to lead the KTDA and that the organization had actually been better off under Karanja. Moreithi himself later concluded that "once Kamau and Karanja were in they could resist further political interference because they were well enough connected themselves."

KARANJA'S GENERAL MANAGERSHIP

One of the first things that Charles Karanja did as general manager was to persuade the board to dismiss the planning officer who had opposed him. He also made it clear that he would deal similarly with any others who failed to carry out his legitimate instructions. This "purge" was an aspect of the way he treated personnel issues more generally. Throughout his career Karanja has been quick to fire those whose performance has disappointed him. This has been as true of him in his own businesses as in the KTDA, and he has applied the principle as rigorously to his relatives and the politically connected as to those of other ethnic groups. Karanja "would not stand fools gladly." This is not to say that his personnel policies were impersonal. The senior positions in the KTDA were filled by a Board committee through an impartial open interview, but personal or political influence might help one make it to this stage in the process. Karanja also exercised patronage over junior positions on occasion. He was adamant, however, that his favors went no further than a chance at the job; to keep it, one had to perform. He dropped those who did not meet his standards and encouraged his supervisors to do the same. He demoted a relative of the minister of agriculture from a senior position in the KTDA and fired two of his own sons from his business. Patronage has quite a different ring to it when those who receive it are subjected to ruthless performance standards, and all agree that this is precisely what Karanja did. Of course his standards did have an element of personal loyalty mixed in with a preponderance of objective merit. Some good people felt his ax, particularly in the early years of his general-managership, but on balance his appointment policies were conducive to good performance.

The other side of Karanja's willingness to fire poor performers is that he was good at career development. He supported his staff against political interference. His expectations were always clear, and he followed up to see that the work was done properly. When he was satisfied he was quick to give public praise and salary increases. Able people rose rapidly under him. The KTDA had more internal promotion of staff than did other parastatals (government corporations). The organization developed an extremely strong esprit de corps among its senior staff and a loyalty to Karanja that long survived his departure.

Karanja enjoyed identifying good work by setting up comparisons and stimulating competition. He adopted the policy of training more people for jobs than he had openings and then making the promotions from among the best performers. This could create some bitterness among those who fell by the wayside. In his early years as general manager he simply handled this problem by dismissing those whose dissatisfaction affected their work.

Karanja was well enough connected to defend the KTDA against political interference, and he was professional enough to believe passionately in doing so. The Authority was under constant pressure to expand its tea-growing areas, since its presence brought both increased agricultural incomes and dramatic improvements in rural roads. Such expansion would have increased the KTDA's operating costs and thereby reduced the incomes of its original producers. L. H. Brown, the then director of agriculture, had prepared a report just before independence defining those areas that were appropriate for smallholder tea production.[10] Karanja vigorously defended those boundaries and only lost once. This concerned Olenguruone, a Kalenjin area, which was included on the orders of President Moi after Kenyatta's death. Otherwise Karanja's easy access to President Kenyatta was sufficient to defend this colonially defined professional standard. The European managers of the KTDA also lost once on this issue, in 1965, when they succumbed to the combined pressure of the Settlement Board and Masinde Muliro, the senior cabinet minister from Western Province, and permitted tea at Cherengani in Kitale.

It is true that the Brown Report legitimated the Central Province Kikuyu's receiving a hefty 42 percent of the Authority's tea acreage and thus might be thought of as representing Karanja's ethnic interests rather than a professional standard. Doubtless it was some of both, but at the end of his eleven-year tenure the Kikuyu's percentage of acreage had slightly decreased, despite a doubling in the area planted and considerable opportunity to have shown them still greater favoritism.[11]

The dramatic increase in the area under smallholder tea and the emergence of the KTDA as a major force on the world market were not solely the result of Karanja's actions. The World Bank had overcome its initial doubts about the Authority in 1965 and joined with the Commonwealth Development Corporation as its principal financier. As the organization went from success to success the Bank provided loans for still greater expansions. To meet the demand for tea plants that these exponential increases in acreage produced, the Authority had to introduce vegetative propagation from mother bushes, instead of growing the plants from seedlings. The new method permitted farmers to develop their own nurseries and thus cost the KTDA its monopoly over the supply of planting material. A fair amount of the organization's control over who planted tea and how much acreage they took on was lost at this point. As a result, the KTDA's careful field-inspection system began to reflect a certain amount of fiction, for the extension agents were being called upon to judge the quality of cultivation of tea that wasn't always where it was alleged to be.[12] The Authority's performance didn't suffer from this loss of control, which strongly suggests that it hadn't been necessary in the first place. Although most of the other colonially inspired controls over growers have remained formally in place, the ideological zeal for their enforcement has waned, save in the area of picking quality. The strong prices for tea and the commercialization of much of the Kenyan peasantry have made the KTDA and the growers partners in a mutually profitable enterprise and erased the conflict of objectives which the controls implied.

What did drive the expansion in smallholder tea were strong international prices for the beverage.[13] The KTDA was responsible for seeing that these were passed through to the growers. Three policies in which Karanja had a hand contributed to this result. First, the Authority was commendable about cutting its own costs and therefore passing on an increased percentage of the profits to the grower. The results are reflected in the decline in real charges made by the KTDA, which were discussed with regard to leaf collection. In the same vein the Authority returned to the World Bank nearly half of the money that it had been lent for its Second Plan period. A senior Treasury official criticized Karanja for having failed to use the money, as the interest rates were subsidized. Karanja's attitude, however, was that it was still a loan; if it went into unnecessary expenses, it would still have to be repaid out of small-holder profits later on.

Second, the Authority decided to pass world price fluctuations directly on to the growers and not try to buffer them with a price stabilization fund. This decision doubtless increased grower profits, for experience elsewhere in Africa suggests that such funds all too often get used for other purposes and are then unavailable when they are needed.[14] The attendant risk to growers was mitigated by dividing the payments for the tea into a guaranteed first payment, which was distributed monthly, and a variable second one at the end of the year.[15]

Under Karanja the KTDA made the link between world prices and producer profits even more direct than it had been originally. Quality of tea varies by the area of growth and the processing factory, which results in different prices on the world market. Initially these revenues had been pooled and paid out to growers as if the quality of their product were uniform. Consistently higher prices were commanded, however, by the tea from east of the Rift Valley, that is, tea grown by the Kikuyu, Meru, and Embu. Karanja proposed that two pools be created instead, east and west of the Rift Valley. The suggestion was vigorously opposed by the board members from the west, for it would lower the income of their growers. The proposal finally carried when Mr. B. Amache, the deputy chairman and a Luhya from the west, became convinced of the justice of such a new arrangement, leaving the Kalenjin members alone against it. Later Karanja persuaded the board to break the payment pools down to the factory level in order to increase the incentive effect still further.

Third, the KTDA fought hard to defend its growers from taxes on its produce, such as those paid by coffee producers. Its objections were finally overcome during the 1977 boom in beverage prices. The economy was awash with extra income and the government (wisely) imposed an export tax above a certain price threshold to dampen the inflationary impact. But the vigorous efforts of the Authority kept still further taxes at bay.

These commitments to economy and market forces were aided by the substantial involvement of the World Bank and the Commonwealth Development Corporation. Threatened changes in government policy could be fended off by saying that they would upset the donors. Donor influence, however, was not an absolute; to have an effect it had to be used by a local institution that shared its objectives. The World Bank failed to get what it wanted for its tea projects in Mauritius, Tanzania, and Uganda.

THE KTDA EXPANDS INTO FACTORY MANAGEMENT

The place where Charles Karanja's impact on the KTDA is best judged is not in its horizontal growth in quantity of tea grown but in its vertical expansion into new aspects of the production process. Under his general-managership the Authority took over from the multinationals the manufacturing, wholesale marketing, and retailing of tea. In all but the last Karanja had startling success.

The saga of the KTDA's movement into factory management was related in chapter 1. The Authority had always contracted out the management of all but one of its factories, as well as the marketing of the tea produced, to the various multinational tea firms in Kenya.* In 1973 Karanja decided that the KTDA should do this work itself. He was particularly dissatisfied with the slow pace at which the multinationals were moving to Africanize the positions of factory manager. In order to get the support of his board, he followed his usual strategy and asked it to let him prepare a policy paper on the issue. This gave him license to use his whole staff to develop the data and arguments that would support the direction in which he wanted to move. His experience was that he could usually carry three-quarters of the board once he had such a sanctioned paper before it. Though he did gain the support of his board for this bold change in the effective operational mission of the KTDA, he was opposed by the donors and the Ministry of Agriculture, which was cowed by the donors. (See plate 21.) To overcome them he had to use his personal standing with Kenyatta. The fact that he was on the side of Africanization gave him an advantage in the argument.

The real sign of Karanja's managerial skill is not that he won the policy debate on this issue but that he implemented it efficiently. The issue of Africanizing the factory managerships was not a new one for Karanja. He and Moreithi had arranged for the placement of KTDA African management trainees in the existing factories from 1968. The dispute with the multinational management agents initially had been over how soon these Africans could be put in full charge of factories. To arrange for the transition Karanja moved slowly but decisively. He decided to leave all the existing management-agent contracts intact and to assume direct KTDA management only of the new factories, as they came on line. This was done partly to avoid taking on too big a task all at once. "When you move into new areas never be in a hurry," he said.

---

*Each tea factory technically is a separate company, and its stock is available for purchase by the local growers who use it. Despite a reasonable amount of such purchases, the majority of the shares in all the companies are owned by the KTDA, which therefore has complete control over their operations.

This tack also avoided provoking still further the opposition of the commercial tea estates that were managing the existing factories. Most important, however, it gave Karanja information. He would have the right to know the costs and operating methods of the commercial management agents and be able to compare them with those of the KTDA's directly managed plants. Both competition and information would be produced. Within a half dozen years he was confident enough of his operations to call in all the remaining management contracts and assume direct control.

Some of the new managers put in place were Africans; others were European. David Venters, a white Kenyan with a Tanzanian wife, was hired as chief factory superintendent to oversee the operation and to train the future African managers. Although Karanja did hire new Europeans to work for him, it was in an overall context of using them to advance Africanization. By the end of the 1970s all posts, including that of superintendent, would be held by Africans. (Venters went on to run Karanja's private tea brokerage after he left the KTDA.) The selection of trainees for factory positions and their subsequent appointment to managerships showed considerable care on Karanja's part about matters of ethnicity. The slates were balanced so that trainees from an ethnic group were approximately proportionate to the numbers of factories planned for their area, and men were generally placed in factories where they wouldn't be seen as outsiders by the local growers.

At the time that Karanja was relieved as general manager in 1981, the KTDA was running twenty-seven factories and had a dozen more under construction. To oversee these operations Karanja expanded the Accounts Department. This department had always been centrally involved in most aspects of the management of the Authority. Its strength was partly a function of the insistence of the World Bank and the Commonwealth Development Corporation. These two had the right to veto the appointment of the chief accountant. A European held the post until the mid-1970s, when a Kenyan Asian was promoted from within to head the department.

This new chief accountant, B. R. Vora, created a management information system that gave breakdowns on the costs of the different aspects of production at each factory. This comparative information was used to identify areas of inefficiency and to reward outstanding managerial behavior. As a result, vigorous competition was set off among managers, and the commercial agents began to modernize and improve their performance. Elsewhere management information systems generally have had a poor record, particularly when they are computerized.[16] The success of Vora's system was due to several factors: First, it was not computerized until it was well established. Second, the system was used by managers who were actively interested in it. Third, it created comparative information and stimulated competition on which direct financial rewards depended.

Karanja also applied the principle of creative competition to the construction of the factories, which had been done before entirely by contract. He didn't like the fact that the architects and consulting engineers were paid a percentage of costs, which seemed to him to give them no incentive to work efficiently. He pushed for the creation of a KTDA Engineering Department to construct some of the factories and install their machinery. As the World Bank favors competitive international bidding, he had to overcome considerable opposition to get this policy adopted. He argued that the KTDA would be better able to maintain these facilities once they were operational if it had had some experience in installing them. The Authority took over only a portion of the engineering work and operated on the principle of charging less than the commercial bids for that which it did. The well-known problems of corruption in construction contracts did arise for the KTDA, however, causing some delays. Karanja found the senior Pakistani staff member in charge to be responsible for the corruption and he was criminally charged and deported.

The general results for factory management of the KTDA's competitive Africanization policies can be seen in table 6.2. All senior positions in the KTDA were filled by Africans by 1980. These included those in factory management and marketing only seven years after the functions were taken over by the Authority. The organization had even done away with expatriate advisers by that time. Despite this fairly rapid localization of managerial staff and despite significant expansions in operations, the KTDA contained or reduced its real operating costs. Industry experts considered these costs to be roughly the same as those of the private estates in Kenya. Increased public management was *not* inefficient. This is all the more remarkable as the accounts for the factories have historically been presented in such a way as to obscure their operating efficiencies to all but insiders. It would have been easy for the KTDA management to hide boondoggles there.

These efficient standards of performance must have been difficult to maintain. To do so required not only managerial vigilance but the political ability to maintain the KTDA's autonomy. Most remarkable in this regard was the Authority's lack of response to the Tri-Partite Agreements. Twice in the 1970s President Kenyatta struck bargains with organized labor that they would forgo wage increases in return for 10 percent increases in employment by large public and private employers. The private sector dealt with the agreements by temporarily increasing its labor force and then using attrition to bring it back down to its pre-

TABLE 6.2
KTDA Factory Costs

Year	Nominal K.shs. Factory Cost per Kg of Green Tea	Real (1976) K.shs. Factory Cost per Kg of Green Tea
1970/71	0.41[a]	0.73[a]
1971/72	0.47[a]	0.78[a]
1973/74	0.44	0.56
1977/78	1.05	0.86
1978/79	0.40[b]	0.31[b]
1979/80	0.80[b]	0.54[b]
1980/81	1.18	0.76
1981/82	1.33	0.78
1982/83	1.35	0.74
1983/84	1.14	0.57

[a] The figure is based on a partial return of factories.

[b] These figures probably are artificially low because of the sale of back supplies during the beverage boom. See the following notes on calculation methods.

NOTE: It is somewhat more common to present these figures in terms of the cost of a kilogram of made (rather than green) tea. Unfortunately the KTDA Annual Reports do not lend themselves to as long a series if that approach is used. A few of the factory costs for a kilo of made tea that are available: 1973/74—K.shs. 1.92; 1980/81—K.shs. 5.03; 1983/84—K.shs. 4.79.

The figures presented were calculated by the author from raw data presented in the KTDA Annual Report for the relevant year. The reports give the prices received by the factories for each kilogram (kg) of made tea [pmt], the payouts for each kg of green tea [pgt], the ratio of the weight of the made tea to that of the green tea [mt/gt], and the percentage weight loss of the green tea between the grower and the factory [wl]. The factory cost is then ((mt/gt) (1 − wl) pmt) − pgt.

There is interyear instability in the cost figures because the factories hold back supplies in abundant years and sell them in the subsequent years. The price quoted for the made tea is for that which was sold that year, not for all the made tea that was manufactured out of green tea that year. This imperfection in the figures averages out over time.

The real (or constant) costs were calculated using the GDP cost deflator and 1976 as a base year.

vious level. In the public sector, however, the number of established (or *authorized*) positions was increased by 10 percent each time, leaving a permanent increase in employees—and of course the associated costs. If the KTDA factories had implemented the agreements, they would have had higher labor costs than their private competitors, and grower incomes would have suffered. Karanja had sufficient commitment to farmer welfare and enough confidence in his political connections to avoid the spirit of the agreements. He skillfully met the requirements by transferring seasonal workers onto the permanent payroll without hiring new or additional labor in the KTDA or its factories.

Another of Karanja's ventures in vertical integration of the KTDA was to expand into the wholesale marketing of its tea, a function that also had been performed by its management agents. This too was a demanding area in which to work, with much opportunity for increasing or decreasing profits, depending on how well one played the market. To get the expertise that he needed, Karanja in 1974 took on G. A. Unsworth, a white Kenyan who was a business partner of his and who had his own tea brokerage. One of Unsworth's conditions for joining the KTDA was that his firm still be able to handle a portion of the Authority's teas. Karanja followed Unsworth's work closely, generally traveling with him abroad, to learn quickly from him and to assure himself that there were no improprieties. Unsworth left the KTDA in 1976 because the potential conflict between his business and managerial interests was too great and too public to be allowed to continue. His successor also was a European. This man was forced out for failing to follow Karanja's explicit policies about the ways in which the Authority's tea was to be sold. Karanja preferred the safety and public integrity of selling most of KTDA's tea through auctions, rather than taking the risks of large profits and losses through private and forward sales, with the attendant possibilities of kickbacks. The marketing position was then taken over by a Kenyan African.

The new areas into which Karanja took the KTDA significantly increased the opportunities for corruption and the potential for conflict of interest. Leaf collection created chances for minor kickbacks or the siphoning off of funds through misrecording of green-tea weights at the local level, and the sales contracts for the trucking fleet created larger temptations. Construction, manufacturing, warehousing, and marketing all increased several fold the dangers of private profit from public trust. Karanja handled these problems by setting high standards of probity for his staff and dismissing those who seemed to have broken them. Various Europeans, Asians, and Africans all were sent on their way because of his doubts about their honesty. There is no evidence in the record of the KTDA to suggest that any one ethnic group had an advantage in moral virtue. The price of a relatively uncorrupted KTDA was eternal vigilance by its general manager and its Accounting Department and ruthlessness in removing the offenders. In the process some people may have been forced out who were not guilty of the charges levied against them. When Karanja was convinced of a case he acted on it; he didn't apply court-room standards of proof. Chapters 8 and 10 will explore the allegations that Karanja did not have the same high standards for himself in conflict-of-interest matters that he applied to others. For the moment it is sufficient to note the benefits to the KTDA of the vigilance that he did exercise and the fact that it had to be constant.

Given the many opportunities for irregularities that the KTDA's expansion provided, it was natural for Karanja to want to oversee personally as many of the operations as he could. In fact, initially he wasn't very good at delegation. In his early years as general manager, for example, he insisted on editing the Authority's Annual Report himself. The centralization and personalization of authority is a common feature and a problem of managers in Kenya.[17] Karanja was forced to begin to delegate more, however, not only by KTDA's growth but by his personal limitations. In 1975 he was on two phones at once raising money for a harambee (self-help) function at which he was to be the guest of honor. He felt a tingling in his chest, got off the phones at once, and went to the hospital, where he collapsed. He was hospitalized for a month with an irregular heartbeat and had to spend another month on the Kenyan coast recovering. Thereafter delegation became a matter of personal survival for him.

CONCLUSIONS

By the end of the Kenyatta presidency, Karanja was running an immensely successful KTDA, which had expanded both horizontally and vertically to an extent that was completely unforseen fifteen years earlier. Later, Karanja suffered a series of reverses and was removed under President Moi. But the KTDA has continued to do reasonably well. The causes of this success have been the subject of thoughtful analyses both by Geoffrey Lamb and Linda Muller and by Samuel Paul. Their views largely converge and may be expressed in the words of Lamb and Muller. The features that explain the KTDA's achievements are these:

> (1) consciously designed and effectively sustained organizational autonomy; (2) control of resources and activities crucial to performance; (3) effective and involuntary accountability; (4) effective and mutually reinforcing incentives for different sets of participants in tea production. The combination of these factors has been so successful, in KTDA's case, in large part because of the strong role of external elements—growers, lenders and prices—in maintaining the Authority's internal discipline [and helping to protect it from political interference].[18]

Others who have watched closely as the KTDA has evolved have also credited its success to the combination of its particular political environment and its structure. To put it somewhat differently, they stress the play of interests and institutional inheritance. I concur, but I would add, as would other observers, that interests and institutions manifested themselves in the managers who were selected to lead the KTDA and that those individuals had an independent impact on the outcome. The

Authority's achievements would not have been as great without Charles Karanja and those whom he assembled around him. How can we parse out these complex causal relationships?

Lamb and Muller argue for the primacy of the three contextual forces: growers, lenders, and prices. It is hard to imagine that the KTDA could have prospered without the buoyant world market for tea that it stumbled upon nor that it could have grown so spectacularly without the resources that the donors provided. As necessary as these two conditions were for success, however, they were not sufficient. Several other African states experienced them and did quite poorly in their tea ventures. To be effective the prices had to be passed on to growers, not siphoned off in taxes or inefficient services, and the concern of the donors had to be enlisted rather than evaded.

The growers are another matter. Because so many of them were Kikuyu and because the prosperity of Central Province was so crucial to Kenyatta's political strategy, small-farmer interests had a prominence in the KTDA that they have lacked for most other African crop authorities. In addition the KTDA had elected grower representatives on its board as part of its institutional heritage. Interests and institutions interacted here to reinforce one another. Karanja's belief in the primacy of grower interests conformed to his political environment.

What of the rest of the structural inheritance that Lamb and Muller identified in the KTDA? All observers remark on the importance of the organization's autonomy, but this actually was not well imbedded in the institution the British created. The board was largely appointed by the government; only the Commonwealth Development Corporation representative was fully independent. The KTDA's autonomy was neither inherited nor granted but was earned by its management. It did so partly through performing well and making few demands on the government for resources. But the policy episodes presented in this chapter make it clear that something much more actively political was involved as well. Charles Karanja was selected to be general manager because he did have the confidence of a president who liked to be able to delegate. Kenyatta gave his attention more to personnel than to the details of public policy. But Karanja also was skilled at building further and maintaining the president's support. Organizational autonomy in the public sector is not simply granted; it has to be politically earned.

The KTDA did inherit an integrated organizational design that gave it control over all the resources that it and its growers needed for success. As was noted above, this institutional format developed out of the colonial authorities' distrust of the market and their belief that they would need to control African peasant behavior if they were to succeed. The KTDA's control over growers weakened somewhat when it lost its monopoly over planting material, and its zeal for enforcing some of its other controls diminished, but it extended its vertical integration when it moved into manufacturing and marketing and displaced its management agents. I think myself that the KTDA didn't require the degree of integration that it had and will explore that issue further at the end of the next chapter. In any case, the extension of the Authority's vertical integration clearly must be credited to Karanja's determination.

The British created a strong accountability structure for the KTDA, selected local staff who believed in it, and socialized them further in its virtues. There is institutional continuity in Karanja's and Vora's commitment to integrity and accounting control. Their willingness to fire transgressors and their zeal with respect to efficiency sometimes went beyond those of their predecessors, but certainly were consistent with them. The KTDA probably would not have had some of its distinctive systems of tight accountability if it had not been institutionalized by the British. Nonetheless, the process of transmission was not automatic. The expansion of the Authority into new domains meant that new routines had to be created. The general political and social environment also offered substantial encouragement to relax these accountability and efficiency standards, as happened in many organizations. The personal and professional socialization of Karanja, not just that of the institution, is responsible for the outcome.

Finally, the KTDA had strong incentives, both for growers and for its staff. These probably assumed an importance in the Authority that went beyond what the British had originally envisioned. The colonial patterns of intervention in agriculture showed doubts about the market and competition and reveal more reliance on controls than on profits to obtain the desired effects. Karanja's policies tightened the link between markets and grower profits and creatively institutionalized competition in a number of different domains. If one were to look for a background variable to explain these policy commitments of his, it would be not the institutional heritage of the KTDA but his own involvement in business.

Interests and institutional heritage thus explain the greater part of the KTDA's success. Neither one can explain it alone. But interests and institutions also worked through specific individuals such as Charles Karanja, who further shaped their impact and must share credit for the Authority's accomplishments.

CHAPTER SEVEN

Muriithi and the Dairy Industry

The success of Kenya's smallholder dairy industry is every bit as impressive as that which occurred for tea. Between 1963, on the eve of independence, and 1980 production increased fourfold (as measured both by the size of the country's grade dairy herd and by the quantity of milk marketed through the Kenya Cooperative Creameries, the largest supplier). Equally striking is the fact that the grade dairy animals owned by African smallholders went from an insignificant proportion of the national herd to 80 percent over the same period.[1] Furthermore, unlike tea, the product produced by the dairy industry was for a domestic, mass-consumer market and faced insurmountable export conditions.

This imposing achievement is relatively unknown outside animal production circles, while the comparable achievements of the KTDA and India's National Dairy Development Board (NDDB) are widely heralded.[2] The difference in acclaim seems due to a single organization's having been responsible in the cases of the KTDA and NDDB, whereas several were involved in the spectacular growth of Kenya's dairy industry. But it is precisely this aspect of the success that is intriguing. How did Kenya defy the apparently unassailable logic of integrated approaches to agricultural development and achieve this expansion in milk production? Because Ishmael Muriithi directed only the veterinary aspects of this effort, this question is tantamount to asking how he was able to promote smallholder dairying when he did not control important parts of the industry's infrastructure.

THE CREATION OF A SMALLHOLDER DAIRY INDUSTRY

That independent Kenya would be successful with dairy products was far from evident in 1964. At the time, the newspapers spoke of a crisis

145

in the industry, as herds in the formerly European areas were down by 20 percent from 1960, and production had declined for two consecutive years.[3]

Dairying had been built around large white farms. Lord Delamere had begun experimenting with the use of European breeds of cattle at the turn of the century and initiated a long series of efforts to get government services that would enable them to survive and be productive. Under the Veterinary Department appropriate preventive measures were found for several of the more serious cattle diseases endemic in Africa, and quarantines to prevent their spread from African to European herds were enforced for the others.[4] In 1935 the department introduced artificial insemination (AI), dramatically reducing the constraint of having to import breeding stock to improve the Kenyan herd. Dairy plants were built, and the Kenya Cooperative Creameries (KCC) was formed in 1925. The KCC gradually came to have a de facto monopoly over most of the formal market for dairy products.[5] Most of these services were skewed heavily toward European producers. The government posted veterinarians disproportionately to white-farm areas, enforced quarantines against African livestock, and centered artificial insemination on European-held stock. The KCC exercised price discrimination between milk delivered under purchased quotas and that outside them. Sale of milk under nonquota terms alone was uneconomic, and the quotas, of course, were all European held. The first African joined the KCC only in 1961.[6]

Milk is central to both modern and traditional diets of Africans, and dairying has always been important to their economic life. European success in this area therefore attracted African attention. The Veterinary Department established a dairy at Mariakani on the coast in 1930 to service African producers, but nothing similar was done up-country.[7] Chief Muhoya illegally imported grade animals into Nyeri District in the late 1940s and helped to found a dairy cooperative society there to process and sell the milk. Ishmael Muriithi's father, Elijah Waicanguru, was centrally involved in both endeavors. This co-op was able to sell only on the local market; no African cooperative was able to join the KCC until 1962.[8] Muriithi's first assignment with the Veterinary Department in the late 1950s involved the introduction of artificial insemination into Kiambu District.

Though the pieces for significant African smallholder involvement in the dairy industry were being created, it took independence for them to be fully developed. Then the components of Kenya's smallholder dairy began to develop rapidly. Improved stock were either purchased with Agricultural Finance Corporation loans or bred through repeated use of artificial insemination on local Zebu cattle. The Veterinary Department provided AI as well as curative animal health services. Cattle dips to prevent tick-borne diseases were built by community self-help under Veterinary Department supervision. The Department of Agriculture provided extension advice on animal husbandry. A combination of local cooperatives and the KCC handled the marketing of milk. But still many of these components were separate from one another and subject only to the overall coordination of the president. Though the Veterinary Department advised the president on policies that affected the dairy subsystem as a whole, as did the KCC and the Department of Agriculture, none of them controlled the others.

DAIRY MARKETING

Nonetheless, the sale of smallholder dairy products was greatly facilitated by the structure of the African milk market, the prior existence of the KCC, and the personal interest of Presidents Kenyatta and Moi in the industry. As incomes increased and became shared more broadly after independence, urban demand for milk increased substantially. Between 1968–69 and 1979–80 KCC sales increased by 15 percent per annum.[9] In addition, in those parts of Kenya with high population density many people needed to buy milk because they were landless or had farms that were too small to support enough cattle. In these areas farmers who upgraded the quality of their dairy animals and began to produce a surplus of milk found a ready market in their neighbors for their product at a price that was even better than that being offered by the KCC to European large farmers. When this neighborhood market became saturated, the smallholders could then form a dairy cooperative to cool their milk and market it in the local town, again at a producer price that started above that offered by the KCC. As the demand in this local market was satisfied and prices began to fall, the cooperative, after 1962, could sell its milk to the KCC for marketing in Nairobi or processing into cheese or butter.

As smallholder dairy production expanded, these three tiers overlapped and supported one another. Farmers typically sold the morning's milk to the dairy co-op and used the evening milking to satisfy the needs of their calves, family, and neighbors. The dairy co-op might sell almost all of its milk locally during the dry season, when milk was less abundant, and pass on a substantial surplus to the KCC during the rains.[10] The advantage of this market structure in areas of high population density was that it required very little external support in the early stages of development of the smallholder dairy industry and called for infrastructural investment and organizational skills only when production was already well established in an area. The usual need to have an elaborate and expensive marketing machinery in place for the very first small dairy producers was thus averted.

The importance of this serendipitous marketing structure is best demonstrated in those areas where it did not exist. Those parts of Kenya in which population densities are modest and in which local families supply almost all of their milk needs from their own herds have had great difficulty in getting a modern dairy industry under way; in these areas farmers who invest in high-producing grade animals must immediately sell their surplus outside their neighborhood, at lower prices and with greater organizational difficulties than were experienced by the innovators in the high-density districts.

Important also was the prior existence of the KCC. It had the technology and organizational skills already in place for managing whatever marketable surpluses were generated. The KCC had even established an export market in fresh milk to adjacent African countries and in canned butter farther afield. Marginal investments in dairy-plant and cooling equipment were all that were necessary to build on this strong, already existing organization.

The final component of marketing smallholder milk was presidential support. Milk production has a considerable natural fluctuation between the dry and the rainy season, with supply often falling short of fresh-milk demand when it is dry, and a surplus sometimes having to be turned into subsidized butter for export when it rains. The KCC coped with this problem in the late colonial period by establishing quotas. Farmers who would guarantee to deliver a certain quantity of milk every day, year-round, would be paid for that quota at a higher price. All other milk would be bought for less. The differential between the quota and nonquota prices was quite high and apparently in excess of the costs of dry-season production, since European farmers sold the quotas to one another for significant sums, whereas African smallholders and cooperatives could not afford to buy their way into this lucrative part of the market.

One of Ishmael Muriithi's highest priorities as director of Veterinary Services was the promotion of smallholder dairy production; he saw the existence of the quotas as a significant brake on its development. The KCC was an independent organization, and the Kenya Dairy Board, which was supposed to regulate it, was ineffective. The only way to force a change was through the president, whose directives no cooperative would dare to defy. The path that Muriithi used to reach Kenyatta lay through Geoffrey Kariithi, a secondary-school classmate who was then head of the civil service and one of the president's prime policy advisers. Once Muriithi and James Mburu, the director of Agriculture, were able to persuade Kariithi of the wisdom of a policy change, he would carry it directly to the president. (See plate 22.)

Kenyatta was moody, and one had to raise a request with him at the right moment if it was to have a chance of success. Kariithi, who spent a great deal of time attending to the president, was extremely tactful at choosing propitious moods. Then, once the seeds of an idea were planted, Kenyatta would make further inquiries on his own. He tended to talk to politicians about such policy matters only after he had made up his own mind. The real decision-making process thus generally excluded the elected members of the cabinet from effective consultation, relying more heavily on the civil service.

In June 1970 President Kenyatta abolished the milk quotas, effectively decreeing a substantial increase in milk prices for smallholders. A year later he increased producer prices a further 45 percent and since that date both producer and consumer prices for KCC milk have been set by presidential decree.[11]

These pricing changes led both to a 35 percent jump in milk sold to the KCC and to more than a tripling in seasonal variation. As elementary economic theory would have led one to predict, not only did an improvement in price lead to an increase in supply, but the elimination of the incentive to maintain production in the off-season caused most of the increase to be concentrated in the rainy season, when costs are less.[12] As a consequence, the KCC came under considerable financial pressure. Consumer prices were raised to maintain the viability of the KCC, but it had to struggle to sell enough of the milk it collected in the lucrative, urban fresh-milk market, which underwrote all its operations. Debates raged as to whether the KCC's problems were due to managerial inefficiencies or to the extra costs imposed on it by the price increases and the increased percentage of smaller producers supplying it. In the absence of the kind of comparative information on costs that would be created by having a competitor in the same market, it is extremely difficult to answer this question.[13] The issue was finally removed in 1979 when President Moi introduced a free-milk program for primary-school children, ending the shortfall in demand for the KCC's fresh milk.

The problem in seasonal variation in milk supplies, however, remained. The historical record is unclear, but Muriithi may have achieved more than he intended when Kenyatta abolished the quota system altogether. Better prices for smallholders were needed to increase production, and the quota differentials seem to have been excessive. But some extra incentive was needed to induce farmers to provide more milk in the dry season, when production is both more expensive and difficult. Once the genie of a uniform price was let out of the bottle, however, it was politically difficult to recapture it. Only in 1980 were the pricing experts, with the influence of Harris Mule and Simeon Nyachae, able to get President Moi to agree to the payment of a dry-season-price premium.[14]

Obviously the politics of milk were and are powerful in Kenya. Both President Kenyatta's Kikuyu and President Moi's Kalenjin had the potential to produce significant quantities of milk for sale to the KCC, and they did so. Many members of the matajiri (well-to-do) from these areas came to be deeply involved in dairying, including Kenyatta and Muriithi themselves.

In addition, dairy development, like tea and coffee, offered the possibility of dramatically expanding and strengthening the Kikuyu petty bourgeoisie, thus marginalizing the landless poor, who might oppose the matajiri regime. Pursuit of this policy had dramatic results. By 1983 three-quarters of the farms in Murang'a District in Central Province had at least one grade cow, and only 7 percent lacked a high-value cash crop. Either criteria would have qualified them for membership in the petty bourgeoisie at the time of independence.[15] The leadership's personal interests and the dictates of constituency politics closely coincided.

The two presidents therefore have been extremely attentive to the health of the smallholder dairy industry and have been willing to "tax" urban consumers with higher prices in order to support producer interests. When Muriithi's urgings supported Kikuyu and Kalenjin smallholder dairy interests, they were quickly heard; when his cautions were counter to their immediate benefit, he found it much harder to command presidential attention. The success of the smallholder dairy industry in Kenya owes much both to this configuration of political interests and to the institutional heritage established by European mixed farmers.

ARTIFICIAL INSEMINATION

The existence of a strong market for milk was only one part of the establishment of a smallholder dairy industry. Not only did there have to be demand, there also had to be supply, and this meant genetic improvement of the Kenyan herd. When Muriithi returned to Kenya in 1964 from his studies at Edinburgh, a consensus had already developed that this would involve the upgrading of traditional African Zebu stock through artificial insemination (AI).[16] This was an approach to which Muriithi was already deeply committed, having helped to introduce AI to Kiambu District before he went to Scotland.

Kenya was fortunate in already having the rudiments of a strong AI system in place. Artificial insemination began to be used by European farmers in Kenya in 1935 to stop venereal diseases; the Veterinary Department was involved from the beginning. By the end of World War II the practice was widely accepted in the "White Highlands," so much so that at the time Kenya bragged that it was second only to the Soviet Union in its use of the technique.[17] Artificial insemination reduced the number of bulls that had to be imported from the United States and Europe and thus dramatically lowered the costs of genetic improvement. The Veterinary Department established the Central Artificial Insemination Station (CAIS) outside Nairobi at Kabete in 1946 to collect and prepare semen, thereby cementing its central role in the system.

By 1956 African interest in AI had been piqued, and five African district councils started insemination programs. However, the charges for the service (K.shs. 40 for a pregnancy) were high enough to discourage the interest of many smallholders in such a new and unnatural procedure, and so African adoption of the innovation was slower than was desired.

As soon as Muriithi became deputy director of Veterinary Services in 1965 he became the central Kenyan figure in negotiations with Sweden for assistance with AI. The discussions culminated in 1966 with an agreement for substantial Swedish aid. The compact was an especially happy one. Not only did the Swedes create a particularly effective and efficient AI field system, they also did a good job in the Africanization of its leadership.

The system that was developed is organized around AI "runs." Deep-frozen supplies of semen are kept in district centers, or "schemes." Inseminators then go out in cars every day from these centers, carrying semen in a liquid-nitrogen container. They drive along preset routes, and farmers who wish to have their cows inseminated gather them at small roadside cattle crushes, where the inseminators stop to provide service and collect fees. The system is intensive in its use of capital and management, requiring both reliable vehicles and liquid-nitrogen deep-freezing facilities. But considerable experimentation and careful economic analysis in the early 1970s established that it was superior to the alternatives. In fact, Kenya's AI Service has been judged to be one of the most efficient in the world.[18]

The administrative intensity of this system led to the development of a simple but comprehensive management information system (MIS). Statistics are compiled for each inseminator, run, and scheme on the numbers of inseminations, the number of inseminations necessary to achieve a pregnancy, revenue collections, and the miles of travel and maintenance costs of each vehicle. The head of the AI Service can quickly tell what the costs of an insemination are for each of the many schemes and compare them with its own past performance. These sta-

tistics are used to identify problem areas, field managers, and inseminators.

It might be thought that the administrative intensity of the AI Service
would have proved a source of weakness when the last Swedish advisers
had left. After all, a lack of administrative capacity is frequently cited as
a cause of failure in African rural development programs. Whatever the
general validity of this perception, routine administration has not been
a problem for AI. The management information system (MIS) that was
bequeathed to it has been maintained and used, fees have been collected
and transmitted to headquarters with relatively little corruption, and the
Service works approximately as well as the combination of its commitments and finances would permit at any given moment. Like any organization, AI has its day-to-day administrative problems, but these are
not the source of its difficulties.[19] The head of the Service, Muriithi's
brother Dan Mbogo, is widely seen as a good administrator.

The administrative success of the AI Service is partly a matter of luck
and partly a credit to the way in which the Swedes handled the issues of
Africanization. Muriithi accepted Swedish technical assistance personnel to run the AI system when he signed the aid agreement with them
in 1966. This was not a popular decision. Kenyan African veterinarians,
although modest in number, were eager to be promoted to positions of
administrative leadership as rapidly as possible. Muriithi argued that
there was no point in promoting a Kenyan vet if doing so simply created
a vacancy elsewhere. He decided to keep African vets in the field, where
they had a language advantage in interactions with smallholders, and to
let expatriates remain for a time in headquarters and research positions.

The Swedes understood, however, that expatriates could only be effective in leadership positions for a short time and moved rapidly to
develop their own replacements. Dan Mbogo was assigned to AI in January 1971 shortly after his return from Bulgaria. He had done well in
his studies and was willing to work extremely hard in order to prove his
worth to the British veterinarians in the department, who were skeptical
about his credentials. Mbogo was extremely resentful of the expatriates
in the department; he had a chip on his shoulder. But the Swedes incorporated their senior Kenyan staff in the daily administration of the AI
Service in a way that both trained them and persuaded even Mbogo that
they were serious about leaving. For example, Mbogo understood the
Swedes' MIS well and was using it actively a decade after they left. He
took over management of the Central Artificial Insemination Station
(CAIS) in March 1972 and was put in charge of the AI Service as a whole
in October 1974.

Muriithi was not particularly helpful in these promotions, even
though he was Mbogo's brother. He was anxious to avoid any suspicion

of favoritism. Muriithi even had the post of head of AI downgraded before he let his brother have it. To get promoted Mbogo had to go against Muriithi's wishes and apply to the Public Service Commission for appointment as provincial director of Veterinary Services in Eastern Province, where he remained for 1978 and 1979. Only then was he able to come back in 1980 as the assistant director of Veterinary Services in charge of artificial insemination. In any case, the combination of Mbogo's availability with sensitive Swedish on-the-job training gave AI strong and professional leadership.

When Muriithi's discussions culminated in the 1966 agreement for Swedish aid, they also brought a significant change in government policy. The fees to Africans for AI no longer were to be set on a cost-recovery basis but were to be subsidized in order to spur adoption of the innovation. The charge for AI on a grade animal dropped from K.shs. 40 to K.shs. 10 and for a native Zebu cow to K.shs. 5. At the same time the AI schemes operated by the county (formerly African district) councils were taken over by the Veterinary Department, making the service a national responsibility.[20]

The results of the combination of national commitment, Swedish assistance, and lowered fees were dramatic. Inseminations per year jumped from 162,000 in 1968 to 326,000 in 1971 and finally peaked at 549,000 in 1979. The number increased by 32 percent between 1968 and 1969 alone, and the ambitious targets that the Swedes had set for the project for 1972 were actually exceeded by 8.5 percent, a rare event in rural development.[21]

The extraordinary rates of growth in AI through 1972 were driven in good part by prices. The real returns on milk production available to African farmers increased significantly with Kenyatta's abolition of the KCC quotas and the rise in prices discussed earlier. Added to this was the decision of the cabinet to reduce the fees for AI still further in 1971, bringing the fee to a nearly insignificant K.shs. 1.

This further subsidization of AI services was not sought by Muriithi nor any of the Veterinary staff involved, as far as can be ascertained. Its origins appear to be purely political. Two-thirds of inseminations were being done in Kikuyu areas at the time, and their M.P.s dominated the government.[22] In addition, the minister of agriculture may have calculated that a further price reduction would spur the use of AI in his Embu District constituency. Thus a policy decision to change a national price had a selective impact on the parts of the country where political power was concentrated.

Although Muriithi and the AI staff had not known that this policy change was coming, they were not unhappy with it when it was announced. They correctly saw it as leading to an increase in the demand for AI and in its centrality to the dairy industry. Nevertheless, in the long run AI was hurt by this decision. The Service's dependence on government subsidy reduced its autonomy and made it vulnerable to variations in budgetary largess. The Hopcraft report of 1976 warned the department of the dangers, but unfortunately its release coincided with the start of the coffee boom.[23] Brazil experienced a serious frost in 1975, which damaged its coffee trees and sent the prices for the rest of the world's coffee through the roof for the next few years. No one was prepared to think about the need to cut government subsidies when revenues were so flush.

Another decision that bore on autonomy was left in limbo. The CAIS was given parastatal status when it was created in 1946. This meant that although it was owned and controlled by the government, it had the authority to operate as if it were a private corporation. In this way it could spend the revenues that it earned without their having to be appropriated (budgeted) by Parliament. It also was exempted from many of the government's more stringent civil service and purchasing regulations. Both sets of provisions gave the CAIS considerably greater flexibility. In 1966 Muriithi arranged for the authority of the parastatal body controlling the CAIS to be broadened, and it was renamed the National Artificial Insemination Board.

Nonetheless, AI field services were developed as a part of the Veterinary Department. Furthermore the board was dominated by Veterinary Department appointees and rarely met after 1971. In effect, the entire system operated under the control of Muriithi as the director of Veterinary Services. On a lawyer's advice the Swedes forced the Veterinary Department to assume direct control of the CAIS in January 1972. However, the purchasing procedures that the CAIS then had to follow were a bureaucratic nightmare, and by July it was permitted to revert to its parastatal status. But the legal ambiguities remained. The Hopcraft report of 1976 recommended that the entire AI system (not just the CAIS) be given parastatal status, but this has never been done. If it had been, the system would have had the autonomy to solve several of the personnel and purchasing problems that later plagued it.[24]

These issues of price subsidy and autonomy, however, were not problems during the Kenyatta presidency. Muriithi gained flexibility with the existing mixed and ambiguous legal status of the system. It was easier to funnel subsidies to a part of the civil service than to an autonomous corporation; and the political support for AI was unshakable. Two illustrations will suffice. In 1973–74 Mbiyu Koinange, Kenyatta's minister of state, came to the CAIS to complain about problems with AI in his home area. The visit was handled by Dan Mbogo, who by this time was head of the Station. Mbogo took the opportunity to point out that the Service was having problems because its application to buy vehicles was being blocked by the Treasury, which was stressing short-term economizing at the expense of long-term efficiencies. Koinange carried the matter to the president, and the Treasury instantly authorized the purchase of thirty-five cars.

Again, at the end of the 1976–77 financial year the AI Service ran out of the budgeted funds that it needed to continue operations, and the permanent secretary (PS) to the Ministry of Agriculture ordered it to stop operations. It would have been poor form and perhaps costly in the long run for Muriithi to go behind the back of his immediate superior and appeal his decision to higher authority. But he did demand that the PS put his order in writing. Dan Mbogo then wrote a circular to his field staff instructing them to shut down and hand their car keys to their district commissioners when their funds ran out. This indirect tactic brought the matter to the attention of Geoffrey Kariithi, the head of the civil service, who called the PS, countermanded his order, and told him to let the Service overspend its budget. Muriithi and Mbogo knew that AI was an essential service to the Kikuyu smallholder and that the politically powerful would never call a bluff that could harm them. They saw no reason to worry about its financial future.

This political context influenced the way Muriithi and Mbogo handled demands for new AI runs. From the very beginning over half of the animals inseminated by the Service were in Central Province; if one includes the settlement areas, probably two-thirds of the cows served were Kikuyu owned. This rendered the Service invulnerable during the Kenyatta presidency, but such gross regional and ethnic disparity was politically embarrassing. Muriithi, Mbogo, and the Swedes felt themselves under pressure to widen the areas served, and their plans regularly called for more rapid expansion outside Central Province than within it. Unfortunately, however, farmer utilization of the new runs consistently has been much higher in Central and Eastern Provinces than in the rest of the country. (As was discussed above with regard to marketing, population density appears to be the major factor accounting for the success of dairy production based on grade cattle, and thereby for the utilization of AI.) Plan targets have been missed in these other areas, often by wide margins, while Central Province met or came close to its projections. The Central Province proportion of inseminated animals continued to climb slowly upward.[25]

As Kikuyus, both Muriithi and Mbogo were vulnerable to charges of ethnic bias in their management of AI. Their response was to draw up and approve ambitious expansion plans for the various areas of the country with dairy potential and then to shelve them pending funding. When a politician demanded AI for his or her constituency, Muriithi and Mbogo could respond that they had been ready to provide it for years and that they only needed the politician to secure the necessary financing. Many schemes have been opened because of political or donor interest, not because of a calculation of their likelihood of success.

The combination of the Service's political responsiveness and the variability in farmer acceptance of AI results in extreme regional differences in the utilization of runs. The costs of an insemination run are determined by (1) the quantity and quality of the road system, and (2) the density of the inseminated-cow population. Thus the regional variations in utilization translate directly into large disparities in costs. In 1979 the average field expenses per insemination in Central Province were literally one-fifth those for the coast. A Swedish evaluation team attributed the 10 percent rise in average real costs of AI between 1975 and 1979 both to unavoidable increases in vehicle operating expenses and to seven new, high-cost schemes. In other respects the efficiency of the Service had improved in these years, with inseminators carrying a 14 percent heavier load.[26]

Political considerations therefore introduced cost inefficiencies into what was otherwise a tightly managed system. The contrast with the KTDA is striking here. Karanja was under similar pressures to expand the area under tea in ways that would have hurt efficiency. He resisted, both because the costs would have hurt producers directly and because he could defend his actions with an "objective" colonial study. Neither of these two conditions applied to AI. In the 1970s these inefficiencies seemed an insignificant price to pay for the overall effectiveness of the Service. Financing them was not the most important problem; it would be much more troublesome in the 1980s.

VETERINARY CARE

The third leg on which smallholder dairy production rests is veterinary care. Grade cows, which are derived from European pedigree stock, are more vulnerable to many African cattle diseases than are the local Zebu stock. Although they are much more productive, they lack the genetic resistance that the local animals have built up by "survival of the fittest" in a hostile environment. They need more careful medical attention if they are to survive in Africa. Furthermore, because they are more productive and thus more valuable, it is economical to treat health problems in grade cattle that simply are accepted as an inevitable hazard for Zebu cattle.

Paralleling the terminology that is used for human medicine, we can distinguish between veterinary services that are curative, preventive, and promotive. The first deal with diseases by curing those animals that have already contracted them. The second prevent the occurrence of disease through the administration of sera, drugs, vaccines, and so forth. The animal and its manager are passive recipients of these treatments; they need neither to understand nor to apply them. Promotive measures inhibit disease and improve productivity through changes in management practices, with the stockkeeper needing to be active and to understand something of what he is doing. Although the curative, preventive, and promotive aspects of veterinary medicine are integrally related, the organizational dynamics associated with their delivery are quite different.[27]

The early work of the Veterinary Department in Kenya was concerned almost exclusively with prevention. Extremely serious epizootics (animal epidemics), such as rinderpest, blackwater fever, anthrax, and foot-and-mouth, had to be brought under control. This is done through a combination of mass inoculations and quarantines separating infected from uncontaminated areas. All veterinary departments consider prevention their first priority; many African countries provide nothing else. The available benefit/cost calculations indicate that this priority is entirely appropriate.[28] By the time of its independence Kenya had succeeded in controlling these epizootic diseases in the areas where dairy production is appropriate and had quarantines around those that remained in the pastoralist beef-producing zones. In the realm of prevention Muriithi's task was largely one of maintaining the department's already considerable accomplishments.

Tick-borne diseases remained the most significant barrier to smallholder dairy production. East Coast fever in particular is usually fatal for grade cattle, which have none of the genetic resistance of Zebu stock. The only way to prevent it is to eliminate the ticks that bear it. This requires regular spraying of the animal or dipping it in acaricide. Shortly after independence the Veterinary Department began to encourage community groups to build and operate dips. Donors were recruited to help with these self-help efforts, and dip construction became a popular activity in those parts of Kenya where dairy production with grade cows was gaining momentum.[29] Muriithi played a personal role in their encouragement in his home district. These self-help dips made smallholder ownership of grade cows possible and played a significant part in the expansion of milk production. Nonetheless, problems with their management sometimes occurred. This led to the department's gradually taking over the operation of many of them in the late 1970s, a development to be discussed in the next chapter.

The other serious gap in veterinary care concerned curative services, which were all but nonexistent in the smallholder areas. Muriithi devoted a major part of his efforts to filling this hole. In the colonial period veterinarians had been concentrated in the White Highlands, where private practitioners provided most curative services. Independence had brought the departure of many of these white veterinarians from both government and private practice, leaving the country with a significant shortage. In addition, smallholders could not afford private veterinarian fees at the time, because of the still nascent commercialization of their part of the dairy industry and because of the expensive pattern of service that had been established for the White Highlands.

Muriithi attacked this problem on several fronts at once. First, into the early 1970s he discouraged the remaining European veterinarians from leaving the country, permitted them to continue to hold headquarters and research positions, and concentrated his small number of African veterinarians in field positions, where they could interact with smallholders. He could see no point in Africanization if it meant a decrease in veterinary services for the country. This decision was both courageous and costly. Many of his African colleagues resented his holding them back from the prized leadership positions held by the European veterinarians.

Second, Muriithi pressed for a doubling of the veterinary faculty at the University of Nairobi at Kabete, where he had been trained initially himself. The expansion was requested in 1968 and was fully achieved in the mid-1970s. As a consequence, the number of veterinarians in government employ climbed from 80 in 1972 to 235 in 1980.[30] Furthermore, Muriithi was able to achieve this leap in the numbers of veterinarians without compromising his high standards for the profession.

Third, as a stopgap measure, government veterinarians, whose duties were mainly in the area of prevention, were authorized to engage in private curative practice after office hours. Although such a policy is frequent among poor Commonwealth nations,[31] Muriithi and his colleagues found it unsatisfying. Disease-control activities were often neglected, and it embarrassed their sense of professional ethics for a government officer to pocket money for a service without providing an official receipt. The conflicts of interest were too great.

This uneasiness contributed to Muriithi's fourth and major policy thrust, the creation of a separate government clinical service. Clinical centers were to be put in areas with a high density of grade cattle but no private veterinarians. These clinics would be staffed with a veterinarian and support staff. Most of the curative work would be done by driving along preset runs and meeting the farmers and their animals at the AI roadside crushes. The combination of paraprofessional support staff and treating the cattle on the runs, rather than going on call to individual farms, would economize on transport and the veterinarian's time and render curative care affordable for smallholders. It was planned that once a practice had been established in an area, it would be taken over by a private veterinarian, and government would step back from curative services there.[32]

The basic policy decision to proceed with clinical centers was made in 1968, and by 1971 Muriithi had succeeded in getting five northern European donors to fund the program fully. The first center became operational in 1974, and the last of the planned eighteen came on line in 1976, together with the four Veterinary Investigation Laboratories that support them.

The availability of curative veterinary medicine to smallholder dairy producers was improved significantly by the program. Unfortunately, however, the combination of donor pressures and political demand undid some of what Muriithi had hoped to accomplish with the clinical centers. During the 1970s donors were preoccupied with reaching the poorest producers and were hostile to private enterprise. The fees that were set for clinical services subsidized drugs as well as the veterinarian's time, whereas drugs had previously been sold at cost. The leap to private practice was made greater, not smaller. When the issue of privatization was broached in 1977, the government was flush with coffee-boom revenues, and the politicians wanted an expansion of public curative services instead. Many of the remaining private practitioners went out of business because of public competition in this period. These pressures accelerated in the early years of the Moi presidency.

The one area in which Kenya clearly failed in these years was promotive veterinary medicine—helping farmers better their animal management. Improper care and feeding of animals often leads to disease, and improvement in management is frequently as important as genetic improvement in increasing milk production.[33] Veterinarians were felt to be too overcome with the professional priority given to preventive medicine and with the profits to be made in curative medicine to give promotive issues adequate attention. Thus in 1969 the several Veterinary Department promotive endeavors were taken away from it, and extension on management issues was made the purview of the Animal Husbandry Division in the Department of Agriculture, where it was a neglected stepchild.

Throughout the British Commonwealth there is an administrative and social distance between veterinarians, on the one hand, and crops and animal husbandry personnel, on the other.[34] This was symbolized in Kenya by the location of the Veterinary Department headquarters at Kabete, on the outskirts of Nairobi, well away from the other government offices, and the refusal of Muriithi as director of Veterinary Services even to have an office at the Ministry of Agriculture, of which it was a part. Given this distance, there was little prospect that animal husbandry extension could be done effectively through the paraprofessional staff members of the Veterinary Department, who were preoccupied with preventive and curative tasks. This left Animal Husbandry with the choice of building its own extension service or cooperating in the use of the general agriculture one. The Range Management Division, which provides advice to pastoralists in areas in which both veterinary and crops personnel are relatively scarce, was able to build its own cadre of agents. To those in charge of the ministry, however, such a course seemed a foolish duplication of resources for Animal Husbandry, which advised dairy producers in regions in which the general extension staff already was strong. The head of the division was nonetheless determined to have his own field presence and for years blocked cooperative ventures in his determination to achieve it. The quality of the management of Kenya's smallholder dairy herd has suffered from this unresolved battle.

WHAT OF INTEGRATION?

For smallholder dairy production to reach its full potential in an area, roads, markets for milk, extension, artificial insemination, preventive and curative veterinary services should all be in place. An approach that integrates these components administratively and assures their simultaneous presence therefore would appear to be highly desirable. Yet Kenya achieved a spectacular growth in milk production without such integration: roads fell to the Ministry of Works; marketing, to the Kenya Cooperative Creameries (KCC) and the Ministry of Cooperatives; extension, to the Department of Agriculture. Only AI and veterinary care were integrated by the Veterinary Department. Was this simply luck? Or is administrative integration sometimes less important than it would superficially appear to be?

To answer this question it is useful to distinguish between components that have an "additive" rather than an "interactive" effect on production and between "minimal" and "incremental" levels of service. When two components of a production program interact to make each other viable, their simultaneous appearance is imperative. For example, AI depends on the existence of dips to control tick-borne disease; otherwise the grade calves will die. Similarly, dipping makes only marginal economic sense when introduced just for the protection of the traditional Zebu stock in East Africa. The two production components thus have an interactive effect. Other services that are only additive in their effects may be highly desirable, but need not be introduced together to have an impact. For example, curative veterinary medicine and improved cattle-management practices both lead to increased milk output, but much of their effects are independent. It is not essential that they be present together or in a particular sequence. Integration is more important for components that have an interactive effect than for those that are only additive.

Similarly, minimal levels of some components are necessary to make a crop or some other production-enhancing component viable. For example, since coffee was not consumed locally in Kenya, a mechanism for marketing it internationally had to be in place prior to farmers' being encouraged to grow it. In the same vein, grade cattle will die without tick control. An industry can survive only after minimal levels of service for its various essential components are established. After that point, further incremental improvements in these components will help the profitability of the crop, but so will increments of other components that were not essential and on which the very existence of the industry therefore never depended. Thus, enhancements in an adequate but imperfect dipping program for tick control and extension on herd management practices (which has no essential minimum) would be alternative incremental contributions to a dairy industry. Integration is more important in achieving the simultaneous presence of the essential minimum level of components than it is for incremental improvements.

Happily for the establishment of a smallholder dairy industry in Kenya, most of the components that have an interactive effect on production had already reached the essential minimum level of service. Local and national milk markets were in place, as were the roads to connect them; and epizootic diseases were under control. All that was needed to make the industry take off was the interaction of genetic improvement (by AI) and tick control. The domains within which simultaneous improvements were needed were therefore limited. This was not just luck. Such a situation is common for crops that are domestically consumed, typically foods. Export commodities demand more integration.

For the all-important interaction between genetic improvement and tick control, integration was provided by the farmers themselves. In the densely populated areas it was sufficiently obvious to farmers that milk sold well, that genetically improved stock were significantly more productive, and that European cattle died without dipping; so they were ready to build dips with only a little encouragement. Other enhancements to production were subsequently made in milk prices, in curative veterinary care, and in improved dipping, and it would have been desirable to have still others in animal husbandry advice. But these components were additive and incremental, not interactive or essential. They added to the attractiveness and growth of the dairy industry, but its survival did not depend on them.

It is one thing to say that integration was not essential, but another to say that it would not have been desirable. Here a weighing of costs and benefits is needed. A single administrative authority would have been able to take up the multiple components of highly productive dairying as they made economic sense, extend the industry into new areas, have the autonomy that comes from self-financing, and command the political visibility necessary to have its policy requirements met. This is what the National Dairy Development Board has done in India.[35]

What disadvantages would have obtained if the Kenya Cooperative Creameries (KCC) and the Kenya Dairy Board (KDB) had played a similar role? First, it would have led to a neglect of other aspects of animal production. The preventive and curative services of the Veterinary Department and Animal Husbandry extension agents also work on the production of beef, sheep, goats, pork, and poultry. An integration that might have enhanced the delivery of these components for dairying would have made it more difficult to coordinate them with other industries.

Second, the KCC or KDB probably would have neglected important parts of the dairy industry more than has been the case with existing arrangements. Only 20 to 40 percent of the country's milk production is marketed through formal channels.[36] An agency that incorporated marketing in its charge would have concentrated on those producers who sold the largest amount of their milk in the formal system and would have neglected those who were producing for themselves and their neighbors. Integration therefore could have slowed the shift of the dairy industry from large farms to smallholders.

Third, the KCC or KDB probably would have tried to undermine the highly efficient local markets that already existed in Kenya. An integrated agency would have been under pressure to finance a large part of its services to producers out of its sales revenues. To do so it would have had to force milk out of the informal markets and into its formal monopoly. The alternatives that would have promoted the widest spread of services with the least controls—financing by fees or general taxes— would have been less likely.

Fourth, once the industry was subject to a single, integrating agency, its health and survival would depend on the management of that one entity, which would have monopoly powers. At present, the failings of any one of the additive, incremental components of dairy production are often compensated by other components, some of which are provided by private entrepreneurs. The present structure, despite its many imperfections, weakens the controls exercised by the state and increases the ability of the farmers to find multiple solutions to their production problems themselves. Furthermore, in an unintegrated industry the several government agencies that serve it are likely to criticize one another's performance and increase the chances of public accountability. The Veterinary Department, for example, has been a source of informed criticism of the KCC.

Finally, it is not clear that a single agency would have had any greater political effectiveness than the existing structure has. It could hardly have done better than the Veterinary Department did under President Kenyatta. The fate of other parastatals, such as the Kenya Meat Commission, suggests that an integrating agency's ability to prosper in the Moi years would have depended on its being free of the need for government subsidies.[37] Given both the interrelationship between dairying and the other livestock industries and the importance of the informal market for milk, it is unlikely that such financial autonomy actually would have been achieved. It is interesting that a preliminary move toward greater integration and control of the dairy industry was defeated by political pressure from farmers in 1967.[38]

An administratively integrated approach to crop development can be effective in many circumstances, as the historical record demonstrates.[39] However, the conditions that obtained in the dairy industry are common for food production in countries that have passed the initial stages of market development. The creation of an agricultural sector with the flexibility to meet changing market conditions requires that the farmers themselves have the ability to choose among production components and to recombine them in ways that meet new problems and opportunities. Administrative integration frequently inhibits that flexibility. Certainly integration is not a prerequisite to further development of food crops *once the first stages of commercialization have been passed.*

BEEF PRODUCTION

Some attention is appropriate here on the impact of the Veterinary Department on beef production as well, for it absorbed much of Muriithi's energies. The economics of beef make curative veterinary care a smaller issue and prevention a bigger one. Kenyan meat is produced both by pastoralists on the open range and by large ranchers in what were formerly areas of white settlement. The livestock of the former generally have undergone little genetic improvement from the traditional Zebu and are sold in local and regional markets. Curative veterinary service is generally uneconomic for this production system. In contrast, the ranchers' stock has been developed from European breeds and is of an internationally marketable quality. Curative care is more economic for these cattle, although it still is not as important as it is for dairy animals.

Both production systems require protection from epizootic diseases. (Recall the decimation of East African herds that was caused by rinderpest at the end of the last century.) The Veterinary Department is aggressive and effective in its preventive work. However, Kenyan livestock are subject to constant reinfection from the pools of disease in neighboring countries with less extensive veterinary services. This problem is exacerbated by the constant movement of pastoralist herds back and forth across these international boundaries. The economic implications of reinfection are greater for the ranchers than they are for the pastoralists for two reasons: (1) their animals are more valuable; (2) their stock could potentially be sold in lucrative international markets from which it would be banned if there were any danger of infection, particularly from foot-and-mouth disease.

Muriithi undertook to deal with the differential importance of epizootic infection for these two production systems by creating a disease-free zone around the ranchers. A buffer zone was legally established, and livestock from outside it (generally owned by pastoralists) could pass through only after being held in quarantine and undergoing inspection.

Muriithi saw that Kenya would be able to realize extra returns from its investment in the disease-free zones and export carcasses to Europe if it was able to convince the rest of the world that it was keeping the areas completely uninfected. A tough-minded, highly professional veterinary service was an essential marketing asset. Muriithi was critical in maintaining its worth. The quality of his performance as a student at Edinburgh, his evident deep professionalism, his conservative commitment to standards, and his personal integrity were all needed to convince the ever cautious veterinary directors in Europe that they could safely import beef that the Kenyan Veterinary Service had certified. Muriithi's service in a number of international veterinary organizations was part of his projection of the necessary image.

A further part of the preparations for the export of fresh meat was the transfer of meat inspection from the Ministry of Health to the Veterinary Department to put Kenya in conformity with international practice. Muriithi got the change through the cabinet in 1969, began training the necessary staff in 1970, had the enabling legislation passed by Parliament in 1972, and set up the new division immediately.

Muriithi then presented the concept of a disease-free zone to the International Organization for Epizootics (OIE), which regulates the international movement of livestock. One of the OIE's stipulations is that fresh meat and livestock cannot be exported to an uninfected country from a country that has had an incidence of foot-and-mouth disease in the last two years. According to a colleague, Muriithi "argued that some countries in Europe are quite small. It was not reasonable to ask a whole country in Africa to be disease free. If an area is as large as some countries and can be proved to be disease free, it should be allowed to export." An OIE team inspected Kenya in late 1972 and agreed that its disease-free zone could be accepted. Thereafter Switzerland began to allow Kenya to send it fresh beef. Its decision was based on the personal confidence its director of Veterinary Services had in Muriithi.

Maintenance of the disease-free zone was difficult, however. Livestock prices were higher inside it because of the privileged access to market that it brought. The temptations to evade the quarantine were high. Presidential intervention was often necessary to stop smuggling by the influential. For example, on one occasion Kenyatta personally had to admonish an assistant commissioner of police from bringing animals illegally into the zone, which he had been doing in police vehicles. Muriithi's access to the president through Kariithi was essential to get the necessary support.

Nonetheless, there were too many incentives for too many people to use influence or bribes to evade the quarantine. Kenya was unable to maintain Switzerland's standards and could not export to it after 1977. But Greece and other nations continue to use beef from the disease-free zone. The initiative has borne some fruit.

CONCLUSIONS

Smallholder dairy production underwent spectacular growth in Kenya between 1966 and 1978, and Ishmael Muriithi was closely associated with many of the developments that were responsible for this achievement. He successfully lobbied the president for the end of milk delivery quotas and thus made the higher price milk market available to African producers. He negotiated the aid agreement with Sweden that extended artificial insemination to smallholders and permitted the genetic improvement of their dairy herds. His brother, Dan Mbogo, became the respected and effective manager of this well-administered system. Muriithi also did an unusually fine job of obtaining donor finance for a major expansion in the Veterinary Department's curative services to small dairy herds and oversaw a significant increase in the numbers of well-qualified Kenyan veterinarians. All of these activities contributed significantly to the quality and profitability of smallholder dairy production. In a parallel set of activities, Muriithi facilitated the sale of Kenyan beef in the lucrative European market by tightening the Veterinary Department's disease-control quarantine system. Throughout the 1970s the department was well administered and operated without scandal. The latter was no small accomplishment when one considers the considerable value of the drugs and acaricides that it handled.

Muriithi was successful because he understood the ways in which his department's services could support small dairy producers and relentlessly pursued opportunities to expand them at a low cost to farmers.

His access, through his friendship with the head of the civil service, to a president who shared these commitments was essential to his accomplishments. His commitment to conservative professional standards and personal integrity both helped to maintain them in his department and gave him a high standing in the world veterinary and donor communities. This reputation made him effective in international negotiations and secured additional markets and resources for Kenya. But it also earned him the criticism of some of his African colleagues, who felt that he slowed down the Africanization of the department. Certainly he had his faults, and other Kenyan veterinarians should share in the credit for what was accomplished in these years. On balance, his term as director of Veterinary Services under President Kenyatta was an effective and eventful one.

Nonetheless, Muriithi's role as an individual, like that of Karanja at the KTDA, must be seen within the context of a favorable configuration of interests and institutions. Smallholder dairy production disproportionately favored a broad spectrum of Kikuyus and therefore fit neatly into Kenyatta's strategy for maintaining the unity of his ethnic political base. Dairying also is central to the farm production of Moi's Kalenjin. Consequently, both presidents were extremely responsive to suggestions that producer prices be increased and that the supply and subsidy of government inputs be expanded. In contrast, the Kikuyu are largely consumers rather than producers of beef, and many matajiri are able to make substantial profits by evading government controls on this subsector. Thus Kenyatta permitted real beef prices to stay low and was less supportive of strict application of the measures that are necessary for success in this part of the livestock industry.

The institutional heritage of European livestock production was extremely helpful also. The basic organizations and practices that were necessary to African participation in the industry were already in place. They had only to be expanded and their focus altered. In the densely populated areas African smallholders already were selling milk to their neighbors; the British had created the Kenya Cooperative Creameries and the Kenya Meat Commission for urban and international markets; the central infrastructure for artificial insemination had been built previously; and the procedures for veterinary care in this tropical environment had been established. Muriithi's energy and vision expanded these components and pressed them into the service of new ends, but the institutionalized patterns were there already.

Kenya was able to accomplish its impressive expansion in smallholder dairy production without the existence of a single integrating agency managing the dairy industry. This was feasible because the commercialization of peasant agriculture had already begun, and the components that were minimally necessary to launch such an initiative were largely in place. It was possible to enhance production through incremental improvements that did not depend heavily on interaction effects for their impact. We argued that integration is generally needed when production-enhancing components are strongly interactive or have not yet reached the minimal levels necessary for commercial production. But integration's administrative problems make it counterproductive when components are only additive and incremental. An incidental benefit of the lack of integration was that dairymen were free of the controls that crop authorities in Kenya usually impose on farmers "in their own interests." Producers gained a valuable flexibility to respond to changing market conditions and opportunities in animal husbandry.

CHAPTER EIGHT

The Moi Presidencies
and Their Impact
on Karanja and Muriithi

THE SUCCESSION

President Jomo Kenyatta died on August 22, 1978, and Vice-President Daniel arap Moi, a Kalenjin, succeeded him. An era had ended, and not all were happy at the way the new one was beginning. The Kikuyu's matajiri leadership believed that it was necessary to provide differential benefits to their ethnic group if its workers and peasants were not to split from them along class lines. Such favoritism required Kikuyu control of the presidency.

At least some Kikuyu had been prepared to take drastic action to achieve that end: When Tom Mboya seemed the heir apparent to Kenyatta in 1969, he was assassinated. Immediately thereafter the Kikuyu engaged in mass oathing, pledging to keep the presidency among their number. The Gikuyu, Embu, Meru Association (GEMA) was founded in 1971 to consolidate the political power of these three closely related peoples. J. M. Kariuki was assassinated in 1975 when his populist campaign for the succession threatened to open up the much-feared class schism among the Kikuyu. And in 1976 a move was made to change the constitution to prevent the vice-president, who was Daniel arap Moi, from becoming president on the death of Kenyatta.

Other Kikuyu politicians, however, felt that it would provoke unnecessary ethnic strife to have another Kikuyu president. Apparently they believed either that the Kikuyu had already gained sufficient advantage and would continue to prosper under equal treatment, or that they could render Moi a figurehead president. Whatever their motives, Mwai Kibaki, then minister of finance and an M.P. from Nyeri, and Charles Njonjo, the attorney general and an ex officio M.P. from Kiambu, opposed the change in the constitution. In the end, Kenyatta also sup-ported the status quo, and Daniel arap Moi succeeded him.

Moi's presidency was quickly confirmed by election, as the constitu-tion required. His candidacy was uncontested; in Africa voters are rarely allowed to determine who will be head of state. In any case, elec-tion to the president's office does not guarantee that one will continue to occupy it on a continent where coups have been rife. It is widely be-lieved that a plot to prevent Moi's succession to the presidency was aborted only by the circumstances of Kenyatta's death.* Moi faced a po-litically mobilized and nervous Kikuyu who also dominated the officer corps of the armed forces and police.

To consolidate his position, Moi declared that his was a "nyayo" gov-ernment, that is, that he was following in the "footsteps" of Kenyatta. He nominated Mwai Kibaki to the vice-presidency and kept him as his minister of finance. Charles Njonjo was retained as attorney general and was subsequently made minister for constitutional affairs. Almost all Kikuyu (and other) politicians and senior civil servants were able to re-tain their positions.

While stressing continuity, Moi created an era of good feeling by re-leasing all political detainees, assembling a broad multiethnic coalition, and instituting popular new government programs. Free milk for school children was one of them. In 1978 and 1979 satisfaction with the Nyayo government seemed virtually universal. Meanwhile, Charles Njonjo emerged as the leader of Moi's political supporters and orchestrated gradually increasing pressure on those Kikuyu politicians who had been most prominent in GEMA and in the movement to change the consti-tution. A leader of both had been Njenga Karume, who had been Charles Karanja's friend and immediate neighbor in Limuru until 1974.

BUREAUCRATIC POWER UNDER THE NEW REGIME

Daniel arap Moi's election to Kenya's highest office changed the power relationships between the presidency and the public service in impor-tant ways. If we apply the Weberian model for analyzing administrative power (see figure 5.2), we can see that Moi was in a much weaker posi-tion than Kenyatta was in dealing with his civil service.

---

*For all of the foregoing, see Joseph Karimi and Philip Ochieng, *The Kenyatta Succession* (Nairobi: Transafrica, 1980). They present the documentary evidence for an anti-Moi plot, but it seems strange that the plan was so easily foiled and that most of those who were behind it continued to live in Kenya afterward. It is conceivable that release of this "infor-mation" was designed to throw off balance those who opposed Moi and to consolidate the power of those who supported him. Either scenario points to the insecurity of Moi's posi-tion.

Of course, on matters of class interest the political elite and the bureaucracy stood together. Both favored a situation in which the lower classes were accommodated through patron-client networks while the direct interests of the matajiri, and to a lesser extent the petty bourgeoisie, received primacy. This led naturally to intense competition among patrons for the resources they needed to maintain the loyalty of their clients.

Thus with regard to ethnic and regional interests neither the elective nor the administrative leadership was united. At the start of his presidency Moi's governing coalition was much broader than Kenyatta's had been. Although the core of his support came from his own Kalenjin group, Moi relied on backing from prominent politicians from virtually every Kenyan ethnic group, including the factions of the Kikuyu headed by Njonjo and Kibaki. Whereas the Kenyatta "inner cabinet" had presented a united front that favored the Kikuyu on issues of regional distribution, Moi's political circle was divided and incorporated most of Kenya's ethnic conflicts.

The bureaucracy was similarly divided, but the police, much of the armed forces, and a number of key ministries were led by Kikuyus who had exercised considerable power on behalf of the president under Kenyatta. Moi confronted a group of public managers whose implicit interests on regional matters were quite different from his own and who controlled a significant amount of the "means of administration."

First, they dominated the air force and held a plurality of the senior ranks in the army.[1] The presumed British military guarantee of Kenya's elected leadership seems to have lapsed, so Moi had to treat a coup as a real possibility if he pushed the Kikuyu too far.

Second, the senior Kikuyu civil servants had enough political support to make it difficult to remove them without "cause." These men commanded considerable expertise and information by virtue of their long tenure in office. This same seniority gave them a "manifest" qualification for their positions, which many of their non-Kikuyu competitors lacked and which considerably diminished Moi's discretion in making appointments. Whereas Kenyatta had had a decision maker in whom he had personal confidence in virtually every public organization that was important to him, Moi quite frequently had to rely on men with whom he had no strong ties and some of whom he distrusted.

Third, the period of rapid upward mobility in the civil service, and the easy access of bureaucrats to new farms and businesses, was largely over. Moi could not reward his public servants for their support as richly as Kenyatta had done.

Moi, however, had his own bases of political support. The personal fortunes of civil servants were still subject to some presidential discretion, and the Kenyan political culture had come to give precedence to the president in matters of public policy. Bureaucrats would not dare to oppose his wishes openly nor to directly subvert them. A failure to take initiative on behalf of his presumed intentions, and a lack of enthusiasm or creativity in implementing his policies, was as far as a civil servant would consider it safe to go. The balance of power still favored the political leadership (in the person of President Moi), as it does in virtually all systems. But the balance had shifted closer to an equilibrium than is healthy for policy effectiveness. The danger was less one of bureaucratic subversion than one of policy stalemate.*

The result of this constellation of political and administrative power was indeed often a managerial deadlock. Many organizations were headed by men who lacked the confidence of the president, who could not get his support for the policy changes that were needed to keep their programs healthy, and who could not force such changes themselves. The magnitude of this problem was not immediately evident. The political centrality of Njonjo and the continuation of Kibaki as minister of finance gave the impression of greater continuity than actually existed. Moi had no desire to provoke the Kikuyu into unity against him. He was prepared to let the old Kikuyu managerial elite continue in office until, individual by individual, it retired or disgraced itself and could be replaced. The only visible signs of change were that the Office of the President intruded much more into the details of implementation, reversing much of Kenyatta's delegation, and that Kikuyu managers often did not find the presidency as responsive to their policy needs as it had been.

KARANJA'S FALL FROM GRACE

Charles Karanja's relationship to the presidency had changed dramatically with the death of Kenyatta. Not only did he have a non-Kikuyu president, but he had been friends with Njenga Karume, who had been one of the leaders of the anti-Moi movement. His position was complicated further when he decided to back Ngengi Muigai for the Gatundu seat in Parliament that was vacated by Kenyatta's death. An ally of Njonjo's was also standing for the seat. Mwai Kibaki supported Muigai as well, but Njonjo had already positioned himself closer to Moi than had the vice-president. As the constituency encompassed Karanja's place of birth, and as he had always been generous in his donations to self-help

*A similar situation in the French Fourth Republic is described by Alfred Diamant, "The French Administrative System: The Republic Passes But the Administration Remains," in *Toward the Comparative Study of Public Administration*, ed. W. Siffin (Bloomington: Indiana University Press, 1957), and "Tradition and Innovation in French Administration," *Comparative Political Studies* 1, no. 2 (1968).

activities in the area, his political influence was significant. Early in the campaign Karanja received signals from Njonjo that public opposition to his candidate would be unwelcome. Karanja underestimated the danger and did not back off.

Karanja did not understand the extent to which his managerial position had changed. He felt that the tremendous success of the KTDA and his outstanding record in managing it rendered him invulnerable. He expected to be judged solely on the basis of his service to the nation and did not foresee how more active political support could be important to him.

In early 1978 the KTDA had taken over the packaging and distribution of tea for the Kenyan market. The beverage is a staple for African households. Its domestic retail price is regulated by the government, and when the international price of tea is high there can be a substantial disparity between the two. In 1977, for example, the local price of tea was only 39 percent of the world figure. In effect, tea producers subsidized Kenyan mass consumption. To assure that this burden was shared equally, all tea producers were required to contribute a portion of their output to a "pool," which ran a blending and packaging plant and sold the tea throughout the country. Since the colonial period this had been run by Brooke Bond Liebig, a multinational firm, which had been Kenya's largest producer.[2]

When the KTDA surpassed Brooke Bond in size in 1977, Karanja decided to challenge its management of domestic sales. His motives were two. First, this part of the market was losing income for tea growers, and Karanja wanted to assure that it was run efficiently and that the burden of its implicit subsidy was equally distributed. His second but unstated objective was to gain experience in retail packaging and sales, laying the groundwork for the KTDA's possible eventual entry into international retailing.

There was intense opposition to the KTDA's assumption of these functions. The representatives of its major financiers, the Commonwealth Development Corporation and the World Bank, argued that such an expansion in the KTDA's mission would strain it unduly, but Karanja overruled them. More seriously, Brooke Bond saw the takeover of its packaging plant as nationalization and feared that it might be a prelude to the nationalization of all its Kenyan operations. British political pressure was applied on behalf of Brooke Bond, and the negotiations were intense. Karanja prevailed regardless, and the Kenya Tea Packers, Ltd. (KETEPA), was formed in 1978 under KTDA control.

Despite the turmoil, the takeover went smoothly. Karanja appointed a Kalenjin to run the packaging plant in Kericho, thereby protecting himself from the charge of tribalism that could have followed if he had sent a Kikuyu to run an operation in Kalenjin territory. The commission that KETEPA charged for its services fell to 4 percent from the 7.5 percent that Brooke Bond had collected, and the price it was able to pay the producers for their tea increased.

Trouble was brewing with the tea, nonetheless. This was the period of the coffee boom, and international tea prices had been pulled dramatically upward as well. Packaged tea on the shop shelves in neighboring Ethiopia, for example, sold for twice what it did in Kenya, owing to the price controls that were being administered through KETEPA. The temptations for smuggling were irresistible, and packaged tea began to be scarce in Kenya. Since tea is basic to the Kenyan diet, a political crisis was in the making.

In August President Kenyatta died, passing responsibility for the welfare of the average citizen to Daniel arap Moi. Karanja was urged to ease the shortage by releasing more KTDA tea to KETEPA for packaging. He did increase the amount by 10 percent but declined to add more, arguing that "you can't fill a bucket with no bottom."[3]

Then, in early December, Stanley Oloitipitip, the minister of home affairs, publicly lamented that smuggling had caused a shortage of tea in his constituency and called on the government to rectify the situation.[4] Karanja lost his temper. Oloitipitip had written to him to secure a tea distributorship in his constituency for "an associate firm of mine" in July,[5] so Karanja informed the press that Oloitipitip was a distributor, suggesting that since the distributors had received their normal allotments of tea plus 10 percent, they were the ones best placed to deal with any smuggling-induced shortages. "We are not accusing anybody of anything. But the distributors . . . should now tell the public where all the tea has gone."[6] Oloitipitip countered by denying that he was a distributor. His political ally Charles Njonjo then intimated in a public rally that a KTDA official was responsible for smuggling.[7]

Karanja prepared his rebuttal to this personal attack carefully. The KTDA hired private detectives to find out where the tea was going. They intercepted a shipment at the airport, and Karanja went to the head of the civil service, Geoffrey Kariithi, with the evidence. Although Kariithi was able to trace the source of the smuggled consignment, he declined to give Karanja the name of the party (presumably for reasons of state). Nonetheless, Karanja proceeded to announce a televised press conference, at which he planned to present his evidence of smuggling and of Oloitipitip's distributorship. As he was dealing with a cabinet minister, he asked for an appointment with the president to brief him in advance on what he would say. He was told that he could not see Moi "until there was tea in Kenya."

Stunned, Karanja canceled the press conference. Instead, the KTDA took out paid advertisements in the newspapers and listed the tea distributors around the country, stated that the shortages were due to smuggling, and suggested that this was a problem for the police, not the KTDA. When the media pressed him for more information, he refused to talk and angrily said, "I hardly have got enough time to educate the press."[8] For it appeared to him to be the instrument of his torture, and he did not know how to fight back when the political odds had so evidently turned against him.

At this point information damaging to Karanja was leaked to the press by a disaffected KTDA employee with links to the Njonjo camp. It was pointed out that Karanja and his chairman, Jackson Kamau, were among the five partners owning a private tea factory and that this factory had enjoyed the services of a KTDA trainee factory manager for a time as part of his apprenticeship. These allegations were true, and the press bayed at the scent of a conflict of interest.* Publisher Hilary Ng'weno complained in an editorial about "public officials who [a]fter serving for many years ... often begin to behave as if they own the public institutions they were appointed to head." Calls were made for Karanja's resignation.[9]

Vice-president Kibaki finally came to the public defense of Karanja.[10] (They had been allied in supporting Muigai against Njonjo's candidate in the Gatundu election.) The government took KETEPA away from the KTDA, made it independent, and forced Karanja to resign from its board. (Moi put in charge the Kalenjin manager Karanja had appointed.) Otherwise the affair appeared to blow over.

A journalist who was close to the coverage of the controversy said in retrospect, "If I were to make a list of people who have profited by their use of public position, Charles Karanja would be *very* far down it." He also indicated that the press did not even receive leads that would have

---

*Charles Karanja has asked that the following additional points be made about the Ngorongo Tea Factory: (1) *Prior* to Karanja's and Kamau's having acquired an interest in the factory, it was already processing green leaf from the KTDA. (2) The owners decided that all surpluses earned by the factory were to be distributed to those who provided leaf to the factory, in proportion to their deliveries. Other than their fees as directors, the owners received the same profits from the factory as did the KTDA. (3) At the time that the factory-manager trainees were placed at Ngorongo, the KTDA was having difficulty finding adequate on-the-job training opportunities. (4) Furthermore, Ngorongo, "like all the KTDA Tea Factories, was required to pay the wages of all the trainees seconded to it." (5) "Finally, let it be known that Ngorongo Tea Factory has been selling good quality tea even after the KTDA Factory Manager Trainees were withdrawn. ... It is also noteworthy that the company's financial position and its ability to pay final payments to its outgrowers did not suffer as a result of discontinuation of delivery of KTDA tea in 1978." "The question of there being a conflict of interest in connection with C. K. Karanja's separate but distinct relationship with the KTDA and the Ngorongo Tea Factory does not arise in light of the arrangements described above."

linked KTDA staff to the tea smuggling. Karanja's major failings appear to have been that he challenged Njonjo and his ally, and that when he got into political trouble, instead of leaking information that would have made the media more sympathetic, he had antagonized it with his defensive anger.

The consequences were serious even if the infractions were minor by Kenyan standards. Karanja had been publicly exposed, which damaged his political effectiveness. He had no presidential support, which meant that initiatives that required policy change were out of the question. His moral authority with his staff was also compromised; he had failed to keep to the letter of the professional code by which they claimed to abide. And his iron managerial hand was weakened; no longer could he simply reassign or fire those whose competence he found lacking. It is indicative that the KTDA's efficiency improved steadily until 1978 (when the controversy erupted), but that it has had cost control problems since then. (See table 6.1.)

Still, President Moi did not remove him from office. He apparently found it convenient to have a weakened manager at the KTDA. More generally, he also has a pattern of not removing someone from office in immediate conjunction with a scandal. Perhaps he wishes everyone to see that the individual in question is no longer effective. Whatever the reason, Karanja was left in suspense and in charge of the KTDA for two more years. He was dismissed without ceremony or advance notice on February 28, 1981. Karanja kept his dignity, called his department heads together, congratulated his successor, and charged them all to continue to work for the benefit of tea smallholders and the country.

After Karanja's departure, the KTDA did not take on any major new challenges, as it frequently had under his general-managership. The Kikuyu who succeeded him did not have the political connections to mold the policy environment as Karanja had done. The KTDA may have lost some of its tight efficiency, for the organization could not be protected as well from political demands for favors. It certainly did not have the élan it once had. Almost all the senior managers remembered Karanja's tenure with great admiration and nostalgia. But the KTDA continued to be a well-run corporation and to prosper. It had been well built.

Karanja "retired" to run his own businesses. He felt humiliated at the way his career in public service had ended. To take his mind off his troubles, he built a hotel at Ruiru outside of Nairobi and named it Ndanga after his wife. (See plate 23.) It may have been bad business judgment to have done so; it seemed too far ahead of demand. But it was well designed, and the attention he gave to it helped to lift his spirits again. His farms and fortunes flourished.

THE "SECOND" MOI PRESIDENCY

The first years of Moi's reign were consensual ones. He made expansive and expensive commitments. Almost everyone seemed to be doing well; no one had a basis for complaint. By 1980, however, the economy had begun to turn sour. The heady revenues of the coffee boom were long past, but the financial commitments they had encouraged remained, creating inflationary pressure. The world economy took a decided turn for the worse, and Kenya reeled in response. Local businesses were no longer prospering, and this upset the Kikuyu, who owned the largest number of them. Government expenditure had to be severely cut at the end of the 1981–82 financial year, disturbing all who depended upon it.

Kikuyu business, administrative, and political leaders began to complain privately that Moi was not managing things well. President Moi started to show signs of insecurity and initiated political detentions again. In the spring of 1982 he pushed through Parliament a constitutional amendment to make Kenya a one-party state. Although the country had in practice had only one party since 1969, many leaders were privately disquieted that opposition was being made more difficult. Moi's governing coalition was showing signs of significant weakness.

A group of radical junior officers in the air force then attempted a coup d'etat in August 1982. The coup was suppressed by the army, and suddenly Kenya's political circumstances were significantly altered. This coup attempt actually proved to be a piece of good luck for Moi. First, it is possible that a group of conservative Kikuyu army officers were planning a coup as well. These men were not going to let a multiethnic group of radicals take over, so they put down the air force coup. But the action preempted their acting to take power themselves. If the army had moved first, it is likely that it would have succeeded. Second, the coup attempt legitimated Moi's reorganizing of the command structure of the armed forces and police. In retrospect it is clear from public statements Moi made in the months leading up to the coup attempt that he had been aware it was coming. But he had been powerless to remove the offending officers without provoking the very event he feared. Once the attempt had been made and suppressed, his opposition stood exposed and disorganized, and he was able to remove its leaders from the positions that were most threatening. The armed forces and the police were neutralized.*

---

*The author has heard people in usually well-informed circles in Kenya discuss the existence of a second coup plot. Such speculation is fueled by the slow and confused response of the army and the paramilitary police in the early hours of the air force takeover. *Africa Confidential*, which is thought to derive much of its information from British intelli-

Moi evidently believed that Charles Njonjo was involved in some way with the various plans to overthrow him. Although the allegation has never been proved, Njonjo was forced out of the cabinet and the Parliament in mid-1983. Politicians scrambled all over one another in their attempts to disassociate themselves from him and to affirm their loyalty to the president. The mood was unpleasantly reminiscent of McCarthy's hunt for Communists in the United States in the early 1950s.[11]

Mwai Kibaki had been transferred from the Ministry of Finance to the emasculated Ministry of Home Affairs in early 1982.[12] He was clearly in disfavor with the president as well. In 1988 Moi replaced him as vice-president with Joseph Karanja, a minor Kikuyu politician and former head of the University of Nairobi. Then in 1989 the minister of finance, Saitoti, a Maasai, was made vice-president. Not only was Njonjo, a man who had seemed second in influence only to the president, gone; suddenly the government lacked any Kikuyu in its influential inner circle.

Those political forces that could oppose Moi had been routed. In relative terms Moi was stronger politically. But on any absolute scale his base of political support had declined.

MURIITHI PRESIDES OVER THE DECLINE IN VETERINARY SERVICES

The Moi years began well for the Veterinary Department. Moi's fellow Kalenjin are nearly as deeply involved in dairying as are the Kikuyu and they produce beef as well. Livestock are an important priority for Moi, and he created a separate Ministry of Livestock Development, combining the Animal Husbandry and Range Management divisions of the Department of Agriculture with the Department of Veterinary Services. Muriithi was promoted from director of Veterinary Services to director of Livestock Development.

Geoffrey Kariithi was retired as head of the civil service, and thus Muriithi lost his direct access to the president. But Charles Njonjo was a fellow Alliance High graduate, and Muriithi hoped to have, through him, the influence he would need. In 1979 Moi introduced the school milk program and removed any danger that there would be a depression in the dairy industry induced by a shortage of demand. Moi also encouraged the Veterinary Department to take over responsibility for

---

gence, doubts that an army coup attempt was in the immediate offing. It does confirm that Moi considered the army and the police negligent and undertook a considerable shake-up in the officer corps as a consequence. *Africa Confidential* 23, no. 17 (25 August 1982); 24, no. 5 (2 March 1983); 24, no. 25 (December 1983).

still more of the communally run cattle dips, in recognition of the fact that their disease-control functions served the interests of a wider group than just the owners of the livestock that were dipped.[13] All the signs were that livestock production enjoyed the highest political priority and that Muriithi's vision of the Veterinary Department's expanding subsidized services to smallholders continued to be propitious.

The new ministry did not do well, however. Neither Muriithi nor any of its other leaders proved to have enough links to the president to get the ministry's urgent problems solved. Muriithi's promotion had not represented a special vote of trust; none of the viable candidates had inspired enough confidence in Moi for him to have ignored seniority. In addition, there was a good deal of turnover in the department's cabinet minister and permanent secretary positions, suggesting that the occupants were not especially influential and in any case did not have time to learn enough about the ministry to represent its positions well. No one could get the cooperation from Animal Husbandry that was necessary to create a meaningful extension program, and so an opportunity for major donor support in this area was lost.[14] The Treasury would not come forward with new funds to support the president's implied commitments for expanded government support for cattle dipping. Neither would anyone announce a reversal of the policy. Muriithi was frightened at his inability to summon support. He probably was already weakened by illness and became more cautious in his decisions. Both his senior staff below him and his permanent secretary above him started to question his authority.

Then economic reality caught up with the country. The coffee boom was over. The revenues with which the government had been awash began to dry up, but the many new projects that had been floated still had to be carried forward. On top of this the international economy stumbled in 1980; export markets turned weak, and the interest on Kenya's foreign debts suddenly leaped upward. Moi could no longer purchase political popularity with governmental generosity.

The crisis of insufficient revenues to meet the bloated government budget was severe and extremely difficult to manage. Not only did real government spending shrink at least 8 percent between 1981 and 1983,[15] it had to be done in a system that was unresponsive to fiscal restraints. During the years of the coffee boom, government officers had been able to overspend their budgets with the confidence that Parliament would always vote a "Supplementary" to bail them out. Once the profligate habit of ignoring red ink had begun, it was difficult to reintroduce fiscal restraint. The Treasury resorted to "cash flow budgeting"— the practice of stopping spending by simply letting the money to pay the bills run out.[16] Even this extreme measure was insufficient; astute spending officers simply stuffed bills in their desk drawers and presented them in the next financial year. An informal government debt of unknown size developed with private vendors, who charged "interest" in the form of higher prices.[17]

Good management practice would have required the setting of priorities for government activities, cutting out those low on the list, and assuring adequate funding for the efficient and effective operation of those activities that remained. Politically, this proved extremely difficult to do, just as it has in the United States. People will fight more vigorously to defend the continuation of an existing service than they will to assure its efficiency or than they will work to create it in the first place. Thus priority setting and program cutting are extremely difficult in a democracy that has multiple sources of power and little centralizing political organization for imposing priorities. It seems fairer to people to freeze budget appropriations at their previous nominal levels, to let inflation erode their real levels, and to let all programs suffer "equally."[18] In a first round of modest cuts this strategy has much to recommend it. Most organizations have some "fat," and a budget freeze will induce them to trim it away creatively to keep vital programs functioning effectively. When the cuts are large or repeated, however, they induce despair, not creativity. The organization lapses into ineffectiveness. This is what overtook the Veterinary Department.

When the budgetary crisis hit the government with full force in early 1982, the Ministry of Livestock Development responded creatively and well. In its submission to the Working Party on Government Expenditures that the president had created, the ministry's permanent secretary proposed new user fees, identified services that could be beneficially privatized, and suggested divestiture of the livestock parastatals whose deficits were being financed out of the ministry's budget and were no longer serving a useful social function.[19] In short, he spelled out the policy priorities that would best serve the livestock industry in a period of serious budgetary constraint. Although this PS was retired, these proposals were fleshed out and further developed over the next two years.[20]

At the micro level, when it became clear that there would be no "Supplementaries" for the 1981–82 financial year, Muriithi made his priorities clear. Disease prevention and artificial insemination (AI) had to be kept functioning; interruption in their provision would occasion long-term, perhaps permanent damage to the livestock industry. Curative veterinary medicine, animal husbandry extension, and other services could be temporarily suspended if need be. The wisdom of these decisions was accepted.

As the budgetary crisis dragged on, however, the ability and willingness of Livestock Development to respond effectively to it was dissipated. None of the innovative policy proposals that the ministry had put up were adopted by the cabinet or the president. This might not have been so debilitating if other priorities had been imposed in their place. But no choices were made between services; all continued with increasingly inadequate levels of budgetary provision. AI, which must be reliable to be effective, was left with a deteriorating fleet of vehicles, too little fuel, and no action on the proposal to increase its fees. The accompanying political cartoon from the *Daily Nation* shows the farm community's despair at its inability to count on this vital service. (See plate 24.) Smallholder production suffered as a result. What had been a well-managed AI service quickly became a professional embarrassment. Dan Mbogo tried several ways to find a solution to its problems but lacked the political connections to effect them.

Other services throughout the Veterinary Department declined as well and morale suffered. Staff could see little point in trying to change things if resources were going to bear so little relationship to real needs and if the cabinet was going to be unwilling to set any deliberate kind of priorities. There was particular despair at the government's failure to shut down the Uplands Bacon Factory. The parastatal had declined to the point where it was serving no useful purpose. But President Moi could not bring himself to lay off workers. The sums that were used to keep it alive would have served livestock producers far better in adequate provision for vital Veterinary Department services.

Without adequate budgetary support, the ambitious design for curative veterinary medicine showed flaws as well. There were inadequate funds for the purchase of required drugs and for the travel of veterinarians. The paraprofessional support staff did an increasing proportion of the work on their own, bought their own drugs, and began to accept illegal payments for their services. This informal commercialization actually had mixed benefits. At least it permitted veterinary care to continue to be available. It also happened that the market distributed veterinary services more widely and equitably than the old patterns of administrative allocation had done. (Poorer livestock producers in Kenya have better access to money than they have to bureaucratic influence.)[21] But the quality of veterinary care declined, for the professional veterinarians were increasingly isolated from its provision. Producers would have been much better served by an officially and openly private veterinary care system, which would have put the paraprofessionals under the supervision of the vets. The great majority of the Kenyan government veterinarians wanted privatization but could not find the formula for making it politically palatable, even though a less-satisfactory illegal version already existed. They were trapped by the embrace of earlier government favor.

In retrospect, Muriithi, Mbogo, and others had failed the Veterinary Department on one of the most critical of all leadership tests. They had not foreseen the damage that could flow from the expansive, subsidized programs that they had adopted in the 1970s. These made both dairy producers and the veterinary profession dependent on a government largess that proved impossible to sustain. As Bruce Johnston and William Clark conclude, "You shouldn't always want what you can get" in the public policy game.[22]

Muriithi was unable to cope with the combination of this new set of circumstances and his lack of support from the president. He was unwell and nearing the end of a long public career. He was awarded the Order of the Silver Star by President Moi for his distinguished service in 1983, retired in late 1984 at the standard age of fifty-five, and died on March 20, 1985, with cancer of the liver and pancreas.

CONCLUSIONS

The accession of Daniel arap Moi to the Kenyan presidency brought a significant change in the nature of political-bureaucratic relationships. Jomo Kenyatta could appoint people in whom he had personal confidence to positions of leadership in most critical organizations. He then was able to give them great administrative discretion and to rely on them for advice on policies that affected their domains. Moi was much less fortunate. He had only a fraction of the personal political stature that Kenyatta had had and found himself constrained to accept leaders in whom he had no particular confidence. President Moi kept reassigning many of his cabinet ministers and permanent secretaries, probably to keep them off balance and to reduce their policy effectiveness. But he couldn't do the same with the technical officers. He therefore was much more interventionist in his relationships with most of his administrators and much less responsive to the demands of many of them for resources and policy support. In the first four years of his presidency many of these matters were handled by Charles Njonjo, who was building his own political machine within Moi's. After the 1982 coup attempt, no other politician had stature even close to the president's, and Kikuyu isolation from the levers of power was much clearer.

The consequences of this struggle for control between the president and his administrators were unhappy for many public organizations. The weakened presidency did not create bureaucratic subversion. Instead, it produced policy stalemate and inaction. In the case of the KTDA it led to Charles Karanja's losing a controversial public battle with an Njonjo ally, having his integrity impugned, and eventually losing his position. The KTDA continued to be a sound organization but lost the strength that it had had for new initiatives.

Although the livestock industry enjoyed favor with President Moi, Ishmael Muriithi found his new political environment unmanageable. As budgetary resources became scarce, the Veterinary Department needed to retreat from the expensive position that it had adopted of providing highly subsidized services. Muriithi was unable to obtain either a retrenchment to a diminished set of higher priority activities, the approval of user fees to keep the existing services viable, or the policies that would have permitted the establishment of strong private services in their stead. He became a shadow of the authoritative administrator that he had been in the Kenyatta years.

Administrative effectiveness is contingent on political support and can vary from regime to regime for the same manager. Not all administration suddenly became ineffective under Moi's presidency. Some officials did enjoy his confidence and operated productively in the new circumstances. Two of them were Simeon Nyachae and Harris Mule.

CHAPTER NINE

Rural Development, Decentralization, and Mule's Apprenticeship

Struggles over three policy issues have stretched over the whole of independent Kenya's history: equity, decentralization, and the priority of agriculture. Harris Mule's career in Planning was intimately connected with all three. Here we will trace his involvement with the development of these three issues during the Kenyatta years and also see how an administrator who was judged outstanding under President Moi appeared unexceptional under Kenyatta. Quality is an interaction effect of managers and their contexts.

EQUITY AND THE ILO REPORT

Although the first decade of Mule's work was largely concerned with agriculture, at the Planning ministry he also was given assignments on employment, an issue of special concern to his permanent secretary, Philip Ndegwa. The African population of the capital city of Nairobi had grown at the astonishing rate of 11 percent per annum between 1962 and 1969, and the port city of Mombasa followed at 9 percent.[1] The city streets were filled with young men and women looking for work. Mule was one of the first Kenyan policymakers to see clearly that urban unemployment is intimately related to rural development. He had become friends with O. Norby, a Ford Foundation adviser in Planning. Norby's Pakistani experience helped to persuade Mule that the only way to keep people out of the cities was to raise rural incomes.

In 1970 Parliament appointed a group of "back benchers" (nonministers) to investigate unemployment problems in the country. Mule was designated to provide staff support to the M.P.s and, together with Peter

Hopcraft, a Kenyan economist at the University of Nairobi, heavily influenced what they wrote. The Select Committee's report concluded:

> At a general level unemployment can be reduced through (a) raising the output of the economy and hence creating jobs; (b) ensuring that increases in output are streamlined to the most labour-intensive means feasible; and (c) reducing the gap between rural and urban living standards by raising the rural incomes and bringing essential amenities to the rural population.... [T]axation and incomes policies have an extremely important part to play [in achieving these goals.][2]

An inquiry that quite easily could have led to a call for more government jobs stressed growth, equity, and rural development instead.

The Select Committee's endeavor fed directly into the famous International Labor Organization (ILO) mission of 1972. The ILO had just completed a study of Sri Lanka and was looking for a follow-up that would assist it in further refining the new "redistribution with growth" strategy it was developing as an alternative to its traditional narrow concern with unemployment. After some negotiations, the Government of Kenya agreed to a mission headed by Hans Singer and Richard Jolly of Britain's Institute of Development Studies at Sussex. The mission created opportunities for a particularly fertile cross-breeding between the new ideas about development of its "international" members and the considerable knowledge about Kenya from the locally based academics on the team. The resulting report thus was a particularly incisive and influential one. Mule was one of the Kenya government officials designated to work with the team. He later considered it to be one of the formative experiences of his life. A careful listener and an astute learner, he became the focus of the other participants' attempts to influence the government. The mission was encouraged in the daring direction that its thinking took by the similar conclusions of the *Report of the Select Committee on Unemployment*, which Mule had influenced.[3]

The ILO report concluded that urban unemployment needed to be treated as a symptom of structural imbalances in the economy as a whole, not as the problem itself. The appearance of unemployment was caused, on the one hand, by the large gap between the wages that were being paid in the "formal" sector of the economy and, on the other hand, by the lower incomes that were generated in agriculture and the "informal" urban sector that escaped official regulation. Men and women thus were encouraged to spend unusually long times as "unemployed" petitioners for formal-sector jobs before finally accepting work elsewhere in the economy. The numbers of true long-term unemployed actually were modest.

To address the "unemployment" problem the ILO mission sought to concentrate on the working poor through vigorous efforts to improve rural incomes and the removal of restrictions on the informal sector. In its report it recommended that Kenya shift its industrialization strategy from an import-substitution one to the processing of agricultural products for export and that labor-intensive approaches to public works and industrial development be promoted. The report suggested that efforts to regulate informal-sector developments in housing and transport be relaxed; that efforts be made to reduce the very high rate of population growth; that primary education be extended and made more practical; and that an incomes policy be devised to freeze the incomes of the wealthiest 10 percent and to redirect the proceeds of growth to the poorer half of the work force. Among the many other recommendations, the ones of greatest concern to this study concern agriculture. Here the report documented that smallholdings in Kenya are both more productive and more labor-intensive than are large farms. Thus it advocated a further intensification and commercialization of smallholder production and measures to promote the breakup of large farms.[4]

Leftist critics such as Colin Leys dismissed the report as politically naive.[5] Doubtless it did underestimate the strength of the vested interests that it attacked, but much of the report was eventually implemented. It touched the same sensitive political nerve that had produced the *Report of the Select Committee on Unemployment*, and it caught the imagination of progressives within the government, such as Mwai Kibaki, the minister of finance and planning. The cabinet responded with *Sessional Paper No. 10 of 1973 on Unemployment*, which formally committed the government to many of the ILO recommendations.

Words are cheap, of course, and the Kenya government has implemented only half of the cabinet's formal policy decisions on some issues.[6] Frequently this lack of implementation is due to the cabinet's having been presented with comprehensive policy papers, the details of which are hard to revise without damaging the coherent logic of the paper as a whole. The cabinet then gives little thought to the specifics of these decisions and does not feel bound by them. Kenya's administrative system is only weakly bureaucratized, and civil servants feel free to ignore formal decisions that are not backed by evidence of serious political intention. Like most planners and analysts, who tend to think like academics, Harris Mule had to learn that official acceptance of plans, papers, and statements is still a long way from their being implemented and becoming effective policy.

The commitment to specifics in *Sessional Paper No. 10 of 1973*, however, was better than average. The paper was drafted under Mule's supervision and edited by David Davies, a planning adviser. The specific decisions were presented in such a way that they did not have to follow from the logic of the analysis and could be easily changed. This encouraged the cabinet to give them more careful attention and produced decisions to which it was more dedicated.

Remarkably, the Government of Kenya declared itself in broad agreement with the ILO report.[7] It did so within the context of giving primacy to economic growth, a priority that it had explicitly adopted in *Sessional Paper No. 10 of 1965 on African Socialism and Its Application to Planning in Kenya.*[8] This policy statement was drafted for the then minister of planning, Tom Mboya, by Ed Edwards, an American economist.[9] Both the logic of that analysis and Edwards's ongoing advice continued to attract Kenya's economic policymakers for twenty years after Mboya's assassination.

The government then adopted policies based on many of the ILO recommendations, the larger number of which eventually were implemented. The cabinet accepted the importance of labor-intensive public works programs; Harris Mule helped to find means to implement them. The government also pledged itself to relax the regulatory pressures on the informal sector. It did so and was rewarded with a dramatic expansion in informal enterprise in housing, transport, food service, and other areas.

Another problem area was the government's industrialization policies, which were heavily focused on import substitution. These policies placed quotas or heavy taxes on selected imports to encourage their local manufacture. The resulting local products were often very expensive and did not save that much foreign exchange. Occasionally the import bill for the component parts of a locally assembled product was as expensive as the imported finished product would have been. The cabinet promised that it would reduce its emphasis on such import-substituting industrialization, but in practice it continued to promote it.

The government reaffirmed its interest in family planning programs, although they did not bear much fruit in reducing the population growth rate. Mule had become convinced of the importance of this issue in the 1960s when he worked on it in Planning, and he continued to find ways to push it gently forward throughout his career. He and his wife Martha personally practiced what they preached by having only two children, both daughters.

The cabinet also accepted in principle the need for fundamental change in the educational system. The larger number of ILO proposals for this sector were gradually introduced, culminating in the nearly universal availability of eight years of free primary education under the Moi regime.

TABLE 9.1
Indices of Real Wages and Incomes
(1970 = 100)

Year	Minimum Wage Earners	Average Civil Sevants	Farmers' Income
1966	104	97	88
1967	104	96	87
1968	103	97	82
1969	103	96	86
1970	100	100	100
1971	93	96	86
1972	90	96	102
1973	78	96	106
1974	93	85	109
1975	103	86	89
1976	94	94	140
1977	91	88	205
1978	80	89	128
1979	74	86	109
1980	90	n.a.	112

NOTE: Farmers' Income is simply the per capita income terms of trade from table 9.2. Minimum wages are taken from various *Kenya Economic Surveys* and are deflated by the low-income consumer price index in the various *Statistical Abstracts*. Civil service earnings are taken from public-sector average wage earnings as given in the *Economic Survey* and are deflated by the middle-income consumer price index as given in the *Statistical Abstract.* The calculations were performed by Barbara Grosh.

The government committed itself to an incomes policy that would reduce income differentials. As can be seen in table 9.1, the gap between urban and rural workers was reduced. The civil service wage scale became more compressed, but the policy was not effective in containing the inequalities in income in the urban private sector. This disparity eventually created problems for the retention of high-level manpower in the public service because business offered markedly higher salaries for this group. This gave Mule second thoughts about that aspect of the policy in later years. But in the 1970s he strongly supported it.

In agriculture, the intensification and commercialization of smallholder agriculture were vigorously promoted through such programs as tea and dairy development. The effects in increased rural earnings are evident in table 9.2. (But also see table 9.3.) In the following decade farm incomes were maintained for domestic crops and improved dramatically for export crops, producing a significant net gain in welfare for the peasantry. The government was evasive about the issue of land

TABLE 9.2
Agricultural Terms of Trade Indices
(1970 = 100)

Year	Net Barter Terms of Trade		Income Terms of Trade		Per Capita Income Terms of Trade
	Export Crops	Domestic Crops	Export Crops	Domestic Crops	
1966	105	131	86	51	88
1967	102	121	73	77	87
1968	92	116	67	96	82
1969	92	110	83	94	90
1970	100	100	100	100	100
1971	84	109	81	107	86
1972	91	113	103	127	102
1973	99	107	120	117	106
1974	154	103	132	113	109
1975	91	117	98	131	89
1976	147	128	186	156	140
1977	198	101	322	149	205
1978	123	106	198	119	128
1979	110	102	167	126	109
1980	106	103	181	127	112

NOTE: Date are taken from the *Kenya Statistical Abstract* (various years). The population growth rate was taken as 3.9 percent. The methodology used was derived from Frank Ellis, "Agricultural Pricing Policy in Tanzania 1970–1979: Implications for Agricultural Output, Rural Incomes, and Crop Marketing Costs" (Dar es Salaam: Economic Research Bureau, University of Dar es Salaam, 1980). The calculations were performed by Barbara Grosh.

reform, although it did pledge itself to a land tax. Despite attempts by a number of civil servants to deliver on the latter commitment, a land tax has remained a dead issue. Similarly, no new smallholder-settlement schemes have been undertaken. But neither did the government do much to maintain large-scale farming; informally, in fact, it promoted the land-purchase efforts of the landless. Through the workings of the market, the size of the large-farm sector underwent significant erosion. The productivity and quality of smallholder rural life were Mule's major priorities throughout his career.

Kenya did in fact give serious attention to an agenda of equity between 1970 and 1975. Mwai Kibaki, the minister of finance and planning, was particularly concerned to reduce inequalities. But international economic events swamped many of the efforts and detracted attention from their full implementation. The shocks of the oil price increases imposed by OPEC in 1974 and 1979 and the mid-decade coffee inflation were the currents that largely determined the direction taken by the Kenyan economy. Given those constraints, much more of the ILO report was implemented than the critics had guessed was possible.

It would be foolish, of course, to see the above patterns of policy as simply the reflection of the idiosyncrasies of individual politicians and civil servants. They were formed within the strong, constraining framework of class interests. Those policies that directly challenged the matajiri (well-to-do)—an end to protection and subsidies for import-substituting industrialization, effective collection of a progressive income tax, ceilings on landholdings, and a land tax—were never implemented, despite the rhetoric. Nothing was done to inhibit the processes of capital accumulation on which this class was already well launched. The one exception was the capping of higher civil service wages. This disadvantage to a part of the matajiri was more than compensated, however, by the availability to senior officials of lucrative opportunities in business and agriculture.

Many of those parts of the ILO report that were adopted promoted the growth of the petty bourgeoisie, particularly among the Kikuyu: the intensification and commercialization of agriculture, an improvement of rural incomes relative to those of urban wage earners, and an end to restrictions on informal-sector businesses. This set of policies often benefited matajiri interests in commerce and farming as well.

Those implemented policies that did directly assist the peasants and workers—extension of primary education and introduction of labor-intensive public works—did not threaten matajiri interests. In fact, because of their popularity and visibility, they were touted by matajiri politicians as patronage benefits for their constituencies. Many of the activities that most advanced the welfare of the poorer half of the population were financed by donors, who were greatly interested in equity issues in the 1970s. These nominally redistributive measures therefore actually were part of a "positive sum game" for the matajiri.

The report thus was implemented in such a way as to strengthen rather than threaten the matajiri. Their most important opportunities for amassing wealth were left untouched, the numbers and prosperity of their petty-bourgeois allies were increased, and their bonds of patronage to the peasantry were reinforced. The best available research indicates that although the incomes of the upper and middle peasantry underwent substantial increase in this period, the welfare of the poorest 40 percent either was static or declined slightly. (See table 9.3.) The impact of these policies was greatest in the Kikuyu areas of the country, thereby averting a split of that ethnic group along class lines, which its political leaders so feared. Issues of regional inequality, the redress of

TABLE 9.3
The Distribution of Smallholder Income
in Central and Nyanza Provinces

	Percentage Change in Per Capita Real Income	
Smallholder Group	Central Province 1963 to 1974	Nyanza Province 1970 to 1974
Poorest 40%	−3.66	−8.6
Middle 30%	+41.03	+18.2
Richest 30%	+38.46	+54.4

SOURCE: Gene Tidrick, "Kenya: Issues in Agricultural Development," mimeographed (Nairobi: The World Bank, 1979), table 2.19, p. 52, from research by Paul Collier and Deepak Lal. Also reproduced in Stephen B. Peterson, "The State and the Organizational Infrastructure of the Agrarian Economy: A Comparative Study of Smallholder Agrarian Development in Taiwan and Kenya" (Ph.D. diss., Department of Political Science, University of California, Berkeley, 1982), pp. 436–37.

which would have blunted the pursuit of intra-Kikuyu solidarity, were largely ignored.

The self-interest of the matajiri, however, cannot explain the pattern of policy implementation by itself. The conception of self-interest pursued in Kenya was broad and enlightened. The leadership of some other African states has followed a narrow and rapacious path.[10] Part of the inclusiveness of the Kenyan matajiri's self-interest is due to the extensive overlap between the types of crops grown by the matajiri and the petty bourgeoisie, a theme to which we will return later. Some of the explanation for the more benign set of policies pursued is that more progressive persons, such as Kibaki and Mule, wanted them. At the margins of others' indifference, they had the positional influence to pursue their vision.

RURAL DEVELOPMENT

Another part of Mule's policy education began with the Kericho Conference of September 1966, which brought together government officials, academics, and donor representatives to discuss Kenya's rural development. The conference gave impetus to the ideas that agriculture and rural development are more important to economic growth than industry and urban development. These themes anticipated the emphasis on agricultural-led development, which became prominent in the 1970s, and rejected the dogma of industrialization-first, which dominated the 1950s.

The Kericho Conference also proposed a pilot program on comprehensive rural development in selected parts of the country. At first the government was reluctant to create a special program to address the conference recommendations.[11] By the time Harris Mule returned from Harvard in 1967, however, the decision to proceed with the Special Rural Development Program (SRDP) had been made and it became part of his portfolio.

The SRDP was one of the earlier and better known of the genre of integrated rural development projects. Ultimately SRDP failed, both because its concrete accomplishments were too modest relative to its level of expenditure and because intense activity in only six small areas attracted jealousy and political opposition. In the face of hostile parliamentary questions, the civil servants involved simply retreated. In late 1971 a decision was made not to extend the program, and by 1976 it was dead.[12]

But the SRDP was an extremely important learning experience for those involved. Out of it came several smaller and successful activities. One of these was the labor-intensive rural access roads program, which was pioneered by the United States Agency for International Development (USAID) in its Vihiga SRDP project. By making minimal use of heavy equipment, this program produced good-quality dirt roads that enhanced rural trade, provided rural employment opportunities that complemented the seasonal demands of agriculture, and increased rural incomes. Harris Mule called the program to the attention of the Ministry of Works, which adopted the methodology for much of its work in 1973. In 1976 he then was able to mobilize donor finance for much expanded labor-intensive construction of rural access roads.*

The SRDP was multisector, comprehensive, and integrated. Mule later reflected that

> in rural development the expressed preference of the population is for social services, for there the total funding is governmental. . . . [But ultimately the resources for] rural development [depend on] agricultural development. . . . Put the maximum on agriculture, for, if it takes off, other things will follow. We spent a lot of administrative energy on all sectors and so dissipated impact.

Kenya's later development initiatives usually were single-sector and concentrated on agriculture.

Among the more important of the next generation of projects were USAID's 1975 Agricultural Sector Loan and the World Bank's 1976 Integrated Agricultural Development Project (IADP). Both were designed

---

*This program has been evaluated as comparing very favorably with conventional road-construction methods in cost per kilometer, capital/labor ratios, share of wages in total costs, and foreign exchange. Ian Livingston, *Rural Development, Employment, and Incomes in Kenya* (Addis Ababa: International Labor Organization, 1981), p. 40.

to stimulate food-grain production among poorer producers and were organized around the provision of credit. Mule favored these programs because they addressed the multiple needs of agricultural production. He also liked them because they were simpler and more focused than the SRDP's integrated rural development projects had been, and their national thrust avoided the particularistic squabbles that had killed the area-centered SRDP. In fact the USAID loan was a direct result of Mule's initiative. He presented the idea to the director of USAID-Nairobi. Perhaps USAID had money that it needed to commit before the end of the financial year, for the project was quickly adopted and funded. There was some skepticism about the program in the Kenya government, but it accepted the idea because $5 million of the $12 million involved was to come through the Treasury and be disbursed in a single check.

The USAID loan was hastily prepared; the World Bank's IADP was designed carefully with contributions from outstanding experts such as Uma Lele. But both failed. They came to be dominated by their credit components, creating problems and complexities that simply overwhelmed them.

The negative dynamics unleashed can be illustrated by the IADP. The idea was to have a project of national scope, with extension provided by the Ministry of Agriculture, and inputs, credit, and primary markets organized through the cooperative movement. The line of credit for the project actually originated in the Sugar and Cereal Finance Corporation, and the ultimate markets for many of the crops were controlled by other government parastatal bodies. Nonetheless, activity focused on the co-ops, with the Ministry of Agriculture (which has supervisory authority over the parastatals involved) providing administrative leadership. As the director of Agriculture was the former director of the Department of Cooperatives, the prospects for integrated activity seemed bright.

The chain of activities in the IADP began with the extension service's recruiting farmers who were interested in the particular package of technical changes that was being recommended for the area. Technical training for these farmers was provided both by extension agents and by the residential farmers training centers of the Ministry of Agriculture. Meanwhile, the farmers' applications for credit to finance the package were forwarded through their primary cooperative societies. These applications then had to be approved by the respective district cooperative unions and the Department of Cooperatives; the loan of the credit money to the district unions needed to be authorized by the Cooperative Bank of Kenya (CBK); and the money had to be released to the CBK by the Sugar and Cereals Finance Corporation, usually with a government guarantee for those co-ops whose credit worthiness the

CBK doubted. When the loans were finally approved, they were paid out through the cooperative societies, partly in cash and partly in vouchers for fertilizer and seeds. The inputs generally then were purchased through the co-op, which should have already laid in the needed supplies. After harvest, the crops were sold through the same cooperative, which acted as buying center for the marketing boards, and the credit payments were deducted from the farmer's proceeds.

Every part of this system supported and depended on the other parts. It was thoroughly integrated, and therein lay the seeds of its undoing. For if any one part of the system failed, the entire structure would be hurt.

As might be predicted from the procedural steps outlined above, weaknesses showed first in the timely delivery of credit. Initially the problem was only that the chain of approvals was too lengthy and the credit arrived late for the start of the planting season. If farmers waited for the loans before planting, as many did, the whole purpose of the IADP was undone. As it happens, early planting does more for maize (corn) yields than fertilizer does, and fertilizer applied late does not provide sufficient returns to cover its cost. The farmer is then in the position of having to repay a loan with insufficient increased production to cover it, and consequently defaults. The problem of inadequate yields was made worse in many IADP areas by poor rains. As both sources of non-payment problems would affect a whole cooperative society, the Cooperative Bank of Kenya would see it as a poor credit risk the next year and refuse to approve its loans until the government guaranteed them. This would cause further delays, producing a vicious circle that assured that the co-op's credit record would be still worse the next year. By the time the World Bank finally put its foot down on IADP, the credit repayment record was only 30 percent.

The rational response of farmers to this situation should be to take a very short-term loan from a relative for the needed seeds and fertilizer, plant the crop, and then repay the informal loan with the proceeds from the formal co-op loan when it arrives. This response was effectively precluded by the credit procedures. The system's designers were concerned that farmers would divert agricultural credit to other purposes. Hence farmers were provided with vouchers, not cash, for the purchase of their inputs. If farmers had already bought seeds and fertilizer, the vouchers were useless. They could not use them to satisfy credit obligations for supplies already obtained.

The sensible response to this situation should be to ignore the credit system altogether and obtain one's inputs without it. Once again, the system made this adaptive response more difficult. Farmers were encouraged to use their input vouchers with their cooperatives, but they were permitted to submit them instead through private stockists, if they wished. The reimbursement process for the trader, however, was a long and difficult one. Furthermore, the natural edge the voucher gave to the co-op cut severely into the private stockists' market. These problems were compounded for rural traders by poor profit margins on fertilizer, which were set at a low level by the government to partly compensate farmers for the low official price on maize. The low margins made it unattractive to traders to pay the transportation costs involved in moving fertilizer to rural centers. As a result of these factors, many traders stopped stocking some inputs, especially fertilizer. The farmer thus was deprived of an alternative channel of supply, one that frequently was closer to his farm than was the co-op.

Another way in which the credit system worked in a dysfunctional, integrated manner concerned the method of assuring repayment. The standard way of guaranteeing recovery of an agricultural loan in Kenya has been the use of an "anchor" crop. Such a crop is one for which there is a state-controlled monopoly to which the producer has to sell, thereby making it "simple" to deduct for the loan at the time of sale. The system actually has not worked well outside the major coffee areas. Farmers have sold to illegal traders, marketed under the names of friends and relatives, and bribed purchasing agents, and thus evaded repayment on their loans. In fact, the anchor-crop system probably works in the coffee areas only because these co-op societies informally extend loans for school fees.[13] This makes them a valued source of credit for an urgent, recurring need, a source to which farmers are eager to protect their access. The belief that monopolies offered the solution to poor repayment of credit persisted, however, and the problems of the IADP created pressures to strengthen the existing monopolies and to institute new ones. These pressures were resisted, fortunately, for many of the existing monopoly marketing boards were highly inefficient. Unfortunately, the pressures slowed the movement to improve marketing by permitting competition. Inefficient marketing almost certainly has a greater impact on agricultural production in Kenya than does the availability of credit, so the fact that the IADP made reform in the former area more difficult was a serious failing.

Meanwhile, the agricultural extension system had organized itself around credit delivery under the IADP. When IADP failed to function properly, extension was left ineffective and helpless, despite the fact that its administration improved greatly in this period. Thus the very integration of the IADP, which was supposed to be an advantage, produced ever-widening circles of problems when the project began to malfunction.

Why should Kenya's experience with integration in the IADP have been so different from the successful experiences that had preceded it? The answer is that the IADP was neither a comprehensive crop-development authority, like the KTDA, nor a concentrated regional-development project, as was Ethiopia's Chilalo Agricultural Development Unit (CADU).[14] It therefore had neither the former's ownership of all the needed services nor the latter's ability to buy the allegiance of all the relevant local organizations. In effect, both of these strategies achieve integration by bringing everything under the control of a single organization, one by virtue of its formal structure, the other by dint of its resources. Neither strategy is possible for a multiple-crop program of national scope, where the existence of several independent service-delivery organizations is inevitable. The amount of money an integrated project has to offer is not as overwhelming to the headquarters of these organizations as it is for their local branches. At the same time, the project's national scope is far more threatening to the policy-making authority of national agencies than requests for regional exceptions would be.[15]

The multiple elements of the IADP could have been funded and provided to farmers independently, making them additive rather than interactive (to use the language of chapter 7). They were not, largely because of the credit component. The experts feared that the loans would not be repaid unless everything was tied together. The colonially inspired traditions of control were still dominant.[16] The irony is that the SRDP experience in Vihiga had already indicated that credit was only a minor constraint on peasant production in Kenya. The tail had been allowed to wag the dog, with disastrous results.

Mule learned two important lessons from the SRDP, IADP, and the USAID Agricultural Sector Loan experiences. The first was admiration for simplicity in project design and a fear of administrative complexity. An integrated conception of development is important at the level of policy, but administrative interdependence is dangerous at the level of implementation. When Kenya and the World Bank redesigned the IADP in the early 1980s they broke it up into separate independent components.

Mule's second lesson was that institutional credit is a minor constraint on peasant agricultural production in Africa and takes a distinct back place relative to direct income incentives.[17] As a result, Mule gave much more attention to agricultural price policy in the 1980s. However, it has not been easy for Kenya to resist credit programs. They are politically very attractive because they provide a visible, discrete benefit, which is distributed to individuals and can be used to reinforce patronage networks.[18] They are appealing also to international assistance agencies because they move substantial sums of money in a way that is administratively simple for the donor to disperse.[19]

DECENTRALIZATION

Another aspect of the Special Rural Development Program (SRDP) and an additional part of its heritage were attempts to provide for decentralized development initiatives.[20] During the first decade of his rule Jomo Kenyatta abolished regional authorities, denuded county (district) councils of their functions, and centralized authority in Nairobi. Most development experts were convinced, however, that a country with the ethnic and ecological diversity of Kenya could not be managed in a uniform manner from its capital city. But because local governments had proved divisive and politically threatening, they pressed for decentralization in another form.

To decentralize means to move resources and authority away from the center.[21] But there are a variety of ways this can be done. Among the several types of decentralization,[22] four are touched upon in this book:

1. Devolution: a grant of authority to geographical subdivisions that are legally autonomous and that have leaders who are not selected by the central government. Such devolution empowers local governments and is what most British and Americans think of first when they speak of decentralization.

2. Delegation to autonomous agencies: a grant of authority to legally autonomous entities, which can have either national or regional scope and which frequently are led by central-government appointees. The KTDA is an example of such decentralization, as is the famous Tennessee Valley Authority in the United States.

3. Privatization: an assumption of formerly governmental functions by autonomous business or voluntary organizations. Many in Kenya's Veterinary Department have been interested in this method of delivering curative animal health care.

4. Deconcentration: the grant of authority to *non*autonomous geographical subdivisions, which are controlled by the field agents of the central government. It was this form of decentralization on which the SRDP built.

The Special Rural Development Program

In the 1960s Kenyatta consolidated authority in the Provincial Administration and used it as his personal instrument of rule, replacing the devolution of the Majimbo constitution with deconcentration. This hierarchy of centrally appointed officers at the provincial, district, and divisional levels was the basic colonial instrument of field administration and had been copied from the Napoleonic prefectorial system.

Those promoting deconcentration hoped that it would accommodate the great variety of local needs and permit some popular participation while still satisfying the desire of Kenyatta and his centralizers for political control. The SRDP tried to use the division, an administrative subunit of the district, as the unit of development.* It also sought to make divisional and district officers of the various ministries responsible for planning and program management and for consulting local people about their priorities. Although the experiment was not a success, a number of basic decisions and lessons about rural development administration emerged from it.

The government concluded from the SRDP experience that the division was too small and administratively weak to be the basic unit of development. The district, of which there are forty outside Nairobi, was selected instead. The District Development Committee (DDC), which also evolved out of the SRDP experience, then was charged with oversight of local planning and development initiatives. The DDCs were primarily composed of the district heads of central departments and were dominated by civil servants. At the same time the government accepted the fact that the existing district staff had proved to be poor planners. It decided to augment them with a district development officer (DDO) "trained in project preparation and development planning." The DDOs were to be selected by the Planning ministry but controlled in the field by the Provincial Administration.[23]

With these decisions began the painfully slow process of making decentralization a reality in Kenya. There was widespread recognition that something had to be done to accommodate the widely differing character of Kenya's forty districts and to give some outlet to local expressions of need. There also was confidence that deconcentration, under the control of the Provincial Administration, would pose no threat of ethnic disintegration. But the Kikuyu political and administrative leadership under Kenyatta feared that too great a role for the district as a unit of development would give attention to the great regional disparities in government services that existed and create pressures for equalization at the expense of their home areas. So, though progress was steady, it was grudging.

At times it seemed that decentralization was being carried forward by

---

*Kenya's districts range in population from 22,000 to 783,000. A typical district will have three or four divisions. See David Leonard, "The Structure of Rural Administration in Kenya," in *Rural Administration in Kenya*, ed. D. K. Leonard (Nairobi: East African Literature Bureau, 1973), pp. 158–65.

the efforts of the Kamba Harris Mule alone. He secured a series of donor grants for technical assistance to the Rural Planning Division of his ministry and from 1974 forward gradually institutionalized and improved the district planning process. These district plans provided a forum where local citizens and administrators could register their priorities and achieve some integration between ministerial efforts. It proved very difficult, however, to incorporate the results of the district planning process into the national plans in any meaningful manner, and the districts could do little themselves with their own resources.[24]

One small source of funds for district initiatives came out of the SRDP, and two more were added as a result of Mule's efforts. The first, initiated in 1971, was the District Development Grants program and was designed to help projects with a large self-help component. The second, the Rural Works Programme, was begun in 1974 and funded labor-intensive works projects initiated by the districts. It was combined with the District Development Grants to create the Rural Development Fund. The third was the European Economic Community's Micro Projects fund. It started in 1977, financing initiatives that are similar to but somewhat larger than those supported by the Rural Development Fund. Mule was able to obtain continuous donor support for these funds, and by 1985 they were supporting district initiatives with K.shs. 100 million (U.S. $6.25 million) a year. Although these sums were significant, they were modest relative to centrally controlled projects. Because the district projects were labor-intensive or involved self-help, they were often difficult to administer. Thus in the early years the money available was underutilized. Mule sponsored a series of administrative innovations to make its use easier.[25]

The Arid and Semi-Arid Lands Program

The Arid and Semi-Arid Lands (ASAL) projects were a much more substantial series of district-oriented efforts. When Britain joined the European Economic Community, Kenya became eligible for EEC development assistance. The EEC project identification team that came to Kenya in 1976 was determined to finance a major area-based integrated rural development program. These projects were extremely popular with the international donor community at the time, but after the SRDP experience they were in disfavor in Kenya. The EEC team wanted a major district, poor but with agricultural potential; it quickly identified Machakos as its desired target. None of the Kenyan officials, including Mule, agreed to this proposal; it was contrary to government policy to single out a district for special treatment, and Mule could hardly seek an exception for his home area. The EEC team went over the head of the civil servants to several cabinet ministers. The minister of finance, Mwai Kibaki, who was among the few in the government to be concerned with equity, gave his consent to the integrated rural development idea and liked the choice of Machakos. The EEC team left with agreement on a Machakos Integrated Development Project (MIDP).

The battle over MIDP did not end there. Kibaki was able to fight off criticism in Nairobi, but opposition coalesced around the views of the Eastern Province Development Committee, which had jurisdiction over Machakos and wanted to spread the EEC funds over all its six districts. A delegation was sent to Brussels to ask the EEC to reconsider. It did agree to some concessions, but it stood firm on its central commitment to Machakos. Mule's "financial diplomacy" may have saved MIDP at this point. The two major alternatives that the Government of Kenya was advocating instead of MIDP were the rehabilitation of the Nairobi-Mombasa trunk road and the Bura Irrigation Scheme. If the road project had been adopted, it would have absorbed all the money the EEC had available. The Bura scheme, however, already had support from another donor and had only a small funding gap. Mule pressed for Bura, which meant that when the EEC accepted it there still was ample money left for the MIDP. The other concession, which also fitted Mule's agenda, was the extension of the EEC's proposed small-projects grant from Machakos to the whole country. This was the origin of the Micro Projects fund.

Mule had not suggested the MIDP and had done his duty by not supporting it initially. Once the idea was launched, however, he was interested in protecting this prospect for major development in his home district. He felt that the project could never survive if Machakos was seen as its sole beneficiary. He also began to see it as an opening for advancing his agenda of deconcentrated, district-based planning and development. He recruited the help of the Planning Division in the Ministry of Agriculture to devise an umbrella proposal for the MIDP. The result was the Arid and Semi-Arid Lands (ASAL) program, which was designed in 1977–78 and which was folded into the 1979–1983 *Development Plan*. ASAL called for district-based integrated rural development initiatives for Kenya's poor and resource-scarce dry districts. The proposal was particularly timely, for it focused on the poor and suggested integrated rural development as a methodology. Both were in great favor with international donors at the time. Mule succeeded in getting financing from seven more donors for ASAL projects in eleven additional districts. He worked particularly hard to secure USAID finance for the ASAL project in Kitui, another Kamba district. ASAL was a giant advance for two top items on Mule's quiet agenda: decentralization and the redistribution of resources toward the poorer regions.

The two evaluations of ASAL efforts that are available to me are both positive. The Kitui and Machakos projects addressed critical problems of soil conservation and water development that would have received much less attention if viewed in a national perspective. They also did well at getting local beneficiaries to participate in project work and devised innovative methodologies for addressing some issues peculiar to the districts. The Kitui project boasted benefit/cost ratios of 1.4 for its soil conservation work and over 2.1 for its water development, both of which are high. Thus it helped to demonstrate that there are economically defensible investments to be made in such "low potential" districts.

As the projects evolved, however, government and donors backed away from the administrative integration of their multiple initiatives. To use the terminology of chapter 7, they found that the components were largely additive and incremental rather than interactive and minimal. In other words, the project pieces were all desirable but did not depend on one another for their successes. Integration was important at the planning and policy-making level but did not prove to be critical in implementation.[26]

CONCLUSIONS

Throughout the 1970s Harris Mule was associated with a large number of different rural development efforts. From them he learned much and consolidated his own policy preferences. He was still committed to improving the general quality of rural life, but he came to see agriculture as central and services as subsidiary in achieving this goal. He had observed the problems created by complexity and had come to favor administratively simple projects. He remained concerned about the unresponsiveness of centralized decision making and about regional inequalities and was convinced that decentralization was the appropriate way to correct them. But he had not yet found the way to promote it effectively.

These rural development initiatives also illustrate a number of the other themes I have been developing in this book. The selective implementation of the ILO recommendations demonstrates the dominance of matajiri class interests and the political need for patronage resources for rural clienteles. But it also shows that Kenyan leaders' conception of their interests was more enlightened and long-term than is common in Africa and that individuals, such as Kibaki and Mule, sometimes were able to give a progressive expression to the implementation of these interests. The latter point is also evident in the creation of the Arid and Semi-Arid Lands projects. The program was shaped by the combination of Mule's desire to help his fellow Kamba, the political impossibility of addressing that concern directly, and the political support that was available for a broad, multiarea approach from Kibaki and others. ASAL can be seen as an interaction effect of the political and the individual, and an expression of the real but dependent character of bureaucratic influence. Mule's inability to keep more than a few minor decentralization initiatives alive in this period is a more negative illustration of the same points.

The importance of institutional heritage is also exemplified in these pages. Kenya's decentralizers have followed the path of institutional least resistance by promoting deconcentration rather than devolution. They have simply extended the colonial pattern of "native" administration and have not challenged its preoccupation with control.

The inherited concern with control and distrust of the market found even less positive expression in the integrated agricultural development projects that were created in the mid-1970s. These projects represented an amalgam of colonial patterns of organization and implementation together with a new concern among donors for the rural poor. The resulting failures finally led the Kenyan government to confine its concern with integration to the policy and planning levels and to permit implementation in an administratively dis-integrated manner. It makes great sense to put farmers in control of integrating the inputs they need themselves when the components are additive and incremental, rather than minimal and incremental.

CHAPTER TEN

Nyachae, Mule, District Focus, and Agriculture

During the presidency of Daniel arap Moi, Simeon Nyachae's interests converged with those of Harris Mule and the two men came to have great influence on decentralization and agriculture.

In 1978, after the death of Jomo Kenyatta, Mule finally became highly visible in public policy-making in Kenya. Daniel arap Moi appointed him permanent secretary to the newly created Ministry of Economic Planning and Development, a natural step, as he had been deputy permanent secretary for Planning in the old Ministry of Finance and Economic Planning. (See plate 25.) However, Mule was assuming the top administrative position in his ministry without one of the requirements for success in the role. He had no relationship of personal confidence with the president and was not particularly skilled in the political arena; he had good judgment about what was politically feasible, but he did not have the personal contacts in the president's inner circle that were needed to make things happen.

The following year, in November 1979, President Moi appointed Simeon Nyachae permanent secretary for Development Coordination in the Office of the President. This was a completely new position. The powerful Geoffrey Kariithi retired from the position of head of the civil service, and his deputy, Jeremiah Kireini, also a Kikuyu, was appointed to succeed him, with the new title of chief secretary. Kireini did not enjoy a relationship of personal confidence with President Moi, such as Kariithi had had with Kenyatta; he probably had been appointed only to reassure the Kikuyu over the succession. Moi needed someone whose policy advice he trusted. When Nyachae was moved from provincial commissioner of Rift Valley to PC in Central Province, some people thought that this was due to his close relationship to Moi. Nyachae and

Moi were also partners in two businesses. Although Nyachae's new permanent secretaryship in the Office of the President gave him few staff, he assumed control of the cabinet secretariat and had Moi's ear on matters of policy.

Most of the senior staff in Mule's Ministry of Planning saw the new office of Development Coordination as threatening because it was taking over functions of policy overview and interministerial coordination that were their prerogative. Mule saw it instead as an opportunity. He liked many of Nyachae's ideas, noted that he was willing to push unpopular programs when he believed in them, and saw that the president listened to him. So Mule approached Nyachae, told him that he wanted to work with him, and offered to assign some Planning officers to his staff. Nyachae accepted, and a firm alliance developed between the two men. Mule contributed his considerable expertise and experience with economic policy, substantial staff support for policy analysis, and skill at handling the international donor community. Nyachae gave his close connection to President Moi, his years of experience with political conflict, and his knowledge of field administration. The two men were well matched.

DISTRICT FOCUS

During the final years of the Kenyatta administration the whole idea of decentralization was under attack. In February 1978 Francis Njuguna, deputy permanent secretary for Provincial Administration, and Harris Mule were asked to prepare a report on the Rural Development Fund (RDF). They toured the country to investigate its operation. Although their starting perspectives were quite different, their views converged as they traveled. It had been expected that the RDF would be seed money that would indirectly influence allocations of ministry funds in the districts. Instead, central influence on spending had been reinforced. The local participants on the District Development Committees (DDCs) focused all their energies on the small RDF allocations and ignored what was going on with the much more substantial ministry spending. Meanwhile, the field officers of the Provincial Administration and the line ministries saw the RDF as making little contribution to their programmatic concerns and were doing little to implement its projects. Njuguna and Mule recommended that the domain of the DDCs be broadened and the districts be made a more meaningful focus of development decision-making. This advice found its way into the Waruhiu Report of 1980, but nothing concrete resulted.[1]

Then in January 1982 President Moi appointed a Working Party on Government Expenditure. It was occasioned by the economic crisis that the second OPEC oil shock and the international recession had caused in Kenya. Philip Ndegwa, who had been Mule's superior for many years in Planning, was the chair, and the other four members were Aaron Kandie, Nyachae, Mule, and Francis Masakhalia, who had studied with Mule at Denver and followed him up the ladder in Planning. All of these men were sympathetic to decentralization. The result was that one of the many recommendations of the working party was a greater deconcentration of authority and functions to the districts. More remarkable, given Nyachae's many years of experience as a PC, a shift in functions and staff from the provincial to the district level was also recommended. The working party's report thus closely reflected the kind of vision that Mule had had for the districts throughout the 1970s and which he had continued to pursue despite only modest progress.[2]

Of course the working party's recommendations were only that—recommendations. Similar ones, such as those in the Waruhiu report, had been made before with little effect. The working party report, however, fell on different ears. Daniel arap Moi had been a part of the decentralist wing of African nationalism in Kenya and had favored the devolution of authority to regions found in the country's first ("Majimbo") constitution. He also received the report shortly before the coup attempt of August 1982. The unrest in the armed forces apparently persuaded him that his four-year quest for political support among the Kikuyu had been pyrrhic. He seems to have decided to revert to his earlier instincts and to seek a wider regional distribution of resources throughout the country. The working party report not only proposed decentralization but did so as part of a strategy to save money for a government that had diminished resources. President Moi called it one of the best reports he ever read. With staff support from Simeon Nyachae he promulgated a "District Focus strategy" for decentralization on September 21, 1982, as part of his general response to the unsettled conditions in the country after the coup attempt. District Focus became officially operational on July 1, 1983, but of course took much longer than that to implement fully.

District Focus was not at all the devolution of authority to elected local governments that Moi had favored before the defeat of "Majimbo" by Kenyatta. Instead, it was a culmination of the fledgling efforts at deconcentration that Mule had nurtured through the hostile 1970s. Its processes are dominated by civil servants. The core institution of District Focus is the District Development Committee (DDC). It typically has over sixty members, of whom the district's M.P.s and the chairmen of its local authorities are the only elected participants. Civil servants constitute at least 75 percent of the DDC. Furthermore, the DDC is served by an executive committee that is composed exclusively of administrators.[3]

These numbers somewhat overstate bureaucratic influence on the

DDC's proceedings. Cabinet ministers and many M.P.s have sufficient sway in Nairobi to make field officers cautious about opposing them. Since the DDCs have begun to make meaningful decisions, M.P.s have participated forcefully in their deliberations and have had an influence on the proceedings that far outweighs their numbers. Such leverage by M.P.s was evident even in the fully centralized system that preceded District Focus.[4]

Another aspect of the deconcentration of District Focus is its primary concern with the management of central resources. No new local taxes have been created; all the funds continue to come through ministerial budgets, and the issues all concern the ways in which the central government's allocations in the district are going to be managed. The opening paragraph of the implementing document for District Focus is instructive:

> The responsibility for planning and implementing rural development is being shifted from the headquarters of ministries to the districts. This strategy, known as the "District Focus for Rural Development," is based on the principle of a complementary relationship between the ministries with their sectoral approach to development, and the districts with their integrated approach to addressing local needs. Responsibility for the operational aspects of district-specific rural development projects has been delegated to the districts. Responsibility for general policy, and the planning of multi-district and national programmes remains with the ministries. The objective is to broaden the base of rural development and encourage local initiative in order to improve problem identification, resource mobilization, and project implementation.[5]

The integration that District Focus hopes to achieve comes from the local expression of priorities and informal coordination among field officers, not from new hierarchical relationships. Ministries still form their own policies, set their own budgets, and supervise the implementation of projects in their domain. Centrally initiated district-specific projects cannot be undertaken without DDC approval, but this is not hard to obtain. Local preferences now can be expressed in a format that will be taken seriously in Nairobi decisions, but the districts cannot force ministries to accept their highest-priority projects if these do not accord with ministerial policies. Integration therefore is more persuasive than authoritative. When decisions are made and influenced by field officers who know one another and see the products of one another's work, there is a greater prospect that they will take account of complementarities and will seek to fill in developmental gaps. The integration provided is one of policy, and even there it is largely advisory. Administrative interdependence, with the attendant dangers of deadlock, is not attempted.

Doubtless this degree of deconcentration seems very modest. Even this has been a major achievement, however. Nothing less than a fundamental restructuring of ministerial budgets was involved. The Government of Kenya budget for each ministry is broken down into programmatic "heads" and "subheads," within which expenditures are authorized on a "line item" basis for specific types of goods or services. The authority to incur expenditure within heads or subheads is held by those in charge of those programs at the national level. Before District Focus these headquarters officials delegated that authority to field units without accountability and as they saw fit. The way the accounts were kept made it very hard to identify where in the country funds were being expended, and program officers had a good deal of flexibility in moving them between areas. The system encouraged program heads to keep funds at headquarters and permitted them to make regional allocation decisions that they would have been loath to defend publicly. Those in charge of the ministries at the district level could not predict easily the resources they would have at their disposal and were often kept without spending authority until well into the financial year.

District Focus requires those in charge of programs in Nairobi to disaggregate their budgets and provide spending authority to the districts early in the fiscal year. For those ministries that had been run in a highly centralized manner and have so far implemented the directive, this disaggregation was extremely difficult to accomplish. In the Ministry of Agriculture, at least, district allocations were provided through a comprehensive authorization booklet that was available to all spending officers in Nairobi and in the field. This made the patterns of spending between districts public to other civil servants. Such openness placed a great deal of pressure on headquarters officials to be more egalitarian in their district allocations. There were no standards set as to what regional spending patterns were appropriate, but officials knew that if they were not to be accused of "tribalism" they would have to be able to justify deviations from equality, particularly those that favored their home areas. Thus what appears at first sight to have been nothing but a technical change in the process of financial management actually was a tool for the redistribution of regional resources. Although such redistribution has been limited so far by the tightness of government resources, it was one of the seldom acknowledged but driving forces behind District Focus.

A great part of the other changes wrought by District Focus were technical as well. Increased emphasis was put on forward budgeting to improve longer-range planning, the operations of the District Treasury were improved, and the authority of the District Tender Boards to make purchases and contracts was expanded, for example. Many of the provincial staff were reassigned to the districts as well, involving them more directly in development work. These reforms resulted in noticeable improvements in the implementation ability of government in the field, filling part of the promise of the Working Party on Government Expenditure to improve effectiveness and efficiency. Joel Barkan and Michael Chege report that the completion rate for RDF projects improved from 40 percent in the early 1980s to 75 percent by 1985.[6] Similarly, a study by Fenno Ogutu of a random sample of district-specific projects in Siaya and South Nyanza Districts before and after District Focus found that the success rate on projects had improved from 25 percent to 68 percent. In the same vein the average amount of time taken to complete water projects had dropped from three years to six months, and to finish classrooms, from three years to one.[7]

As mechanical as these reforms appear, they were difficult to design and implement. The early stages of the District Focus reform were handled by the staff in the Office of the President, who had a strong background in the Provincial Administration and were sensitive to the political ramifications of their actions. As the implementation process accelerated, however, the expertise that Mule had assembled on decentralization in Planning was increasingly used as well.

Several of these experts were expatriate advisers, whose role sometimes appeared to loom large. Many of them were academics who were analytically inclined and wrote easily and well. They therefore often played a major part in drafting key documents and could point to ideas that they had inserted into the program. Their contribution to the implementation of the many District Focus reforms is unquestionable, but their influence was less than a simple "word count" would imply.

Kenyans feel little bound by the written word in official documents and take their real cues from the spoken words and actions of those with power. Despite the expatriate gloss on much of the District Focus program, the aspects that have been implemented are those that have been validated and pressed by Kenyan actors themselves. The real work of making District Focus a reality was the day-to-day commitment of senior administrators to persuading other officials to do things they would rather not do. Simeon Nyachae and those immediately around him were particularly good at doing precisely this. When he was promoted to the office of chief secretary in July 1984, he took on much-expanded duties and could no longer give District Focus his full attention. As a result, some of the momentum of the reform was lost, and the center of energy passed to those around Mule at the Treasury. In its initial years, District Focus was very much a creature of the efforts of Nyachae and Mule, acting of course on behalf of their president.

Kenya's deconcentration efforts are unusual in their economizing intent. Decentralization has usually been seen as increasing governmental expenditure, both by giving vent to new political demands and by up-grading the local officers needed to design and implement activities. Kenya hoped to deal with the additional staffing requirements of decon-centration through training and redeployments from national and pro-vincial headquarters.[8]

The savings that were expected, however, were to come from the gen-eration of a new political dynamic. As long as local leaders directed their demands for development toward the national Treasury, they had no incentive to economize or to assign priorities to their needs. The waste-ful expenditures of all forty districts added together significantly dimin-ished the government's ability to meet the country's requirements. But the benefits of restraint by the politicians in any one district were dissi-pated in the rest of the nation, to their competitive loss. Thus the coun-try was presented with a classic "Tragedy of the Commons," where that which is rational for the collectivity as a whole is not rational for its constituent members acting individually.[9]

Mule and Nyachae hoped to break out of this tragic trap by redefin-ing the political game. By assigning resources more equitably among Kenya's districts and giving to them the authority to decide how these are to be used, local politicians would be induced to fight one another over the relative priority of their favorite projects, relieving the budget-ary and political pressures on the center. In this way the inflationary character of political demand would be contained, and it would be easier to bring national expenditure back under control. Local politicians would have to bear increased responsibility for choosing what could not be done, making the burden at the center more bearable. It is interest-ing that Mexico's decentralizers, responding to the same international economic crisis, have an almost identical set of economizing hopes.[10]

The hope for an economizing political dynamic from District Focus has not been realized so far. In good part this failure is due to the fact that districts have not been assigned fixed resources over which they have a great deal of discretion. The portion of the national Develop-ment Budget at the full discretion of the districts rose from 2 percent in 1976 to 8 percent in 1983.[11] This is a significant and impressive shift, but it still leaves the bulk of the budget in ministerial hands. Unless and until districts can easily get ministries to reassign funds from one pro-grammatic activity to one that enjoys higher local priority, it is not ra-tional for district M.P.s to treat their budgetary pies as fixed. Thus pres-sure is still directed at the center.

The decentralizers tried to bring local demand under control in the interim by directing that funds should be used to complete existing proj-ects, not to initiate new ones. In the absence of an effective mechanism for keeping communities from starting projects on their own, this direc-tive proved counterproductive. Ogutu's research in Nyanza Province found a frenzy of new, incomplete project activity as communities and politicians strove to get something started before the ban became effective.[12]

A good deal of decentralization, then, was concerned with administration and its impact on efficiency, effectiveness, and equity. One aspect of District Focus was not technocratic, however. A part of its purpose was to increase the ability of local citizens to influence government decisions. Although District Focus was deconcentration, not devolution, and remained firmly under the control of national field administrators, the shift in the locus of decision making to the district was intended to make it more accessible to local influence. Consultative committees were created for subordinate units of administration, in some cases even reaching to the level of the village. These committees were designed to add to the possibilities for popular participation in the development decision-making process, albeit not control over it. In this way the decentralizers hoped both to increase local political satisfaction with government and to induce communities to bear greater financial responsibility for development in their areas. Ogutu's study shows only a marginal improvement in popular satisfaction with project activity, but the proportion of projects completely dependent on the central government for their finance declined from 23 percent to 6. Ogutu also found more projects being initiated at the village level and a decline in civil-servant-proposed projects from 37 percent to 24. However, he did not consider this a victory for participatory democracy, for the initiative over projects was lodged even more decisively with local elites, who were using them to pursue their patronage agendas and not necessarily to address community needs. Given the nature of the Kenyan political system, little else could have been expected.[13]

The record on District Focus, then, is a mixed one. Such is always the case for major governmental reforms. It is extraordinarily difficult to reorient a large, well-institutionalized organization. That which has been accomplished, however, has been positive and appears to have brought modest advances in effectiveness, equity, and participation. It is impressive that Mule, using donor support, was able to keep the embryo of decentralization and integrated regional development alive in the hostile 1970s and that Moi was able to use Nyachae and Mule to achieve as much as they did in the 1980s against the centralizing traditions of the Kenyan state.

AGRICULTURAL PRICES AND MARKETS

In the early 1970s Harris Mule's ideas for increasing agricultural production had focused on inputs. The projects he had helped to initiate provided new hybrid seeds, extension, fertilizers, credit, roads, and so on. By the end of the decade he became much more concerned with price incentives. In this too he found himself allied with Simeon Nyachae.

The potential impact of the government on marketing in Kenya is great. In 1983–84 the government played at least some role in marketing 78 percent of Kenya's agricultural production, and 34 percent of the crops and animal products were owned at some point by government agencies. The five most important agricultural commodities are maize (corn), milk, beef, coffee, and tea, and the government is involved in marketing all of them. Kenya permits the farmers' prices for the commodities it exports to be determined by the world market, so the story of price policy was played out most clearly on domestically consumed crops. The producer prices that the cabinet sets annually include maize, milk, and beef as well as wheat, sugar, cotton, and others.[14]

In the late 1960s Kenya's major concern with food-grain prices was that they might be too high. Colonial agricultural policy had been designed to give economic support to the white-settler mixed farmers, who produced maize, wheat, and milk. As a consequence of this generosity, production was robust, and the government was troubled with surpluses of maize that had to be exported at a loss. Price policy consisted of pushing the producer price of maize down toward *export* parity, that is, the price that it would normally command if it were *sold* onto the world market. An internal decision in the Ministry of Agriculture to do the same to wheat was blunted by the opposition of matajiri civil servants and politicians who were producing it and who had argued that such a low price was inappropriate, as Kenya had to import much of its wheat requirements.*[15]

The 1970–74 *Development Plan* envisioned improvements in agricultural inputs as able to maintain production despite the disincentive of declining prices.[16] The accepted wisdom of the time was that peasant producers grew food grains largely for their own consumption, sold only a small portion of their crop, and therefore were insensitive to price signals from the market. Adoption of high-yielding varieties of maize and other improvements in technology would have a much greater effect on production than prices, it was thought. This view underestimated the importance to smallholders of market-based profits to finance the increased costs of adopting these yield-enhancing inputs. Those African states that let producer prices deteriorate severely have had difficulty in feeding themselves.[17]

Given that Kenya had consistent surpluses of food grains through the

---

*Nominal maize prices fell to 69 percent of their 1966 level in 1969, rose to 83 percent in 1971 and to 97 percent in 1972. In contrast, wheat prices stayed above their 1966 level through 1970, dropped to 86 percent in 1971, and were up again to 97 percent in 1972.

1960s, the decision to lower their prices was a correct one. It was reversed in 1970 when the government had to import a large amount of maize following a drought. But a new, coherent set of pricing policies did not result. Both decisions were taken in a context that paradoxically both regulated prices and gave them little importance in determining smallholder production. Little analytic attention was devoted to prices in the 1970s.[18]

The "methodology" for setting prices in this second half of Kenyatta's presidency became even more political than it had always been. Farmer presentations of their costs of production and periodic lobbying efforts were balanced with a concern to keep down urban costs of living. These forces led both to wide fluctuations in prices and to their being kept somewhat low.

The process is illustrated by maize. In 1976 Jomo Kenyatta decreed a 23 percent increase in the producer price. This decision was the direct result of a concerted effort by the Kenya National Farmers Union, representing large producers, who presented evidence to the president on their costs of production.[19] The new price was nearer to *import* parity than maize prices had been at any other time since independence. That is to say, it was close to what maize that was *bought* on the world market would cost if it were sold in Kenya.[20]

The result was a dramatic spurt in maize production. The Maize Board, which buys all maize that is not locally marketed, was overwhelmed, could not pay for deliveries on time, and exhausted its storage capacity. The producer price was dropped to its previous level in 1978, and arrangements were made to export the surplus at a loss. Drought and the price reduction combined to lower significantly the amount of maize offered for sale to the board in 1979–80. The government found itself embarrassed by a maize shortage within months of its exports.

Robert Bates is convinced that this kind of government intervention in grain markets, far from stabilizing prices, accentuated free market fluctuations.[21] This "policy-induced cycle" was driven by periodic shortages, on the one hand, and the huge losses run up by the board when it had to buy bumper crops, on the other. The government never recognized the inherently costly character of the board's stabilization function, did not make financial provision for it, and thereby exacerbated the board's crises in the periods when it needed to import or export.

The financial straits of the Maize Board, combined with the political desire to keep consumer prices low, on average kept the producer price low. A similar, although less dramatic dynamic, was at work on other commodities. Kevin Cleaver and Mike Westlake estimate that producer prices that were set by the government were 24 percent below the import parity level in 1980, leading to a 7 percent loss in farmer income. Still, these prices were not as bad as they were in many other African countries. Kenya's matajiri leadership is itself too deeply involved in agriculture to let the sector be damaged too much.[22] As a result, Kenya has managed to maintain a rate of agricultural growth only just below the pace of population increase.[23]

Concerned, among other things, at the degree to which pricing policy lacked a technical rudder and was simply being buffeted by competing political pressures, Mule secured multidonor support for technical assistance to the Ministry of Agriculture's Development Planning Division in 1976. The number and complexity of the pricing decisions was too great for all the economic analysis to be handled in the Ministry of Finance and Planning. From the late 1970s on, the depth, quality, and sophistication of Agriculture's economic analysis grew. The improved technical capacity devoted to price review came to have a major impact when it was coupled with Simeon Nyachae's interest and influence.

The review process that emerged began with an analysis of producer prices by economists in the Ministry of Agriculture. In 1981 the ministry succeeded in having the cabinet adopt its *Sessional Paper No. 4 on National Food Policy*, which pledged the government to set maize prices at import parity.[24] As is so often the case in Kenya, this broad declaration of policy was not followed with a commitment to implement the details that followed from it. But the Ministry of Agriculture had taken the unusual step of convening a large conference of political, civil service, and agricultural leaders to discuss the policy paper. This had resulted in a broad consensus supporting its thrust of increased support for agriculture, if not to its policy details. Thus, although government prices frequently differed from import parity, Agriculture's economic analysis and recommendations moved ever closer to it.

After the producer-price recommendations were cleared out of the Ministry of Agriculture's Development Planning Division, they went to an interministerial Price Review Committee, which the head of Planning in Agriculture chaired. The committee was composed of technical personnel from the Office of the President (i.e., Nyachae's adviser), the Ministry of Finance and Planning, Agriculture, and other ministries with an interest in specific commodities. The price controller also was present, as one of the important innovations of the late 1970s was to bring producer and consumer price recommendations before the cabinet at the same time.

The price controller tended to play the role of consumer advocate. In the early 1980s she did this, not by opposing producer-price increases, but by squeezing the margins of the intermediaries. By the middle of the decade she had begun to pull back from this strategy and argued directly for restraint on producer prices because of the large number of marketing boards that were in financial difficulty. Her concern for consumers in the setting of producer prices found support from other committee members, who were concerned that the cabinet might agree to an increase in a producer price without a corresponding retail one. The so-called technical analysis thus internalized the political concerns of the cabinet.

The parity-price-based recommendations of Agriculture's economists were usually considered in conjunction with the cost-of-production analyses prepared by the director of Agriculture's agronomists. The latter figures would show how unprofitable farming was and would imply price increases even higher than those proposed by the economists. So the general atmosphere of the meetings was pro-farmer, tempered by a fear that price increases for urban consumers might not be politically feasible and by a desire not to force the intermediary marketing corporations into financial difficulty.

Generally, recommendations were developed by consensus at this level, although with much argument. No votes were taken. If agreement was not reached, Agriculture's Development Planning Division determined what would be recommended to the next level.

The next stage was a meeting of the permanent secretaries to the Office of the President (Nyachae), Finance and Planning (Mule), and Agriculture, with Agriculture's chief price economist in attendance. Some price adjustments might be made at this level, but generally very little substantive change occurred. "After all, they are all farmers themselves." Finally, the recommendations went to the cabinet, where they were virtually always accepted as presented.

The consequences of this process were a gradual rise in producer prices. By 1986 the weighted average of producer prices was only 5 percent below import parity, compared with 24 percent in 1980.[25] One of the most significant accomplishments concerned beef prices. Various economists had been advising the government since the 1960s that domestic beef prices were too low, but all attempts to improve them significantly had been defeated, out of concern for urban consumers. In the 1980s, however, price controls were lifted, first on top-quality cuts and then on all beef products. The result was an increase in prices and a significant increment to the incomes of pastoralists and other beef producers.

Why were Nyachae, Mule, and the technicians able to get producer prices raised in the 1980s? The answer lies both in Kenya's balance-of-payment difficulties and in the way the government's policy analysts saw them. Economists Mule and Philip Ndegwa were persuaded by their advisers that deficits in foreign currency could only be met by producer incentives to increase exports and decrease the need for imports. Thus when the first OPEC oil-price increases created balance-of-payment problems in 1974, they immediately began to look at agricultural prices. This effort was stalled by the boom in coffee prices and the temporary glut of foreign exchange that it brought. When the second oil-price shock hit at the end of the decade, however, they immediately returned their attention to producer prices. Mule had already put in motion the steps needed to improve the technical quality of price analysis. A strong consensus developed quickly among the technicians as to the kinds of measures that were needed, and this is what swayed the cabinet. Other African states relied on other measures, such as import controls, and met with much less success than Kenya experienced, with serious consequences for their economies. Thus Kenya's policy shift on agricultural prices was shaped both by events and by how decision makers perceived them.

The political forces that previously had molded prices did not simply disappear. The considerable stake and experience that Kenya's political and administrative leadership had in agriculture obviously made it receptive to arguments that would raise prices and serve these interests. But fears of the political costs of raising consumer prices were temporarily finessed rather than overcome. Urban retail prices were not raised enough to match producer prices. The intermediary marketing corporations were squeezed instead.

Simeon Nyachae brought with him considerable experience with these corporations when he moved to the Office of the President in 1979. He had been chair of the Wheat Board since 1972 and became chair of the National Cereals and Produce Board in 1980 when it replaced the Maize and Wheat boards. Although neither position was an executive one, Nyachae was close enough to operations to be aware of the considerable inefficiencies, corruption, and profiteering by senior politicians that had overtaken them in the late years of the Kenyatta presidency. It seems reasonable to suppose that he hoped to square the circle of raising producer prices while containing consumer prices by decreasing these problems in the marketing parastatals. In addition to reducing their margins, he created elaborate control mechanisms to try to eliminate abuse. He did succeed in cutting down the patronage that had engulfed the National Cereals and Produce Board when it extended its buying centers in 1980.[26] But in general this strategy did not yield the returns expected of it. Barbara Grosh's excellent study suggests that it may even have been counterproductive for some boards by creating inefficiencies from inadequate operating capital.[27]

Whatever the hoped-for legerdemain, the political accomplishment of these producer-price increases should not be underestimated. The fact that the process was so completely dominated by technicians may make it appear apolitical. Instead, the image of a purely technical process was a coup of high bureaucratic politics. It resulted from a careful laying of the groundwork for economic analysis by Harris Mule and courageous and skillful lobbying on its behalf by Simeon Nyachae. Without Mule's feel for economic policy and Nyachae's devotion to Daniel arap Moi's long-term political interests, the confidence that the president and cabinet gave to the recommendations of the technicians would not have been possible.

ECONOMIC MANAGEMENT IN ADVERSITY

No better illustration of the strength of economic policy-making in Kenya can be found than the events of September 1982. Recall that the country had experienced an attempted coup d'etat in early August and was in political turmoil. Economically it was in perilous condition as well. Most developing countries had hoped that the OPEC oil-price hike of 1979 would be like that of 1974, producing an economic pause, readjustment, and then renewed global growth. Thus they borrowed to get themselves through what they expected would be a short, difficult time. They found themselves instead in a prolonged world recession and with debt burdens that were quickly getting out of hand. Kenya was one of many countries so affected.

The bill for these debts came due, so to speak, in September 1982, right after the August coup attempt. A team from the International Monetary Fund (IMF) arrived in Nairobi, ready to provide the country with bridging finance but demanding the usual package of reforms in return: budget cuts, increased interest rates, and a devaluation of the shilling. Such austerity measures are painful, and governments have been known to fall when they accepted them. Given the unsettled conditions already prevailing in Kenya, none of its cabinet ministers would even meet with the IMF.

Yet Kenya's senior economic managers were convinced that it would be dangerous for the IMF to leave without an agreement. The country's responses to this and subsequent economic crises were greatly influenced by Harris Mule, at the Treasury, and by Philip Ndegwa, when he later became Central Bank governor. (See plate 1.) They saw the economy in similar terms despite the personal conflicts they had sometimes experienced in the past. Ndegwa had been Mule's superior in Planning and the Treasury, and both had been deeply influenced by Ed Edwards, an American economist who had advised Kenya off and on since the 1960s. The three looked to external trade, agriculture, and strong private business within a framework of government direction to keep the economy healthy. Mule, in particular, had always paid close attention to the series of foreign economic advisers and international donor representatives that Kenya had had. He had learned a great deal from them, and although his thinking was more progressive than the current international vogue, it was consistent with it. Mule and Ndegwa both wanted to see the economy restructured to meet the crisis of the 1980s. Through devaluation, for example, they hoped to promote agricultural and other exports. This would raise farm incomes, increase rural development, and reduce the pressures on the cities. The IMF's medicine was what they would have prescribed themselves. They did not want simply to reschedule Kenya's debts and thereby postpone or prolong the agony of readjustment. They wanted a profile of debt repayments that would peak in 1989 and leave the country in strong economic shape thereafter.

Mule was handling the IMF visit and had to decide what to do when no cabinet minister would negotiate with it. He turned to Simeon Nyachae. Although Nyachae lacked the economic training and exposure that Mule had had, he had a similar outlook, perhaps because of his personal interests. He is a wealthy man with substantial investments in both industrial and agricultural firms. He seems to have been inclined to protect those investments, not by seeking special favors, although he has had some, but by maintaining an economy that is favorable to business and farming. Where necessary, he has been willing to cut government services to achieve that end. In short, he pursued his long-term class interests rather than his short-term purely personal ones.

Nyachae was persuaded by Mule of the wisdom of the IMF's bitter medicine. One of his distinguishing characteristics has been his willingness to take risks for policies that he thinks are right. This does not mean that he pays no attention to the political consequences of his actions. If he thinks a position is correct but cannot be won at the time, he will back away from it. But where he thinks he has a chance of success, he will publicly expose himself to risk in a most "unbureaucratic" manner in order to achieve it.

Nyachae thus brought the matter to Moi, who decided to approve the IMF package. This kind of access was possible because Nyachae was known to give priority to the president's long-term political interests. Moi also is a skilled political tactician and doubtless saw that the aftermath of an unsuccessful coup was actually a good time for difficult actions. His opponents were disorganized and unsure of themselves. He accepted the IMF package, and structural readjustment began.

Nyachae played a similar role with Philip Ndegwa in the Central Bank in early 1983. Ndegwa, whose advice also was respected by Moi, wished to initiate a new policy for the rate of foreign exchange. He wanted to undertake a substantial immediate devaluation and also to continue incrementally and unobtrusively to revalue the currency thereafter in line with inflation and the terms of trade. Ndegwa went to Moi, together with Nyachae and the minister of finance. The president adopted the policy after careful consideration, and it has proved particularly effective. Not only has it kept Kenya in a good trading position internationally and encouraged agriculture, the resulting devaluations, being frequent and very small, have been invisible to the public and therefore have not become political issues.

Kenya adopted these difficult economic policies not because of but almost in spite of international pressure. Other issues that the donors have pushed aggressively have provoked a nationalist response and gone nowhere. Like most countries, Kenya is jealous of its sovereignty and is willing to endure discomfort rather than have it impugned. In these instances, however, the relevant civil servants were persuaded of the wisdom of the course of action first and were willing to use donor pressures as a vehicle for advancing their own views.

These readjustment policies had to be implemented once the president had taken them. Ndegwa had the expertise and temperament to do so in the Central Bank for monetary matters. Mule had the knowledge and vision to do as much for budgetary matters, but not the personality. He is not good at saying no. But he understood this deficiency. He made sure that he had officers serving under him who were good at enforcing fiscal discipline, and he was careful to delegate to them the authority that they needed. The results, as is evident in table 10.1, were really very impressive. Between 1981–82 and 1983–84, at the height of the crisis, real spending by the government was reduced at least 7.5 percent, which is extremely difficult to do. Strict financial discipline was

TABLE 10.1
Total Kenya Government Expenditures
(in billions of K.shs.)
(base year = 1982/83)

Year	Nominal Expenditures	Real Expenditures as adjusted by GDP Deflator	Real Expenditures as adjusted by Consumer Price Index
1981/82	22.4	24.8	27.4
1982/83	23.8	23.8	23.8
1983/84	25.1	23.0	21.8
1984/85	30.7	25.9	24.6
1985/86	33.0	25.3	23.9
1986/87	42.7	29.9	29.2

SOURCE: Some economists working on Kenya consider the Consumer Price Index to be more reliable than the deflator implicit in the government's calculation of its GDP per capita. Government of Kenya, *Economic Survey* (Nairobi: Government Printer): *1984*, pp. 8, 17, 80; *1985*, pp. 8, 16, 76; *1986*, p. 69; *1987*, pp. xii, 9, 75.

maintained until 1986–87, in the middle of which both Mule and Nyachae retired.

Nyachae retired in February 1987 on his fifty-fifth birthday. Moi had instituted a strict policy of retirement at age fifty-five in order to gracefully clear out many of the senior Kikuyu administrators who had served Kenyatta. Nyachae could not sidestep this policy without creating political embarrassment for the president. In any case, Nyachae's high and increasingly political profile in his final year in office caused him to slip in presidential favor. Mule retired at the same time, even though he was only fifty. He was tired from the strains of managing the Treasury and wanted to earn enough money in the private sector to send his daughter abroad to university. Perhaps he was influenced in his decision as well by the fact that Nyachae was retiring and could no longer give him the influence that he felt he needed to control the budget and economic policy.

CONCLUSIONS

Michael Lofchie has suggested that one indicator of a state's strength is its ability to make policy in its long-term interests. A weak state is constantly buffeted by its short-term political needs. Kenya was a strong state through almost all of the period reviewed in this study, while a majority of other African nations have been weak.[28] Kenyatta's preeminent political stature and skill made it relatively easy for him to keep a longer view. Further explanation for the country's relative constancy to its long-term economic interests can be found in two other factors. First, Kenya's African leadership developed a stake in the economy, which gave it interests that closely coincided with those of most peasant producers and the economy as a whole. During the time when this matajiri class was forming and had a weak conception of itself, Kenyatta provided the long view for the state. Afterward, this class exerted influence for a stabilizing vision of its own. Second, the preeminence of the civil service in the Kenyan political system has kept near the center of power and decision making men who are professionally and temperamentally inclined to be guided by the future rather than immediate political convenience.

Nyachae and Mule illustrate the latter pattern well. Mule developed his policy positions out of a long series of interactions with fine economic analysts and experiences with the making and implementation of policy. A moderately progressive commitment to the prescriptions of neoclassical economics was well institutionalized in Kenya's ministries of Finance and Planning. Once Mule's basic views were formulated he showed a remarkable ability to adapt them and nurture them through difficult times. He never acted contrary to the wishes of his political superiors, but he could stall when he thought their decisions unwise and would move the machinery of government rapidly when their decisions did support his predilections.

Nyachae had personal interests that coincided well with those of the economy. Once elevated to a role at the center, he came to see those interests in broad, class terms, rather than particularistic ones. Furthermore, he was willing to take risks to pursue that longer-term vision. He was skilled at understanding both the political requirements of his president and the technical arguments of other civil servants. He used that skill to mediate between them in a way that was extremely productive for public policy.

As a consequence of the actions of men like Mule and Nyachae, Kenya has maintained policies that have been favorable to agricultural growth and have kept the country in a relatively competitive position internationally. Matajiri interests and the desire to protect Kikuyu peasant clients kept Kenya's farm-gate prices from falling as disastrously as they did in other African countries in the 1960s and 1970s. The solidification of matajiri class interests, mediated by the skilled advocacy of Nyachae and Mule, raised these prices to competitive levels in the 1980s. These same interests, combined with the institutionalization of neoclassicalism among Kenya's economic administrators, caused the country to respond quickly and well to the global recession of the 1980s.

Kenya also pulled away from its centralized past and deconcentrated enough authority to its districts to achieve some degree of local integration and participation in development and to produce somewhat greater regional equity. Consistent with the lessons of the 1970s, the integration sought was more one of policy than of administrative implementation. The modest pace at which these reforms progressed was not at all due to the political context, which had become quite favorable to deconcentration. Instead, it illustrates the difficulties of altering deeply institutionalized governmental practices, in this instance particularly those of financial management. The degree of progress made on these reforms was due in great part to the groundwork laid by Mule and to the commitment to fight through the detailed obstacles to implementation that he shared with Nyachae.

CHAPTER ELEVEN

The Unofficial Lives

The behavior of most African public servants cannot be understood if we confine our observations to the office place. The demands of private life have an especially profound effect on the official actions of African administrators.[1] Of course the informal has a significant effect on the way formal roles are performed in American organizations too, as we have known for over half a century.[2] But the ideal of the separation of personal and job roles is very strong in the West, and it is possible to describe official actions there without referring to administrators' private obligations. Africa simply does not permit such a narrow, focused view. Kinship duties frequently impinge on work roles, and unless we understand how our four administrators handled the unofficial demands on their lives, we will not unlock some of the most important secrets to their official successes.

To appreciate fully the behavior of the four men we have been studying we have to put it in the context of what was going on around them. The stereotype of African bureaucrats would be something like the following: They are overwhelmingly concerned with the welfare of their family and ethnic brothers and sisters. Considerations of the broader public or national interest have distinctly lower priority for them. They have private businesses on the side, and these occupy a good deal of their attention during official working hours. The story is told of the official who has two jackets so he can hang one over his office chair and then leave for most of the day to handle his business. More commonly, they come to the office late, leave early, and are slow to answer messages. What does motivate these bureaucrats in their official duties is the prospect of personal gain. Contracts routinely require a 10 percent kickback to the responsible official. Vital permits are more easily and quickly obtained through the payment of a bribe. Much of this income will be used to support relatives and community projects at home. Officials may hope to become popular enough in this way to run for Parliament someday. Outside the bureaucrats' offices will be knots of petitioners from their home areas, hoping to use their influence to secure government jobs. As a result of this patronage, the ministry's offices and halls will be filled with junior staff who have little to do and whose conversation interferes with the work of those who are needed. Patronage leads to much incompetence in the public service, and there seems to be little ability to get rid of it. This stereotype is precisely that—an exaggeration. But it does have its grounding in reality. Only a minority of civil servants fit all the parts of this stereotype, but the behavior of a large number conforms to at least one of its components. John Montgomery comments in his study of managerial behavior in southern Africa that this "personalistic interpretation . . . is perhaps oversimplified [and the corruption part of it exaggerated], but [it] turns out to be a recognizable explanation of observed realities."[3] Jon Moris, using his Tanzanian experience, would agree.[4] David Gould, writing about Zaire, Nigeria, and Ghana, would even reject the qualification about corruption.[5]

WORKAHOLICS

As we seek to differentiate the four administrators from the stereotypical African bureaucrat, let us begin, as we would with a manager anywhere in the world, by asking how they handled the pressures of their jobs. All four men held extraordinarily demanding positions and reveled in their work. Ishmael Muriithi spent so much time traveling, both internationally and domestically, that his wife "used to joke, 'You only come here [in] passing.'" When Simeon Nyachae was chief secretary, each day he got up at 5:00 A.M., arrived at the office by 7:00, had a meal sent in so he could work through the lunch hour, and did not leave the office until 7:00 P.M. Harris Mule needed only four hours of sleep and frequently did professional reading until two in the morning. He often did not leave the office until 8:00 P.M. Charles Karanja was infamous with his family for his inability to sit still and his need to be always at some kind of work. All four men had the stamina to put in more hours on the job than most of their colleagues and the powers of concentration to make that time highly productive.

For relaxation Ishmael Muriithi was an avid tennis player until late in his career. When Simeon Nyachae was a provincial commissioner he used to walk regularly; as chief secretary he had a squash court installed at his home and would play by himself and do exercises every night, retiring regularly by 10:30 P.M. His entire life was run with a military-like discipline. Harris Mule was able to turn off the pressures of work quickly and relax into conversation. He used to enjoy going to bars with his friends when he was a young man—the usual relaxation for Kenyan men. But as his responsibilities increased he reduced his alcohol consumption and no longer frequented bars. He often spent the evening talking with a couple of very close friends instead, usually in a room at the back of his sister's Nairobi shop. None of the four administrators used alcohol to relax. Charles Karanja's drinking was very modest. Nyachae abstained completely and would not even take coffee, remnants of his Seventh-Day Adventist upbringing.

SONS OF THEIR VILLAGES

The character of risk in the agricultural systems of preindustrial society causes small producers to invest heavily in personal relationships as a hedge against adversity. Not only do close ties with social equals, such as relatives and neighbors, provide help when one experiences calamities such as drought or illness; bonds to one's social or economic superiors can also result in personalized assistance. For these latter, unequal types of relationships, the recipient promises support in return for the help that he or she receives. This social dynamic lies at the root of the patron-client relationships that pervade preindustrial societies and dominate most of their political processes.[6]

Men such as Karanja, Mule, Muriithi, and Nyachae were valued "sons" of their villages. Their upward mobility gave them access to resources that could make a large difference to the life-chances of their parents' neighbors and kin, most of whom were relatively poor. Their communities would not let them go. Relatives and neighbors gave these "sons" great status, insisted that they still belonged to the village (no matter how long they had lived away from it), and did everything possible to help them protect their positions. One senior official told me: "Once you reach that level, there will be so many people from your home and tribe helping you. They will not want to see that position of influence lost to them, so they will inform you and warn you of what they hear, even coming to your house at night." In return the villagers expect contributions to community projects, assistance with jobs, help with school fees, and emergency aid. If unchecked, these expectations can suffocate the financial well-being even of the well-to-do. How did this book's four "sons" manage these village ties?

The first expectation of adult males is that they build houses in the communities of their birth to reaffirm their membership, even if they are living elsewhere. Furthermore, for those in senior positions, these houses have to be "modern" and substantial—houses that reflect their status and to which they might plausibly retire someday. Three of the four men accepted this obligation; only Mule did not.

For Nyachae the decision was straightforward; two of his wives continued to live in Kisii after he left, and he needed housing for them. He provided it in a particularly impressive manner. The home consists of three large buildings, only one of which is used by his wives. On the spot that Chief Nyandusi had indicated his son should build, Nyachae constructed a round house of several rooms with a peaked roof. The design is striking and distinctly modern, but its shape evokes the filial piety and tradition out of which it was built. (See plate 26.) The home as a whole is impressive, enough so that President Moi has stayed in it when visiting Kisii. The buildings are a strong, visual statement that Nyachae's "home" is Kisii. (However, Nyachae lived most of the time in his large and extremely elegant Nairobi house.)

Charles Karanja built a house at his birthplace of Karatu in 1961. (See plate 27.) He was interrupting his career to go to Canada for further studies and needed a place for his wife and children while he was gone. He bought a farm in upper Kiambu in 1964, after his return, and lived there until 1974, a considerable distance from Karatu. He then bought a coffee estate in the same administrative division as his birthplace and built a very large house there, where he now lives. (See plate 28.)

Ishmael Muriithi built a house near Nyeri town on land given to him by his father. He rented it out, however, and never used it himself. This action was sufficient to meet community expectations, but he never developed real ties to the property. Instead of his being buried there when he died, as would have been traditional, his grave was placed higher up in the Aberdares at his mother's house, where he was born. (See plate 12.) (Muriithi lived outside Nairobi in a modest stone house that had been built by the European from whom he bought his farm.)

Karanja, Muriithi, and Nyachae were able to make reasonable use of the houses that they built at home. But this should not obscure the fact that these houses also fulfilled the important symbolic purpose of affirming their community memberships. Many other Kenyan men build such houses without having any practical use for them, lending them to relatives or using them for vacations a few days a year. They are nothing but monuments to the strength of their communal ties.

Harris Mule was alone among the four in not building a house in his place of birth, although he bought a farm there and visited it at least once a month. He identified with the community and assisted it, but he did not see the practical purpose in constructing a house there—it was too far from Nairobi for commuting yet close enough so he could make day visits to it when he had business to conduct. In any case, his mother had a good house in which he could visit if necessary. He put his money into the purchase of a moderate home in Nairobi instead. People in Mbooni were troubled that he had not built there, and it was one of several things about Mule that the villagers could not understand.

PATRONAGE

One of the basic forms of assistance that villagers expect from their well-placed "sons" is jobs. Outside the doors of the influential there frequently will be long lines of those seeking an "in" to employment. Most of these petitioners will be modestly educated, looking for entry-level jobs. But a few among them will be well credentialed and in pursuit of plum positions.

The administrators in charge of public entities in Kenya generally have complete discretion in hiring their most junior staff and therefore have considerable scope for the exercise of influence there. If they have openings at this level, they can easily employ those who have direct or indirect claims on them and can trade appointments with other senior managers with the same authority. (Thus an administrator's own hiring may result in a reasonable ethnic mix and still be an instrument for favored employment for his kinsmen throughout the government.)

The weak controls on the exercise of patronage at the junior level creates great temptations for the expansion of this part of the public payroll. During the period in which President Moi was consolidating his presidency, the numbers of junior staff in the government may have doubled. For example, the National Cereals and Produce Board increased its employees from one thousand to three thousand in order to staff the new buying centers created for the 1980 season (when Nyachae was chairman). Many valuable patronage opportunities were thereby created in localities around the country,[7] although Nyachae emphasizes that "at no time, during the period I served as chairman of the Wheat Board of Kenya and the NCPB did I request the management to recruit any relative or friend from my home district or any other area."

Senior appointments, however, are strictly controlled. The Public Service Commission, a parastatal board of directors, or some other control body will be involved in employment and promotion decisions. As demonstrated in Appendix A and discussed in chapter 4, the processes at this level are much more difficult (although not impossible) to manipulate.

Favoritism in employment is an important and highly emotional issue in Kenya. When people obtain positions for which they are not best qualified, they may perform poorly or treat the jobs as sinecures and do little at all. Productivity will suffer as a result. Villagers are innocent of these consequences, however, and are unrelenting in the pressures they apply to their relatives and "sons" for help. Other employees are alert for signs of favoritism, are demoralized, and speak bitterly of "tribalism" when they see it, and warmly praise an administrator who resists it as being "a nationalist."

The four administrators clearly deviated from this norm of patronage, although to different degrees. Ishmael Muriithi handled the pressures for patronage in the manner of a proper Weberian bureaucrat, strictly distinguishing between his private and public roles. The career of Dan Mbogo was probably hindered rather than helped by having his brother as his director. Muriithi was anxious to avoid even the appearance of favoritism. He instructed his family members *not* to send him job applicants. "If there is work, let them apply" through the proper, regular channels. Conversations with those close to him at his birthplace of Ihithe did not reveal a single case in which he had helped a person find employment. Many of those questioned had difficulty understanding why a man who was generous in other respects should have failed to help in this way. One relative, referring to Muriithi's farm near Nairobi, speculated, "You know that person has stayed as if he is a Kiambu man and [maybe] that is where he has helped much." If those in Muriithi's home village didn't appreciate his probity on employment matters, his professional colleagues in the Ministry of Livestock Development did. They considered him a "true nationalist."

Charles Karanja's record in this area is intriguing. On the one hand, some of those working with him felt that his employment decisions sometimes involved favoritism. Karanja holds that "in order to enhance faith and confidence in government [among the large numbers of unemployed], I have always deemed it my duty to see job seekers and to help where possible. The process is straining and time-consuming in a busy office, and . . . I have only been able to help a small fraction." He stresses that those employed were qualified and that the "record shows that I helped all on the basis of first come first served." Still, those who had some personal ties to him, either by kinship, by hailing from his parents' village, or by having been at school with him, would have felt more able than others to approach him. When he helped these people, it was possible for others to interpret this as favoritism, even though the ethnic mix of his employees is reasonable. By and large, the positions involved were junior ones, either at the KTDA headquarters or on his own farms. (The latter were not what the petitioners usually had in mind, as such work is hard.) He did not control the hiring of senior staff, but if someone about whom he had favorable personal knowledge seemed qualified, he would try to put them on the short-list for a board interview.

On the other hand, Karanja insisted on excellence on the job. He himself did not see any bias in helping those who came to see him and would have abhorred it if he had.

> I maintain that to obtain the best results . . . , one must hire the services of the best-qualified people and show no favor, as to do so will always discourage the other workers. . . . If appointments were made on the basis of favoritism rather than merit, efficiency and performance would have been seriously jeopardized.

Whatever favoritism he did exercise did not hurt the effectiveness of his organizations. He strongly believed that work standards should be high and that his personal obligations ended with giving someone a chance at a job and did not extend to keeping them there. When he did hire people with whom he had a personal link, he would hand them over to someone else to supervise and would urge that they be fired if they did not perform adequately. There is no doubt that he meant this. He let one of his own sons be dismissed from one of his businesses. With respect to senior positions, Karanja's help ended with getting someone to the job interview. Once there, they were on their own and strict merit criteria prevailed. Promotions too were governed by performance alone.

Patronage, in the sense of helping someone with whom one has personal ties, has a radically different meaning if it is tied to strict performance criteria. In some circumstances it may even be conducive to superior organizational performance, for not only are those doing the work good people with strong incentives, they also have distinct feelings of personal obligation to their superior that can lead them to perform beyond the formal requirements of their roles.[8] But Karanja's methods sometimes cost him the loyalty of those few who felt outside the net of his patronage. These people contributed to his troubles when his political problems erupted.

Simeon Nyachae was politically astute in his appointments. The nature of his positions gave him little direct control over junior staff hiring. Thus to the extent that people in his home district of Kisii talked about his assistance with jobs, the reference was generally to employment in his businesses, not in the government. During the years that Nyachae held the confidence of President Kenyatta, he learned to work well with Kikuyus. When he emerged on the stage of power in his own right, he maintained a preference for working with a multiethnic staff. His professional staff in the office of the chief secretary reflected a wider ethnic mix than that of his predecessors in the position. He regarded the civil service as too important to the nation for ethnic meddling. University students from Kisii sometimes criticized him for *not* helping the careers of fellow Gusii.

Nyachae had a reputation for working his staff hard, getting rid of those who were lazy or untalented, and rapidly promoting those who served him well. Thus, though he did exercise patronage in the civil service, it was meritocratic. Those he helped were those who had been skilled at anticipating and meeting his wishes for action. Similarly, when he was angered with a decision, a career that he had previously accelerated could be suddenly stalled.

Nyachae was not above using patronage in its more classical form, but it appears that he restricted it to domains that he considered political and thus more appropriate. Several relatives and associates (including a former schoolteacher of his) received positions on parastatal boards through his influence. Not all of the beneficiaries of his patronage in this domain were Gusii, but certainly many were. These appointments were highly visible, and in some cases the qualifications of the recipients could be questioned. In this way he gained a reputation among the wider public as one who could take care of those close to him. However, these board positions had long been used in Kenya as political sinecures, and they had little practical effect on the operations of the parastatals they nominally oversaw. Nyachae appears to have distinguished areas in which he felt that traditional patronage would damage the performance of public organizations from those in which it would not and to have confined his favors to the latter. It is symptomatic of the difficulties of administration in Kenya that the general public and some civil servants could not appreciate the distinction.

Harris Mule also seems to have made fine but principled distinctions about patronage. There was not even a hint of favoritism in his appointment and promotion of professionals. In a wide range of interviews with Mule's colleagues, some of whom were very critical about certain aspects of his handling of personnel, no one ever suggested that he was anything other than scrupulously fair. Such was his reputation for being above ethnic and family considerations that one senior official remarked, "I would be surprised if he helps people [from his home] with work, for I have never seen a job seeker in his office."

The view in Mbooni, from which he hailed, was quite different. There many people remarked on the aid he had given people in finding employment, sometimes citing specific cases they knew well. It was known that he did not like to see job seekers at his office, but villagers found him sympathetic when they approached him in Mbooni. Much of the help that he gave was simply the advice that the well informed can provide to the uninitiated, steering them toward the places where people with their qualifications are most likely to find success. Instances were also reported in which he had taken a petitioner's qualifications and called the person when he had found an appropriate spot. It appears that these positions were never in Mule's ministry.

Evidently Mule succeeded in a remarkable balance. His open personality and genuine desire to help people convinced supplicants in Mbooni that he was doing everything he could for them. At the same time he was keeping this assistance sufficiently far removed from his office that his fellow professionals saw him as a model of integrity.

HARAMBEE, PATRONAGE, AND POLITICS

Kenya has a distinctively strong tradition of community self-help.[9] Rooted in customs of mutual assistance and communal labor, self-help began very modestly in the colonial period as a means of raising the resources needed for school classrooms beyond those that the missions and the government would provide. After independence self-help was raised to the level of an ideology. President Kenyatta dubbed it *harambee* (Swahili for "let's pull together") and exhorted communities to help themselves first if they expected government assistance and challenged politicians to demonstrate their value to their constituencies by mobilizing such efforts.[10]

Gradually harambee shifted from a vehicle for self-help to one for patronage. When it began and in the early years after independence, the sums raised were modest and comprised large numbers of small contributions. Often a measure of coercion was applied by the local chief and subchief to get these "gifts," but they did come primarily from those living in the community itself. As the matajiri class emerged, however, many harambee functions took on a distinctly different cast. Rural residents were transformed from the prime actors into appreciative audiences as their leading "sons" vied with one another to show who were the most generous patrons and to claim the prominence that followed. Peasant contributions may have been as great as before, but their significance as a percentage of the whole declined dramatically.

Ishmael Muriithi's role in this heady competition was an unpretentious one, as befitted his modesty and lack of claim on community leadership. In the first decade after he became director of Veterinary Services, Muriithi made the expected K.shs. 100 to 200 ($11 to $22) contributions to school projects in his home area and was visible only on livestock harambees. Grade dairy cattle need to be dipped regularly in acaricide to protect them from tick-borne disease. The Ministry of Agriculture was encouraging smallholders to form community groups to build and maintain cattle dips, and some donor funds were available to match locally raised money. Muriithi personally promoted this endeavor in the areas around his home in the early 1970s. Then, when asked, he would come in person to add his resources to the fund-raising effort. For the dip at Hubuini, near his birthplace in Ihithe, he matched the K.shs. 7,000 ($1,000) raised locally with an equal amount of donor funds that he controlled as director. On occasions like this, he himself would donate about K.shs. 1,000 ($111 at the time), some of which he would have collected from others in his office in Nairobi. A few times he served as guest of honor for these harambees, and he would then bring K.shs. 5,000 to 10,000 from himself and his associates in the capital. When Muriithi participated in opening these cattle dips he would donate a five-gallon can or two of acaracide, which probably had been given to him by the suppliers. There were approximately thirteen dips around his birthplace that he supported in these various ways.

In 1976 Muriithi raised his harambee standing in Ihithe. He was invited to a fund-raising event for a new Presbyterian church at Hubuini. Isaiah Mathenge, his friend and a former provincial commissioner, was the guest of honor and brought K.shs. 12,000. Muriithi surprised everyone by presenting K.shs. 18,000 ($2,570). The total raised that day was K.shs. 54,000, with the two patrons responsible for over half. Had both men had political ambitions, Muriithi's upstaging of the guest of honor would have represented a serious challenge. As it was, it seemed to cause no rancor.

Muriithi became known as a special patron of the churches in his home. He traveled too much to attend church regularly; very few of the matajiri do. But the Presbyterian Church of East Africa was central to the lives of Muriithi's parents, and he had a deep emotional tie to it.

In 1979 the Hubuini church was ready for the next step in its building program. A delegation went to visit Muriithi at his home in Nairobi, led by a church elder who had been to primary school with him. They asked Muriithi to be guest of honor for a harambee, and he promised to think about it. A month later he gave his consent and spent about five months on personal fund-raising endeavors in Nairobi. On the appointed day he brought two other prominent people from the area and K.shs. 14,000 ($2,000) of the K.shs. 44,000 raised that day.

Muriithi was asked to be guest of honor again in 1981, but this time after reflection he declined and recruited Mathenge to take his place. On this occasion, of the K.shs. 52,000 raised, Mathenge brought K.shs. 10,000 and Muriithi, K.shs. 4,000 ($400 by then). It is likely that Muriithi was careful not to upstage his friend this time and may even have redirected some Nairobi contributions to him. Over the years Muriithi donated K.shs. 36,000 to the Hubuini Presbyterian church, or about 18 percent of its completed cost. (See plate 29.)

The reputation Muriithi gained for his endeavors at Hubuini earned him an invitation to be guest of honor for a harambee for another Presbyterian church at Kariguini in 1984. The place is about fifteen kilometers (ten miles) from Ihithe, but a cousin of Muriithi's who was an elder approached him twice on behalf of the church. Muriithi finally said that since this was a church of God he would come and help, but he did not have much money, as he had contributed to other harambees recently. Such protestations are common among guests of honor, who try to contain inflated rural expectations. It did not work. Muriithi brought K.shs. 31,000 ($3,100) and only K.shs. 3,000 more were raised locally. This was the epitome of "self-help" as a spectator event. Muriithi's efforts on behalf of this church had raised its stone edifice to the top of the walls before he died. The community was hopeful that the family might consider it a memorial to him and help to complete it.

During the last decade of his life, Muriithi probably contributed about K.shs. 100,000 to his community, about K.shs. 10,000 ($1,000) a year. Of course the large contributions that he brought were not only from himself but from his friends and associates as well. Since he would have been expected to reciprocate these gifts by his peers, our assessment of the final, net outlay would remain much the same. These annual sums were more than double the average family income of the villagers they benefited, but they seem feasible, if generous, for Muriithi's.

Harris Mule entered the world of harambee prominence in 1977. He was asked to be guest of honor for the Kiumi Water Project, which would bring piped water to farms in four sub-locations, including his own. The event raised K.shs. 30,000 ($4,300), of which about K.shs. 15,000 was brought by Mule from himself and his friends. Some large donors like to enhance their reputations by blurring the line between their own contributions and those of their associates and thus have their gift announced simply as coming from themselves "and friends." Mule is one of those who insists instead on enumerating the sources and amounts of the funds he has raised. At least as important as the immediate cash that Mule gave was the promise that he secured from Lois Richards of the United States Agency for International Development (USAID) to provide a matching contribution through CARE. This ultimately resulted in about K.shs. 100,000 in materials for the project. Many donor representatives were fond of Mule because of the ease with which they were able to talk with him and because of his reputation for personal integrity. He was the sort of government official they liked to help. USAID's promise had an amusing side effect. In announcing it, "I told the harambee that I would bring a woman who would match whatever they raised. The Kamba word for woman and wife is the same and the women [in Mbooni] thought she was my second wife. They mobbed her in excitement when she came [to make the presentation]." After another harambee this water project was ultimately taken over and completed by the government's District Development Committee.

Mule used his contacts with donors to assist with two other small projects in his home. For the Kikima Farmers Cooperative Society he helped get Dutch funding for a community center, a dairy, and a revolving loan fund for the purchase of grade cattle. He also gave advice on how to get American assistance for over forty women's poultry-keeping groups in the location.

Philip Mule, Harris's father, had helped to build both a church at Tawa in 1938 when he was working there and the Mbooni Boys High School after independence. Philip served on the board of the school until he died in 1980, and Harris "inherited" his place on it. The school library is named after Philip. Harris was guest of honor at a harambee in 1979 at which the school raised K.shs. 102,000 ($14,500) in cash and materials. Harris was responsible for about K.shs. 70,000 ($10,000) of this sum, a large part of which were materials from CARE, which he had secured through the good offices of the Canadian embassy. He also found guests of honor for subsequent harambees for the school and obtained foundation scholarships for some of its poor students.

Harris Mule became chairman of the new Utangwa Secondary School in Mbooni Location in the mid-1970s. In 1985 he persuaded Chris Musau, a prosperous Kamba businessman near Machakos town, to be the guest of honor for its harambee. By the standards of smaller, struggling schools, this was a very successful event. It raised K.shs. 193,000 ($12,000) in cash and K.shs. 300,000 ($18,700) in materials. Musau brought contributions of K.shs. 56,000, and Mule, of K.shs. 40,000 ($2,500), both in cash. Mule's gift had been obtained from a British American Tobacco fund. Mule subsequently remarked: "I created a big problem for myself in bringing [such a large gift]. In self-help the more you do the more they expect. . . . In my next harambees they then were disappointed by my K.shs. 2,000 to 3,000."

The scale of Mule's personal gifts to various harambees was modest, for so was his personal wealth, and he was unwilling to sell favors at the Treasury for contributions. He was well liked for his assistance, however, because he knew how to tap into donor resources and had a generous, open spirit. The community's way of expressing this popularity was to insist that "he would get 95 percent if he were to stand for this seat in Parliament." It did not distinguish between the patronage roles that were appropriate for a politician and those for a civil servant.

Charles Karanja's involvement with harambees began in 1964. Their scale at that time was very modest. "We then might collect K.shs. 100 ($14) in a meeting. At one I offered to match anything they gave and they came up with K.shs. 371 ($53). I wouldn't dare do that today."

His earliest and enduring interest was in primary and secondary schools. In 1964 and 1968 he became chair of the boards of Mururia Secondary School, in Gatundu, and Kanunga High School, in Kiambaa. He was made board chairman of Loreto High School, Limuru (a Catholic girls school from which his wife had graduated), in 1969 and continued in that position through the end of the 1980s. For a time he served as the chair for the Loreto Teacher Training College in Kiambu as well. These schools are scattered widely in his home district.

Later Karanja added Catholic churches and some independent ones to his list of favored projects. In the area around his birthplace he was known to support "virtually every [church and school] project." (He himself would claim only "many.") But he did not accept involvement in harambees that concerned any sort of business. "It must be in the public interest." Similarly, although he obviously was dedicated to schooling, his sympathy with requests for the educational expenses of individuals was limited.

For the types of projects he favored he was exceedingly generous and active. Once established at the KTDA, he never gave less than K.shs. 1,000 ($143) personally to a project and averaged a couple of these a month. Most of the harambees he supported were within Central Province, and he would travel as far as Kirinyaga to attend one on a great many weekends. During his years at the KTDA he would be guest of honor at up to four harambees each year. After his retirement he accepted up to three a year. These would be mainly in his home division of Gatundu, with some others elsewhere in Kiambu District.

When Karanja was at the KTDA the highest contribution he brought to a harambee as guest of honor

> was K.shs. 140,000 [$20,000], but then my personal contribution was less then than it is now. . . . I delivered more money then, for I would have my officers to collect money [for me]. Also business people give you more when you are in a position like that where they expect that you may be able to help them in return. Once I get K.shs. 20,000 to 40,000 [$1,250 to 2,500] I stop collecting now, although I gave K.shs. 60,000 [$3,750] last time. Normally you reach K.shs. 60,000 to 80,000. . . . I always ask those involved what the target is. I [have] never brought less than K.shs. 25,000 [$1,600].
>
> I always read the names of friends who gave [contributions through] me. . . . The type of people I ask will almost always give K.shs. 1,000 [$63]. I rarely have to read [the names of] more than thirty people. . . . In recent years there has been a tendency for people to give publicly and not announce where the money is from. I don't like it when people say only "myself and friends." . . . You don't know where he got it from, nor whether he has given it all.

The particular harambee game in which Karanja was playing was one with high stakes. Many times he was giving more than his salary at the

KTDA; this was possible only because the income from his businesses was always at least as great as that from the KTDA after 1969. Even at this level, the volume of giving and the newly amassed wealth in Kiambu were such that Karanja was considered to be only in the top two or three for generous contributors in his home place.

Simeon Nyachae began to play the role of guest of honor in harambees shortly after independence, as his meteoric rise to provincial commissioner gave him resources and influence with businessmen which relatively few possessed at the time. Much of this harambee activity was conducted in his official capacity and therefore benefited government-blessed projects in the areas in which he was working. Those in which he did participate in Kisii were close to his home and attracted little attention in the rest of the district. His contribution to one harambee, which he conducted at home in the 1960s, was big enough to make the then member of Parliament for his constituency, James Nyamweya, feel threatened by it. It seemed to him to be challenging his position as prime patron for the area and to portend a challenge by Nyachae for his seat. In fact Nyachae had no such ambitions, and it was two decades later before Nyachae expressed any interest in elective office. He seemed instead to be driven by a diffuse sense of responsibility for the welfare of the people his father had served.

Nyachae's pattern of harambee activity changed significantly after Kenyatta's death and his move to the Office of the President in Nairobi. He no longer had responsibilities for a particular province, and he did not have to worry about appearing to neglect the welfare of the Kikuyu he was governing for the benefit of his fellow Gusii. He continued to be a prominent and generous participant in harambees "in very many parts of Kenya, which shows the breadth of his friendships." Such spread earned him the praise of some as "a true nationalist." But his activities in Kisii also became more visible and eventually widened to cover much of the district. For example, in 1985 he was guest of honor for four harambees in different Kisii constituencies.

His harambees became very substantial affairs. For instance, the one that he conducted in the Majoge Bassi constituency in 1986 benefited 202 primary schools and raised K.shs. 6,000,000 ($378,000). Nyachae brought K.shs. 136,000 ($8,500) from himself and his friends and delivered a contribution of K.shs. 20,000 ($1,250) from President Moi. The M.P. from the constituency, Chris Obure, brought K.shs. 86,571 ($5,410).[11]

NYACHAE'S POLITICAL DOWNFALL

Nyachae's efforts were widely known and appreciated in Kisii. At the same time they were seen as a bid for leadership: "He is trying to make his influence felt with the people." Once again, we see that citizens in Kenya do not distinguish between the roles that are appropriate for civil servants and for politicians. A small, rural shopkeeper in Kisii commented:

> The difference between a cabinet minister and a chief secretary is that a chief secretary can give more in harambees. There is no other difference in the ways in which it is permissible for them to help.

But there *are* differences in the roles. A senior government official remarked of Nyachae:

> It is not an asset as chief secretary to be so visibly political. . . . It is a powerful position with defined positions of chief adviser to the president, control of the civil service, [management of] security, etc. That in itself draws resentment, and if one is politically visible in addition, the resentment becomes too much. . . . I believe that in Nyachae's case he is not in harambee because of political ambition. He does it because he likes it. He likes to be appreciated; he likes applause. . . . [But it creates jealousy.] Politicians, including cabinet ministers, resent the fact that they can't extract as much, and they suspect that you are up to something. . . . I don't think any politician likes to see other politicians do better.

Indeed, Nyachae did involve himself in political matters in the 1980s. He was known to have supported Omanga's successful bid for Parliament in 1979 in his home constituency. But many civil servants have done as much. More seriously, he became deeply involved in KANU party politics at the Kisii District level. This district had always suffered from factionalism, and Nyachae sought to promote greater unity among its M.P.s so as to give them greater bargaining power at the national level. To this end he suggested in 1985 that the KANU branch chairman for Kisii not be a sitting M.P., and Lawrence Sagini, who had been Kisii's first M.P., was selected for the post. Many Gusii, however, did not interpret this as a neutral action on Nyachae's part. Sagini, a brother-in-law of Nyachae's, had been displaced from Parliament by Zachery Onyonka, who was then the sitting district KANU chair. Onyonka had been compromised with a murder charge arising out of the 1983 Parliamentary election campaign (although the courts ultimately found him innocent, placing the blame on one of his supporters). The scandal persuaded Nyachae that it would be wise to replace him. In acting on this conviction, he sealed a feud with Onyonka and made the other M.P.s uneasy that his influence might be eclipsing their own.

As long as Nyachae remained chief secretary and had the support of President Moi, his position was unassailable. After his retirement, however, he reversed his oft-repeated disinterest in elected office and declared himself a candidate for Parliament. Many former provincial commissioners have attempted election in Kenya, but only one has ever succeeded. The frequently heavy-handed, authoritarian behavior that goes with the role of PC does not go over well at the polls. Nonetheless, informed observers not only considered Nyachae the favorite but gave him a good chance at carrying allies in surrounding constituencies to victory with him.[12] But he never got to try. Kenya is a one-party state; although elections are contested, candidates must be cleared by KANU in order to stand. Nyachae's "papers disappeared mysteriously at the KANU Headquarters," and his candidacy "did not therefore reach the executive committee for [the required] clearance." The president declined to intervene in this and thirteen other similar cases elsewhere.

How could such a powerful man fall so suddenly and so far? Onyonka's opposition to Nyachae was a foregone conclusion, and it is understandable that the other Kisii M.P.s may have been reluctant to yield primacy of place to him. Because Kenya is a one-party state, significant policy disputes cannot be resolved by elections, and highly personalized factionalism frequently takes their place. Nyachae himself attributed some of the antagonism to his attempts to get some of the M.P.s to account for harambee funds that were collected under their leadership and may have been misappropriated.[13] These are insufficient explanations. President Moi had the power to intervene on behalf of Nyachae's application to stand for election. Furthermore, Nyachae's businesses suddenly began to have severe difficulty getting the various government permits that they needed to operate; this trouble had to be coming from somewhere in Nairobi. Moi appeared to have turned his back on Nyachae for reasons that have never been made public.[14]

Although many details in Nyachae's "fall from grace" are not clear, some general observations can be made. His career had been built by always putting the interests of his president first. Although his loyalty to President Moi never shifted, he violated this principle in minor but important ways in his tenure as chief secretary. First, he was highly visible. This is standard for a provincial commissioner, who is representing the president in a purely local setting. But civil servants in the capital are expected to be invisible. The attention Nyachae was receiving in the press could have been seen as detracting from the stature of Moi and therefore would have been unacceptable.

Second, as chief secretary Nyachae was head of the civil service and of the cabinet secretariat. As such he felt obliged to represent the interests of the public service, to defend individual bureaucrats from unwarranted political attack, and to protect the integrity of basic governmental procedures. If this representative function were perceived to have conflicted with service to the president, it could have strained Moi's favor.

Third, Nyachae was outspoken and willing to take risks. These attributes first brought him to Kenyatta's attention and aided his advance to the post of chief secretary. But it is possible that they also led him to advocate some policies that finally tried the president's patience. Paradoxically, great careers cannot be built without taking risks, but in the end they can be undermined by such gambles as well.

Finally, a civil servant is not likely to be successful in the long run if he challenges elected politicians for their constituency support. Several times Nyachae in his role as provincial commissioner confronted members of Parliament, but he was seen as doing so on behalf of President Kenyatta. His activities in Kisii in the mid-1980s threatened to take him across a vague and invisible boundary and strained his effectiveness. After his retirement he attempted to convert the immense power he had exercised on behalf of the president into an elective political base. This is extremely difficult to do, for power that is delegated from the top is radically different from that which comes from popular support. The combination of an electoral base with high civil service experience in sensitive positions also can be threatening to senior politicians, who may find themselves suddenly challenged on their own ground. If Nyachae had succeeded in his campaign in Kisii, he would have dominated his district's politics in a way that no new Kenyan politician has been able to do since independence. In other words, he would have gone from being his president's "most obedient servant" to one of the powerful "peers of the realm." There were many who would have found that menacing.

ILL-GOTTEN GAINS?

The wealth of men such as Karanja and Nyachae, and the substantial sums that are sometimes dispersed in Kenyan harambees, immediately raise the question of where this money is coming from. There can be little doubt that much of what is gained and given in the country has been corruptly obtained. It would be remarkable if it were otherwise. The political system is based on patronage. Citizens do not ask their elected leaders to deliver national policies; they ask instead for immediately tangible benefits delivered to themselves and their communities. This patronage is dispensed in the form of jobs, individual gifts, and harambee donations. Nor do voters inquire where the money necessary for this largess comes from; they ask only how much, not how.

Corruption has grown steadily in Kenya over the past twenty-five years. Although it still is not as pervasive as in West Africa, it is confronted in many aspects of public life. Rumors of 10 percent kickbacks on government contracts and purchases are frequently mentioned by usually well-informed people. Permits of various kinds also are said to be obtained often by bribes. The incentives for ill-gotten gains are powerful and the disincentives quite limited. The police find it difficult to keep up with all but a fraction of the corrupt activity, and the powerful most often are prosecuted only if they "fall from grace." In most of Africa the indictments for corruption come *after* one has lost office; they do not precede and cause the loss of power, as they do in some other political systems. In any case, the boundaries on the legitimate pursuit of private gain are poorly defined in Kenya. During the colonial period senior civil servants were allowed to possess farms of up to fifty acres, thereby encouraging their solidarity with the white settlers. With the Ndegwa Commission report of 1971 a public servant was permitted to own virtually any business or property. The doors to conflict of interest were opened wide.[15]

How do the four men conform to these values of public life? Remarkably, their behavior has generally been quite different from the prevailing standards. The next chapter will argue that this is part of the reason for their success as civil servants.

It is easiest to certify the ethics of Harris Mule, because his personal wealth was so clearly limited and what he gave away came largely from foundations and international donors. There is no unusual cash-flow to explain. The belief in his integrity was widespread and unanimous.

Considerable search revealed only one instance of what might remotely be called conflict of interest on Mule's part. He had used the Ministry of Agriculture's Farm Mechanization Unit to clear and plow his newly acquired farm in Kibwezi in 1984 and 1985. The unit was created to provide exactly these kinds of services to farmers like Mule, and he paid for the work. Nonetheless, he had argued against its highly subsidized services in the past and felt that they probably would not have gotten around to helping him if it were not for his position. He did nothing wrong, but he had gained a kind of advantage from his office. In any case, Mule did not continue to use the unit's tractors. Though the charges were low, the slowness of its work in 1985 substantially reduced his yields.

Mule's relatively simple life-style, selflessness, and humility were appreciated by people at his birthplace but were incomprehensible to them. One remarked, "This person eludes us." He did not play the role that they expected of a "big man." His failure to take better care of himself lay outside their system of values. The same behavior evoked similar admiration from his professional colleagues, but much better comprehension. They understood that it greatly enhanced his ability to perform his duties well and felt themselves challenged by it to greater integrity.

Harris Mule's generosity and integrity were inspired by his father, Philip, but they were also greatly aided by the simple tastes and support of his wife, Martha Ngina. Unlike many wives of the upwardly mobile, she does not press him for expensive things or urge him to make more money. "She is not demanding," a relative remarked. "I think he was just lucky in choosing her; I don't think he saw it clearly in her" when they met.

This does not mean that questionable decisions never came out of his office. Such unbending integrity would lead to one's being kept from the centers of decision in Kenya. Mule

> gives his professional advice on what should be done but he has been willing to accept and implement political decisions when they are given to him. He has proved accommodating in that respect. But unlike others who have long accommodated . . . he has retained a professional vision of where he wants to see public policy go.

In other words, he has not been overtaken with cynicism and become self-serving.

Ishmael Muriithi's values on private gain from public office were similar to those of Mule, but his image with his colleagues was slightly tarnished in the later years of his career. He came to the civil service with the stern moral values of his Presbyterian parents. At the time of independence he was the district veterinary officer (DVO) in Eldoret. There were multiple chances for him to have undertaken some private practice on the side, and, indeed, many of the British DVOs had done so. However, Muriithi adhered rigidly to the formal regulations and kept strictly to his public practice.

The position of director of veterinary services, which Muriithi held for eighteen years, would have offered him a vast number of opportunities for corruption. The profits earned on the marginal costs of the chemicals and pharmaceuticals used in veterinary medicine are substantial. (Some of the biggest costs in this industry are for research and development, which have to be paid up front. Because the actual costs of manufacture represent a modest portion of the price charged for each unit sold, the incentives to sell additional units are very high.) Thus, bribes and other inducements to purchasing officers are common around the world. Confidential inquiries with well-placed people in Kenyan pharmaceutical businesses did not reveal even a rumor of corruption on Muriithi's part in dealing with them or their competitors. In fact, he even declined to accept for private use on his farm gifts of returned drugs that could no longer be sold.

Muriithi's standing was somewhat tarnished with his professional colleagues, however, over an episode that was perfectly legal in Kenya. When the Government of Kenya ceded the land outside Nairobi on which the International Laboratory for Research on Animal Disease

(ILRAD) was built, a piece across the road from the site was unneeded. It was divided into three parcels, and Muriithi bought one of them. As Muriithi was instrumental in securing the site for ILRAD, and as he was subsequently on its board, he obviously had advance knowledge that the extra parcels were going to be sold and, in this sense, may have profited from his position. (There is no suggestion that he paid anything other than the standard price for the land.)

Later there were serious problems at ILRAD, and the board (including Muriithi) felt that it needed to remove several of the top managers. In the midst of this controversy one of those removed accused Muriithi's wife of having sold hay to ILRAD from this plot. As ILRAD is an international organization, it is considered unethical for board members to have financial dealings with it and thus create a possibility of conflict of interest. This charge was not pursued, Muriithi did not have an opportunity to reply to it, and some people doubt that it was genuine. Whatever the truth of the matter, the incident did make the purchase of the land parcel more widely known in the veterinary profession and compromised the reputation for absolute integrity that Muriithi had had with his colleagues. As the charges did not involve anything that is illegal in Kenya, they passed unnoticed by the general public. They may have been one factor, however, in Muriithi's subsequent decision to resign from the ILRAD board. This incident highlights once again the great gap that exists in Kenya between societal and professional ethical standards over conflicts of interest.

That Muriithi had high personal standards of integrity is not necessarily to say that the organizations he was associated with had the same. There is only so much that the man at the helm can do when he lacks the support of society and the state's monitoring institutions. Informal extra payments to veterinary field staff for their services had become frequent by the end of his career.[16] There also were many rumors of irregularities around the purchase of livestock at the Kenya Meat Commission, including during the years that he chaired its board.

Charles Karanja's fall from power at the KTDA was occasioned in part by his being caught in a relatively minor conflict of interest. He probably would not have made this error in the early 1970s. During that time he had substantial private interests in trucking but was careful not to do any business with the KTDA, to avoid even the appearance of impropriety. However, the coincidence of President Kenyatta's declining health and acuity with the flush coffers of the coffee boom led to an explosion of questionable acquisitiveness among the political and administrative elites after 1976. Many were tempted into changing their ethical standards during this period; to a minor extent Karanja was drawn along with them.

The Achilles heel in Karanja's ethical system was Africanization. He was passionate in his commitment to advancing African participation in the previously white and multinational bastions of the tea industry. Most often this involved extending the functions of the KTDA, but he was pleased to advance private Kenyan entrepreneurs as well. In domains where other Africans were offering their services to the KTDA, Karanja was scrupulous in not tendering his own, so as to avoid even the appearance of impropriety. But in the areas where Africans were not represented, Karanja came to feel that it was legitimate for him to involve companies in which he had an interest of his own, so as to promote Africanization of the economy. It was in this way that the compromising decision was made to place trainee managers in the Ngorongo tea factory, in which he had an interest. He persuaded the KTDA board that this arrangement would speed the training of African managers for the KTDA factories.

There were other decisions that also might have been questioned. A company of Karanja's had indirect shareholdings in a newly created Kenyan tea brokerage firm that handled some of KTDA's business. Combrok provided good service at the same prices as other brokerages, so KTDA was not harmed in any way. Nonetheless, some eyebrows might have been raised if the Karanja-Combrok connection had been known.

Again to promote Africanization, a Karanja company acquired an interest in a Mombasa warehouse that was to handle some of KTDA's tea. When the major shareholder tried to charge a slightly higher price than his competitors were offering to the KTDA, its business had to be withdrawn to protect KTDA's interests and Karanja's reputation.

Most of those close to Karanja within the KTDA felt that "when he helped his business it was in ways that wouldn't hurt the KTDA." But this point and the nuances of his Africanization ethics were not apparent to all, and this cost him support both inside and outside the KTDA. It is certainly true that Karanja's use of his position for personal profit appears to have been legal and minor by Kenyan standards. His businesses flourished after his "fall from grace," whereas those businesses built on the use of influence usually do not, for their profits depend on favoritism. Even though Karanja's breach of integrity was minor, it damaged his ability to manage his organization aggressively and autonomously.

Simeon Nyachae was a man of great wealth and power. The combination created recurring suspicions that the former came from his abuse of the latter. From time to time members of Parliament, the press, and the rumor mills of Nairobi have all made allegations of corruption and conflict of interest against him.[17] Nyachae has effectively responded to many of the public accusations, and there is evidence that some of the other rumors were false.[18] But it is beyond the capacity of a single investigator, lacking legal powers, to establish the full truth in such a thicket of innuendo.

Still, we can suggest why rumors of wrongdoing would have arisen even if Nyachae may never have made a corrupt decision. First, he was a political inside player. He did not get to the pinnacle of the civil service by being a neutral technocrat. On behalf of his presidents he skillfully managed the interface between the political and the administrative. Payoffs and questionable business deals are a regular part of Kenyan political life, financing the patronage networks that are essential to political survival. As so much of Nyachae's work touched on sensitive political matters, people naturally would assume that he was privy to its shadier side as well.

Second, Nyachae was a wealthy man. When offices or parastatals with which he was associated made questionable decisions, people simply assumed that he had received a bribe. After all, reasoned the public, how else could he have gotten his money? Yet the decision could have been executed under political orders or because of a bribe to someone else. Nyachae's prosperity is easily explained by his business acumen, his early entry into the highly propitious climate for African business at independence, and his father's wealth. When similarly questionable decisions were made around Harris Mule, people simply assumed that he had not been involved. After all, he had nothing to show for it.

Third, Nyachae most likely did derive some business advantage from his government position without necessarily having sought it. He argued that since he consciously took himself out of the day-to-day running of his businesses and was ignorant of the specific points at which the government might help them, his interests could not affect the way he performed his public duties. He congratulated himself on having refused to bid on projects where he was conscious of a conflict of interest. Others were not so sure he had enjoyed no advantage.

> Once you submit an application with his name on it as a director, no one would give it any problems. . . . He never had to get on the phone. . . . His name was enough. He's benefited by his position without having tried to.

> The mere fact that he is associated with a business leads it to get government preference without his having to ask for it. Of course it becomes more difficult if you ask for help, which he does in the same way as a normal [citizen would]. You can only be at par if you discriminate against yourself, which he doesn't do.

That Nyachae had a quick temper and great influence over civil service careers led bureaucrats to err in favor of his interests without his even knowing it. That he had held powerful positions without interruption since independence could have left him unaware of how difficult it can be to get permits and contracts if one is not connected. Such advantages, even if they were unintended, created great resentment. This partly explains why many officials sought to block his business interests after his "fall from grace."

Even as chief secretary, Nyachae was conscious that something was not working with the government's conflict of interest regulations. He did not believe that civil servants should be kept out of business. The civil servants of the previous generation, like his father, Chief Nyandusi, not only had been permitted to have parallel business interests but had been actively encouraged to do so by the British colonial government. But Nyachae did wish that the irregularities could be controlled and the rumors quelled. His solution would have been

> a standing committee of well-respected, honest, professional people who would deal with individual investments of people in public office [both elected and appointed]. One should be required to submit to them a report [each year] of all one has and account for every single cent one has invested. They should have a staff to analyze returns and investigate where investment has been very large. That would curtail abuse.

But he was unsuccessful in getting his proposal accepted.

CLASS AND THE NEXT GENERATION

Most people are concerned to provide not only for themselves but for the future of their children as well. The four subjects of this study had stood on the shoulders of their parents and joined the small percentage of the truly advantaged in Kenya. It would be unnatural if they did not want to help their children achieve a similarly privileged status. As we are about to see, they largely succeeded. Their offspring differ considerably in how well they are doing, but most of them belong in the same broad status group as their parents. In their occupations, friendships, and social orientations they are part of the matajiri (well-to-do), although not yet in terms of their independent wealth. The successful transmission of this group membership to the next generation is one of the clearer indications that class formation is well advanced in Kenya.

All of Charles Karanja's six children went to respected primary and secondary schools in the Nairobi area, and four of them received post–A-level training. Karanja was a strong family man and was usually home to eat with his wife and children each night. He also was a passionate believer in the importance of education and was strict in his insistence on study and good grades. His wife, Philomena, gave up her teaching career to manage their farms and raise the family. This was somewhat unusual. Most educated Kenyan women stay in paid employment, as they have servants to run their homes and as they are not required to participate in the social side of their husbands' careers. Philomena put strong pressure on the children to succeed as well. But the traditional formality and discipline of the African father-child relationship did not work well for Karanja in the new affluence in which his family was being raised. He was careful not to spoil his children with too-ready access to money, but as they got into their teenage years they could not attach the same importance to school grades that he did. "He sees your report [card] and tells you off for one hour. It made me feel rebellious. The more he pushed, the less we did. . . . You felt you could never do enough for him." In short, the social setting was more like the one in which American middle-class families find themselves. It was not at all like the one in which Karanja had grown up, where a lapse in effort consigned one to a lifetime of farm work.

At different points rebelliousness undid most of his children. Two sons made it to the University of Nairobi but failed because of alcohol-related problems. Two other children insisted on setting their sights below the university level. One son went to Canada to pursue his B.A. but dropped out after two years to become a lay preacher.

Despite these educational disappointments the children were launched on careers that seemed likely to keep most of them part of the matajiri, at least when they inherited their father's property. One daughter was married to a successful businessman. The other children all eventually joined his businesses in various capacities. Karanja was struggling with learning to delegate enough responsibility to them, and it seemed likely that they would become good enough to at least hold onto their father's gains. Despite Karanja's best efforts, none of his children were yet as successful as he was, but they hadn't dropped out of their father's newly formed class either. All of them had their own cars, and they were quite urban and matajiri in their social lives and orientations.

Harris and Martha Mule have two daughters, Nthenya ("early morning"), born in 1971, and Ndinda ("stayed for too long"), born in 1983. Nthenya was in an elite Catholic girls high school in Nairobi—Loreto Convent, Msongari—when the interviews for this study were conducted. (See plate 30.) Although she was bright, she was doing only moderately well in school at that point. She remarked that with regard to her studies her father was

> "cool." You know he wants you to do well, but he never shouts at you when you don't. He says, "I see you had a problem. What was it?" He always goes to parents' days, et cetera. You can talk to him if you need to. Mother is the one who applies more pressure. She's always saying how well she did and how I'm not studying hard enough.

Her parents were uncertain how to handle Nthenya in the atmosphere of relative affluence in which she was being educated. Harris was pessimistic about the ability of parents like himself to surmount their children's privileged environment. He remarked:

> The children of the old chiefs have not done well. (Nyachae is an exception—and is only one of his father's hundred-odd children.) [The] same will happen to the children of today's rich. They don't do well in school and are poorly disciplined, poorly motivated workers.

Nonetheless, the Mules did succeed with Nthenya. Martha had given up her job as a secretary to raise the two daughters. They found the marginal income tax rates on her earnings too great to justify the sacrifice. They regularly took Nthenya with them to work on their farm, hoping to keep her grounded in Kenyan reality by so doing. She also was taught to cook and liked it. She passed her O-level exam in the First Division, did A-levels at Kenya High, and went to Grinnell College in the United States with a scholarship.

Although Ishmael and Martha Muriithi lived right outside Nairobi, their children had a different experience from that of most matajiri offspring. They were raised neither in a housing tract, as were the Mules, nor on a large estate, as were the Karanjas. Instead, they grew up working a small, family farm.

> From the start it was manual labor—feeding chickens, milking the cows, grazing the cows before [the farm] was fenced, [helping] to clear the new land [with] father. . . . There is nothing [we] have not done. . . . [He taught us] "The more you do, the more you get."

All four children were sold on farm life and wanted to work their own someday.

The Muriithis went to Hospital Hill Primary School, one of the best of the government schools. The two eldest then boarded at Alliance High School, where their father had gone. They went on to the University of Nairobi, and Ann Wangeci became a dentist and Elijah Waicanguru a medical doctor. These educational institutions gave them a peer group of upwardly mobile rural youth, not the children of the affluent. (Grace had gone to England to take a degree in music, and Munene was in Jamhuri High School when this study was done.)

It seems likely that the environment was more responsible for the success of the four than was their father. He cared about and advised them, but he was away a great deal. "He'd come [home] after you were asleep or be gone before you were up. [You] never knew when he'd be there." To compensate, his wife Martha also quit her job and worked the farm full time. The rearing of the Muriithi offspring took place in a setting more like that of their father's than that of the other matajiri children.

Despite his large number of children,* Simeon Nyachae devoted considerable time to them. They obviously mean a great deal to him. "When he works hard he says he is doing it for the children." Even when he was chief secretary he would be home at 7:30 each night and spend an hour playing with the small children. He then would dine with his wife and the older children.

He had observed that children in polygamous marriages usually pull away from their father, identify with their mothers, and are factionalized accordingly. Nyachae was determined that this should not happen to his family, "so he raised us together to give everyone an equal opportunity." Once they were in secondary boarding schools, rather than separating to their mothers' homes, they would spend half their holidays working on their father's farm near Nakuru and the other half with their paternal grandmother on the Sotik farm.

> [Nyachae] has always been a disciplinarian [with us children. The farm labor that we did] was for the purpose of making us realize that everything one got had to be worked for. . . . We probably did more work on average than other well-to-do kids.

The discipline was particularly strict around education.

> At the end of each school term he would read the [grade] reports in detail in front of all of us and reprimand us where necessary. He followed progress in studies very keenly. He followed Charles's reports closely even when he was in Britain as a graduate student.

Despite his demanding schedule Nyachae visited their many schools for their parent conferences himself. He did have the traditional African formality in his relations with his offspring. "At the same time he made an effort to understand us as individuals" and tailored his careful advice accordingly.

Nyachae's wives devoted full time to the family's affairs. Although educated Kenyan women generally do subordinate their careers to their husbands', it is unusual for them to give them up altogether. The fact that the wives of all of the four men did so speaks to the great strain that the men's workaholic devotion to their senior positions put upon their families.

Most of Nyachae's children went to rural secondary schools, thereby having the same kind of upwardly mobile peer group as the Muriithis.

---

*It is contrary to Gusii custom for one to enumerate one's children. Out of respect for the wishes of Simeon Nyachae and his family, I neither give the number of his children nor provide a listing of their names.

Five of them subsequently went overseas to Britain, India, and the United States for university. None of them attended Kenyan universities. They entered professions such as nursing, hotel management, law, business management, and insurance sales. Nyachae was disappointed in the performance of only one of his children, and he was having him trained to enter one of his businesses.

Thus most of the progeny of these four men entered the matajiri class with their fathers. It seemed unlikely that many of them would achieve the same prominence or startling increase in wealth. Yet the new class had succeeded in reproducing itself. There were two important differences between this second generation and the first, however. The second did not have its parents' roots in rural villages. The friends of these young people were primarily like themselves—urban and from affluent families. This generation would not have the same ties of obligation to the peasantry as their fathers had. And very few of these children went into the civil service, unlike their fathers and grandfathers. This phenomenon is general among the offspring of senior civil servants. What had seemed to be the beginning of family dynasties in the public service (similar to those on the continent of Europe) was not to be.[19] It appears that the civil service is to be populated, not with a hereditary administrative elite, but with new waves of upwardly mobile rural refugees.

CONCLUSIONS

By virtue of their senior positions in the public service, all four men achieved incomes and standards of living far higher than those of their parents. They also came under incomparably greater financial pressures. Village neighbors and relatives wanted help with jobs. Expectations for harambee contributions were on an unending escalator. And they had to provide for the education and future of their children. They themselves had worked their way up through publicly supported institutions and had won their own positions through intelligence and hard work. However, their very affluence often sapped their children's will to work. The four men were forced to pay for expensive private schools and universities and to worry about businesses that their children could enter, so as to pass on membership in the matajiri class they themselves had struggled so hard to create.

These pressures were distracting in themselves and made opportunities for extra income very tempting. Many of those in their positions succumbed and became corrupted. By and large, the four men we are studying did not, meeting the financial strains through either modest living standards or business acumen instead. The extent of this self-denial was an important factor in determining the degree of their success. It gave them the respect and cooperation of their professional colleagues and made them less vulnerable to damaging accusations in the rough-and-tumble of bureaucratic politics.

The unofficial lives that we have reviewed here illustrate how Kenyan senior public servants become patrons to their communities and secure matajiri class membership for their children, whether their careers accomplish something for the public good or not. These breakthroughs were easier and more lucrative for the first generation of African public servants because new business opportunities were so numerous. The later generations would be jealous of their wealth and, finding it harder to achieve, be much more tempted to cut corners to get it.

The patronage role civil servants played gave them local political status and blurred the distinction between administrator and politician in the public's eyes. Civil servants who were tempted to play political roles often did so at the peril of their administrative careers. Visible participation in electoral politics by Simeon Nyachae and Charles Karanja ultimately cost both of them presidential favor. The power that a civil servant exercises in Kenya derives from the person of the president. Attempts to amass support from the grass roots, far from contributing to one's influence, will be seen as threatening to the president's power and probably lead to one's "fall from grace."

CHAPTER TWELVE

African Managerial Success:
Conclusions about Individuals

Many have expressed concern lately about the quality of public management in Africa.[1] The performance of Kenya's public organizations is generally held to be above average for the continent of Africa. But "above average" is still not satisfactory. Focusing on public corporations (parastatals), where performance can be quantified more easily, the Kenya government's *Working Party on Government Expenditures* found that "examples of unsound and poorly controlled investments can readily be found. . . . [The sector is frequently characterized by a] lack of advance planning, adequate safeguards for Government investment and good management, which has resulted in uncontrolled cost escalations, inefficient technologies and unprofitable enterprises."[2] Similarly, Barbara Grosh reports that half of the corporations she studied had serious problems.[3]

To see what the administrative histories in this study can teach us about the aspects of management that are most critical in the African context, I will begin with a summary evaluation of the managerial performance of the four administrators. I will then argue that in contemporary African conditions the effectiveness of individual managers is particularly important to organizational achievement. We will examine the attributes of the four administrators that seem to have been responsible for their positive impacts, and conclude by asking how this kind of good management can be promoted.

THE VARIETIES OF MANAGEMENT

In reality public management is not one thing but many, so it would be well to acknowledge the plurality of the phenomena and the tensions that sometimes exist between them. For example, an attempt by the United States Agency for International Development to address management issues begins by speaking of "how to use scarce resources efficiently to produce development results."[4] Then its focus shifts to project management and factors ranging from project impact and sustainability, on the one hand, to accountability for funds and cost overruns, on the other. Four different types of management behavior are involved in these shifting foci: public policy-making, organizational leadership, internal administration, and what we will call bureaucratic hygiene. These activities are not at all the same; what's more, excellence in one of them can frequently be purchased at the expense of one of the others.

Public policies, of course, are the most important way in which a state affects development. For example, development specialists are in substantial agreement that the more efficient methods of promoting agricultural production in Africa today include righting distorted prices, devaluing inflated currencies, and generally decreasing the extent to which the state is extracting resources from the farming sector of the economy. The emphasis often is not so much on improving the operations of the state as on keeping its overall policies congenial to agriculture and on finding ways to decrease the negative role it has often played in the past.[5] These are important issues of public management because they are among the most critical variables affecting program success and sustainability. Kenya's success in agricultural development owes much to the fact that it has not permitted its currency to become seriously overvalued and to the generally favorable prices it pays its farmers. We have noted ways in which Ishmael Muriithi, Charles Karanja, Harris Mule, Simeon Nyachae, and Philip Ndegwa promoted these policies for the commodities with which they were most concerned. In many African countries the best program may well be one that does somewhat less to manage its environment directly and leaves more to the play of market forces. The evidence that we have about the commercialization of Kenyan veterinary services certainly supports such a conclusion.[6]

Organizational leadership is the second variety of management. It entails goal setting and the mobilization of the human and material resources that are necessary to achieve them. The largest part of a leader's efforts is probably directed at factors that are external to his (or her) organization: funds and authorizations are secured; the cooperation of other agencies is negotiated; the support of clients is obtained; and political threats to a program's image and mission are averted. Even many of the internal aspects of a leader's task are political in character—obtaining consensus on goals, inspiring commitment, negotiating interunit conflicts, and so forth. This part of management is an art, not a science, and it is second only to public policy in determining whether a project or a program will be successful. The most important managerial contributions of Karanja, Mule, Muriithi, and Nyachae fall under the rubric of leadership.

Internal administration is what we usually think of as management. It entails the organization of work and already secured resources to achieve agreed-upon goals. Important though it is, it is clearly subordinate in importance to a congenial policy framework, an appropriate set of goals, and the acquisition of resources to administer. Charles Karanja was gifted at internal administration; Harris Mule and Ishmael Muriithi were sometimes criticized for not being as skilled in this domain. Excellence in one aspect of management does not necessarily connote its presence in another.

Bureaucratic hygiene: Particularly in the public sector, internal administration also requires the operation of certain control systems that have been designed to assure those outside the organization that its resources are not being misused (e.g., accounts, audits, civil service regulations, contracting mechanisms, and administrative law). These functions, which might be said to maintain "bureaucratic hygiene," are not directly productive themselves. Although organizations that function very badly in these systems often have difficulty securing and managing the resources they need, those that are too scrupulous about them also often fail to meet their objectives. We then appropriately speak of goal displacement and bureaucratic red tape.[7] A recent USAID study found that during the flush period of donor involvement, poor financial management (if unaccompanied by serious corruption) did not hurt the achievement of project goals.[8] Karanja had little to worry about in this area, as the KTDA kept fairly high standards of bureaucratic hygiene. But the regular government ministries often had difficulties with some of these functions, particularly accounting. There was little that Muriithi could do about them, as British practice, which Kenya inherited, divides technical duties from the administration of these bureaucratic control systems. Simeon Nyachae's responsibilities also rarely touched on these matters. Mule tried to get improvement in those parts of his ministry that were suffering from poor bureaucratic hygiene, but this was not his highest priority, and he had only mixed success.

When we consider the factors that affect the success of programs and projects, the hierarchy of importance begins with public policy, is followed by leadership and general internal administration, and ends with bureaucratic hygiene. External criticisms of management, however, often imply a reversal of this rank order. This is partly because failures at the policy and leadership levels are more diffuse and harder to gauge. But it is also due to the special role that the bureaucratic hygiene systems are designed to play. These bureaucratic controls were established in the late nineteenth century in Europe and the United States, over considerable resistance, in order to eliminate the abusive use of public goods for private ends. They have been quite successful in that regard in the Western democracies, and their general objectives (although not the detailed consequences of their operation) enjoy considerable public support there. The misuse of public office is certainly a serious problem in much of Africa, but the control systems needed to prevent it receive only sporadic popular backing. Shortcomings in accounting, procurement, and recruitment are often used as pretexts for dismissal but generally against someone whom one opposes for other reasons.

Another external group that often focuses its criticism on bureaucratic hygiene is made up of the international donor agencies. When donor officers move money that will not subsequently withstand an audit or that violates certain procurement regulations, they know they are taking a risk, and they will put pressure on aid recipients to run their control systems in a way that will avoid the danger. Once things begin to go wrong, a vicious cycle sets in: unsuccessful projects invite tighter control and are more vulnerable to audit criticisms; if the host country's control systems are weak, donors will impose their own; both the multiplicity of systems and the pressures to meet these external standards demand more and more host-country managerial attention, pulling it away from policy and leadership and making project failure more likely. Although there have been increasing problems with Kenya's accounting and procurement systems, they have functioned well enough in the areas of donor concern to avoid the worst aspects of this vicious cycle.

The point here is not that bureaucratic hygiene can be neglected, for without it serious corruption can overtake a system. Officials and citizens then become distrustful of one another's greed and engage only reluctantly in constructive cooperative activity. Government's production of economically and socially useful goods then declines. Management has multiple components, however, and the drive for bureaucratic hygiene must be kept in perspective. What ultimately matters most is that the state sets socially useful objectives for itself and achieves them.

CAN MANAGERS AFFECT THE PERFORMANCE OF THEIR ORGANIZATIONS?

Do these variations in the performance of the four individual administrators actually matter? For example, Barbara Grosh sees the managers of Kenyan public corporations much more as victims than as villains.[9] She was able to develop a twenty-year time series of performance indicators for thirty-three parastatals. Based on the analysis of these data, she focuses her attention on the occurrence of adverse economic conditions and on problems with the policies governing many of the enterprises. The very difficult international economic climate in which Kenya has found itself since 1979 is certainly responsible for many of the problems of public corporations.

On the policy front Grosh is impressed with the damage that can be done to parastatals by inflexible controls over the prices at which they buy and sell their products. Some corporations suffered from having to compete against unregulated private firms while their own prices were fixed by the government. Others worked with regulated prices that were appropriate on average but which responded too slowly to the swings in supply and demand and which therefore left them with debilitating surpluses and shortages.

Grosh also stresses problems with the financial structure with which many of these firms worked. Several of the enterprises were seriously undercapitalized, or were deprived of adequate working funds, or both. Others had highly leveraged financial structures, with most of their capital coming from loans rather than equity. These parastatals were highly vulnerable to sudden surges in interest rates. Grosh's analysis draws attention to a number of other, less frequent policy problems as well. Many of these derive from the all too common propensity to give parastatals inherently unprofitable social mandates without providing them with the resources or means that would compensate for the costs involved.[10]

There is little doubt that the policy problems that Grosh cites are real and that they account for much of the poor performance of Kenyan public corporations. In a comparative study of parastatals in Botswana and Tanzania, Rwekaza Mukandala concludes that performance is largely determined by the political context and government agenda within which these corporations operate.[11] By extension, the same argument that performance problems are based in the framework of public policy applies to the regular government ministries as well. Are we then to conclude that management accounts for little in the variation in effectiveness of these organizations?

The Policy Responsibilities of Management

The analyses by Grosh and Mukandala imply that policy-making and management are separable functions; they are not. Philip Selznick's classic *Leadership in Administration* stressed that the most important role of chief executives is not internal administration but setting the objectives for their organizations and mobilizing the resources to achieve them.[12] This view was presaged in the work of Chester Barnard,[13] and it has been strongly reinforced by organizational studies since.* It is reflected in the way we defined management in the preceding section.

The four administrators were not the passive recipients of public policies, but exhibited the kind of leadership and skill at manipulating the environment of their organizations which the organizational literature describes.[14] The examples of these men confirm that the best managers are active in shaping the policy framework within which they operate. Charles Karanja was able to secure authority for the KTDA to take over the international marketing and processing (or manufacturing) of its tea from the multinationals. He also successfully evaded the burdensome increase in payroll costs for KTDA factories that was threatened by the Tri-Partite Agreements between government, labor, and business. Ish-

---

*Peter Vaill's research has led him to stress what he calls "purposing" by managers. By this he means the "continuous stream of actions by an organization's formal leadership which have the effect of inducing clarity, consensus, and commitment regarding the organization's basic purposes." He argues that "there are three characteristics of the actions of leaders of high-performing systems which I believe appear one hundred percent of the time. . . . (1) Leaders of high-performing systems put in extraordinary amounts of *time*. (2) Leaders of high-performing systems have very strong *feelings* about the attainment of the system's purposes. (3) Leaders of high-performing systems *focus* on key issues and variables." Peter B. Vaill, "The Purposing of High-performing Systems," in *Leadership and Organizational Culture: New Perspectives on Administrative Theory and Practice*, ed. Thomas J. Sergiovanni and John E. Corbally (Urbana: University of Illinois Press, 1984), pp. 91, 93–94. Emphasis in the original.

In his recent study of eighty chief executive officers Warren Bennis concluded that "effective CEOs . . . viewed themselves as *leaders* not *managers*, which is to say that they were concerned with their organization's basic purposes, why it exists and its general direction. . . . [These] CEOs possessed the following competencies:

Vision: the capacity to create and communicate a compelling vision of a desired state of affairs . . . that clarifies the current situation and induces commitment to the future.

Communication and alignment: the capacity to communicate their vision in order to gain the support of multiple constituencies.

Persistency, consistency, focus: the capacity to maintain the organization's direction, especially when the going gets rough.

Empowerment: the capacity to create environments . . . that can tap and harness the energies and abilities necessary to bring about the desired results.

Organizational learning: the capacity to find ways and means through which the organization can monitor its own performance, compare results with established objectives, have access to a continuously evolving data base against which to review past actions and base future ones, and decide how, if necessary, the organizational structure and key personnel must be abandoned or rearranged when faced with new decisions." Warren Bennis, "Transformative Power and Leadership," in *Leadership and Organizational Culture*, p. 66. Emphasis in the original. For a fuller statement, see Warren Bennis, *The Chief* (New York: Morrow, 1983). For the manager of a public organization, Vaill's purposing and the first three of Bennis's competencies translate directly into the ability to define and obtain the public policies and resources that it needs to prosper.

mael Muriithi secured the intervention of President Kenyatta to stop the evasion of livestock quarantines by powerful government officials. Simeon Nyachae and Harris Mule were able to persuade President Moi to negotiate a structural adjustment loan with the International Monetary Fund in the difficult circumstances of September 1982. Nyachae played a similar role with Philip Ndegwa of the Central Bank in early 1983 over devaluation. The best and most effective administrators have taken the initiative and helped to shape the policy environment within which they operate.

Of course they have not always been successful. The KTDA lost control of the domestic marketing of packaged tea during the Moi administration because Karanja mishandled a public controversy over the smuggling of tea to Ethiopia. Mule and Nyachae had to back away from a liberalization of grain marketing, which they favored but which had become too hot politically. Some issues cannot be won even by skillful and well-connected managers, who then have to know how to detour around them. Even though the executives of public organizations can win only a portion of the policy battles in which they engage, that portion is critical nonetheless to the health of their organizations.

The successful managers, then, will focus on the issues that are central to their firms' performance and will assemble the resources necessary to address them. To the extent that those issues are matters of public policy, they will seek to find policy alternatives that are viable within their political context, to present them cogently to those with the power to influence their acceptance, and to mobilize support for them.

Management does make a difference. It is necessary for setting direction and securing external resources and policies. It also is needed to focus the organization's internal energies and to motivate and empower the efforts of subordinates. Organizational leadership thus has both external and internal faces. Charles Karanja's performance in the KTDA is a particularly striking illustration.

Of course, Karanja, and by extension management, was not solely responsible for the success of the KTDA; the Authority inherited a sound institutional structure and operated in generally favorable economic and political environments. Nonetheless, those advantages had to be translated into concrete organizational initiatives, and the Authority's high standards of performance had to be maintained, defended, and extended. It is easy to imagine that the KTDA would have been much less successful if it had had more passive and less skilled management. The political, economic, and institutional context explains much of the KTDA's accomplishments, but several of the positive features of that environment were shaped by the management itself.

Similar points can be made about the Veterinary Service and Ishmael

Muriithi in the 1970s and about Mule's and Nyachae's initiatives over decentralization and agricultural pricing in the 1980s. Political leaders, institutions, and administrators have an *interaction* effect on performance. Managers cannot act alone, but the best ones are not passive victims of their context, for they frequently can influence the policy context in which they operate. Even more clearly, good managers are needed to take effective advantage of a congenial context when it does arise.

Can Individual Managers Make a Difference?

The stress on the importance of leadership made by the organizational literature and the preceding discussion of Karanja does not necessarily lead one to a "great man" theory of organizational accomplishment. Herbert Kaufman concluded that the U.S. federal executives he studied made only modest incremental impacts on the policies and programs of their agencies.[15] Certainly most administrators are able only occasionally to shift significantly the public policies governing their organizations. Their leadership skills are more commonly employed in coping with their policy environment, not changing it.

A vigorous dissent to the view that individual management makes a difference is advanced by James March. He casts the issue of managerial impact in a new and insightful light. In a pair of articles on the careers of Wisconsin school superintendents, he suggests that the pattern of apparent failures (dismissals) and successes (promotions to better districts) is really random. "Most of the time superintendents are organizationally nearly indistinguishable in their behaviors, performances, abilities, and values."[16]

Reflecting on these results several years later, March was careful to interpret them in a way that nonetheless acknowledged the importance of administration. As a result of the many promotional filters through which management candidates pass on their way to the top, he said, the variation in chief executives is smaller than the measurement errors involved in evaluating their performance. Because the criteria for successful management must be vague to reward adaptability and because events beyond organizational control are important, the identification of an outstanding manager is imprecise.

> Toward the top of an organization, it is difficult to know unambiguously that a particular manager makes a difference. Notice that this is not the same as suggesting that management is unimportant. Management may be extremely important even though managers are indistinguishable. It is hard to tell the difference between two different light bulbs also; but if you take all light bulbs away, it is difficult to read in the dark.
>
> [In my] view, managers *do* affect the ways in which organizations func-

tion. But as a result of the process by which managers are selected, motivated, and trained, variations in managers do not reliably produce variations in organizational outcomes. In such a conception, administrators are vital as a class but not as individuals. Administration *is* important, and the many things that administrators do are essential to keeping the organization functioning; but if those vital things are only done when there is an unusually gifted individual at the top, the organization will not thrive. What makes an organization function well is the density of administrative competence, the kind of selection procedures that make all vice-presidents look alike from the point of view of their probable success.[17]

March's is the dissident view. Most others take the role of the top executive more seriously. His generalization that *individual* managers are unimportant is most likely to hold true for mature organizations that have achieved stable personnel systems at a high level of performance. Thomas Peters and Robert Waterman, who think managerial leadership is exceedingly important in the early stages of a firm's development, agree with March that "the excellent companies seem to have developed cultures that have incorporated the values and practices of the great leaders and thus these shared values can be seen to survive for decades after the passing of the original guru."[18] Note, however, that this stable personnel system in which individual managerial candidates are themselves interchangeable is itself initially a managerial creation.

The pool of African qualified managers is newer in Kenya and therefore likely to be thinner. Moreover, many of the country's public organizations are young and have not achieved organizational stability. It is reasonable, therefore, to expect much greater variation in managerial performance there, even by March's criteria. March's analysis is helpful, however, for it directs our attention away from the individual, exceptional, chief executive officer and leads us to focus on the attributes that one would like almost all of the managerial cadre to share. It also causes us to look at the personnel system through which managerial candidates are generated and selected and to ask if managers with these attributes are likely to come out of it.

THE ATTRIBUTES OF SUCCESSFUL KENYAN MANAGEMENT

If management does matter, then what makes a good manager? This study has been conducted in search of the keys to African managerial success, and the task has not been easy. The four Kenyans whose biographies have been pursued have managed rural development initiatives, that domain of public activity in which failure is most prevalent.[19] All of these men were responsible for important successes, but they had fail-

ures as well.* For example, Mule was less effective at internal administration than he was at policy-making and leadership. Similarly, Muriithi's
leadership faltered seriously after the death of Kenyatta. And Nyachae
can be criticized for centralizing too much authority in his own hands.
Each of these men had his weaknesses. The assessment of their managerial attributes that follows therefore is a subtle one, giving greater
weight to those factors that are associated with the successes and steering away from those elements that seem to be responsible for their failures. I have been aided in this assessment by the wide range of interviews that I conducted with the associates of these men, of whom at least
one hundred expressed opinions about the managerial attributes of one
of the four administrators.

Political Connections and Organizational Autonomy

One of the older pieces of wisdom on public enterprises is that their
effective management requires political autonomy. Organizations are
expected to prosper to the extent that their leaders are appointed for
their technical and not political qualifications.[20] It is evident from this
study that this analysis is too simple.

Although all four of our administrators were professionally well qualified for the positions they held, their managerial success and the autonomy of their organizations was critically dependent on their political
connections.† The quantitative evidence presented in Appendix B supports this point. So do the multiple instances we have encountered in
which these managers were able to influence their political environment
to suit the policy needs of their organizations. A few examples are Karanja on tea processing and marketing, Muriithi on milk and artificial
insemination prices, Mule and Nyachae on agricultural prices, and
Ndegwa and Nyachae on devaluation.

The converse—that loss of political connections can threaten organizational performance—is also illustrated by this study. When Kenyatta
died, Karanja lost his direct contacts with the president, but he was so
confident of the importance of the KTDA and of the quality of his management that he continued to act with the same independence and decisiveness. Ultimately this cost him his position, through the crisis en-
gendered by the smuggling of tea to Ethiopia. Similarly, when Kenyatta

---

*Mixed records are characteristic of great American public administrators as well. See
Jameson W. Doig and Erwin Hargrove, eds., *Leadership and Innovation: A Biographical Perspective on Entrepreneurs in Government* (Baltimore: Johns Hopkins University Press, 1987),
p. 12.

†This is true in the United States as well. See Doig and Hargrove, eds., *Leadership and
Innovation*, p. 15.

died and Geoffrey Kariithi retired as head of the civil service, Ishmael Muriithi was deprived of his connections with the Office of the President and was unable to protect the Veterinary Services from the conflicts and mindless budget cutting that then undermined its effectiveness. In his final years as director he lost his characteristic vigor and decisiveness and came near to a despairing lethargy, probably only partly due to his declining health.

In all of these cases we see public servants pursuing professionally dictated policies and striving to protect the integrity of their organizations against inappropriate political pressures. Their ability to do so was directly contingent on their personal connections, direct or indirect, with the president. When these relationships of confidence were lost, so was their managerial effectiveness. Thus we see that the autonomy of an organization from undue politicization is not something that can simply be granted to it in a single constitutional act. It has to be earned and then maintained through political connections. As is illustrated by the work of Rwekaza Mukandala and Barbara Grosh, virtually all public organizations need favorable policy decisions and additional resources at critical junctures if they are to prosper.[21] They also need protection from unwise policy initiatives and politicization. All of these requisites, even depoliticization, are achieved as a consequence of political action. In Kenya and most other African states the relevant political intervention comes from the president.

In John Montgomery's quantitative study of managerial behavior in the public sector in southern Africa he was struck by the absence of the kind of bureaucratic politics he is accustomed to seeing in the United States. Permanent secretaries and their equivalents almost never try to build support for the policies they favor with legislators, party personnel, interest groups, or any other "structural coalitions of like-minded partners." Instead, they resolve problems through the use of personal relationships.[22] This is a sign, not of the absence of politics, but of the presence of a very different form of politics. Power in African political systems is aggregated out of patronage networks, is highly personalized, and generally is concentrated in the hands of the head of state.

Effective public servants are able to mobilize support at critical junctures, *not* by building independent political bases of support for themselves or their organizations, but from personal access to, and the confidence of, the president, either directly or through others who are close to him. Politics is more like the court intrigue of an earlier era than like what one is accustomed to seeing in industrialized societies today. By and large, these crucial connections were not accidental for the four men studied here. They resulted from loyalty and careful network building and are a tribute to the men's administrative astuteness in an underbureaucratized environment.[23] Thus political considerations are important in the appointment of the most senior public servants if political autonomy and effectiveness are to be maintained.

Professional Concern with Public Policy and Organizational Mission
Not everyone who has the confidence of a president is going to use it to advance the performance of the organization that he or she leads. This is particularly true for those who come to positions of leadership in Africa through a political career or because of their ability to mobilize support in the larger political community. They are apt to see their positions and the powers these convey as a reward for the delivery of their support to the president, not as a resource to be used to advance the effectiveness of the organization. Managers with this type of political support tend to sap, not strengthen, their units.

The problem goes well beyond politicians. Montgomery's study of southern African managers left him troubled about the ends toward which they were administering their organizations. Development goals did not play a prominent role in their decisions and activities. Money and turf were the most frequent causes of bureaucratic conflict; policy matters came a distinct fifth. When resources were at stake, "there is not much concern over their relation to their public origin or to the public interest. . . . Arguments . . . center about the convenience of the individual users more than about the mission of the organization to which they are assigned."[24]

The four administrators differed dramatically from this characterization. They had very well defined organizational missions they wanted to accomplish, were activist and entrepreneurial in their pursuit, devoted considerable attention to the public policies affecting them, and were concerned that the resources they managed served the public interest. They saw internal administration as grounded in a larger set of purposes and felt some responsibility as well for the factors outside their organization that affected them. Their entrepreneurship and concern with policy came from the leading role Kenyatta accorded to the civil service and from their recognition that they were necessary to the achievement of their goals. But those goals and their public-regarding character came from still deeper and more exceptional roots.

The effective managers in our "sample" were committed professionals. Harris Mule and Ishmael Muriithi were trained overseas as an economist and a veterinarian, respectively. Both men were deeply committed to their professions and dedicated to maintaining their standards in Kenya. Charles Karanja was trained in Uganda as a civil engineer. Such a background was unnecessary to the leadership of the KTDA, but it did seem to shape Karanja's ideas about public service and efficiency. In all three of these cases professional identity gave these men a strong commitment to the goals of the organizations they headed and caused them to resist their use for inappropriate personal gain by themselves or others.

Simeon Nyachae was prepared to be a provincial administrator, first by his father, Chief Nyandusi, and then by training in Kenya and England. This background gave him a very strong identification with the state and a principled determination to serve the interests of those who hold political power. In his years as a provincial commissioner these values did not give him a particularly strong commitment to the goals of some of the organizations with which he was involved, and he was willing to see them taxed to serve the personal interests of those who held political power over him. When he came onto the national scene, however, Nyachae increasingly came to see the interests of the "nation," conceived in a conservative sense, as coincident with the interests of his president, the state, and the business class of which he was a part. This broadening of vision gave him a set of values that made him quite open to the policies advocated by the economist Mule.

Professional Integrity

All four men were careful to place the interests of the organizations that they served above their own pursuit of personal gain. Although their conceptions of what constitutes conflict of interest were generally more lax than those applied in the United States today, they definitely had ethics and adhered to them. They also differed among themselves. Muriithi's and particularly Mule's personal ethics were the strictest, and their personal wealth upon retirement was consequently modest. Karanja and Nyachae had laxer conceptions and left the public service rich. Nonetheless, their wealth was due to hard work and business acumen and probably only to a minor degree to the positions they had held, particularly for Karanja.

The question is, as long as they care well for their organizations, does it matter for their effectiveness whether public managers use their positions to advance their personal wealth in Africa? I have concluded that the answer is yes. Certainly the general political and social environment of which these men were a part was quite unconcerned about corruption and effectively encouraged it. In much the same way as Robert Price demonstrated for Ghana,[25] the question in the popular mind was never how prominent officials got their wealth but whether they were personally transferring resources to their relatives and home areas. My interviews revealed, however, that a different set of values usually prevailed *inside* public agencies among the professional subordinates and peers of the managers I studied. The respect and support that a manager of a professional organization received from his subordinates and from his peers in related organizations appeared to be heavily contingent on his perceived personal integrity. This does not mean that these subordinates and peers were always behaving with integrity themselves. Unlike members of the general public, however, they understood the concept of conflict of interest and felt that they owed effort and support to those who were faithful to it, even if they were not. Conversely, they felt free to be slack in their duties if they were asked to do something by someone whose integrity they doubted. I'm not suggesting that Kenyan professionals always or even usually practice what they preach, but they do believe what they preach. Their values on integrity have something of the same status as American values on marital fidelity in presidential politics: even those who do not practice the ethical code themselves believe that those who break it do not deserve to hold leadership positions. Thus in Kenya those whose integrity is in doubt are unlikely to be effective managers of professional organizations. Indeed, the decline in the careers of Karanja and Muriithi can be traced in part to revelations that they had profited from minor conflicts of interest.

I have carefully limited the above generalization about the relationship between integrity and managerial effectiveness to professional organizations. Interviews with Simeon Nyachae's colleagues in the Provincial Administration did not reveal much concern with the issue of conflict of interest. It is possible that this part of the Kenya government is so closely tied to the regulation and practice of politics that it has no distinct professional code of ethics on such matters.

Access to Donor Resources

Another attribute that proved critical to managerial effectiveness was the ability to inspire the confidence of international actors. African economies are relatively small and weak, and international markets together with gifts and loans from international donors are unusually important to them. Those managers who are skilled at acquiring these resources are able to use them to gain flexibility in an environment that is usually severely constrained. They also perform for the economy a function that gives them support from other powerful domestic politicians and public servants.

Harris Mule was particularly well known for his skill with donors; this attribute was independently raised by eight quite different interviewees. It is interesting that whereas the foreigners tended to say that Mule "*gets along* well with donors," one of the Kenyan respondents said that "he *handles* donors well," a subtle but significant difference in perspective.

Mule was useful in international economic negotiations because he both understood donor objectives and was able to make them understand Kenyan political constraints in turn. Thus he was invaluable in advancing some of the reforms that donors regarded as important and in getting them to accept the fact that others were unachievable at the time. In this way he was crucial to obtaining IMF, World Bank, and bilateral donor resources at critical junctures for the economy. Mule's skill in this regard was immensely aided by, and may well have depended on, his reputation for professionalism and absolute personal integrity, which made donors trust what he said. One donor even funded a small project in Mule's home area to reward him for being so incorruptible that he was unable to finance any significant projects himself.

Ishmael Muriithi's professional reputation was similarly responsible for inspiring international confidence in his Veterinary Services and thus giving Kenya access to the lucrative European beef market, despite the continued presence of foot-and-mouth disease in the country. In a similar way, the high regard with which he was held in international veterinary circles helped him to bring the International Laboratory for Research on Animal Disease and other, even more direct, forms of donor assistance to Kenya.

Charles Karanja's reputation for efficient management of the Kenya Tea Development Authority facilitated its continued access to substantial amounts of assistance, particularly from the World Bank, and thus gave it the resources and flexibility to grow beyond what Kenya's domestic capital constraints would have allowed.[26] The KTDA's size and international reputation in turn gave Karanja weight in many domestic policy struggles.

The only one of the four who was not particularly gifted with the international community was Simeon Nyachae. As a provincial commissioner, Nyachae had been one of President Kenyatta's primary instruments for the control of domestic politics.[27] When Nyachae came to the national policy scene he had very little international experience and was tainted by his past political connections. He and the donors did not understand each other very well, and the donors were not certain that they could trust him. It was here that Nyachae's alliance with Mule was of such great importance; just as Nyachae provided Mule with political connections, Mule provided donor access to Nyachae.

Africanization

Frequently there was a downside to donor confidence, one that reduced the loyalty that managers inspired in their own staff. Three of the managers in our "sample" felt that they had to use some non-Kenyan staff in order to maintain high professional standards in their organizations, standards that gave them a strong international reputation. The morale and allegiance of their Kenyan staff depended, however, on a vigorous Africanization program, replacing foreign with local staff.

Charles Karanja handled this dilemma best. He concentrated expatriate staff in training positions and in those parts of the organization where new functions were being added. By externalizing the conflict he was able to rally nationalist sentiment for his personnel policies despite the continued use of foreigners. He argued that the important issue was not the exact distribution of positions inside the organization but whether it would be the Kenyan-controlled KTDA or the multinational corporations that would control critical aspects of the domestic tea industry. For the technically demanding role of factory manager, he was able to point out that the multinationals did not believe it was possible for any Kenyan African to do the job in the near future. Thus when he hired an expatriate to head the factory division and to train managers, he could argue that he was promoting, not hindering, Africanization. In the process he was able to unleash a nationalist determination among his recruits to do their jobs well and prove the multinationals wrong.

Ishmael Muriithi was not so adept. He was under great pressure to replace expatriate veterinarians with Kenyans as they became available. He argued that this was not an issue. As the country had a shortage of veterinarians anyway, both should be employed. But he also felt that his highest priority was to assign African veterinarians to field positions, where they would be able to interact with African producers of livestock. This meant that he was seen as keeping expatriates in the highly prized headquarters positions. Consequently, he developed a reputation among his Kenyan staff for being insufficiently attentive to their advancement and lost some of their loyalty. This was unfortunate, for the circumstances closely parallel those in the KTDA, where Karanja was able to engender the extra incentive of nationalist competition. The measure of an "Africanizer" may be as much subjective as objective. The manager who is able to give reality to an external promotion standard that he is *helping* his staff to meet will outperform one who is seen as being the gatekeeper himself.

Harris Mule also had trouble with Africanization, a problem he inherited from his predecessor, Philip Ndegwa. In Finance and Planning, the replacement of expatriates with locals in line positions took place relatively rapidly, perhaps too rapidly. For it was then felt that certain critical skills were still in short supply, and foreign advisers were brought in to provide them. Mule's Kenyan subordinates frequently resented the influence that some of these advisers had, as well as the fact that the foreigners often seemed to get the more challenging work. There was something of a vicious circle here, for as Kenyans grew discontented with foreign advisers they sometimes became more lax in their own work, and the need for expatriates increased. Something like Karanja's device for making this competition functional rather than destructive was needed.

Being a "Nationalist"

The nationalism inherent in the pressures to Africanize was not directed only against foreigners; it was also a force against undue parochialism. Interviews with the colleagues of the four frequently provoked strongly felt comments that one or another was or was not "a nationalist." It quickly became clear that this term was not meant to describe that person's attitudes about matters external to Kenya but instead indicated whether he was favoring his own group in the allocation of resources, particularly those related to employment.

All public institutions in Kenya employ a mixture of ethnic groups throughout their hierarchy. If the organization is to perform effectively, these ethnically diverse staff must be able to work well together. Not only will a manager typically have to rely on the efforts of crucial subordinates who do not belong to his group, but a staff member also usually finds that the hierarchy that controls his or her promotion has someone from another group in it somewhere.

This need for interethnic cooperation and trust creates tension, for even senior, highly educated officers naturally will draw their friends disproportionately from among those who share their mother tongue.[28] Kenyan staff believe that their career prospects are improved if their supervisor belongs to their ethnic group. This perception may be true for junior staff appointments and promotions, but the data analyzed in Appendix A do not bear it out for senior officers. Nonetheless, even if the belief is false, it has real consequences. Staff *expect* ethnically based favoritism among their superiors, seek out fellow tribesmen who may be able to help them accordingly, and are ever alert to signs of parochial ties being used against them.

Simeon Nyachae did exercise some of the powers of patronage that were expected of him by his community and his political superiors. But he was careful to exercise them only over symbolic positions where poor performance would not greatly affect the organizations involved. His own immediate staff comprised a wide range of ethnic groups. These officers had confidence that parochial considerations did not influence his promotion of their careers. As a consequence, they had great loyalty to him and performed well. A similar impartial concern for ability to do the job well seemed to guide the influence he exerted on operational senior executive positions throughout the Kenya government.

Harris Mule was even more clearly above ethnic ties in his personnel decisions and commanded strong loyalty from his officers as a result. In both Nyachae's and Mule's ministries senior officers who belonged to ethnic groups that were at one another's throats in the larger political arena cooperated well under their leadership.

Charles Karanja did not do quite so well in convincing his staff that he was "a nationalist," and this contributed to his downfall. We have seen that his high standards for performance were applied without favor and that he was careful to maintain some ethnic balance in key positions. Nonetheless, the perception persisted among some staff that Kikuyus, especially those from Kiambu, were being given an edge. This belief may well have been largely unjustified, but Karanja's admitted willingness to give those personally connected with him a first chance to prove their worth lent credence to the perception. The beneficiaries of Karanja's patronage, if we are to call it that, did excellent work. He never compromised on that. But those who felt outside his circle of favor sometimes withheld their enthusiasm from their work as a result. If these employees could not be fired for political reasons, the KTDA suffered—and so ultimately did Karanja. It is likely that one of these disgruntled employees leaked to the press the information that irreparably damaged Karanja's career.

The pattern of values with regard to ethnic favoritism is similar to the one we found for corruption. Society expects that senior administrators will provide assistance to those from their home areas and applies a good deal of pressure toward that end. Civil servants also expect such behavior from their colleagues, but they, unlike the general society, are ambivalent about it. Many will use junior staff appointments they control to satisfy the pressures of petitioners from their villages, and some will try to find ethnic allies to help them promote their own careers, although usually without too much success. But these same civil servants do not want to see signs of parochialism among their own superiors. They expect it, but admire its absence. A superior who is "a nationalist" commands their respect and commitment. The organization then performs well. Superiors who are parochial are given only the cooperation they can coerce and are often undermined by those outside their group.

Staff Management

Africanization and nationalism are really Kenya-specific attributes of the more universal issue of staff management. All four of the administrators showed good judgment in selecting and promoting the staff who worked with them. Mule even had the sense to put strong "naysayers" in charge of budgetary matters in his ministry, knowing that he himself was weak in that area.

The four also set high standards for their staff once they were in place. Karanja and Nyachae were particularly firm in this regard. Both men would quickly rid themselves of staff whose work disappointed them. As Karanja was in a parastatal corporation, he could and did fire them. Nyachae, in dealing with tenured civil servants, was more constrained and instead transferred them to harmless "punishment" posts. But Nyachae had a temper, and this made him somewhat unpredictable. As a consequence, some of those working with him were overly cautious. Mule and Muriithi were less ruthless, and their organizations lacked the discipline of Karanja's and Nyachae's as a result. But their standards and expectations were clear, measured, and fair, which also helped to produce good work.

The other side of the high-standards coin was the protection and support given to those officers who were doing well. Karanja and Nyachae worked hard to advance the careers of the officers whose work pleased them. Muriithi was much less aggressive in this area, and this clearly cost him support among his senior staff. Nyachae also was unusual in his willingness to defend civil servants publicly when he thought they were being attacked unfairly by politicians. Mule supported his officers by refusing to listen to rumors about them. He would only receive complaints against a staff member if it was delivered in the subordinate's presence. All four men were easily accessible to those working with them and sympathetic to their problems. In this variety of ways Karanja, Nyachae, and Mule generated particularly strong support among their officers and could count on their loyalty and effort in return.

For these men staff management became staff development.[29] The kinds of personal rewards they provided and loyalties they developed are important to organizations everywhere. But they may be especially important in Africa where the *institutional* standards and incentives are often weak.

Competition and Management Information Systems

One attribute of successful management that we found was at first surprising. A strong management information system (MIS) seemed to be at the root of much of the effectiveness of Charles Karanja and Dan Mbogo, Ishmael Muriithi's younger brother. Such systems have a checkered record.[30] The typical MIS in Africa is a highly technical device that is developed in isolation from the top managers who need to use it. Once information is alienated from authority, it loses its effect. But Karanja and Mbogo each understood his MIS well and knew how to use it to make decisions.

Another attribute of these two management information systems was that they produced *comparative* information. In the typical MIS a wealth of technical detail is created, but it is hard to interpret. The systems used by Karanja and Mbogo monitored the performance of comparable local field operations. The information produced by this type of MIS can be used to influence the careers of field officers; and it was so used in the KTDA. The field staff thus often paid attention to their comparative standing themselves, not waiting for the feedback of their superiors.

Thus the really important management innovation in the KTDA was the institutionalization of competition among field units. The MIS was important, not so much for its own sake, but as the device that produced information about the competitive standings.[31]

Delegation

One attribute of good management, the skill of delegating, did *not* come easily to most of the four. An organization is limited to the time, energy, and attention span of its chief executive if there is no delegation. Dating back into the colonial era, senior civil servants in Africa have had trouble delegating. Jon Moris has described this as the hub-and-wheel pattern of administration. The senior officer places himself at the hub of all decisions and delegates the execution of straightforward tasks only. Little real discretion is permitted to subordinates. This style of administration arises most frequently in settings in which there is a great gap between the skills of the person in charge and his or her subordinates and is widespread in Africa.[32]

Karanja's instinct was to do all the important work himself. He even insisted on editing the KTDA's annual report. He learned to delegate only when his heart objected and his overwork threatened to take his life.

Mule delegated to those staff who inspired his confidence (including foreign advisers), but there were not enough of these for the work that had to be done. He never did discover how to delegate progressively more responsible tasks to his junior subordinates so as to help them learn new skills and eventually give him confidence in their ability to undertake major decisions.

Nyachae generally was willing to delegate, but he fell victim to officers who were afraid to exercise the authority they had. At the time he became chief secretary many heads of government departments no longer had the confidence of the president. They sometimes had difficulty in making their decisions stick, and they rightly felt that the president was waiting for them to make mistakes that could be a pretext for their removal. Nyachae clearly did have President Moi's confidence. And so they turned to him for advice and support. Once asked to make a decision, Nyachae would do so and take full political responsibility for it. He also had an instinct to exercise control over units in which he lacked confidence, rather than finding good new executives to exercise discretion within them. Thus, despite Nyachae's calls for department and ministry heads to exercise the powers officially delegated to their offices, more and more authority was centralized in his office. He made a prodigious number of decisions, but those matters he did not get to were neglected.

Unless delegation is institutionalized, organizational attention is limited by the capabilities of the individual who heads it. The custom in Kenya is *not* to delegate. Karanja overcame this disability only when his health demanded it. Mule's and Nyachae's impacts were limited (in different ways) because they were not able to delegate effectively.

Risk Taking

A further attribute that emerges from our case studies is the willingness to take risks, an attribute that seems to be rare among African managers.[33] All four men occasionally faced circumstances in which they had to put their own careers at stake by making decisions or advocating policies that were critical to their organizations. Karanja, Mule, and Nyachae were willing to do so when they calculated that the political odds gave them some chance of success, and they usually won. Muriithi was a more classically "conservative" bureaucrat, and his organization may have suffered at some critical junctures as a result.

Why were these three managers willing to risk their careers? Karanja and Nyachae both said that it was because they were already well-to-do and had always intended to make their careers in private business rather than the public sector anyway. Mule had always been dedicated to a public career, and his personal property was modest, but he too felt that his welfare did not depend on his continued government service. His family was small and his living standards were within the means of his pension. Also, since he had been incorruptible, he could make more as a private or international executive. Although I think that all three men, in different ways, loved the exercise of power, that love did not outweigh their drive to accomplish certain goals that they had set for their organizations, and they felt that they had the financial independence to take that risk. Business or other executive positions awaited them outside the public sector.

Paradoxically, the fact that the Kenyan state does not have a monopoly control over positions earning higher income seems to have given it better service from its managers by making them less averse to risk. Muriithi's unwillingness to take the same risks as the other three men may have been due to the extremely limited possibilities for private veterinary practice in Kenya, which his own policies had helped to create.[34]

Drive

Finally, it is not surprising that all four men had extraordinary drive and an ability for hard work that was sometimes of legendary proportions. This is one of the attributes of successful executives that Warren Bennis and Peter Vaill found in the United States, and we noted earlier that our successful Kenyan shared all those same attributes.[35] The enumeration of managerial attributes has concentrated on those aspects of Kenyan management that seem to supplement or give a special twist to the U.S. features. Nonetheless, the four administrators were different from many other ambitious Kenyans in the way in which they exhibited their drive, and special note should be taken of this. They worked exceedingly long hours and were extremely self-disciplined. Mule read voraciously and into the early hours of every morning. Nyachae was famous for the speed with which he gave written reply to memos. All four were unusual for being extremely temperate in their drinking.

SELECTION POLICY AND ORGANIZATIONAL PERFORMANCE

Problems with the Current Kenyan Analysis

Management does matter, but how is the state to get good practitioners of the art? The way the Kenyan government has been trying to achieve this recently may be exacerbating rather than solving the problem. The State Corporations Act of 1986, which was recommended by the two Ndegwa reports, is oriented toward establishing controls over parastatals management. It not only strengthens accounting and financial reporting procedures, which indeed are needed for effectively evaluating managerial performance; it also mandates detailed cost controls and central approval of parastatal budgets, measures that reduce managerial flexibility. One-fourth of the Act's sections provide for the personal prosecution of parastatal managers and board members for failure to comply with government directives.[36]

It is well established in organization theory that controls induce formalism and rigidity and are ill-suited to positions that require problem solving and the exercise of discretion. The performance of researchers, professionals, and senior executives is most enhanced by careful attention to the selection of appropriate personnel and the removal of those who fail to perform satisfactorily. Attempts to control the details of their behavior will tie the organization up in bureaucracy. In the words of

Martin Landau, "To manage is not to control."[37] Thus A. H. Hanson's classic work on public corporations stresses the need for managerial autonomy.[38]

Precisely because of the importance of the contextual factors that Grosh emphasizes, good management comes from the selection of managers who understand their environments and are able to obtain the resources their organizations need, including favorable policy decisions. If they are to operate effectively in Kenya, organizational heads cannot be selected simply for technical excellence. They must have direct or indirect access to the president and be able to inspire him to have confidence in their recommendations.

Kenyatta's Selection Policies

The personnel policies of Jomo Kenyatta appear to have been consistent with this model of management, at least for the first decade of his presidency. It is evident that Kenyatta appointed many ministers, assistant ministers, parastatal board members and chairmen, and sometimes even chief executive officers of public organizations, solely for political reasons. But somewhere at the top of each organization there usually was at least one individual, often a Kikuyu, who was competent and motivated and in whom the president had great personal confidence. Kenyatta followed this person's advice and was responsive to his pleas for supportive policies, just as he was to Charles Karanja at the KTDA. It would quickly become evident who this individual was, and the informal authority structure of the corporation would be organized around him (or her). In many cases it appears that Kenyatta's ability to find an executive in whom he had confidence was aided by there being at least a few people on the board of the corporation who were experienced in the area and from whom he could get advice. Thus, although *most* board appointees may have been strictly political and gained from, rather than contributed to, their organizations, a minority had the competence and inspired the confidence necessary to manage effectively. Kenyatta clearly delegated a great deal of authority to these individuals.

These chief executives who combined formal office with the informal authority of the president were often able to build effective teams of junior officers. Because they had the influence to make promotions and because they had the vision to use it in their organization's interest, they were able to stimulate élan and effort among their subordinates. These junior men and women not only contributed to the immediate performance of their organizations, they also formed a cadre out of which future senior executives could be selected. Where this process worked well, as it did in the KTDA, those promoted to senior management from within were very likely to succeed. The job socialization and filtering processes worked to create a pool of administrators who were imbued with their organization's values and who were in many ways indistinguishable from one another when promoted. For organizations like the KTDA the depersonalization and continuity of internal administrative excellence of which March and Peters and Waterman speak was achieved.[39]

It appears that this pattern of "planting" an excellent executive deteriorated in Kenyatta's final years as his health failed. His judgment in personnel appointments was no longer so sound, and many of those around him manipulated his decisions for their personal benefit. Thus when Kenyatta died many Kenyans were more impressed with the rapaciousness of the more recent, generally Kikuyu, appointees than they were with the quality and reliability of the more numerous and still-serving earlier group. This impression legitimated a view that saw senior administrative positions as more concerned with the distribution of benefits than with the creation of value.

Moi's Personnel Policies

Daniel arap Moi found himself in an awkward position when he succeeded to the presidency in 1978. He inherited a large group of Kikuyu senior officials, some good and some not, who had inspired Kenyatta's confidence. Since the Kikuyu were an important part of his governing coalition through 1982, he could not simply remove these executives. But they did not enjoy Moi's confidence, and they therefore were unable to get supportive decisions from him in the same way in which they had with Kenyatta. As the economic environment had taken a sudden turn for the worse and new policies were frequently urgently needed, the organizations managed by these individuals began to fail.

Meanwhile President Moi played a game of attrition. He established a mandatory retirement age of fifty-five, which enabled him to dispense with the services of many of Kenyatta's appointees. He would wait for the rest to make some error or for their organizations to show signs of failure. The offending executives could then be dismissed with legitimacy in the public's eyes. Whatever its political necessity, this strategy was terribly debilitating for the quality of public management. Executives were not only unable to get the policy decisions and resources that they needed, they also experienced great uncertainty and insecurity about their jobs. They became cautious and managed by the rule book instead of taking the initiatives that were needed to solve their organizations' problems.

The preceding are only transitional problems, however. If these "holdover executives" were replaced one by one by others who were skilled and also enjoyed the new president's confidence, all would eventually be well. The administrative system then would be guided by a new set of values—the president's agenda. If the new appointees had the attributes outlined in the preceding section, the administration would pursue those objectives with great effectiveness, as it did under Nyachae, Mule, and Philip Ndegwa.

If the new crop of top executives lacked energy and intelligence, were not dedicated to their organizations' professional standards, were unable to command the respect of their subordinates, or were self-serving and corrupt, the performance of the public service would begin to deteriorate. The negative effects would not be immediately evident. For a time the habits of good work by holdovers who had been wisely recruited would carry the organization forward. Eventually, however, their morale would be sapped, and their critical mass of quality would be diluted by new staff who were not as gifted or as dedicated.

The difference between these two scenarios would *not* be the use of political considerations in making appointments. Kenyatta used them, and it is inevitable and necessary that they come into play when the goals that the state is pursuing are at stake. The difference would be how gifted the appointees were and whether those goals were broadly or narrowly conceived.

In any case, the Kenyan experience strongly suggests that a president's personnel policies are among his most important and have effects over a long term. No president can know enough, or work hard enough, to make good decisions by himself. He needs subordinates upon whose values *and competence* he can rely for guidance. If he neglects one or the other of these dimensions in his personnel decisions, he will still have a few good managers by chance alone. But the density of quality will be reduced and will deteriorate over time.

Internationalizing Professionalism

The lessons for outsiders wishing to enhance African managerial performance are somewhat different. From their point of view the ability of a manager to inspire presidential confidence is an exogenous variable, over which they can have little influence. All they can do is assure that the other attributes of managerial effectiveness are widely distributed, increasing the probability that someone who has them will also be close to the president. Of these other attributes three are of greatest importance and are in fact related to one another. Concern with organizational mission, professional integrity, and risk taking are all influenced by professionalization. A manager who is deeply imbued with the values of his or her profession is focused on the goals toward which organizational resources are to be directed and will keep his or her own interests from interfering with their pursuit. Furthermore, someone with internationally recognized professional qualifications, standing, and reputation has a wide range of options as to how and where he or she can earn a living and therefore is in a good position to take risks.

Rigorous training in a professional discipline is the first step, for the techniques and methods of analysis that are learned have public-regarding values imbedded in them. Best at this socialization are the traditional professions, such as medicine, engineering, accounting, and law, all of which have clear minimum training requirements for membership, which often are internationally recognized. Economics also has imbedded public-regarding values, although it lacks recognized entry qualifications.*

The value socialization imparted in the process of professional education must be reinforced if it is to be sustained over time. The individuals who enter these professions must identify with them and look to their fellow professionals for reward. Traditionally the social processes of reinforcing professional values have taken place within national associations, which have met regularly, determined membership requirements, and expelled those who failed to maintain ethical and technical standards. In :nost of Africa, however, these professional bodies are still only weakly institutionalized and often have difficulty in resisting societal pressures by themselves. They need the fortification of involvement with international professionals to sustain their value and technical commitments. Formal and informal interactions by African professionals with their counterparts elsewhere, which expose them to judgments about their professional standards, are an important international contribution to the continent's development. At a minimum this internationalization of a profession must accord status and moral support to those who maintain high standards. Better still, it should provide channels to employment for those who find advancement at home blocked despite or because of their professionalism.

CONCLUSIONS

The problem of public organizations in Kenya today is both one of management and one of policy; the two are intertwined and mutually reinforcing. Some of the Kenya government's recent attempts to deal with these problems have been going in the wrong direction. By creating controls over management, it probably has been making administration worse. Managers to whom decisions can be delegated are needed instead. The focus needs to be on the selection of chief executives who

---

*Training in business administration imparts values, but its profit motive too easily reinforces the pursuit of self-interest. Public administration is insufficiently professionalized as a discipline to impart a reliable value content.

can give appropriate direction to their organizations and inspire sufficient confidence in the president for him to give them the resources and policies they need. Only in this way can the state *create* the resources the president politically needs to distribute.

The kinds of executives needed are those who share the distinguishing attributes of the men we have studied. "Type A" personality attributes and the ability to give purpose to an organization are a common part of the folklore of executive success everywhere. Of greater interest are the attributes of political connections, professionalism, integrity, access to donor resources, skill at maintaining staff quality and commitment through the trials of Africanization, the institutionalization of competition, and the ability to take risks. These attributes have a distinctively African character, one that is consistent with the universal tenets of organization theory but which could not have been easily predicted from it.

The State and Administrative Development: Conclusions about Institutions and Interests

Why were the development initiatives described in this book successful? More generally, why does Kenya's rural development over the last twenty-five years look so good when held up against the accomplishments of most of the rest of Africa?[1] Many have suggested that the answer lies in the character of the Kenyan state.[2] But what does that mean?

THE STATE

First of all, what is the state? Max Weber defined it as that body which exercises a monopoly over the legitimate exercise of force within territorially defined boundaries.[3] Thus a state exists when there is an overall organization whose right to use coercion on those living in a given geographical area* is supported by other power holders in the society.[4] The entirety of the organization that exercises this legitimate coercion is also known as the government. In Theda Skocpol's words, the state is "a set of administrative, policing, and military organizations headed, and more or less well coordinated by, an executive authority."[5]

Why then not simply use the term "government" instead? The term "state" can sometimes connote something more comprehensive than a government. In international politics it suggests as well the territory and citizens of a country as they are officially represented by a government.[6] But, more important, the scope of the term "government" is frequently ambiguous. Definitions range from the highly comprehensive "complex of political institutions, laws, and customs through which the function

---

*Certain precolonial African political systems exercised legitimate force over groups of *citizens* and not over territory and therefore have traditionally been called "stateless." See E. E. Evans-Pritchard, *The Nuer* (Oxford: The Clarendon Press, 1940).

of governing is carried out" to the specific "small group of persons holding simultaneously the principal political executive offices of a nation or other political unit and being responsible for the direction and supervision of public affairs."[7] Thus at one extreme the government is almost the same as the political system, and at the other, in a parliamentary system, it is the cabinet. Compared with this ambiguity, the term "state" is much more precise.[8]

Therefore, when we say that the character of Kenya's state is responsible for its accomplishments in rural development, we are indicating that its political authorities and administrative agencies have behaved in such a way as to promote that success and have had the capacity to do so.

The task of specifying what we are to explain is not complete, however. We could see the state simply as a creature of the various societal forces that have shaped it, in which case the focus of our explanation would be the larger political system. Alternatively, we might hold that in important respects the state is able to act autonomously of society's political forces, in which case at least part of our explanation must target the internal mechanisms of the state itself. In the first case the state is thought to act simply as a mechanical transmitter of external political pressures, and we can treat it as an unexplained "black box." In the second, we hypothesize that the state itself is modifying and transforming the societal forces operating on it in some significant way, and we need to "get inside the black box" and understand its operations.

Some theoretical traditions in political science have concentrated so heavily at times on the external forces operating on the state that they have seemed to deny it any causative power at all.[9] Recently, however, there has been a series of studies demonstrating that there are important instances in which the state does act autonomously on public policy.[10] I suggest that both the character of Kenya's political system and the capacity of its state for relatively strong and autonomous action explain its development success.

The processes of causation described here are deeply affected by the historical sequence in which they occurred. There is some element of chance associated with all events. But in an institutional setting these chance occurrences accumulate instead of averaging one another out. Seemingly small events affect later ones, thereby aggregating into large causes. They are not counteracted by other random occurrences. The partly accidental solution to one problem becomes part of the baseline for solving the next and is no longer a random element. James March and Johan Olsen refer to this attribute as a "policy martingale" and write:

This martingale property . . . seems a prototypic institutional characteristic. Policies, once adopted, are imbedded into institutions. They are associated with rules, expectations, and commitments. By affecting attention and aspirations, they affect the future search behavior of political participants. . . . In a martingale process all events are forks; the policy paths of two political systems with identical underlying political conditions will be radically different simply because of the way in which (possibly small) perturbations shift the focus of political pressure.[11]

THE POLITICAL FORCES DIRECTING THE STATE

That Jomo Kenyatta became president of a newly independent state in the aftermath of the Mau Mau "peasants' revolt" had four important consequences for Kenya. First, there were unmistakably powerful demands for urgent attention to the welfare of peasant producers. Any new government would have had to undertake some degree of land reform and to promote small-farm productivity.

Second, in response to the rebellion, the British had forced an ethnic fragmentation in Kenyan politics. Thus Kenyatta's primary base of political power was among the Kikuyu, and he could not afford to fragment it further by pursuing policies that would pit poorer Kikuyu against the better-off ones. This dictated public policies on his part that were relatively conservative and also provided visible benefits to the Kikuyu peasantry. The former attribute set the general direction of economic policy. The latter attribute was consistent with the first only if resources were directed unevenly toward the Kikuyu. The policies produced thus maintained Kenya's ethnic tensions.

Third, within these broad boundaries Kenyatta had considerable flexibility, for he had symbolized the struggle for independence and was immensely popular during the early years of his regime. Fourth, Kenyatta's own Kenyan African Union (KAU) was banned by the British during the rebellion, and he was in detention when the Kenyan African National Union (KANU) was created to replace it. The governing party therefore was not his political agent, and he had little confidence in it. He chose to use the administrative apparatus of the state as his instrument of political governance instead.

It follows then that in its early years the independent Kenyan state was constrained by its political environment to promote simultaneously the welfare of the African well-to-do and of the peasantry, particularly among the Kikuyu. It was able to square this circle by redistributing white-settler large farms, by redirecting state subsidies from the European to the African sectors of the economy, and by giving the Kikuyu a somewhat disproportionate advantage.[12] Within these very broad parameters the state had considerable flexibility of action, and this autonomy was used in ways that fitted both Kenyatta's personal vision and the proclivities that were built into the institutional structure of the administrative apparatus of the state.

Kenyatta's vision included the creation of an African propertied class to replace the Europeans and Asians. This reallocation of economic power to correspond more closely with the transfer of political power that had already taken place went well beyond the usual extension of patronage to the supporters of the regime. As we saw in chapter 4, Kenyatta explicitly encouraged civil servants to use their salaries as collateral for government-facilitated loans that would purchase large-farm, commercial, and, eventually, small industrial properties. (Many used their positions to acquire wealth illegally as well.) Thus the new matajiri (well-to-do) class that eventually emerged was grounded simultaneously in commerce, small industry, agriculture, and the higher civil service. Public servants constituted an unusually large portion of this new class.

Also important were the facts that virtually all members of the emergent matajiri class owned moderately large farms and that there was a substantial overlap between them and most small farmers in the crops they grew and the technologies they used (except for wheat). As was seen in chapters 6 through 10, both the politicians and the higher civil servants who determined Kenya's public policies were supportive of agricultural interests in a way that usually reinforced those of middle peasants and petty-bourgeois smallholders. Only the poorest 40 percent, particularly the landless, were left out, and even their condition did not get worse. This coincidence of elite and peasant interests also explains the success of agriculture in Botswana, Malawi, and the Ivory Coast.[13]

Kenyatta apparently saw those on whom he bestowed property not just as a collection of privileged individuals but as an emergent class that could compete with Europeans. This class vision committed Kenyatta to think in collective rather than just individual terms and to undertake public policies that would work to the advantage, not of individuals, but of the class as a whole. For example, he was deliberate rather than rushed in transferring Asian commercial property into African hands. He wanted to make sure that the change was not so rapid as to damage the economy. He was more concerned with the welfare of African property owners as a collectivity than he was with advancing the personal interests of the particular individuals who might have taken over the businesses. Kenyatta seemed to see himself first as the trustee of an emergent African propertied class and only second as a patron dispensing individual favors.

THE STATE AS A "COMMONS"

Kenyatta's behavior as the trustee for a still-emerging ruling class was of fundamental importance for the nature of its public policies. To see that this is so, we must examine what has happened under a different conception of governance elsewhere in Africa.

The state not only creates and manages many collective goods for society; it is a collective good itself. It has long been recognized that services such as roads, security, and a stable currency benefit many more people than those who would pay voluntarily for their creation and that it thus is not profitable for private parties to develop them to the degree that would be efficient for society as a whole. These services are said to lack excludability, because it is difficult to exclude those who have not paid for them from "free riding" on the benefits they produce. Some collective device for the provision of these services is needed.[14] Dietrich Rueschemeyer and Peter Evans note:

> The state offers, in the context of a capitalist economy, a contribution that is both unique and necessary—unique because it transcends the logic of the competitive market and necessary because a capitalist economy requires, for its development as well as its maintenance in the face of changing conditions, the supply of "collective goods" that cannot be provided by the competitive actors in the economy.[15]

Some of the collective goods produced by the state, such as national defense, are consumed jointly by all citizens together, and the distribution of their benefits is therefore automatic and self-regulating. Elinor Ostrom designates these as pure public goods and distinguishes them from what she calls common-pool resources. Common-pool goods are consumed separately and can be exhausted, but, unlike privately owned resources, they are managed collectively, and it may be hard to exclude those who are not cooperating in their upkeep.[16] These resources are particularly vulnerable to the "tragedy of the commons." If a commonly owned field is not subject to sound collective management, it can be destroyed by overgrazing as each individual cattle owner tries to increase his share of the benefits by grazing more and more livestock on it. State control is usually seen as one of the alternatives to private ownership as a way to avert the "tragedy of the commons." But this presumes that the state has the capacity to manage its resources and services in the collective interest.

Not only can the state create and manage collective goods, it is one itself. It is a potential device for creating and sustaining societal benefits, but that potential will only be realized if the state itself is managed in the collective interest. Just as with the collectively owned field, if those who control the state continuously use it only to maximize their own narrow, individual interests, they will soon run it down, and it will produce less and less benefit for society as a whole. The ability of the state to function effectively is destroyed when the public payroll is expanded beyond the useful work to be done, when employees are hired out of patronage and without regard to merit, when decisions to undertake massive public expenditures are based on the size of bribes that the contractors offer,[17] when regulations are implemented to advance the fortunes of the particular businesses of the well connected and without regard to their larger economic impact, when agricultural prices are suppressed so as to subsidize credit or other services for political clients,[18] when local projects are created without regard to need or the ability to sustain them simply in order to advance political careers, and so on.

Such unrestrained depredation on the state and its resources, sapping its ability to produce and manage collective goods, is precisely what has happened to many African states. Crawford Young and Thomas Turner write of Zaire, "Worse than a mere *pagille* [shambles], the state risks becoming an irrelevancy, as well as a mechanism of predatory accumulation by those associated with its eroding power."[19] Richard Joseph makes only a slightly more moderate statement about Nigeria.[20]

Why are some states run in something like the collective interest while others are torn apart by self-serving special interests? Mancur Olson has suggested that we look at the structure of the political organizations that influence and control the state. He argues that the narrower the interests of the groups and organizations that dominate the political system, the more likely we are to have a "tragedy of the state commons."

> On balance, special-interest organizations and collusions reduce efficiency and aggregate income in the societies in which they operate and make political life more divisive. [In contrast,] encompassing organizations have some incentive to make the society in which they operate more prosperous, and an incentive to redistribute income to their members with as little excess burden as possible, and to cease such redistribution unless the amount redistributed is substantial in relation to the social cost of the redistribution.[21]

The African state is particularly vulnerable to the "tragedy of the state commons" because the interests that control it tend to be so narrow. The exercise of political power is inclined to be highly personal and bound by few institutional constraints.[22] The building blocks out of which political power is constructed usually are patron-client networks and ethnic appeals. Clientage puts primary emphasis on those benefits that can be appropriated and distributed on an individual basis, thus devaluing the production of collective goods.[23] The satisfaction of ethnic constituencies is broader but still involves the creation of services that can be distributed locally. Obviously, the members of client networks and ethnic alliances have many collective interests, but these are devalued by the way politics is organized.* Even though ethnic groups are collectivities, the only group in sub-Saharan Africa that is sufficiently large or politically dominant to treat the state as if it were acting as the guardian of its own exclusive interests is South African whites. In other states some degree of ethnic power-sharing is a political necessity, and self-restraint by one ethnic group will simply result in extra benefits for more selfish groups.

Given these attributes of most African political systems, we can better understand the comment of Rueschemeyer and Evans that

> in its early development the state is likely to have a thoroughly parasitic and even predatory character. Greater autonomy of such a predatorial state is likely to have negative rather than positive consequences for economic transformation. Under these circumstances, reducing the autonomy of the state, trying to make it the "handmaiden" of dominant economic elites, should also make it a more effective agent of accumulation.[24]

If a particular class captures a large portion of the benefits created by the state, has a firm collective identity, and is able to control the political system, then it will find it desirable to manage the state in the interests of the class as a whole and not run it down in the pursuit of purely individual interests. In African conditions it is possible for an economically privileged class to so dominate the political system as to treat the state as simply the guardian of its own interests, whereas almost no ethnic group can do the same.

This is not to suggest that such "class management" is selfless or will govern for the "common good"—far from it. Those who are disadvantaged by the political system will remain relatively disadvantaged. But management in the name of even a dominant class interest will produce more collective goods for society than would the depredations of more narrow interests. In the long run society will be still better served when the ruling class is challenged by the political participation of associations of the less advantaged. But in the meantime it would be less well served

---

*Roddie Cole has pointed out to me that African patron-client networks have been fruitful in producing some collective goods in the areas of health and education, but not in agriculture. In these areas services can be delivered to collectivities that have developed a sense of community and have the ability to manage their collective interests *at the local level*. But in agriculture, collective goods tend to be for social units that transcend the existing boundaries of African communities.

by the unrestrained and unstructured pursuit of the interests of patron-client or ethnic interests.

If we speak of "a collective interest" when a class uses the state to manage its group interests, we obviously mean collective interest in a sense quite different from "the greatest good of the greatest number." We intend instead something more like what others have called "enlightened self-interest." Such self-interest suggests the following: the pursuit of the greater gain of the larger number of members, rather than the ruthless pursuit of advantage by some members at the expense of others in the group; a concentration on long-term interests, rather than on immediate, short-term benefit; and sufficient care for the welfare of those outside the group so as to maintain the stability of the system, rather than nonmembers' being so deprived that they challenge the order's continued existence. This concept of self-interest tends to eschew zero-sum games in favor of positive-sum ones. Even though this enlightened self-interest is definitely oriented toward producing benefit for the members of one's own group, it pays much more attention to issues of collective benefit, leads to greater aggregate gain in the long run, and is not as destructive as is its narrow, purely individual counterpart. Political analysis is not helped by the usual failure to distinguish between an enlightened and a narrow self-interest. To make this point more forcefully I shall speak of the enlightened varieties of self-interest as class-based visions of the collective interest.

Kenyatta's role in the first decade of his presidency as a self-appointed trustee for the nascent matajiri class was critical. It led him to use the decision-making autonomy given him by his political security to manage the state with a greater view to collective interest than was the case in many other African countries. Even more important, the class on whose behalf Kenyatta was acting has different interests than its counterpart in a majority of other African states, for its wealth comes not only from commerce, industry, and wages but from agriculture as well. The matajiri own farms of reasonable size and grow much the same crops as smallholders. Thus it is in their interest to maintain healthy terms of trade for agriculture and to support services that will keep it expanding. These interests have led to public policies that are much more supportive of agriculture than are found in most of the other countries on the continent.

Kenyatta's health slipped in the final years of his reign, and he no longer controlled those around him well. Many Kikuyu insiders began to use their positions to promote the personal and special interests that could, in time, render the state a shambles. This change was partly countered and controlled by Mwai Kibaki, the minister of finance, Charles Njonjo, the attorney general, and Geoffrey Kariithi, the head of the civil service. The values of these men had been shaped by a socialization process that was quite similar to the one for professional civil servants I will describe shortly.

The dangerous narrowing of the interests pursued in the late Kenyatta years was partly reversed when Daniel arap Moi became president. This correction in the course of the ship of state was reinforced by cabinet ministers such as Njonjo, Kibaki, and later, Vice-President Saitoti, who tended to think of policy in terms that were broader than immediate personal interest. But of course political necessity dictated the presence in the government of other ministers, who were concerned only with fueling patronage machines. Of even greater assistance in the correction of the country's direction were civil servants like Simeon Nyachae, Harris Mule, and Philip Ndegwa. The influence of administrators like these is always tenuous. They have no power other than their own professional competence, integrity, and persuasiveness. They are influential only so long as the president recognizes their quality and listens to them. If they are to be effective, he has to be willing to hear advice that sometimes is unwelcome. Otherwise, only sycophants become "advisers." Nyachae, Mule, and Ndegwa belonged to the category of those who could be counted on to express their honest best judgments as to what was in the national interest. Through 1986 (which is as far as this study goes) President Moi generally valued their advice.

Thus parts of the civil service became visibly important as a repository of the collective interest; in fact, they had been so all along. This is why Kenyatta's reliance on the civil service as his instrument of governance was so significant for public policy. A strong bureaucracy is usually somewhere at the heart of autonomous action by the state.[25] But where did this commitment to the "common good" of the matajiri by critical figures in the civil service come from?

THE FORCES DIRECTING THE STATE FROM WITHIN

There is no inherent reason why the civil service should represent society's (or the ruling class's) collective interests. Bureaucrats have their own special interests: salaries, unpressured work, and growth in the size and prestige of their offices are fairly universal.[26] In the United States civil servants identify with the priorities and special-interest groups associated with their own departments, not with the government as a whole.[27] In Nigeria and many other places in Africa public office is often seen as a place from which to care for one's own network of clients.[28] The truth is, civil servants are perfectly capable of being predators on the state as well. Something special must happen if they are to have a larger vision. We will look at two forces shaping the views and actions of bureaucrats: their socialization and the procedures institutionalized in the existing state structures.

Socialization

People pursue their interests, but they don't always seek to maximize their *material* interests. In other words, they pursue their own values, broadly construed. But where do those values come from? Even when people work to advance their material interests, some individuals concentrate on their immediate interests and others on their long-term ones. Similarly, some individuals conceive of their material interests quite personally and others think of them in terms of the groups to which they belong. What determines these perspectives? What decides the group identity that one assumes? The experiences that cumulatively determine one's values and sense of identity are known as socialization.

We learned in chapter 2 that a disproportionate number of Kenya's highest civil servants, like Muriithi, Mule, and Nyachae, had fathers who had served the colonial government. Bureaucracy was a part of their family tradition. The bureaucracy into which they were socialized, however, was not the same one that Europeans joined. The white and black parts of the administration were rigidly segregated. British officers had usually spent their secondary-school years in an English public (i.e., prep) school. Although they had been trained to rule, they had been socialized to do so within the confines of democracy and had been imbued with traditions of service, collegiality, and teamwork.[29] These values were further reinforced by their peers after they joined the colonial service. Africans who worked for the colonial government had none of these experiences.

The state served by the fathers of today's African administrators was strong and authoritarian, with few legal constraints on its actions. It had crushed the opposition by force of arms, without much subtlety, and it had put down several rebellions, of which the most recent and most serious had been the Mau Mau. The decision to transfer power to an elected African government had been made in London in response to global, more than Kenyan, conditions. These men all accepted that the state should be strong and should have a primary concern with the maintenance of order.

The colonial African also experienced government service as extremely hierarchical. Orders were given and followed; they were not discussed. There was no collegiality and little teamwork. The authority of the governor was absolute; it was the duty of the civil servant to follow his instructions without question. There was no velvet glove on the iron fist of state; power was open and harsh. The African administrator was subject to authoritarian behavior from above and exercised it in turn on those below.[30]

The colonial state was relatively unconstrained by law as well. From an African point of view, Europeans made laws to suit their interests; law could not be used to challenge or limit them. Similarly, the colonial attempts to put legal limits on the African chiefs' exercise of power were unsuccessful. Rulers, not the law, ruled.[31]

In a similar vein colonial administrators were accustomed to playing political roles. European administrators, of course, did their best to manipulate and control African political expression. Appointed African chiefs were extensions of this endeavor and were frequently asked to play representative roles that one might have expected would fall to elected delegates. From the African point of view, there was no differentiation between administrative and political roles.

Finally, African colonial administrators were actively encouraged to use their positions to acquire wealth. European officers were hedged with conflict-of-interest regulations. But African civil servants were encouraged to expand their agricultural enterprises and to create commercial ones. They were to be the instrument whereby Africans were incorporated in the market, a development on which much of the prosperity of the colonial state rested.

When the sons of these colonial African administrators became senior civil servants, it is no surprise that they were dedicated to a strong, authoritarian state, one that was deeply concerned with order but little limited by law. They believed that their duty to the head of state was absolute, but otherwise did not see much reason why they should subordinate their judgment to that of elected leaders. They themselves were leaders, and leadership was an undifferentiated role. They also felt that it was appropriate and desirable that they use their positions to launch themselves into membership in a new African economic elite that could replace the European one.

It is a misrepresentation to say that the British conceptions of democratic rule, a bureaucracy oriented to service and development, and a civil service bound by strict conflict-of-interest ethics failed to take root on African soil. The truth is that the attempts to plant these ideas and the institutions to support them came very late in the colonial era and were quickly choked out by the already vigorous authoritarian conceptions that the British themselves had planted and nurtured earlier.[32]

These strains of bureaucratic socialization give a great deal of strength to the Kenyan state. The senior civil service accepts subservience to the president and the stability of the political system as primary goals. The mechanisms whereby the will of the government could be imposed on the general population also were well developed, and those who administer the state believe that it is their duty to use them.

Nonetheless, if these values had been the only ones guiding the bureaucracy, Kenya would not have had the many developmentally minded and service-oriented civil servants that it had. This socialization and the administrative structures that went with it explain the capacity of the Kenyan state for action, but not the positive manner in which it actually was used. Five other forces mitigated and partially redirected the colonial heritage.

The first was the African educational system. Throughout the colonial period African education was dominated by the missionary and English public school traditions. These combined to put great emphasis on moral rectitude, service, and public employment. As most of the secondary-school educators in this system were European, their African students did not fully identify with them, and the teachers' attempts at socialization did not have as much effect as did those of their counterparts in the English public schools. However, these schools were the gateways in an extraordinary narrowing in the path of advancement. Those who passed through them were members of a tiny meritocracy. Like most other elites, they had some identification with the values of the institutions that served to legitimate their claim on status and position.

Second, many of those who came to play a central role in Kenya's development entered the civil service by way of a profession. Just as Karanja was an engineer, Mule an economist, and Muriithi a veterinarian, many civil servants acquired an identity and values that were independent of their government position. Very often the referents for their professional standards were international, sometimes acquired in study overseas. This professional socialization developed alternative role conceptions. Many professions legitimate their elite status by their service to a set of larger societal interests. These "collective-regarding" values are heavily emphasized during the education that one needs to enter the profession and are reinforced by one's superiors in one's early job experiences. Commitment to these values is praised by the other members of one's profession, and one is encouraged to give these opinions priority over those of outsiders. In Africa these professional reference groups include international organizations and peers, making the standards truly independent of purely local considerations.

Professionalism therefore created the potential for pockets of autonomous performance within the public service. It is not unusual for some parts of a civil service to maintain highly professional standards of performance and integrity even while the bureaucracy as a whole is dismal.

A few islands of quality remained in the American public service through its deepest floods of corruption and patronage.[33] When Brazil's military launched that country on rapid economic growth, it too created offices of excellence within a bureaucracy that generally was ineffective.[34] And eighteenth-century England maintained a skilled navy and ship- building industry while its army was patronage ridden and much less competent.[35]

A third factor, international donors, was closely related to professionalism and greatly reinforced it. Because of their aid the Kenya government has many technical-assistance personnel, who generally have been recruited for their competence and who tend to uphold the values associated with their professions internationally. The donors also cajole Kenyan civil servants into maintaining standards on their projects and reward those who do so with access to more funds.

Fourth, the struggle for independence had imbued all who lived through it with a deep nationalism. The British colonial masters had said that Africans were not fit to rule, and they were determined to show that they could. The propertied Europeans and Asians wanted to continue to dominate the economy, and the new public servants were eager to demonstrate that Africans could compete with them. Most of these Africans also had studied overseas, where their "Kenyan-ness" and the need to compete internationally had been impressed on them.

Fifth, in Kenya the strength of the private economy gave potential independence to most of its higher public servants. Karanja, Mule, and Nyachae were all explicit about this. Many public servants became independently wealthy with the opportunities that the Africanization of the economy created. Others were confident that well-remunerated private-sector or international jobs awaited them if they left the employ of the Kenyan state. They could afford to risk the displeasure of their political superiors to pursue their professional visions of their roles, knowing that the state did not have a monopoly over their chances for prosperity and prestige. At the same time, they knew that these alternative income opportunities could be lost if they were forced out of the public service because of incompetence or corruption, and they were thereby encouraged to maintain their professional standards.

The statist orientation that many of Kenya's new higher civil servants inherited from their fathers, and the professional and nationalist orientations that they developed for themselves, combined to give them various visions of a collective interest and the sense of distinctive group identity that was necessary to pursue these. This cadre of statist and professional officers probably were a minority among administrators. But in the early years after independence they sufficiently dominated the civil service that they frequently were able to socialize others who had not shared their experiences into their own collectively oriented values.

Socialization experiences do not last forever; they need to be reinforced if they are to retain their influence. Unfortunately, there were other forces at work countering the generally positive ones just described. The pull of ethnic identity is very strong, as is the siren call of easy wealth. The positive values that shaped the civil service not only are distinctive to it but are actively opposed by the general society and its elected political representatives, who think in narrow, sectional terms. The Europe-like custom of administrative careers as a family tradition,[36] which was so evident among the first generation of African higher civil servants, is not being maintained. The children of today's matajiri administrators usually are going into the private sector.

Furthermore the countervailing forces of nationalism have been weakening, as the memory of the independence struggle wanes. There is the possibility that the public humiliation of Africa's subordination to the sway of the International Monetary Fund and the World Bank in the current economic crisis could be used creatively by heads of state to regenerate this nationalism and the sense of collective purpose that goes with it. General Babangida did as much in Nigeria, and Jerry Rawlings used a neutralist populism to work a similar wonder for a time in Ghana. Nationalism is a powerful mobilizing force when used creatively and positively.

The more constant of the remaining collectivizing socializing forces is professionalization. This is far from trivial. Professionals have maintained pockets of distinctive performance in other governments. Furthermore, many of the Kenyan professions have the advantage of still having strong international ties. Economics is the most important profession from the point of view of general public policy, and it is still true that everyone who advances in government in this field in Kenya has been overseas for at least one higher degree and has frequent interactions with international counterparts.

Institutionalization

The patterns of socialization that have been described work at the individual level. Added to these are the organizations and standard operating procedures of the state, which often become institutionalized or valued for their own sakes. These institutions have an independent influence on state actions and are not simply a pass-through for the interest structure of the political system. Although they were *formed* to serve a constellation of interests that existed at the time of their creation, they frequently outlasted it. Thus they represent an amalgam of present and past interests. Furthermore, neither the politicians nor the administrators nor the interest-group leaders who create these organizations and standard operating procedures act with perfect knowledge; they often bring into existence institutions that do not serve their intended beneficiaries in the way they anticipated.

The colonial Kenyan state existed to control its African populace and to serve the interests of white-settler agriculture. Its "native" administration was centralized and authoritarian. At the same time, most of the state organizations that were involved in agriculture were not designed to extract a surplus for the benefit of the colonial power, as was the case in most of Africa, but instead were intended to benefit farmers, albeit large ones. Because the white settlers organized themselves along associational (or class) lines and not patron-client ones, the organizations were oriented more toward collective interests than individual ones. These agricultural support services had grown to prominence during the Great Depression and reflected the distrust of markets that characterized the era. They added up to socialism for the well-to-do.

The institutionalized momentum of these organizations and habits of action carried over into the postcolonial period. The state stressed control, distrusted the market, but was supportive of agriculture and continued to emphasize policies that were more oriented toward the interests of farmers as a collectivity. The state was not transformed by independence; instead, its energies were refocused. In agriculture it shifted and broadened its clientele from large white farmers to large and small African ones.[37]

The particular ways in which the independent Kenya state served African farming was often determined by the accidents of the already existing institutional framework or the precise shape of the political interests existing at the moment of the creation of the new organizations. Several examples were discussed in chapters 6, 7, and 9. The colonial European dairy industry was served by two well-organized entities, the Kenya Cooperative Creameries for marketing, and the Veterinary Department for artificial insemination and animal health. This unintegrated structure was simply stretched to meet the needs of smallholders and worked well. The Kenya Tea Development Authority was created just before independence specifically to work with African small growers and reflected the then dominant view that a vertically integrated organization would be necessary to accomplish the task. It too functioned very well. But when the United States and the World Bank moved to stimulate peasant food production in the 1970s, they adopted the then fashionable position that horizontal integration was necessary. This approach was a failure. The arrangements used for each agricultural venture were more influenced by the interests and ideologies prevailing at the moment when the relevant organization was created than by a rational calculation of what was needed for a particular crop at the time of the new initiative.[38] The analysis in chapters 7 and 9 suggests that the necessity for integration and control usually was seriously overestimated.

The political demands accompanying independence also led to the institutionalization of different patterns of staff socialization in different parts of the public service. The Provincial Administration was the symbol and substance of colonial rule. President Kenyatta had been in detention when his governing KANU party was created and did not feel in full control of it. The Provincial Administration became his primary instrument of governance and political control. To give legitimacy to the new regime and to improve Kenyatta's grasp, the Provincial Administration therefore had to be Africanized very rapidly. This cadre had been the elite of the colonial civil service and had been drawn from a small, well-socialized group of Englishmen. The rapidity of transfer broke the chain of socialization. Many of the new African recruits, like Nyachae, had worked for the colonial government and had absorbed the priority it gave to order. But they did not assume the values of impartiality and respect for democracy that were latent among the British provincial administrators and saw their tasks more simply as the president's instruments of political control. Most of those in the cadre today have been successfully socialized into a role that permits the kind of political manipulation on behalf of the government of the day that characterized nineteenth-century French prefects.[39]

Similarly visible were the positions on the boards of Kenya's many parastatal enterprises. The colonial state had used these positions to secure expertise and to represent client interests. With rapid Africanization, expertise was less available, and the new government was more anxious to control competing bases of political power than to give them independent vehicles for articulating their interests. Board memberships therefore were increasingly used as patronage for the purposes of co-optation and control. The contributions of the boards to policy formulation therefore declined precipitously, and they became vehicles for patronage pressures on the parastatals.

Junior staff appointments in the colonial government had not been subject to supervision by the Public Service Commission. The junior staff were always African, and the supervising senior staff who controlled them were always European then. Therefore there seemed little reason to worry about abuse of the powers of appointment and promotion. However, after independence the supervising officers were African and were subject to great personal pressures to take care of unemployed educated kin. The nontechnical junior positions have become the major vehicle for patronage in Kenya today, and the people who occupy them often show the same laxity about the performance of their duties that characterized similar employees under the nineteenth-century spoils system in the United States.[40]

The professional and technical staff in the Kenya government were affected quite differently than was the general civil service. The members of the Provincial Administration are an example of senior, generalist civil servants. Their qualifications were forged largely by apprenticeship and experience and were not formalized. As suggested in chapter 5, such qualifications are ruler-acknowledged: they exist only to the extent that the president sees them. Professional qualifications, however, are publicly manifest; they are formalized and require defined periods of institutional education and externally defined standards of performance. These qualifications are much more difficult for rulers to ignore (which, as was demonstrated, gives technical officers greater influence on government action). The need for manifest qualifications made Africanization slower and more deliberate among the ranks of the professional senior staff. The attempts of their European predecessors to socialize them in their roles were consequently more gradual and effective. This was important, as there is some evidence that early job experiences may have an even greater effect on organizationally relevant values than education and background have.[41] These more deliberate Africanization processes accounted for the careful selection of effective administrators such as Karanja, Mule, and Muriithi.

This first generation of African professional leaders then institutionalized similar selection procedures for their successors. Socialization was further aided by the technical education that was required for these posts and the identification with a larger profession that it induced. The occupants of these positions therefore are generally less political and are more committed to the formal purposes of their organizations than are those in other parts of the public service. These offices are the ones in which a concept of some kind of collective, long-term interest is most likely to be maintained, as noted earlier in this chapter.

Professional pockets of productivity are easiest to maintain in those parts of the civil service that perform distinctive tasks that are visible and widely seen as keys to the economy or to powerful groups within it. Excellence is harder to sustain in offices that provide diffuse indirect benefits.[42] Pockets of productivity also are more likely in agencies that are separate from the general civil service, can at least influence the selection of their own personnel, and can maintain continuity in their staffing. All these factors help to sustain their distinctness and are found most frequently in parastatals and in agencies run by the traditional professions.[43]

Political Responsiveness

The portrayal of values institutionalized in organizations and staff socialization might lead one to conclude that the bureaucracy was dominating the policy process and shouldering aside the politicians. This would be a mistake. All the evidence indicates that the politicians are and have been firmly in charge. Little or no effective state action takes place without the support of the president in Kenya. This is demonstrated quantitatively in Appendix B and is illustrated in numerous instances by the policy initiatives in which the four administrators were involved.

This subservience of the civil service is part of a common pattern. In the last century numerous heads of government expressed concern about their ability to control their bureaucracies. But almost all of them actually succeeded. In Britain the fears of the postwar Labour government that its socialist policies would be sabotaged by the conservative administrative class were not realized. Hitler emasculated the powerful German civil service with little trouble.[44] The Soviets controlled their "bourgeois technicians" easily,[45] and the Chinese "experts" melted before each "Red" campaign, culminating in the Cultural Revolution.[46] American presidents have complained that they cannot control parts of their bureaucracy. But the best evidence indicates that they have done far better than they acknowledge.[47] The deviance from presidential will that does exist is supported by Congress and therefore must be seen as responsive to the political will as it is defined by the peculiarities of the American constitutional system.[48] Even the much-vaunted French civil servant has been responsive to direction when the political leadership has been united.[49] Military bureaucrats have a base of independent power with which they can resist the explicit will of their political masters and even supplant them, but the instances in which civil servants have been able to do the same are extremely few and far between.*

Civil servants have not even been very successful in assuming the policy-making function when the political leadership has been divided and hopelessly ineffective. During the Fourth French Republic the civil service was unable to give direction to government even when there was no effective political hand at the rudder of state. The bureaucracy had plenty of ideas but could not make them coherent or make them happen without political support.[50] In a similar vein John D. Montgomery has

---

*The only example of civil service dominance of the political leadership of which I am aware is that of nineteenth-century Germany. The influence of this case on the writings of Max Weber helps to explain why the fear of bureaucratic dominance is so disproportionate to the reality. Hans Rosenberg, *Bureaucracy, Aristocracy and Autocracy: The Prussian Experience: 1660–1815* (Boston: Beacon Press, 1966), pp. 202–28.

observed that senior civil servants in southern Africa seem paralyzed when they lack clear political guidance.[51]

There is much politics in good administration, and effective politics requires some attention to administrative detail, but the core roles of the politician and the administrator are different. Administrators are involved in policy-making, but they need politicians to aggregate disparate interests, to mobilize the political resources needed for action, and to provide the energy needed for change.[52] Without a good political leader's hand at the tiller, the wind seems to go out of the sails of the ship of state. Not all heads of government are able to provide this direction, but the bureaucracy is unable to take their places if they do not.

Nonetheless, without a good civil service there will be neither compass nor charts for the political leadership to follow, and the sails of the ship of state will be rotten and will tear. Bureaucracies are not the adversaries of heads of government; they are the equipment with which politicians can achieve their goals. This is not to say that the civil service will realize the political government's every wish. A ship at full sail cannot be brought instantly to rest; nor will a freighter be able to function as a racing sloop, or vice versa. The head of government is limited by what he or she has at hand. Civil servants as individuals rarely offer concerted resistance to the will of a united political leadership, but the service's preexisting institutional characteristics will determine how well it is able to serve that will. Bureaucracies have generally proved malleable with regard to the explicitly political parts of their agendas, for politicians are skilled at recognizing and dealing with challenges at this level. They have been more inflexible with regard to their structure, personnel, and standard operating procedures, and these have sometimes had unanticipated secondary effects.[53]

The nature of the administrative apparatus of the state can be changed, but it takes time and the investment of considerable effort to do so. This lack of instant response is not due to some subversive opposition on the part of a coterie of bureaucrats; most civil servants are eager to serve the wishes of their presidents or prime ministers. It derives instead from the size and complexity of the organizations involved, the individual competencies and incompetencies that have been assembled within them over time, and the values that are imbedded in their procedures. An excellent basketball team cannot be made into a good football club without a great deal of training and new personnel. When the values, competencies, and experience of the civil service are consistent with the objectives of a skilled and popular head of government, remarkable things can be accomplished. When the two are out of synchronization with each other, the going will be very slow. The cause of effective policy formation and implementation is neither political will nor administrative competence but the *interaction effect* of the two. In Chapter 5 and Appendix B we established that technical and professional officers can have a major impact on administrative outcomes, but the existence of this effect depends on presidential support.

Thus our attention is directed not to who is winning the struggle for control over the apparatus of state—a zero-sum game—but to the quality of governance—a cooperative game between heads of government and their administrators whereby benefits are created for society. By and large, such a congenial partnership existed between President Kenyatta and his new civil service. As a consequence, the economy developed reasonably rapidly, and the country's political and social structures evolved in ways he wanted. President Moi was less fortunate. Many of his goals required a reorientation of objectives and competencies in the civil service, as he wished to stress greater regional equality in the state's programs. It took time to achieve this. When there was consistency, as there was with Nyachae and Mule, there was rapid forward movement.

If a Kenyan president works with the dedicated professionals in the civil service and nurtures their growth, the collective interests of various groups in the society can be effectively served. If, however, he or she wished to prey on the state for the narrow, selfish benefit of selected individuals and small groups, the professionals would question the wisdom of these actions and might slow them down for a time. But there would be other civil servants who were willing to cooperate. Similarly, if the president's agenda were repression and the control of independently expressed opinion, parts of the colonially created administrative apparatus would be ready instruments.

Multiple policy opportunities exist within the Kenyan state. The professional, collectivity-regarding pockets of performance within the civil service have been central to Kenya's development performance to date. But that has been due to the willingness of the presidents to use them. Otherwise they are a weak force in a society that generally has little regard for nationwide collective purposes. If these pockets of excellence were not nurtured, they could eventually be destroyed and would be hard to re-create. A president who swept over them in the name of political necessity would gain many short-term benefits but would pay dearly with the country's long-term prosperity.

The matajiri are the *social* force that is most likely to support and sustain the vision of Kenya's collectivity-regarding professional civil servants. The matajiri have begun to emerge clearly as a class and seem to be beginning to understand their collective interests and to wish to protect them. They are *capable* of countering the factionalizing, narrow agendas of patron-client politics. When the two ultimately confront each other, it remains to be seen if the matajiri will actually prevail.

THE STRONG STATE

Is the Kenyan state strong and autonomous? If so, does this explain its relatively successful rural development? Or is it instead being overwhelmed by the antidevelopmental forces in its own society? Let us hold the answers to these questions up against more general theories about the state.

Joel Migdal defines strong states in terms of their capacity to make the programs of their leaders real and effective in the larger society.[54] Michael Lofchie has suggested that one indicator of a state's strength is its ability to make policy in its long-term interests. I have argued that this latter attribute is an aspect of state autonomy and the ability to pursue some form of collective interests. A weak and nonautonomous state is constantly buffeted by its short-term political needs. It engages only in the "politics of survival."[55]

It would be possible to have an autonomous state that lacked the administrative capacity to impose its programs on society and therefore would be judged weak. But an administratively effective state that lacked autonomy would hardly appear strong, for it would have no separate agenda to work on society and therefore would have little independent impact upon it. It therefore makes sense to follow Lofchie's explicit and Migdal's implicit intention and to fold the concept of autonomy into that of the strong state.

Throughout the Kenyatta years, Kenya had a relatively strong state by African standards. Why? Migdal suggests that its emergence depends on the existence of one or more of four conditions. He holds that one of these

> is the existence of a social grouping with people sufficiently independent of existing bases of social control and skillful enough to execute the grand design of state leaders. Bureaucrats of the state, both those at the tops of agencies and the implementors in the field, must identify their own ultimate interests with those of the state as an autonomous organization. . . . [Another condition is] skillful top leadership [which] must be present to take advantage of the [other] conditions to build a strong state. . . . They must carefully select bureaucrats who can and will proffer strategies of survival to the population based on the principles of the leaders. Also, they must have a keen eye toward the changing risk calculus. Leaders must know when to move and against whom.*

*Migdal, *Strong Societies and Weak States*, pp. 274–75. Migdal also holds that a precondition of strength is a "massive social dislocation which severely weakens social control." This precondition was met in Kenya by Mau Mau and its suppression. I have doubts, however, about the validity of this hypothesized precondition. Malawi, Cameroon, and Ivory Coast have done well without such a dislocation. Nigeria, Ethiopia, and Mozambique had such dislocations and certainly do not have strong states.

Colonial Kenya had developed an unusually strong bureaucratic apparatus in order to crush the Mau Mau, and the core of the new Provincial
Administration were men who had identified with the state against this
particular manifestation of society. Kenyatta had the vision and political
skill to use this administrative apparatus to advance his conservative
preferences for Kenya's future.

From a worldwide rather than an African perspective, however, the
Kenyan state appears to be only moderately strong. Goran Hyden comments that the all-pervasive pressures of the peasant "moral economy"
for patronage constantly threaten to penetrate the state apparatus and
corrupt its ability to act in the service of any larger, collective ends.[56] A
politically weak president could undermine the still-fragile strength of
the Kenyan state by practicing the "politics of survival." He or she then
would be afraid to permit any social or political organization that was
not subject to the control of the president. If they could not be dis-
banded, intimidated, or rendered peripheral, then their leaders would
have to be co-opted. The pervasiveness of the need for resources for co-
optation would play into demands from below for patronage, weakening the state.[57]

The civil service is one of the keys to the survival of a relatively strong
state in Kenya, and hence to its ability to address any version of its long-
term collective needs. When one considers the tremendous gap that exists between the values of the general public and those that guide the
professional bureaucrats, it is remarkable how much the Kenyan state
has been able to accomplish. At the same time, that social gap threatens
the ability of the civil service to maintain its autonomy. The better that
senior civil servants are integrated into the general workings of society,
the more difficult it is for them to maintain the distinctive values on
which the smooth functioning of the state depends. Whereas in the
United States the professions are being urged to become less distant and
to abandon their elitism so as to be more accessible to the concerns and
perspectives of average citizens,[58] the opposite prescription seems more
appropriate for Africa at this stage of its development. The professional's sense of specialness and separateness is a precious asset in this context.

The other key to the future of a strong state is the emerging matajiri
class. By its nature it is dependent on economic growth,[59] and it ultimately has the capacity to frame and pursue its collective interests.

The combination of matajiri class interests and strong professionalism offer the best prospects at the moment for the continued strength
of the Kenyan state and its economy. This is not to say that the matajiri
and the professionals represent "the common good." Their vision of so-

ciety's future is self-serving in important respects. But it is *a collective* vision, one that would build the state as an instrument of the group's common interests. In this respect it is superior to the patronage-driven urge to raid the state for private goods, which debilitates its capacity for purposive action and leaves it a shambles. The professional civil servants also bring a significant leaven to the class-based interests of the matajiri. Their training and international contacts make them more likely to interpret those interests in long-term and enlightened ways, thus creating a wider spread of benefits in Kenya and lessening the likelihood of serious social conflict.

The matajiri/civil service professional vision of Kenya's future is far from perfect. It deserves criticism by international progressives and political competition from associational groupings of Kenya's disadvantaged. The more it is tested the less shortsighted and narrowly self-serving it is likely to be. But it is this vision that has brought Kenya as far as it has come already, and it is the one that is likely to carry it farthest in the next decades.

WHAT OF THIS CAN BE GENERALIZED?

Are the lessons gained from this book of any utility in understanding and improving the quality of public management in other African states? The pessimistic reader might say, "No, the developmental path portrayed here was unique to Kenya and no other society can pass that way again. If a country didn't have a Kenyatta, a Mau Mau rebellion, and white-settler agriculture, it can hardly recreate those ingredients thirty years after independence. History is irreversible. In fact," this devil's advocate might add, "in the future Kenya itself is not going to be able to draw on some of the factors that were important to its past success. Kenyatta is dead, and the family tradition of civil service employment, which was responsible for three of the distinguished administrators the book describes, is no longer being sustained." Can we gainsay such a sweeping critique?

I think we can, and in the process suggest propositions of wide applicability. It is true that this book is a case study of Kenya and not a piece of systematic comparative research. The latter would be necessary to verify any generalizations that we might want to make. In the interests of laying the groundwork for such larger research, however, I now propose to extend my hypotheses to cover other African countries.

It is true that historical chains of events are cumulative in their effect and are heavily influenced by a complexity of context that is specific to each case, as indeed I have argued on several occasions in this book. One cannot simply take the institutions and developmental patterns that worked for one country, plop them down elsewhere, and hope to achieve the same results.[60] But one can identify the most important elements in a success and see if their essential character might be replicated by different means, with causal chains that are themselves unique to the new case.

The essential ingredients in Kenya's agricultural development have been (1) a coincidence of elite interests with those of peasant agriculture, and (2) pockets of strong professionalism in the civil service, which give the state some strength and autonomy. The interaction of these two factors created pockets of administrative productivity that sustained the growth of small-farm production. The first arose from Kenyatta's vision of how to Africanize the benefits of white-settler agriculture and how to prevent the reeruption of Mau Mau. The second derived primarily from colonial patterns of civil service training and socialization. These primary causes cannot be recreated, but the essential nature of their effects can be.

Kenya was one of a small group of countries in which the new African economic and political elites developed (or already had) substantial interests in agriculture. Furthermore, these new African large farmers generally grew crops and employed technologies that were quite similar to those on small farms. Thus it was in their interests to promote agricultural research, the development of economic infrastructure, and prices that helped smallholders as well. The latter suffered by having reduced access to land; a land reform that broke up these remaining large farms would have reduced Kenya's landlessness. But the peasantry gained far more from the resulting economic structure, which produced dramatic increases in the incomes of middle peasant and petty-bourgeois farmers.

Bruce Johnston and others have long argued for the benefits of unimodal agricultural systems, in which farm sizes and incomes are relatively equally distributed.[61] The Kenyan case requires a modification of his proposition, for bimodalism has persisted there, and the country still has done reasonably well. A relatively egalitarian (unimodal) farming system *does* have powerful economic and developmental benefits. And the large farms in the typical bimodal system *do* siphon off resources from the small-farm sector, choke off its growth, prevent its members from providing a mass-consumer base to local industry, and thereby create severe structural impediments to economic development. But Kenya's African large farmers were not typical of bimodalism. Their farms were still generally moderate in size and their production systems were similar to those of smallholders. The net effect of their political and economic influence was to make new resources available to peasant agriculture, rather than diverting them or choking them off. These political benefits more than offset the purely economic disadvantages. Thus moderate deviations from equality into bimodal agriculture can be beneficial to development if they create the political conditions for public policies favorable to large- and small-scale farming alike.

However, similarities in the crops and technologies on large- and small-scale farms are not enough in themselves to produce benefits for little producers. The bigger farmers, with political influence, have to demand policies that advance their *collective* rather than their purely individual interests. If they derive their incomes from patronage (special loans, licenses, and subsidies, etc.), which benefit them alone, the small and the noninfluential will be hurt. But if they press for better prices, relevant research, strong markets, and so forth, all the relevant producers benefit. Kenya has emphasized a preponderance of collective over purely individual benefits for agriculture. In the years right after independence this was achieved through a combination of Kenyatta's vision of a new African ruling class (the matajiri) and the momentum of the institutions that had serviced the white settlers. Today, however, that emphasis on the collective comes from the political strength of the matajiri, which now has a reasonable sense of itself as a class.

It seems to me that it is possible for many other states on the continent to recreate the essentials of these political components to Kenya's agricultural success. First, the economically advantaged throughout Africa are increasingly becoming a socially distinct and self-conscious class, similar to Kenya's matajiri. Where this upper class has continued to draw its income predominately from commerce, it appears to have pursued its political interests primarily in the form of patronage. But as it has moved into directly productive sectors of the economy, particularly industry, it has defined its interests much more in class and therefore collective terms.[62]

Second, the crisis in food production throughout the continent and the improvement in agricultural prices by structural adjustment have led increasing numbers of this upper class to begin farming seriously. As this is a directly productive activity, to the extent that they already see themselves as a class they seem likely to advance their new interest through collectively beneficial policies more than patronage. If their production requirements are similar to those of peasant producers, the enhanced political standing of agriculture is likely to produce broad benefits and a resulting regeneration of agricultural growth. Such a process appears to be well advanced in Malawi, Botswana, Ivory Coast, and

Cameroon and to account for their better performance in this sector over the last fifteen years.

The other component in Kenya's agricultural success story has been the presence of professional pockets of excellence in the civil service. The distinctive values of these professionals came initially from socialization in the colonial period and its immediate aftermath. Many other African states (although by no means all) had similarly socialized and competent men and women in the civil service at independence, but their effectiveness was undermined by the absence of the necessary supporting political conditions. Now that the political requirements for agricultural development are closer to being met, is there any prospect of regenerating the professional pockets of productivity to complement them, give the state some strength, and produce public policies and programs supportive of farming? And, in countries like Kenya, can the existing pockets of excellence and state strength be sustained now that the earlier socializing conditions no longer exist?

As was suggested in the discussion of President Moi's personnel policies in chapter 12, over time, high standards in the civil service are very sensitive to the appointment and promotion practices of the head of state. Strongly institutionalized systems can resist attacks on their core values for a considerable period of time, but without some external reinforcement they will eventually crumble. Once these institutionalized standards have been destroyed, they are difficult to recreate. The civil service as a whole has deteriorated severely in most African states and it is unlikely to be resurrected as a positive force in the near future. But where the waste has not been complete, small pockets of good performance can be expanded where they persist and created where they do not, as is suggested by the experience of other societies.[63]

The necessary conditions for the existence of a pocket of excellence appear to be political demand for its particular services and a professional group sustaining its values. The creation of the political aspect was discussed above. Historically, the professional aspect was sustained in Europe by the guild structure of urban society.[64] In Africa, however, national professional cultures have been weak. For this reason international professional referents and contacts are generally needed to help sustain them—that is, to give them institutional strength. At the end of chapter 12 I argued that international bodies and donors can play an important role in promoting this sustenance and institutionalization. When heads of state want to draw on professional expertise, they then will find it there to help them, and they will be able to design personnel policies to expand on the existing base.

The future of Africa's agriculture thus rests, I submit, on an interaction of managerial and political factors. Successful policy outcomes derive from the intersection of interests, institutions, and individuals. Their particular combination in Kenya produced a number of notable rural development successes, but for most of Africa their configuration produced dismal results in its first quarter-century of independence. The prospects for a more propitious combination for many states now exists on the horizon, I believe. If subsequent research confirms the hypotheses advanced in this book, we not only will have discovered the keys to the successes Africa has already experienced but will have uncovered the means for creating more of them.

APPENDIX A

Ethnic Determinants of Civil Service Promotions

When I was teaching future civil servants at the University of Nairobi between 1969 and 1973, it was widely believed by my students that their ethnic identity would influence their career prospects. Not only did they think that some groups (particularly the Kikuyu) were being systematically favored over others, they also were convinced that the ethnicity of their superiors in the civil service would shape their promotion prospects. Specifically, they believed that if those who were responsible for recommending their advancement belonged to the same ethnic group as themselves, their prospects would be enhanced.

In 1974 I began to collect data that would enable me to test these assumptions systematically. I discovered that through 1970 the Government of Kenya annually had published a book that listed every senior civil servant and the following data concerning them: salary, ministry, position, qualifications, tenure in present position, and seniority in the government service. Changes in salary are an obvious indicator of career advancement. The objective factors that might properly weigh on promotions, such as qualifications and seniority, were given in the publication. Furthermore, the data were presented in such a way that it was possible to determine the supervisors of at least the more senior officers.

These personnel books were available on the open shelves in one of the ministry libraries. I made copies of these data from the social service and development ministries and undertook their analysis. (I felt that it would be unwise to collect these data on those parts of the public service that the Government of Kenya might regard as especially sensitive, such as the Ministry of Defense, the Police, and the Provincial Administration.) The lines of supervisory authority were evident furthest down the hierarchy in the Ministry of Agriculture, which included the Veterinary

Department at that time. Thus the largest number of cases I analyzed came from this ministry. The other ministries examined were Cooperatives, Economic Planning and Development, Education, Housing, Labour, Social Services, and Works. Because the data in Agriculture were deeper than they were for the other ministries, I always checked my findings on it and the others separately.

We began by identifying the ethnic identity of every senior civil servant and cabinet minister.* This was first done by Kenyan research assistants, who determined ethnicity from the person's name. This methodology has an 80 to 90 percent reliability in Kenya. For the ministers and the occupants of the highest civil service posts, the ethnicity was confirmed with a respected Kenyan political scientist who knew them.

Salary data were available to us from 1966 through 1970, but after some preliminary analysis of the material it became evident that studying the change in salaries between 1968 and 1970 would give us the largest number of cases to examine.

The following data were coded and rendered computer readable for every case: salary in 1968 and 1970, the ethnicity of the individual, his or her qualifications, tenure in post, seniority in government service, and the ethnicity, qualifications, and tenure of those in the various positions that might be able to influence their careers: the division head, the department's chief technical officer, the ministry's personnel officer, the permanent secretary, the cabinet minister, those at the Public Service Commission, and so forth. A total of 724 cases were usable for analysis.

A thorough search of the data was made, looking for patterns of advantage and influence. The results were largely negative, but this in itself is significant. The one determinant of promotion that was discernable from these data was formal qualifications ($r = .154$; $N = 694$; $p < .0005$). The modest size of the correlation is to be expected, given that most people will be promoted less often than every two years. The effects were not small, however. A staff member with only an Ordinary-level high school certificate generally received a 9.87 percent increase over the two-year period, while those with university degrees averaged 14.24 percent. Length of time in post and seniority in the government service had no effect on advancement prospects.

By and large, there is no evidence of ethnic discrimination nor of supervisory favoritism along ethnic lines. Europeans received above-

*At various stages in this project I received research assistance from M. Louise Fox, Lizz Kleemeier, Catherine Akinyi Muketi, and Herzon Olouch, and advice from Professor John J. Okumu. I am grateful for their help.

TABLE A-1
The Determinants of the Percentage of Increase
of a Civil Servant's Salary between 1968 and 1970

Dependent Variable: Percentage of increase of a civil servant's salary between 1968 and 1970 (mean = 12.15; std. dev. = 13.54)

Multiple Regression Coefficient = .189
N = 694; F = 8.52; p < .0005

Independent Variables:
• Years of post-secondary education; B = 1.01; F = 20.53; p < .0005
• 1968 salary in Kenya shs.; B = −0.0688; F = 5.82; p = .016
• Perm. sec. of same ethnic group; B = 1.94; F = 3.60; p = .058

---

average salaries, but once they were removed from the analysis there was no sign that ethnicity played a role in determining either one's base salary or one's increase from it.

We made multiple attempts to discover evidence that having someone from the same ethnic group in an influential position advanced one's salary prospects. All our probes failed to pass the test of statistical significance, despite the large size of our sample. The variable that came closest was having a permanent secretary of the same ethnic group as oneself. When all the personnel cases were aggregated, a small relationship appeared that could occur by chance alone 6 percent of the time. (See table A-1.) The statistical significance of the apparent relationship declined still further when the cases were disaggregated into the Ministry of Agriculture and other ministries sets. Even if such influence were in existence, its effects were modest. Having a permanent secretary of the same ethnicity as oneself would, on average, increase one's salary over the two-year period by only 1.9 percent (less than half the effect of having a B.A.). We believe that even this appearance of influence by the permanent secretaries was simply a statistical artifact. The structure of the promotion process, rumor, and the analyses presented in Appendix B lead us to believe that an officer's chief technical officer would be more influential with promotions than his or her permanent secretary. The fact that we found absolutely no evidence of such influence makes it more likely that the appearance of possible influence by the permanent secretaries is simply a chance occurrence and does not reflect reality.

Given the strength of the rumors that ethnicity and influence were determining promotions, the weakness of the evidence supporting them is striking. Chapter 4 considers the reasons for this unexpected finding.

APPENDIX B

Bureaucratic Influences and the Regional Allocation of Government Services

Everywhere the modern state is undergoing bureaucratization. But whether the power of bureaucracy within the polity is universally increasing must here remain an open question.

—MAX WEBER

Max Weber's dictum that history involves a continuous struggle between political chiefs and their administrators for control over the resources of the state is well heeded today.[1] The literature of political science is rich with assertions and analyses of bureaucratic power.[2] Yet despite the attention, the relative power of politician and civil servant is hotly debated for almost every system, and we really don't seem much closer to answering Weber's "open question" than he was himself.[3]

Commentators on Kenyan politics also see bureaucratic power as important but, like other comparativists, offer vague and somewhat conflicting interpretations of its significance.[4] This lack of either precision or consensus is simply a manifestation of a problem affecting the whole of political science. "Power" and "influence" have proved to be complicated to conceptualize and extraordinarily difficult to operationalize.[5] A direct measurement of bureaucratic power in Kenya is much too difficult even to be attempted.

Nevertheless, in the process of examining other issues in Kenyan administration I have developed an indirect indicator of bureaucratic power in that particular system, an indicator that provides harder results and more useful quantitative estimates than most direct-measurement techniques have yielded to date. This methodology enables me to demonstrate (1) that members of the elite, general cadre of the administration probably have only indirect influence over the regional alloca-

I have accumulated an impressive list of debts in the preparation of this appendix. M. Louise Fox, Lizz Kleemeier, Catherine Akinyi Muketi, Patrick Muzaale, and Herzon Olouch served as my research assistants at various times. My colleagues Christopher Achen, Steven Rosenstone, John Okumu, and W. Ouma Oyugi provided invaluable advice and assistance at critical points.

tion of public goods and services in Kenya, (2) that senior technical officers do have significant potential influence, and (3) that both groups of civil servants are able to exercise influence only with the support of the president.

ANECDOTES AND QUESTIONS

Anecdotes on bureaucratic power are common in informed Kenyan circles. One incident for which my sources are particularly good occurred in the Ministry of Agriculture in 1969. Government price-support policies were undergoing extensive review at that time, and an overall decision had been taken to reduce the price on those foods for which there was a domestic surplus. The price had already been reduced on maize, which is produced in marketable quantities in Western Province (the Luhya area) and on some large Rift Valley farms. A similar decision was made to lower the price of wheat, which was grown only on large farms. The minister of agriculture (a European) had approved the decision and was due to promulgate it in a public speech. At the last minute he fell ill and the chief technical officer (CTO) of the ministry was delegated to deliver the speech but omitted the section on wheat prices. The price never was lowered.

Clearly, power was exercised in this incident, but it is impossible to specify the source and base of that power from the anecdote alone. First, was this CTO actually exercising influence in this instance or only anticipating its use by another power figure? The president of Kenya had some of the largest wheat farms at that time. It is quite plausible that the CTO was anticipating—or had been informed of—the president's intention to reverse the decision. This would make the CTO only a pawn, not an influential actor himself. Second, if the CTO was the source of power in this instance, what was the base of that influence? Was it an attribute of his office? If so, was it the hierarchical or technical character of his office that was important? Alternatively, was his power due to his Kikuyu ethnicity and consequent close links with the president? Or was his influence idiosyncratic to him alone, and no others who held his position would have been able to behave in the same way? As will become clear from the evidence subsequently presented here, the answer is that the power probably had its source in an interaction between the president and the CTO. The former has political power, and the latter had information and proximity to the decision. Action would have been difficult for either without the support of the other. It will also become evident later that the base of the CTO's influence was not idiosyncratic but came from his technical status and senior position (although his specific post at the top of the technical hierarchy was not very important).

Conclusions like these cannot be drawn from the anecdote itself, however. They can emerge only from the analysis of relatively large numbers of comparable decisions. Unfortunately, direct, comparable information about any quantity of decisions is almost never available in comparative politics and administration.

Happily, there is indirect evidence available in Kenya for a good number of decisions, and this evidence points to answers for the tantalizing puzzles posed by the insiders' anecdotes.

METHODOLOGY FOR THE STUDY OF INFLUENCE

During the first decade of Kenya's independence (from 1963) the regional distribution of government benefits was one of its most prominent political issues. Intense attention was paid to which ethnic groups or districts were getting a favored share, whether it be of new roads, hospital beds, or agricultural loans. Public and private political discourse was based on the assumption that decision makers in the various ministries were able to redirect resources toward their "own people" and that the tribal distribution of cabinet ministries and senior civil service posts therefore was immensely important.

This ethnic/regional category of decisions has two attributes in Kenya which make it peculiarly useful for the analysis of bureaucratic influence. First, except in the urban areas, the major African ethnic groups live in separate parts of the country. Districts are almost always overwhelmingly dominated by one ethnic group, and, with the exception of the Kikuyu, no group has significant numbers in more than one province. As a consequence, figures on the regional allocation of government services can be translated into ethnic ones with reasonable accuracy. A large number of statistics are therefore available that bear direct testimony to the results of ethnic political and administrative conflict.

The various regional distributions of new government services can be seen as caused by a multiplicity of factors, some of which are exercises of influence. This image has two advantages: It permits questions of influence and power to be situated firmly *within* the larger issue of cause and to be pursued as matters of *degree* of impact in multicausal situations. These attributes enable us to escape one of the more unfortunate connotations of the concept "power." The term implies that an individual or a group has the ability to cause an outcome by itself—that it is a necessary and sufficient condition for the event. Causes such as these are exceedingly rare, however.[6] The more usual situation is that several factors have differing degrees of influence on the outcome. Furthermore, some of the immediate determinants of the event have themselves been caused by other factors and have little *independent* influence on the outcome.[7] By using a multicausal model to explain government outputs we can avoid the implication that any actor can *determine* the final outcome, even if he is the final decision maker, and can focus instead on the relative *degrees* of *independent* influence various actors may be having on the final distribution of goods, no matter how far they may be removed from "the decision" itself. To reiterate, our approach does *not* permit us to say who the final, authoritative decision maker is and what his latitude for action is. It does allow us to suggest what actors probably have influence on the outcome and how much. We are setting aside the concept "power" and concentrating on direct *and indirect* influence instead. This frees us from a fixation with the mechanics and final act of decision making and is a great advantage in the end. Among other things, it enables us to measure influence with a unit that is inherently meaningful, degrees of difference in the quantities of public goods received by groups of citizens. Influence then has direct policy consequences, rather than being concerned only with effects upon people who in turn determine policy.

A second characteristic of the Kenyan situation that is advantageous to the study of bureaucratic influence is that preferences of decision makers on ethnic/regional allocations can be known relatively simply and accurately. A person's ethnicity can be deduced in Kenya from his name with about 90 percent reliability, and an a priori desire to favor one's own group and region can safely be assumed. The latter assumption is possible because all Kenyan Africans have close relatives and good friends living in their rural areas of origin, and the family and peer pressures for assistance for one's "own people" are well-nigh irresistible. Of course a few do resist these ascriptive demands, but the pressures are sufficiently strong that the resistance itself requires some kind of explanation. One rationale often given in Kenya is subordination to organizational pressures, which is exactly what we are trying to uncover. Virtually all Kenyans and observers of Kenyan politics are certainly willing to make the general assumption of ethnic preference. Even Leys, who sees "tribalism" as a problem of "false consciousness" that diverts attention from the more important distributional issues of class, acknowledges its potency in Kenya.[8]

This is not to say that ethnic preferences in Kenya are pathologically strong or unsavory. There are limits on the extent to which most actors would be willing to favor their own. Most see their actions as righting past inequalities or protecting their group from the selfish depredations of other ones. These attitudes are common to most political systems. The pressures to honor them are probably stronger in Kenya because most of its elites still have poorer friends and relatives to whose interests they are happily sensitive. The only assumption necessary for this analysis is that almost all influentials will wish to resolve the ambiguities and uncertainties in a decision-making setting in favor of their own group (although stronger preference than this is usually involved). Even such a limited assumption has important methodological benefits.

An act of influence results from several factors. Roughly following Robert Dahl,[9] it can be represented in the following manner: a (Preferences of Actor) causes b (Influence Attempt by Actor) which interacts with c (Resources of Actor) and d (Skill of Actor) in order to produce (in P proportion of times) e (Magnitude of Response) of f (Scope) by g (Respondents).

Dahl defined degree of power (or influence) as equal to P, which is the proportion of the times that an Actor's influence attempts are successful. The difficulty with this formulation, which Dahl recognized, is that a and b are not independent of P; that is, the Actor is apt to change his or (rarely in Kenya) her wishes about what he wants (or at least his statement of them) in accordance with his perceived chances of success in achieving them. This gives rise to what I call "Dahl's dilemma": he cannot tell the genuinely highly influential figure from one who tries to exercise his small influence only when he is sure it will be successful or, worse, from the chameleon who pretends to try to influence that which is going to occur anyway.[10] This is an exceptionally important problem in the study of influence, for large numbers of prominent officials claim to will that for which they would lose their positions if they did otherwise. Thus they profess and appear to have influence in situations in which they are actually relatively powerless.[11]

The fact that we can know a high official's initial preferences on regional distribution questions in Kenya, independent of his subsequent adaptations to the limitations of his role and free from his dissembling about his objectives, greatly simplifies the analytic problem. If the Actor can be assumed to wish an influence attempt (as can be done in Kenya on distributional issues), then elements a and b in the equation above are held constant.

The degree of influence is then a function only of the Actor's resources (c) and skill (d). The scope of influence (f) is defined for this appendix as matters of regional distribution of public goods in Kenya, and the respondents (g) are defined as the (unspecified) set of individuals who make the final regional allocations. (This set of respondents, g, is of only incidental importance now, as our focus of concern is with influence on policies rather than on those who decide and implement them.) The magnitude of response (e) is variations in regional allocations, is known from the data, and now can be presumed to be the resultant of $c \times d$ only, that is, the interaction of the Actor's resources and skill. We still cannot separate out the importance of these two elements, but with preferences (*a*) known we have escaped Dahl's chameleon problem. As a result, we are now quite close to what we intuitively consider to be influence—the *capacity* to change events.

As a consequence of the two special features of the Kenyan situation that have been analyzed in the preceding several paragraphs, we have a data set that meets almost all the scientific requisites for testing causal hypotheses about the influence of politicians and bureaucrats.[12]

1. We have *variations* in the regional preferences of cabinet ministers and senior administrators, the independent variables, and in the regional distribution of new public goods, the dependent one.

2. *Covariations* between the independent and dependent variables can be readily and accurately identified.

3. A *temporal sequence* can be established in which the allocation of positions of potential influence and preferences for their use precede the distribution of new government services, which are hypothesized to be caused by them.

4. The relations between the independent and dependent variables generally is *asymmetrical*, in that the distribution of positions could influence the allocation of goods, but not vice versa. In order for the relationship to be symmetrical, it would be necessary for those regions that are favored by a ministry to come to dominate it. Of the thirty-four allocations of new government goods examined in this appendix only eleven are distributed in patterns that are consistent with the historical ones for that service. Hence most of our data seem quite safe from the dangers of symmetry.

5. Our analysis is subject to the danger of *spurious correlation* (falsely considering something a cause when in fact it is only correlated with the true cause). Almost all scientific study shares this problem. At least the use of regional allocation data permits us to control for a large number of other factors, since statistics on a good range of socioeconomic variables are available on a regional basis in Kenya. This reduces the danger of spuriousness.

6. With these statistical data alone we cannot, however, satisfy a criterion that is missing from the usual checklists but is important in the Weberian tradition. The nature of our quantitative data permits us to establish only statistical regularities between the independent and dependent variables and does not allow us to demonstrate the exact mechanisms through which the cause produced the effect. Unless we make our statistics "understandable" in this latter sense, we would have to qualify the generalizations that result from our analysis.[13] The policy case studies of this study's main chapters serve the function of making evident these causal mechanisms, giving us the "understandability" we need.

To the extent that problems do arise at steps 4–6 above, they would apply only to *positive* statements about causal relations. There would be no problem at all with a proof that a causal relationship does *not* exist. Some of our most interesting and important findings concern those actors who do not have influence; the scientific status of these statements is very strong.

REGIONAL ALLOCATIONS: THE DEPENDENT VARIABLE

A thorough search of published and unpublished Kenyan documents provided regional allocation figures for thirty-four sets of actual or planned additional government goods or services provided from 1963 (independence) to the early 1970s. It is well known that existing allocations of services (the "base") are usually accepted as given in the budgetary process and that policy changes are reflected largely only in the distribution of new funds (the "increments").[14] Kenya is no exception to this general rule; hence our focus is only on new services, or increments. Where totally new funds were being spent (as with housing construction or World Bank loans to small farmers) it is possible to look for manifestations of policy and influence in the allocation as a whole. Where we are dealing with ongoing services, however (as with teachers or hospital beds), the politics of allocation will be manifest only in the handling of the increments. For this latter type of service it is necessary to have figures on regional distributions for two periods of time in order to gauge the changes or increments.

The thirty-four sets of regional allocation decisions represent all those for which the full necessary data were available. They are not a random sample of all distributional decisions, and it is conceivable that a different group of decisions would yield different results. The allocation decisions examined do come from six ministries, which control almost all public service expenditures. (See table B-1 at the end of this appendix for the full list of outputs investigated.) Of the thirty-four sets of decisions, eight were for planned, rather than actual, allocations, and one (growth in numbers of outpatients in government hospitals) might not have been the result of a decision at all. The remaining twenty-five decisions therefore have been examined separately to see if they produce different results; they do not. The analyses and tables that follow are based therefore on the full thirty-four allocation decisions. Data exist on the distribution of the goods and services to provinces for all thirty-four decisions, and the analyses based on them are identified as "Province" ones.

Figures are available at the district level (the next smallest unit) for only thirteen of the allocations. This is unfortunate, as the districts are ethnically homogeneous and therefore well suited to a test of our hypotheses, whereas the provinces sometimes contain more than one group. The thirteen decisions with district data have been analyzed separately according to ethnic grouping. (They are identified as the "Ethnic" analyses.) The results are largely the same as with the Province analyses.

In all analyses the allocation sets were rendered comparable by converting the absolute increase in service that each province or ethnic group received into a percentage of the total increment (new service). This made it possible to compare how well a group did across different types of services, to combine the data sets, and to perform analyses with large enough numbers of cases to produce statistically reliable results.

CATEGORIES OF CAUSE: THE INDEPENDENT VARIABLES

Causes for the regional allocation of new services can be grouped into four broad categories: (1) general environmental, (2) particular environmental, (3) institutional, and (4) positional. The first category incorporates those general political, economic, and social characteristics of a group that cause it to be systematically favored or disadvantaged in all areas of allocation. For example, the politically powerful, numerous, literate, economically developed, and centrally located Kikuyu systematically do well, while the various northern ethnic groups almost always receive the least, for they are politically and geographically marginal, illiterate, poor, relatively few in number, and they live in an arid region.

The second category, particular environmental factors, includes those features that dictate broad boundaries for the allocation of specific types of services. For example, there is no point in building secondary schools in areas that have no primary school graduates to use them.

The third, institutional, category identifies the allocational decision rules that are traditionally followed by the professional group that dominates a particular ministry. Thus agronomists are oriented toward increasing marketed crops, rather than farmer subsistence welfare, and allocate funds accordingly. Public health doctors of medicine, however, are concerned with the reduction of death rates, and this leads them to favor more egalitarian distributions for health facilities. Decision premises like these are not the attributes of particular officeholders in a ministry but instead are a part of its total institutional character. Since institutional decision premises typically involve the identification of one particular part of the environment and its use as a criterion for allocation, it is often difficult to tell this third category from the second.

The fourth, positional, category of causes is the focus of interest in this appendix. This grouping deals with the influence on allocations that goes with various positions (or roles) in the government hierarchy. Figure 5.1 in chapter 5 indicates the structure of positions at the top of a typical Kenyan ministry. What influence do cabinet ministers (CMs), permanent secretaries (PSs), and chief technical officers (CTOs) actually have on the allocation of services? Formal authority resides either with the minister or the permanent secretary, depending on the decision. But are they able to make their own wishes felt? Or do they usually end up only putting a stamp of approval on decisions that have been made and influenced lower or higher in the hierarchy? In asking these questions we are investigating the influence inherent in the position or role itself. We are not inquiring into the influence of particular occupants of these roles, which may be greater than that inherent in the position itself by virtue of other, extra resources or skills brought to the position. In other words, we are asking, not whether any permanent secretaries, for example, are influential, but whether they are influential by virtue of occupying that position. This means investigating whether the average occupant of the role has discernable independent influence on allocations.

The various roles in a Kenyan ministry headquarters have distinctive characteristics, which give them larger theoretical interest. The ministers are elected politicians with independent power bases but subject in this period to the general control of President Kenyatta, who was politically secure. It is expected and legitimate in Kenya for ministers and assistant ministers to use their positions to favor their ethnic constituencies. As we shall see, their independent influence is limited, and they usually have an impact only with the support of the president and the active assistance of their administrative staff. This appears to be a classic case of Max Weber's famous assertion that "under normal conditions, the power position of a fully developed bureaucracy is always overpowering. The 'political master' finds himself in the position of the 'dilettante' who stands opposite the 'expert.'" [15] This proposition is actually an overstatement, however, for our evidence will indicate that the president of Kenya *was* the master of the situation in this period.

The second set of roles of general interest are the permanent secretaries and other senior members of the general cadre of the administration (senior generalist officers, SGOs) in a ministry. (Senior officers, both generalist and technical, are defined as those earning at least K.shs. 36,000 [U.S. $5,140] per annum in the late 1960s time period of this study.) The Kenyan general cadre is the equivalent of the other elite, generalist cadres of the former British Empire—the British Administrative Class, the Indian Administrative Service, and so forth. Throughout the Commonwealth this cadre occupies the peak of the administrative hierarchy, signs all decisions, and mediates the relationships between the ministers and the technical personnel. Almost all administrative studies for the Commonwealth simply assume that this cadre is the most influential bureaucratic group, by virtue of its elite status, hierarchical position, wide experience in government, and monopoly of the flow of information to the ministers.[16] Our evidence will suggest that this assumption of influence has been misplaced; the technical level is the true locus of influence. In retrospect, one realizes the importance of Weber's dictum that control of the machinery of government "is possible only in a very limited degree to persons who are not technical specialists."[17] Nonetheless, that the resource of expertise so outweighs the other advantages of the general cadre was not clear from the literature.

Finally, there is the possibility of influence for the role of senior technical experts. Weber would have us place our bets on this group, but several important questions would remain even then. Is influence centered in the top technical position, that of the CTO, or is it diffused more widely among the technical heads and deputy heads of departments or even the senior technical officers as a whole? I suggest that it is diffused. Does the influence of technical experts exist against political leadership, as Weber suggests, or only with political support? Our evidence will indicate that technical experts were able to exercise positive influence only with presidential support in Kenyatta's Kenya. And last, what degree of influence for technical experts is involved? The answer will be a significant amount.

THE QUANTITATIVE EVIDENCE

Presentation of the issues to be investigated has anticipated the conclusions. How have they been reached? Some of the more important findings concern the *absence* of independent influence for several sets of positions. The strongest validation of these conclusions comes if we make the most generous possible assumptions in *favor* of positional power and look only at general environmental and positional correlates of allocations. In doing so we would be assuming that there exist no significant environmental constraints particular to the allocations (category 2 of cause) and that any apparent technical rules governing allocation decisions (category 3) are actually manifestations of positional influence. These assumptions seem to me to be too strong to be reasonable, but it is striking that even they lead to confirmation of most of the negative conclusions suggested by using stricter assumptions.

After extensive multiple-regression analysis using these generous assumptions, the following two points are clear (Since the results are negative and based on several analyses, the tables are not presented.):

1. In no case was it possible to find an administrative position or group of positions that has influence by itself.

2. Neither the permanent secretary nor the other senior members of the general cadre in the ministries are found to have direct influence, either by themselves or with political support.

These conclusions are based on assumptions that are generous for positional influence. What if we impose much more rigorous assumptions? Let us now reverse ourselves and argue that there are important particular environmental constraints and institutional policies (categories 2 and 3 of cause) that do affect regional allocations and that are not simply manifestations of positional influence. This seems eminently reasonable. To execute an analysis under these assumptions each individual set of outputs was examined and the socioeconomic variable(s) was identified that best predicted it and that could reasonably be assumed to be related to a technical-decision rule for allocations in that area. (In fact, each individual set of outputs was subjected to separate statistical analysis for socioeconomic *and* positional determinates *prior* to any of the aggregating analysis that is reported here. Many of the conclusions drawn here were clear already in these discrete analyses, but aggregation was needed for generalizability and statistical reliability.) For example, primary school enrollment was identified as the probable basis for allocation decisions in education, and the market and export crop sales were the most frequent likely criteria for decisions in agriculture. Each of these socioeconomic correlates was entered in the regression for its respective output only.* The resulting equations for all four categories of cause are given in tables B-2 and B-3.

The results of analysis with the strict assumptions are broadly similar to those with the loose ones. Conclusions (1) and (2) above are reaffirmed, along with four positive points.

3. Technical experts do have influence, but only with political support. This always involved the president (a Kikuyu).

4. Influence is probably diffused among the top expert officials. It is the combination of the chief technical officer, the heads of departments, and their deputies who are found to have influence, when they are supported by the president.

5. The Ethnic analysis indicates that cabinet ministers (CMs) have positional influence, independent of any dependence on the president or their administrative staff. This conclusion is not substantiated by the Province analysis (table B-3), but it is consistent with the perception of informed observers in Kenya. The amount of influence involved is not

---

*The full list of correlates is given in table B-1. I am indebted to Christopher Achen for teaching this procedure to me.

overwhelming, but it is significant—the presence of a CM nets an ethnic group an estimated additional 6.3 percent of the increments in that ministry's output.

6. Ministry policies and environmental constraints *peculiar* to an output are the most important determinants of allocation decisions. Together they account for over 55 percent of the observed variance in regional allocations, leaving a much smaller (although quite important) impact for general environmental factors and positional influence. (Note that percentage of variance is different from percentage of output.* The detailed percentage of variance figures for the impact of technical-decision criteria are these: 57.5 of 69.3 percent for the Ethnic analysis, and 56.6 out of 61.8 percent for the Province analysis.)

Are the apparently technical criteria embodied in the socioeconomic correlates of the outputs really apolitical, however? The seasoned observer of Kenyan politics is left with the strong suspicion that primary school enrollments are used as a decision criterion for education precisely because the politically powerful Kikuyu are so far ahead in them. It seems likely that the reality about positional influence is somewhere between the strict and loose assumptions made above. Before I can indicate the quantities of positional influence in Kenya, I need to make estimates as to what component of the technical criteria is really a manifestation of bureaucratic politics.

To make such an estimate, I have created a new variable, which is the predicted value of regional allocations if only the technical criteria were used to decide them. I will call this new variable (created separately for each analysis) the Technical Decision Criteria. The extent to which general environmental and positional influence factors are associated with this new variable is indicated in tables B-4 and B-5.

7. Our caution seems well founded, for there is evidence of modest but significant positional influence on Technical Decision Criteria. Probably about 10 percent of its observed variance is due to senior officials' selecting Technical Decision Criteria that will favor their regions. (Positional-influence factors account for 17.2 percent of the variance in the Ethnic analysis and 8.9 percent in the Province.) Still, the greater part of the regional impact of the Decision Criteria really is due to technical and other policy considerations. Positional politics accounts for a modest but significant residue.

---

*Variance is simply the amount of variation in the distribution of output that was observed. Since this variation could be greater or less in other circumstances, statements about variance are not generalizable to other situations. They are reported here to give a general idea of the relative magnitude of various causal factors observed to be at work in this situation. In contrast, statements about the amount of increase in output that various degrees of positional influence carry are potentially generalizable to other situations.

8. Even with respect to the specification of technical criteria for allocation decisions, experts do not seem to have purely personal discretion. Only those administrators who had presidential support were able to get criteria accepted that favored their regions. Of course, experts may well have had substantial independent influence on purely professional matters that have no direct bearing on regional allocational issues. That would not be evident in this analysis.

9. The analyses of Technical Decision Criteria are the one point in this entire study in which the permanent secretaries seem to have an impact. They have this impact only in conjunction with the president and heads and deputy heads of departments, but an effect is evident nonetheless. The impact occurs primarily in the Ministry of Education, where the combination of Kikuyu department heads with a Kikuyu PS was strongest. This ministry's decisions are more readily mastered by a generalist than those of almost any other ministry. The finding therefore does not threaten our conclusion of the primary importance of technical officers. In any case, the role of the PS seems to be that of a dependent generalist. He does not have independent influence as the ministers probably do, but instead serves as an instrument of the president in providing political support to Kikuyu experts in senior positions.

10. The evidence strongly suggests that most of the positional influence of administrators is exercised by Kikuyu CTOs and heads and deputy heads of departments, who have political support. All of these officials combine expertise with hierarchical position. If influence is exercised by the experts without authority (the other senior technical officers) or the top authorities without expertise (the PS and other headquarters' members of the general cadre), it is slight in comparison with that of those with expertise and authority. The CTO, who has more of the latter, is the more influential figure, but only by degree.

11. We are now in a position to make quantitative estimates of the impact of civil servants on regional allocations. My best judgment is that positional influence, operating both directly on allocations and indirectly through the choice of Technical Decision Criteria, accounts for between 6 and 20 percent of the observed variance in the distribution of the *increments* in outputs. As was noted earlier, however, this estimate is not readily generalizable.*

*This estimate was obtained as follows: The Ethnic analyses put the figure at 11.6% under our strict assumptions and approximately the same for the loose ones. As the Technical Decision Criteria used under the strict assumptions do show evidence of positional influence at work in their creation, it seems reasonable to adjust the strict-assumption estimate upward a bit. If we were to multiply the percentage of variance explained by positional influence on Technical Decision Criteria times the percentage of variance in output

The regression coefficients from our equations in tables B-2 to B-5 provide estimates of positional influence that are more likely to be applicable to other, later, Kenyan situations. Unfortunately, however, they are difficult to interpret. As they are frequently based on variables that are in log form or are the results of complex interaction effects, the units of influence are rather difficult to visualize. Thus the following summary statement is provided.

The Province analyses indicate that the *direct* influence of Kikuyu senior civil servants, with presidential support, in principle *could* produce a 9.4% addition to the *incremental* outputs for Central Province. (The actual maximum was 7.1%). The Ethnic estimates of direct positional influence by technical staff are substantially higher: in principle a possible 32.1%, in practice a maximum of 18.2%. The Ethnic estimates have the advantage of being based on precise units of analysis, but the Province estimates are derived from the analysis of a much larger number of allocation decisions. My inclination is to err on the conservative side and suggest that *the positional influence of politically supported bureaucrats has a potential direct impact on up to 10% of allocations of increments and was observed to have an effect on 7%.*

Civil servants also have a substantial effect on allocations through their choice of the technical rules of thumb that are to be followed in distribution. This indirect impact of positional influence can be estimated by multiplying the regression coefficients of positions on Technical Decision Criteria by the coefficients for the Criteria on Outputs. (The latter are Ethnic—.692; Province—.931.) The Province and Ethnic analyses suggest that *the positional influence of bureaucrats in principle could have an indirect impact on 36% (ethnic) to 50% (province) of allocations of increments and was observed in the Ministry of Agriculture in 1970 to have an indirect impact on 18%–11%* (and in the Ministry of Education in the late 1960s of 10%–9%).

An example of the various factors at work in determining allocations for one set of outputs is the Agricultural Finance Corporation loans to small-scale farmers in 1969. Careful analysis indicated that the provincial distribution of loans was effectively determined in the Ministry of Agriculture, which administered the loans in the field, rather than by the AFC board. The Province analysis produced a set of predicted fac-

---

accounted for by the Criteria, we would get an additional 17% of variance for positional influence, giving us a total estimated impact of approximately 21% (17.2 × 57.5 = 9.9 + 11.6 = 21.5). Both the loose- and the strict-assumption analyses for the Province give low estimates of positional influence (1.5 and 1.2%). But the Technical Decision adjustment suggested above would raise both estimates to about 6% (3.9 × 56.6 = 5.0 + 1.2 = 6.2%).

tors influencing the allocation of loans and these are given in tables B-1, B-3, and B-5. On the side of general environmental influences we note that Northeastern Province generally does poorly. The particular environmental determinants of the allocation of agricultural loans and the ministry's institutional policies are combined in the tendency to provide loans to those areas most deeply involved in cash-crop production. It is no accident that Kikuyus largely live in Central and Rift Valley Provinces, which are heavily advantaged in this regard, and positional influence was probably involved in the choice of cash crops as a criterion. In fact, on the basis of the combined presence in 1969 of a Kikuyu president, strong assistant minister, and chief technical officer, we should have expected a decision criterion to be chosen that would have produced about 8 percent of loan funds additional for Central Province. Since the permanent secretary was not Kikuyu that year, no indirect benefit was to be expected from that base of positional influence. Direct positional influence produced a further boost of 9 percent of funds for Central Province (where 70 percent of the Kikuyus live), this time through the interaction of the president with the CTO, heads, and deputy heads in the ministry. The sum of all these factors produces a "predicted" value for the allocation of loans, which is very close to what actually occurred (r = .94).

To sum up, we have encountered evidence of substantial direct and indirect influence by civil servants on regional allocations. This influence is not independent, however, but is instead dependent on political support—at least by the president and often at the ministerial level as well. This positional influence seems largely to be concentrated among technical officers at the top of the hierarchy; generalist officers have substantially less influence, if any at all.

TABLE B-1
Outputs and Their Correlates

Government Outputs Studied	Strongest Socioeconomic Correlates of Respective Outputs
Ministry of Agriculture	
1. Grants made to farmers, 1966	1. Graduated Personal Tax revenues (an indicator of personal income)
2. Development loans made to farmers, 1967	2. Agricultural cesses revenue (an indicator of export-crop income)
3. Development loans made to farmers, 1968	3. Value of crops marketed, 1970
4. Loans made to large-scale farms, 1963–69[a]	4. Hectares of high-potential land (same)[a]
5. Agricultural Finance Corporation small-scale loans, 1969[a]	5. Value of crops marketed (high-potential land)[a]
6. International Development Association–financed small-scale loans, 1969[a]	6. Agricultural cesses revenue (Graduated Personal Tax revenues)[a]
7. International Development Association–financed small-scale loans, 1970	7. Agricultural cesses revenue
8. Increases (or decreases) in agricultural extension officers (degree or diploma) between 1964 and 1968	8. Nothing
9. Increases in Agricultural Assistants (certificate) for extension between 1963 and 1968	9. Nothing
10. Increases in agricultural extension officers between 1968 and 1970	10. Agricultural cesses revenue
11. Increases in Agricultural Assistants between 1968 and 1970	11. Value of crops marketed divided by Agricultural Assistants in 1968
Ministry of Education	
12. Increases in number of aided Form I (first year of secondary school) classes between 1964 and 1967	12. Primary-school enrollment in 1966

TABLE B-1 (continued)

Government Outputs Studied	Strongest Socioeconomic Correlates of Respective Outputs
13. Projected increase in aided Form I classes from 1967 to 1970, made in 1967[b]	13. Primary-school enrollment in 1966
14. Increases in number of aided (maintained and assisted) secondary schools between 1967 and 1971	14. Primary-school enrollment in 1971
15. Increase in number of all primary-school teachers between 1966 and 1971[a]	15. Primary-school enrollment in 1971 (same)[a]
16. Increase in number of most highly qualified (P2 and above) primary-school teachers between 1966 and 1971[a]	16. Primary-school enrollment in 1971 (same)[a]
Ministry of Health	
17. Increase in number of government hospital outpatients between 1963 and 1966[b]	17. Nothing
18. Increase in number of government hospital inpatients between 1963 and 1966	18. Nothing
19. Increase in government hospital beds between 1966 and 1971	19. Population
20. Decreases in numbers of dispensaries funded by government between 1966 and 1972	20. Dispensaries in 1966, negative (i.e., proportionate cuts)
21. Increases and decreases in numbers of health centers and sub-health-centers funded by government between 1966 and 1972	21. Population divided by health centers and sub-health-centers in 1966
22. Increases in government hospital beds between 1971 and 1973	22. Nothing
23. Planned increases in government health centers, sub-health-centers, and dispensaries between 1972 and 1975, made in 1972[a,b]	23. Population divided by health centers, sub-health-centers, and dispensaries in 1972 (same)[a]

24. Planned increases in government health centers between 1972 and 1984, made in 1972[a,b]

25. Planned increases in government sub-health-centers between 1972 and 1984, made in 1972[a,b]

26. Planned increases in government dispensaries between 1972 and 1984, made in 1972[a,b]

27. Value of houses built by the National Housing Corporation in 1969

28. Number of site and service sites provided between 1970 and 1973

29. Value of houses built by the National Housing Corporation between 1971 and 1973

30. Number of unemployed placed in jobs during the Tripartite Agreement employment-creation scheme, 1970[a]

31. Planned kilometers of new trunk roads, 1969 for Five Year Plan[a,b]

32. Planned kilometers of new major roads (nontrunk) 1969[a,b]

33. Planned kilometers of new secondary and minor roads, 1969[a,b]

34. Expenditure on road construction, 1973

24. Population divided by health centers in 1972 (same and health centers in 1972, together)[a]

25. Population divided by sub-health-centers in 1972 (same)[a]

26. Population divided by dispensaries in 1972 (same)[a]

Ministry of Housing

27. Income of modern-sector employees, 1970

28. Urban population in 1969

29. Urban population in 1969

Ministry of Labor

30. Modern-sector employment, 1968 (same)[a]

Ministry of Works

31. Value of crops marketed, 1970 (existing Class A roads and high-potential land, together)[a]

32. Value of crops marketed (income of modern-sector employees, 1968)[a]

33. High-potential land (income of modern-sector employees, 1968)[a]

34. Value of crops marketed

NOTE: All the above outputs were used for the Full Province analyses ($N = 236$).

[a] These outputs were the only ones for which complete district data were available and were used in the Ethnic analyses ($N = 130$). The correlate given in parentheses is the one used for this Ethnic analysis.

[b] These outputs were excluded from the Strict Province analyses ($N = 173$) on the grounds that they were planned rather than actual outputs or (in the case of 17) that the numbers may not have been subject to government influence.

NOTES TO TABLES B-2 TO B-5

Alphabetic Key to Computer Variable Labels

ACRDA	Existing Class A roads in kilometers to one decimal
CCCESSES	County Council Agricultural Cesses in thousands of K.£ (K.shs. ÷ 20)
CM/AM	Cabinet Minister or (in the case of the Ministry of Agriculture) Assistant Ministers
COAST	A province made up of various coastal ethnic groups, primarily the Miji-Kenda and the Taita
CROPSMKD	Crops marketed in 1970 in thousands of K.£
CRPYAA8	Crops marketed in K.£ divided by Agricultural Assistants in 1968
DEPVARI	Dependent variable: government outputs expressed as the percentage of a particular service received by an African ethnic group or province
DISPEN66	Dispensaries in 1966
GDLAND	Quantity of high-potential land in thousands of hectares
GPT	Graduated Personal Tax revenues in thousands of K.£
HC72	Health centers in 1972
HIPOLAND	High-potential agricultural land in thousands of hectares
EARN68	Earnings of modern sector employees in 1968 in thousands of K.£
EMPINC70	Income of modern-sector employees in 1970 in thousands of K.£
EMPLOY68	Number of modern-sector employees in 1968
ENROL71	Primary-school enrollment in 1971 in thousands
LOG-(PR) × (CM) × (CTO)	The log base 10 of the president (PR) times the minister (CM/AM) times the CTO
LOG-(PR) × (PS) × (D/HD)	The log base 10 of the president times the permanent secretary (PS) times the percentage of heads and deputy heads of departments (D/HD)
LUHYA	An ethnic group that lives in Western Province
NEG	A dummy variable to accommodate the fact that there was a loss of health centers and sub-health-centers between 1966 and 1972
NOREAS	A poor and remote province in which some of the northern ethnic groups live, especially the Somali

NORTHERN	Those ethnic groups living in the northern part of Kenya
PENROL66	Primary-school enrollment in 1966 in thousands
PENROL71	Primary-school enrollment in 1971 in thousands
POP	Population in thousands for 1969
POPDIS72	Population in thousands divided by dispensaries in 1972
POPHC72	Population in thousands divided by health centers in 1972
POPHLF72	Population in thousands divided by health centers, sub-health-centers, and dispensaries in 1972
POPSHC72	Population in thousands divided by sub-health-centers in 1972
POPYDIS2	Population in thousands divided by dispensaries in 1972
POPYHC72	Population in thousands divided by health centers in 1972
POPYHCS6	Population in thousands divided by health centers and sub-health-centers in 1966
POPYHLF2	Population in thousands divided by health centers, sub-health-centers, and dispensaries in 1972
POPYSHC7	Population in thousands divided by sub-health-centers in 1972
$(PR) \times (CM) \times (CTO)$	President times minister (or AM) times CTO
$(PR) \times (CTO + D/HD)$	President times percentage of chief technical officers (CTO), heads and deputy heads of departments (D/HD)
TECHDEC	The product of a regression equation using the socioeconomic variables that predict output in the Ethnic group analysis
TECHDEC6	The product of a regression equation using the socioeconomic variables that predict output in the full Province analysis
URBANPOP	Population of urban areas of 5,000 or more in thousands

Technical Notes on the Regressions

All positional influence variables in the equations are accompanied by examples indicating the strength of their impact. The examples given are always the maximum impact case, and the minimum impact case if it is anything more than zero.

Nairobi Province is not included in any of the Province analyses. Statistics for it frequently were not available, and it receives very special treatment in allocations because it is the capital, all urban, and made up of residents from all the major ethnic groups.

The basic component of any position variable is the percentage of those who have occupied the office who came from a particular ethnic group or province. For example, with senior technical officers (STO) it is the percentage of all such experts in a ministry who come from a particular area. Alternatively, when an output is a composite of several years of decisions, even a position that never has more than one occupant at a time will be represented as the percentage of the relevant time period in which the post has been held by someone from a particular area. This percentage is the variable for the Ethnic analyses.

The percentages of position holders just explained required further adjustments for the Province analyses. Presumably an officeholder who is directing resources toward his ethnic group will not assist the other ethnic groups in his home province and will divide his benefactions among the provinces in which his ethnic group lives. (Only the Kikuyu have significant numbers in more than one province.) Therefore the percentage of officeholders of an ethnic group was multiplied times the percentage of the ethnic group that lived in a particular province and again times the percentage of that province's population that belonged to that ethnic group. Thus, for example, a Kikuyu CTO's impact on Rift Valley Province would be represented as 2.4 percent—the product of his 100 percent time in the position times 15 percent for the proportion of all Kikuyus who live in Rift Valley Province times 16 percent for the portion of Rift's population that is made up of Kikuyus. The comparable figure for Central Province is 68.5 percent. This formulation for the impact of influence seemed to us a priori to be the best, and experimentation with several other possible alternatives produced nothing that worked better in the analyses.

TABLE B-2
Ethnic Analysis of the Distribution of Service Increments

Dependent Variable:		DEPVARI		
Multiple R	.85	Analysis of Variance		DF
R Square	.71	Regression		14
Adjusted R Square	.68	Residual		115
Std. Deviation	6.24	Coeff. of Variability		62.4%

Variables in the Equation

Variable	B	Std Error B	F	Significance
GDLAND	.0089	.0018	24.05	.000
EMPLOY68	.00021	.000037	32.62	.000
POPDIS72	.1508	.0331	20.73	.000
GPT	.0255	.0052	23.79	.000
HC72	−.0757	.1514	.25	.618
POPHLF72	.4312	.0934	21.30	.000
POPSHC72	.0446	.0113	15.50	.000
EARN68	.00084	.00021	16.03	.000
ACRDA	.00035	.00058	.36	.549
ENROL71	.000046	.0000092	24.58	.000
POPHC72	.0723	.0219	10.91	.001
CMAM	.0625	.0217	8.29	.005
LUHYA	4.3200	1.9313	5.00	.027
(PR) × (CTO + D/HD)	.00046	.000067	46.61	.000
e.g., Ag (hi)	+ 18.2%	5.23%		
Ed (lo)	+ 9.3%	2.7%		
CONSTANT	.7612	.9317	.67	.416

TABLE B-3
Province Analysis of the Distribution of Service Increments

Dependent Variable:		*DEPVARI*	
Multiple R	.79	Analysis of Variance	DF
R Square	.62	Regression	21
Adjusted R Square	.58	Residual	214
Std. Deviation	9.41	Coeff. of Variability	74.5%

Variables in the Equation

Variable	*B*	*Std Error B*	*F*	*Significance*
GPT	.0128	.0056	5.32	.022
POPYDIS2	.1455	.0539	7.28	.008
HIPOLAND	.0110	.0027	17.11	.000
EMPLOY68	.00016	.000044	12.53	.000
CRPYAA8	.0003	.000099	9.10	.003
EMPINC70	.00051	.00022	5.50	.020
DISPEN66	−.2286	.0345	42.89	.000
POPYHC72	.1014	.0447	5.15	.024
URBANPOP	.1558	.0235	44.02	.000
POP	.0052	.0023	5.35	.022
POPYSHC7	.0409	.0169	5.86	.016
POPYHLF2	.542	.1723	9.90	.002
POPYHCS6	.8111	.2229	13.24	.000
PENROL66	.0515	.0166	9.67	.002
CCCESSES	.1100	.0175	39.40	.000
PENROL71	.0367	.0095	14.92	.000
CROPSMKD	.0012	.00022	27.92	.000
NEG	−69.81	13.75	25.79	.000
COAST	−5.56	1.858	8.96	.003
NOREAS	−7.247	1.984	13.35	.000
(PR) × (CTO + D/HD)	.0000029	.0000011	6.83	.010
e.g., Ag '69 (hi)	+7.12%	5.33%		
CONSTANT	8.566	1.17	53.57	.000

TABLE B-4
Ethnic Analysis of the Technical Decision Criteria Guiding Allocations

Dependent Variable:		TECHDEC	
Multiple R	.47	Analysis of Variance	DF
R Square	.22	Regression	3
Adjusted R Square	.20	Residual	126
Std. Deviation	7.47	Coeff. of Variability	74.7%

Variables in the Equation

Variable	B	Std Error B	F	Significance
NORTHERN	− 5.13	2.19	5.49	.021
Log-(PR) × (PS) × (D/HD)	3.618	.9638	14.09	.000
e.g., Ed (hi)	+ 12.8%	6.7%		
Log-(PR) × (CM) × (CTO)	.0050	.0013	14.25	.000
e.g., Ag (hi)	+ 16.5%	8.6%		
CONSTANT	9.824	.7061	193.6	.000

TABLE B-5
Province Analysis of the Technical Decision Criteria Guiding Allocations

Dependent Variable:		TECHDEC6	
Multiple R	.35	Analysis of Variance	DF
R Square	.12	Regression	3
Adjusted R Square	.11	Residual	232
Std. Deviation	10.47	Coeff. of Variability	89.3%

Variables in the Equation

Variable	B	Std Error B	F	Significance
NOREAS	− 5.16	2.15	5.76	.017
Log-(PR) × (PS) × (D/HD)	1.559	.4499	12.00	.001
e.g., Ag 1966 (hi)	+ 8.4%	4.7%		
Log-(PR) × (CM) × (CTO)	.000053	.000023	5.52	.020
e.g., Ag 1968 (hi)	+ 12.4%	10.4%		
CONSTANT	11.38	.7557	226.8	.000

APPENDIX C
Persons Interviewed

Name	Identification
Name	*Identification*
Abere, S.	Gusii student at University of Nairobi
Adams, James	Resident Representative of World Bank for E. Africa
Annette, Sister	Teacher, Precious Blood Secondary School
Ayot, Dr. Henry	Kenyatta University
Barclay, H. P.	Chair, Kenya Meat Commission
Bates, Prof. Robert	Duke University
Belsoi, Edward	Former Provincial Police Officer, Rift Valley
Bereki, Ali	Economist, Agriculture
Bosibori, Pauline	Mother of Nyachae
Brigden, Gerard	Architect
Bwisa, Edward	Senior Economist, Office of President
Chege, Dr. Michael	University of Nairobi
Chele, E. B. M. B.	Undersecretary, Budget Supply Department
Chema, Dr. Samuel	Head of Veterinary Research
Cleaver, Kevin	World Bank, Nairobi
Cohen, John	Head, Harvard Team, Planning
Court, David	E. Africa Rep. of Rockefeller Foundation
Cox, Pamela	East African Projects, World Bank
Creek, Michael	Food and Agricultural Organization
Davies, David	World Bank
Davis, Dr. R. H. K.	Private Veterinary Surgeon

Edwards, Prof. Ed	Former Economic Adviser, Finance
Enswinger, Jean	Anthropologist
Fountain, Robert	Former Kenya Director of Pfizer
Fowler, W. J. D.	Board Member, KTDA
Galgalo, Luka D.	Provincial Commissioner, Central
Geist, Judith	Adviser, Planning
Gerhard, John	The Ford Foundation
Githae, G. K.	Senior Assistant Secretary, Livestock Development
Githuku, J. W.	Permanent Secretary, Planning; past Financial Secretary
Gitonga, David	Former Chief of Thegenge Location, Nyeri
Gitonga, William	Cousin of Muriithi
Goldman, Richard	Economic Adviser, Agriculture and Livestock Development
Gotsch, Prof. Carl	Stanford University
Gray, Dr. A. R.	Director General of International Laboratory for Research on Animal Disease
Grey, Clive	Economic Adviser to Government of Kenya
Grosh, Barbara	Research Associate, University of Nairobi
Haddow, Paul	Economic Adviser, Agriculture
Holmes, J. Anthony	Economic Affairs, U.S. Embassy
Hook, Richard	Former Adviser, Planning
Hyden, Prof. Goran	Past E. Africa Representative, Ford Foundation
Irungu, Cyrus M.	Company Secretary, KTDA
Isaksson, Neils	Management Adviser, Livestock Development
Ithau, Mrs. Phoebe	Sister of Mule
Jando, John	Manager of Mule's farm at Kambu
Kalikander, F. M.	Senior Planning Officer, Planning
Kamau, Magda	Daughter of Karanja
Kamau, Peter N.	Son-in-law to Karanja
Kamau, Philomena	Secretary to Karanja, 1970–1985
Kamau, Simon	Elder of Hubuini Presbyterian Church
Kamuyu, Simon M.	General Manager, KTDA
Karanja, Charles	Former General Manager, KTDA
Karanja, John M.	Son of Karanja
Karanja, Njeri	Mother of Karanja

Karanja, Philomena	Wife of Karanja
Karega, Geoffrey	KTDA Factory Manager, Mataara, Kiambu
Kariithi, Geoffrey	Formerly Head of the Civil Service
Kariithi, Peter	Senior Editor, *Weekly Review*
Kariuki, J. N.	Marketing Manager, KTDA
Kasioki, Aaron	Friend of Philip Mule
Katuku, Ruth	Mother of Mule
Keli, Ester	Planning
Kemoli, R.	Commonwealth Development Corporation
Kiarie, Thomas	Son of Karanja
Kiarii, Karanja	Father of Karanja
Kibera, David	Undersecretary, Budget Supply Department
Kibinge, Leonard	Former Permanent Secretary, Livestock Development
Kidenda, J. H. O.	Chief Planning Officer, Planning
Kiere, Dr. S. M. W.	Executive Officer, Central Artificial Insemination Station
Kiiti, Peter	Manager of Mule's farm at Mbooni
Kimatu, Julius	Clerk, Mbooni Location, Machakos
Kimeu, John	Laboratory Technician, Precious Blood Secondary School
Kioko, Francis	Formerly of Shell Chemicals, Ltd.
Kipligat, B. A.	Permanent Secretary, Foreign Affairs
Kithome, Joseph M.	Former Chief, Kangundo Division
Lewis, Prof. David	Former Adviser, Planning
Macharia, B. N.	Deputy Director, External Aid Department
Magaki, Daniel	Pastor and first teacher of Nyachae
Maina, Andrew	Chief Veterinary Field Officer, Livestock Development
Makhanu, M. S.	Former District Commissioner, Kisii
Maranga, Elijah	Shopkeeper, Ibacho, Kisii
Martin, William K.	Former General Manager, National Cereals and Produce Board
Mathenge, James	Permanent Secretary for Provincial Administration
Mbaka, Charles	Senior Assistant Secretary, Office of President
Mbate, George	Programme Officer, Machakos Integrated Development Project

Mbaya, Moses	Agricultural Manager, KTDA
Mbindyo, Charles	General Manager, Agricultural Finance Corporation
Mbogo, Dan E.	Brother of Muriithi and Assistant Director, Livestock Development
Mbugua, Simon	Retired Chief Engineer and Permanent Secretary, Transport and Communications
Mbula, Dr. Judith	Sister of Mule
Mburu, James	Former Director of Agriculture
McDonald, Ian	Economic Adviser, Agriculture and Livestock Development
Mogaka, Zeverino	Research Assistant, University of Nairobi student
Mokaya, Andrea	Former Chief, Wanjare, Kisii
Moreithi, F. I. H.	Former General Manager, KTDA
Mule, Harris	Permanent Secretary, Finance
Mule, Martha Ngina	Wife of Mule
Mule, Nthenya	Daughter of Mule
Munguti, P. N.	Chief, Mbooni Location, Machakos
Muriithi, Ann W.	Daughter of Muriithi
Muriithi, E. Waichanguru	Son of Muriithi
Muriithi, Grace	Daughter of Muriithi
Muriithi, Martha	Wife of Muriithi
Muriithi, Munene	Son of Muriithi
Muriuki, Nicodemus	Executive Chair, Mercantile Finance
Musya, Joseph M.	Headmaster, Mbooni High School
Mutambuki, Kamene	Research Assistant, University of Nairobi student
Muthenge, D. J.	Deputy Secretary, Office of President
Mutiso, Dr. Cyrus G.	Mutiso Consultants
Mwangale, Elijah	Minister of Foreign Affairs
Mwangi, Njuguna	Principal Economist, Planning
Mwango, Martha	Wife of Nyachae
Mwansa, O.	Headmaster, Utangwa Secondary School
Ndata, Kaunda K.	Foreman of Mule's farm at Kambu
Ndegwa, Philip	Governor, Central Bank of Kenya
Nderitu, Peter	Brother of Muriithi and Mbogo
Nderitu, Waicanguru	Nephew of Muriithi

Ndeti, Jackson	Former Deputy Director, Veterinary Services
Nellis, John	World Bank
Ng'ang'a, Dr. J. M.	Chief Health Officer, Veterinary Department
Ngigi, Samwell	Research Assistant, University of Nairobi student
Ngulo, Dr. W. K.	Deputy Director, Veterinary Services
Njenga, James	Commissioner of Lands
Njeru, Elphas N.	Principal Economist, Planning
Njoroge, Dr. W. M.	Director of Veterinary Services
Njoroge, Peter	Factory Operations Manager, KTDA
Nowrojee, Pheroze	Attorney-at-Law
Nyaboke, Esther	Wife of Nyachae
Nyachae, Charles	Attorney-at-Law, Son of Nyachae
Nyachae, Grace	Wife of Nyachae
Nyachae, Kenneth	Son of Nyachae
Nyachae, Mary	Daughter of Nyachae
Nyachae, Simeon	Chief Secretary to Government of Kenya
Nyamora, Pius	Reporter, *Daily Nation*
Nyankarania, A.	Deputy Head, St. Stephen's School, Kisii
Nyariebo, Elijah	Deputy Head, Kionyonyi Primary School, Kisii
Obure, Stephen	Former District Revenue Officer, Kisii
Oduol, A. O.	Administrative Services Officer, Veterinary Department
Ogessa, S. W. O.	Assistant General Manager, KTDA
Oiruria, James	Brother of Nyachae; Chief of Kisii Town
Ojany, Prof. F. F.	University of Nairobi
Ongendi, L.	Old man, Bassi Location, Kisii
Osiemo, Alfred	University of Nairobi graduate student
Othieno, Antipa	Chair, Kenya Sugar Authority
Otieno, James O.	Deputy Chief Planning Officer
Ouko, Dr. Robert	Minister of Planning and Economic Development
Owino, Dan	Former General Manager, Maize Board
Owiro, Z.	Deputy Director, Animal Production, Livestock Development
Oyugi, Dr. Walter	University of Nairobi
Patel, Jagdish M.	Provincial Accountant, Rift Valley

Peterson, Stephen	Adviser, Finance
Pritchard, Prof. William	Chair of Board, International Laboratory for Research on Animal Disease
Raikes, Philip	Donor Consultant in Kisii
Ramakrishnan, Subramaniam	Management Adviser, Finance
Rhodes, Rev. William	Former Chaplain, University of Denver
Roe, Emery	Former Adviser, Planning
Roemer, Michael	Senior Economic Adviser, Finance
Ryan, Prof. T. C. I.	Director of Planning
Ryanga, Reuben	Deputy Director of Agriculture, Office of President
Sagini, Lawrence	Chair, KANU, Kisii District
Shitemi, Simeon	Permanent Secretary, Health
Tench, Andrew	Economic Adviser, Office of President
Thomas, Ruth	Library of Congress, Nairobi
Thorne, Anthony	FAO Adviser, Livestock Development
Tuva, W. J. A.	Senior Assistant Secretary, Finance
Unsworth, Gerry	Former Marketing Manager, KTDA
Venkatesen, K.	Former Financial Secretary, Tamil Nadu, India
Venters, David	Former Factory Superintendent, KTDA
Vogel, Sister Maria-Pacis	Headmistress, Precious Blood Secondary School, Kilungu
Vora, B. R.	Former Chief Accountant, KTDA
Wachira, Naphtali	Leaf Collection Manager, KTDA
Waicanguru, Elijah	Father of Muriithi and Mbogo
Walton, Christopher	Former Acting General Manager, KTDA
Wangeci, Lydia	Mother of Muriithi and Mbogo
Wanjohi, Philip	Animal Health Assistant, Gathuthi, Nyeri
Weir, Andrew	Head of EEC Team, Machakos Integrated Development Project
Weisel, Peter	USAID, Nairobi
Wells, Dr. Kenneth	Board Member, International Laboratory for Research on Animal Disease
Westcott, Clay	Adviser, Finance and Planning
Westlake, Michael	Economic Adviser, Agriculture
White, Harold	Former Chairman, KTDA
Wilson, J. G. Alistair	World Bank, Nairobi

The following unnamed persons also were interviewed:

Twelve villagers from Gatundu Division, Kiambu District: two female (from Mataara and Gitwe) and ten male (three from Gacharage, two each from Gitwe and Kanyani, and one each from Gakoe, Ituramiro, and Mataara)

A worker at the KTDA Factory, Gituamba, Kiambu District

Eight residents of Kisii: three female (from Biringo, Kiamokana, and Sameta) and five male (two from Nyaribari Borabu, and one each from Keroka, Nyaribari, and Taracha)

A woman from Kitundu and a man from Utangwa in Machakos

NOTES

PREFACE

1. Arturo Israel, *Institutional Development: Incentives to Performance* (Baltimore: The Johns Hopkins University Press, 1987), pp. 19–23.

CHAPTER 1

1. Samuel Paul, *Managing Development: The Lessons of Success* (Boulder: Westview, 1982), pp. 11, 60–62; *Standard* (Nairobi), 23 November 1982, quoting R. Kemoli of the Commonwealth Development Corporation.

2. International Tea Committee, *Annual Bulletin of Statistics: 1985*, p. 37.

3. Denys Forrest, *The World Tea Trade* (Cambridge: Woodhead-Faulkner, 1985), p. 76.

4. For example, The World Bank, *Accelerated Development in Sub-Saharan Africa* (Washington, D.C.: The World Bank, 1981); Paul Collins, "Current Issues of Administrative Reform in the Nigerian Public Services: The Case of the Udoji Review Commission," in *Administration for Development in Nigeria*, ed. P. Collins (Lagos, Nigeria: African Education Press, 1980); David Gould, *Bureaucratic Corruption in the Third World: The Administration of Underdevelopment in Zaire* (New York: Pergamon-Maxwell, 1980); Goran Hyden, *No Shortcuts to Progress: African Development Management in Perspective* (Berkeley and Los Angeles: University of California Press, 1983); Jon R. Moris, *Managing Induced Rural Development* (Bloomington: International Development Institute, Indiana University, 1981); Robert M. Price, *Society and Bureaucracy in Contemporary Ghana* (Berkeley and Los Angeles: University of California Press, 1975).

5. Israel, *Institutional Development*, pp. 19–23.

6. Rwekaza Mukandala, "The Political Economy of Parastatals in Tanzania and Botswana" (Ph.D. diss., Department of Political Science, University of Cali-

fornia, Berkeley, 1988); Barbara Grosh, "Improving Economic Performance of Public Enterprises in Kenya: Lessons from the First Two Decades of Independence" (Ph.D. diss., Department of Economics, University of California, Berkeley, 1988); Robert H. Bates, *Markets and States in Tropical Africa: The Political Basis of Agricultural Policies* (Berkeley and Los Angeles: University of California Press, 1981).

7. Barbara Grosh, "Performance of Agricultural Public Enterprises in Kenya: Lessons from the First Two Decades of Independence," *Eastern Africa Economic Review* 3, no. 1 (1987): 51–64; Geoffrey Lamb and Linda Muller, *Control, Accountability and Incentives in a Successful Development Institution: The Kenyan Tea Development Authority*, World Bank Staff Working Paper, no. 550 (Washington, D.C.: The World Bank, 1982).

8. The World Bank and the United Nations Development Programme, *Africa's Adjustment and Growth in the 1980s* (Washington, D.C.: The World Bank, 1989); Michael F. Lofchie, *The Policy Factor: Agricultural Performance in Kenya and Tanzania* (Boulder: L. Rienner, 1989).

9. The World Bank, *World Development Report 1987* (New York: Oxford University Press, 1987), pp. 264, 266.

10. Bruce F. Johnston and Peter Kilby, *Agriculture and Structural Transformation: Economic Strategies in Late-Developing Countries* (New York: Oxford University Press, 1975).

11. The World Bank, *Accelerated Development in Sub-Saharan Africa* (Washington, D.C.: The World Bank, 1981); The World Bank, *World Development Report 1988* (New York: Oxford University Press, 1988), tables 1, 2, 7.

12. For example, see Lofchie, *The Policy Factor*; Colin Leys, *Underdevelopment in Kenya: The Political Economy of Neocolonialism: 1964–71* (Berkeley and Los Angeles: University of California Press, 1974); J. Heyer, J. K. Maitha, and W. M. Senga, *Agricultural Development in Kenya: An Economic Assessment* (Nairobi: Oxford University Press, 1976); Gavin Kitching, *Class and Economic Change in Kenya* (New Haven: Yale University Press, 1980); Robert H. Bates, "The Politics of Food Crises in Kenya," in *The Political Economy of Kenya*, ed. M. G. Schatzberg (New York: Praeger, 1987).

13. For example, Leys, *Underdevelopment in Kenya* v. Carl Rosberg and Robert Jackson, *Personal Rule in Black Africa* (Berkeley and Los Angeles: University of California Press, 1983) v. Gerald Holtham and Arthur Hazlewood, *Aid and Inequality in Kenya* (London: Croom Helm, 1976).

14. See also David K. Leonard, "Class Formation and Agricultural Development," in *Politics and Public Policy in Kenya and Tanzania*, rev. ed., ed. Joel Barkan (New York: Praeger, 1984).

15. John Armstrong, *The European Administrative Elite* (Princeton: Princeton University Press, 1974); Y. P. Ghai and J. P. W. B. McAuslan, *Public Law and Political Change in Kenya: A Study of the Legal Framework of Government from Colonial Times to the Present* (Nairobi: Oxford University Press, 1970).

16. Peter B. Evans, Dietrich Rueschemeyer, and Theda Skocpol, eds., *Bringing the State Back In* (Cambridge: Cambridge University Press, 1985); Alfred Stepan, *The State and Society: Peru in Comparative Perspective* (Princeton: Princeton University Press, 1978); Stephen Krasner, "Approaches to the State: Alterna-

tive Conceptions and Historical Dynamics," *Comparative Politics* (January 1984): 223–45.

17. See, for example, Armstrong, *European Administrative Elite*; Ezra Suleiman, *Elites in French Society: The Politics of Survival* (Princeton: Princeton University Press, 1978); Jeremy R. Azrael, *Managerial Power and Soviet Politics* (Cambridge: Harvard University Press, 1966); Jerry F. Hough, *The Soviet Prefects: The Local Party Organs in Industrial Decision-Making* (Cambridge: Harvard University Press, 1969); and Franz Schurmann, *Ideology and Organization in Communist China* (Berkeley and Los Angeles: University of California Press, 1966, 1968).

18. Henry Bienen, *Kenya: The Politics of Participation and Control* (Princeton: Princeton University Press, 1974), pp. 58–65, 192–93; Cherry Gertzel, *The Politics of Independent Kenya* (Nairobi: East African Publishing House, 1970), pp. 166–70; Colin Leys, *Underdevelopment in Kenya*, pp. 193–98; John Okumu, "The Socio-Political Setting," in *Development Administration: The Kenyan Experience*, ed. G. Hyden, R. Jackson, and J. Okumu (Nairobi: Oxford University Press, 1970).

19. Joel Aberbach, Robert Putnam, and Bert Rockman, *Bureaucrats and Politicians in Western Democracies* (Cambridge: Harvard University Press, 1981); Graham Allison, *The Essence of Decision: The Cuban Missile Crisis* (Boston: Little, Brown, 1971); Francis Rourke, *Bureaucracy, Politics and Public Policy*, 2d ed. (Boston: Little, Brown, 1976); Peter Woll, *American Bureaucracy*, 2d ed. (New York: W. W. Norton, 1977).

20. Max Weber, *The Theory of Social and Economic Organization*, trans. A. M. Henderson and T. Parsons, ed. T. Parsons (London: Free Press of Glencoe, Collier-Macmillian, 1974), p. 384.

21. For example, see Ezra N. Suleiman, *Politics, Power and Bureaucracy in France: The Administrative Elite* (Princeton: Princeton University Press, 1974) v. Alfred A. Diamant, "The French Administrative System: The Republic Passes But the Administration Remains," in *Toward the Comparative Study of Public Administration*, ed. W. Siffin (Bloomington: Indiana University Press, 1957), and "Tradition and Innovation in French Administration," *Comparative Political Studies* 1, no. 2 (1968).

22. Peter M. Blau, *Exchange and Power in Social Life* (New York: John Wiley, 1964).

23. This basic point underlies much of the argument in John P. Powelson, *Institutions of Economic Growth* (Princeton: Princeton University Press, 1972).

24. Hugo F. Reading, *A Dictionary of the Social Sciences* (London: Routledge and Kegan Paul, 1977), p. 108.

25. Arthur Stinchcombe, *Constructing Social Theories* (New York: Harcourt, Brace and World, 1968), pp. 107–8.

26. James G. March and Herbert A. Simon, *Organizations* (New York: John Wiley, 1958), pp. 140–41.

27. Weber, *Theory of Social and Economic Organization*.

28. Stinchcombe, *Constructing Social Theories*, p. 112. Emphasis omitted.

29. David K. Leonard, *Reaching the Peasant Farmer: Organization Theory and Practice in Kenya* (Chicago: University of Chicago Press, 1977) and David K. Leonard, ed., *Rural Administration in Kenya* (Nairobi: East African [Kenyan] Literature Bureau, 1973).

CHAPTER 2

1. G. Muriuki, *A History of the Kikuyu: 1500–1900* (Nairobi: Oxford University Press, 1974), pp. 155–56.

2. M. F. Hill, *Permanent Way: The Story of the Kenya and Uganda Railway* (Nairobi: East African Literature Bureau, 1976; reprint), p. 161.

3. Colin Leys, *Underdevelopment in Kenya* (Berkeley and Los Angeles: University of California Press, 1974), p. 28; Hill, *Permanent Way*, pp. 34, 49, 65. Other reasons, among them suppression of the slave trade and economic development, were offered at the time as well, but Leys rightly sees the strategic motives as primary.

4. Leys, *Underdevelopment in Kenya*, p. 28.

5. Roger van Zwanenberg with Anne King, *An Economic History of Kenya and Tanzania: 1800–1970* (London: Macmillan, 1975), pp. 25–27, 147–51.

6. E. A. Brett, *Colonialism and Underdevelopment in East Africa: The Politics of Economic Change: 1919–1939* (New York: NOK Publishers, 1973), pp. 122–23, 146–47, 218–19.

7. Jomo Kenyatta, *Facing Mount Kenya* (London: Heinemann, 1961; first published 1938), chap. 9.

8. Lucy Mair, *Primitive Government: A Study of Traditional Political Systems in Eastern Africa* (London: Scholar Press, 1977), pp. 12, 69.

9. Leys, *Underdevelopment in Kenya*, p. 31.

10. Van Zwanenberg, *Economic History of Kenya and Tanzania*, p. 30, 37.

11. Helge Kjekshus, *Ecology Control and Economic Development in East African History: The Case of Tanganyika: 1850–1950* (Berkeley and Los Angeles: University of California Press, 1977), pp. 126–37.

12. Carl G. Rosberg and John Nottingham, *The Myth of Mau Mau: Nationalism in Kenya* (Nairobi: East African Publishing House, 1966), pp. 4–7; Leys, *Underdevelopment in Kenya*, pp. 40–50; Brett, *Colonialism and Underdevelopment in East Africa*, pp. 172–73; van Zwanenberg, *An Economic History of Kenya and Tanzania*, pp. 9–12.

13. Bruce F. Johnston and William C. Clark, *Redesigning Rural Development: A Strategic Perspective* (Baltimore: Johns Hopkins University Press, 1982).

14. Y. P. Ghai and J. P. W. B. McAuslan, *Public Law and Political Change in Kenya* (Nairobi: Oxford University Press, 1970), p. 97. Also, Leys, *Underdevelopment in Kenya*, pp. 39–40.

15. Leys, *Underdevelopment in Kenya*, p. 31.

16. Brett, *Colonialism and Underdevelopment in East Africa*, pp. 186–91; Ghai and McAuslan, *Public Law and Political Change in Kenya*, pp. 83–84, 94–97.

17. Leys, *Underdevelopment in Kenya*, p. 40.

18. Rosberg and Nottingham, *The Myth of Mau Mau*, pp. 243, 249–51.

19. Ibid., pp. 80, 86, 112, 113.

20. Judith Mbula, "The Impact of Christianity on Family Structure and Stability: The Case of the Akamba of Eastern Kenya" (Ph.D. diss., Department of Sociology, University of Nairobi, 1977), pp. 69–70. Dr. Mbula is a daughter of Philip Mule and a sister of Harris Mule.

21. See the discussion of the *asomi* in Gideon-Cyrus Makau Mutiso, *Kenya*

Politics, Policy and Society (Kampala: East African [Kenyan] Literature Bureau, 1975). This pattern is also the point of Chinua Achebe's novel, *Things Fall Apart* (London: Heinemann, 1962).

22. Republic of Kenya, Central Bureau of Statistics, Ministry of Economic Planning and Community Affairs, *Statistical Abstract: 1978* (Nairobi: Government Printer, 1978), p. 16, table 19(a). For this age group educational opportunities were apparently relatively equally distributed between men and women. Republic of Kenya, Central Bureau of Statistics, Ministry of Finance and Planning, *Women in Kenya* (Nairobi, July 1978), p. 21.

23. Thomas S. Weisner and Susan Abbott, "Women, Modernity, and Stress: Three Contrasting Contexts for Change in East Africa," *Journal of Anthropological Research* 33, no. 4 (Winter 1977): 412–51; Thomas Weisner, "The Structure of Sociability: Urban Migration and Urban-Rural Ties in Kenya," *Urban Anthropology* 5 (1976): 199–223.

24. Robert A. and Barbara B. LeVine, *Nyansongo: A Gusii Community in Kenya* (New York: John Wiley, 1966), p. 71.

25. Rosberg and Nottingham, *Myth of Mau Mau*, pp. 30–31.

26. William R. Ochieng, "Colonial African Chiefs—Were They Primarily Self-Seeking Scoundrels?" in *Politics and Nationalism in Colonial Kenya*, ed. Bethwell A. Ogot (Nairobi: East African Publishing House, 1972), p. 59.

27. Sarah LeVine, *Mothers and Wives: Gusii Women of East Africa* (Chicago: University of Chicago Press, 1979), pp. 43, 46, 59, 60–61.

28. LeVine, *Nyansongo*, pp. 66–71. B. A. Ogot, ed., *Kenya Before 1900* (Nairobi: East African Publishing House, 1976). W. R. Ochieng-Opondo, *A Traditional History of the Gusii of Western Kenya from Ca. 1500–1914* (Ph.D. dissertation, Department of History, University of Nairobi, 1971).

29. The point that the role of chief was an artificial, British-created one in Kenya is also made in Robert L. Tignor, *The Colonial Tranformation of Kenya: The Kamba, Kikuyu and Maasai from 1900–1939* (Princeton: Princeton University Press, 1976).

30. Silas Ita, "The Changing Role Expectations of the Chiefs in Mbere Division: 1900–1971" (B.A. diss., Department of Government, University of Nairobi, 1972, Mimeo.).

31. Ochieng, "Colonial African Chiefs," pp. 47, 59–60.

32. Ita, "Changing Role Expectations."

33. Ochieng, "Colonial African Chiefs," pp. 59–60, 64.

34. Robert Maxon, "The Years of Revolutionary Advance, 1920–1929," in *A Modern History of Kenya: 1895–1980*, ed. W. R. Ochieng (Nairobi: Evans Brothers [Kenya], 1989), pp. 103–4.

35. LeVine, *Nyansongo*, pp.75–76.

36. Arthur Stinchcombe, *Constructing Social Theories* (New York: Harcourt, Brace and World, 1968), pp. 150–51, 162.

37. Ita, "Changing Role Expectations."

38. Ochieng, "Colonial African Chiefs," pp. 47, 59–60.

39. Gavin Kitching, *Class and Economic Change in Kenya: The Making of An African Petit Bourgeoisie* (New Haven: Yale University Press, 1980), pp. 307–8.

40. LeVine, *Nyansongo*, p. 75.

41. Cherry Gertzel, *The Politics of Independent Kenya: 1963–8* (Evanston: Northwestern University Press, 1970), p. 33.

42. LeVine, *Nyansongo*, p. 76.

43. Ita, "Changing Role Expectations."

44. David K. Leonard, *Reaching the Peasant Farmer* (Chicago: University of Chicago Press, 1977), pp. 197–200.

45. Thomas Mulusa, "Central Government and Local Authorities," in *Development Administration: The Kenyan Experience*, ed. G. Hyden, R. Jackson, and J. Okumu (Nairobi: Oxford University Press, 1970), pp. 234–36, 239–40.

46. James C. Scott, *The Moral Economy of the Peasant: Rebellion and Subsistence in Southeast Asia* (New Haven: Yale University Press, 1976); Peter Blau, *Exchange and Power in Social Life* (New York: John Wiley, 1964).

47. David Leonard, "Class Formation and Agricultural Development," in *Politics and Public Policy in Kenya and Tanzania*, 2d ed., ed. Joel Barkan (New York: Praeger, 1984), pp. 142–45.

48. Kitching, *Class and Economic Change in Kenya*, pp. 309–11, 438–55.

49. This figure is based on an unpublished sample survey taken at the University of Dar es Salaam by the author in 1975. Similar demonstrations of the advantaged character of university students is contained in Joel D. Barkan, *An African Dilemma: University Students, Development and Politics in Ghana, Tanzania and Uganda* (Nairobi: Oxford University Press, 1975), pp. 27, 28, 30.

50. Ghai and McAuslan, *Public Law and Political Change*, pp. 109–21.

51. John P. Powelson, *Institutions of Economic Growth* (Princeton: Princeton University Press, 1972).

CHAPTER 3

1. Judith Mbula, "The Impact of Christianity on Family Structure and Stability: The Case of the Akamba of Eastern Kenya" (Ph.D. diss., Department of Sociology, University of Nairobi, 1977), p. 174.

2. Rupert Wilkinson, *Gentlemanly Power: British Leadership and the Public School Tradition: A Comparative Study in the Making of Rulers* (New York: Oxford University Press, 1964). The British edition is titled *The Prefects*.

3. For full treatments on the rebellion, see David Throup, *The Economic and Social Origins of Mau Mau* (Athens: Ohio University Press, 1987), or Carl G. Rosberg and John Nottingham, *The Myth of Mau Mau: Nationalism in Kenya* (Nairobi: East African Publishing House, 1966). On the nature of the Home Guards, see p. 295. For a novel that vividly portrays the conflicts of the period, see James Ngugi (Ngugi wa Thiongo), *A Grain of Wheat* (London: Heinemann, 1967).

4. *Prospectus of the Course in Public and Social Administration for Overseas Students* (Torquay: South Devon Technical College, undated). This document was located and provided to the author by J. L. Strudwick, head of Business Studies in the college. (Cover letter ref. JLS/MG of 29 May 1986.)

5. Rosberg and Nottingham, *Myth of Mau Mau*, pp. 47–52.

6. David W. Throup, "The Construction and Destruction of the Kenyatta State," in *The Political Economy of Kenya*, ed. M. G. Schatzberg (New York: Praeger, 1987), p. 37.

7. Cherry Gertzel, *The Politics of Independent Kenya: 1963–8* (Nairobi: East African Publishing House, 1970), pp. 7–8.

8. David Goldsworthy, *Tom Mboya: The Man Kenya Wanted to Forget* (Nairobi: Heinemann, 1982), p. 29.

9. Y. P. Ghai and J. P. W. B. McAuslan, *Public Law and Political Change in Kenya* (Nairobi: Oxford University Press, 1970), p. 177.

10. Colin Leys, "Administrative Training in Kenya," in *Administrative Training and Development: A Comparative Study of East Africa, Zambia, Pakistan, and India,* ed. Bernard Schaffer (New York: Praeger, 1974).

11. Aristide R. Zolberg, *Creating Political Order: The Party-States of West Africa* (Chicago: Rand McNally, 1966).

12. L. B. Greaves, *Carey Francis of Kenya* (London: Rex Collings, 1969), p. 63.

13. Ibid., chap. 4, esp. pp. 63–66, 76–82, 88, 91. Compare the foregoing with the classic English model of the public school as described in Wilkinson, *Gentlemanly Power.*

14. Greaves, *Carey Francis of Kenya,* p. 83.

15. The respondent remembered the date as 1950, but the histories of the rebellion make 1952 more likely. Goldsworthy, *Tom Mboya,* p. 18.

16. Arthur Stinchcombe, *Constructing Social Theories* (New York: Harcourt, Brace and World, 1968), p. 112.

CHAPTER 4

1. This formulation owes much to that of Marx in "The 18th Brumaire of Louis Bonaparte." Karl Marx and Friedrich Engels, *Basic Writings on Politics and Philosophy,* ed. Lewis S. Feuer (Garden City, N.Y.: Doubleday, 1959), pp. 338–39.

2. Ralf Dahrendorf, *Class and Class Conflict in Industrial Society* (Stanford: Stanford University Press, 1959).

3. Colin Leys, *Underdevelopment in Kenya* (Berkeley and Los Angeles: University of California Press, 1974), p. 64, n. 4.

4. Mahmoud Mamdani, unpublished lecture to the TANU Youth League University of Dar es Salaam, 1975; E. A. Brett, *Colonialism and Underdevelopment in East Africa* (New York: NOK Publishers, 1973), pp. 186–91; Y. P. Ghai and J. P. W. B. McAuslan, *Public Law and Political Change in Kenya* (Nairobi: Oxford University Press, 1970), pp. 83, 84, 94–97.

5. Leys, *Underdevelopment in Kenya,* pp. 178–81.

6. Issa G. Shivji, *Class Struggles in Tanzania* (Dar es Salaam: Tanzania Publishing House, 1975), pp. 45–48; Mahmoud Mamdani, *Politics and Class Formation in Uganda* (New York: Monthly Review Press, 1976).

7. David Throup, "Moderates, Militants and Mau Mau: African Politics in Kenya, 1944–52" (unpublished paper, Northeastern University, n.d.).

8. Peter Marris and Anthony Somerset, *The African Businessman: A Study of Entrepreneurship and Development in Kenya* (London: Routledge and Kegan Paul, 1971), pp. 119, 156; Leys, *Underdevelopment in Kenya,* p. 175.

9. See also, Leys, *Underdevelopment in Kenya,* p. 177.

10. Giovanni Arrighi and John Saul, "Socialism and Economic Development in Tropical Africa," *Journal of Modern African Studies* 6 (August 1968): 156.

11. Throup, "Moderates, Militants and Mau Mau."

12. Cherry Gertzel, *The Politics of Independent Kenya: 1963–8* (Nairobi: East African Publishing House, 1970), pp. 7–8, 11.

13. Henry Bienen, in *Kenya: The Politics of Participation and Control* (Princeton: Princeton University Press, 1974), pp. 131–33, insists that Kenyan politics cannot be explained without reference to ethnicity (or tribe). Leys, in *Underdevelopment in Kenya*, pp. 198–206, argues that "tribalism" is simply an expression of deeper, class-related phenomena, but acknowledges that it has potent political force. My own position is between the two, but closer to that of Leys.

14. Joel Migdal, *Peasants, Politics and Revolution: Pressures Toward Political and Social Change in the Third World* (Princeton: Princeton University Press, 1974).

15. James C. Scott, "Patron-Client Politics and Political Change," *American Political Science Review* 66, no. 1 (March 1972): 91–113.

16. Robert Bates, *Markets and States in Tropical Africa: The Political Basis of Agricultural Policies* (Berkeley and Los Angeles: University of California Press, 1981).

17. Gertzel, *Politics of Independent Kenya*, p. 43.

18. Leys, *Underdevelopment in Kenya*, pp. 52–53; Roger van Zwanenberg with Ann King, *An Economic History of Kenya and Tanzania: 1800–1970* (London: Macmillan, 1975), p. 49.

19. Republic of Kenya, Statistics Division, Ministry of Economic Planning and Development, *Economic Survey of Central Province 1963/64* (Nairobi, 1968), table 57, p. 44; as cited in Gavin Kitching, *Class and Economic Development in Kenya* (New Haven: Yale University Press, 1980), p. 341. The average cash income of Central Province families from all sources at this time was K.shs. 1,677.

20. Gerald Holtham and Arthur Hazlewood, *Aid and Inequality in Kenya* (London: Croom Helm and the Overseas Development Institute, 1976), pp. 105–9; Christopher Leo, *Land and Class in Kenya* (Toronto: University of Toronto Press, 1984), pp. 95, 99–101.

21. Leys, *Underdevelopment in Kenya*, pp. 37, 87–88.

22. Holtham and Hazlewood, *Aid and Inequality in Kenya*, p. 113; Leo, *Land and Class in Kenya*, pp. 174–77.

23. Bruce Johnston and William Clark, *Redesigning Rural Development* (Baltimore: Johns Hopkins University Press, 1982), pp. 70–89; Diana Hunt, *The Impending Crisis in Kenya: The Case for Land Reform* (Aldershot, England: Gower, 1984).

24. International Labor Office, *Employment, Incomes and Equality: A Strategy for Increasing Productive Employment in Kenya* (Geneva: ILO, 1972), pp. 165–72.

25. Leo, *Land and Class in Kenya*, p. 177.

26. Ibid., pp. 184–85; Leys, *Underdevelopment in Kenya*, pp. 84–85; Arthur Hazlewood, *The Economy of Kenya: The Kenyatta Era* (New York: Oxford University Press, 1979), p. 33.

27. Leo, *Land and Class in Kenya*, p. 178.

28. Gertzel, *Politics of Independent Kenya*, p. 49.

29. Quoted in Leys, *Underdevelopment in Kenya*, p. 224.

30. Leo, *Land and Class in Kenya*, p. 185.

31. John M. Cohen, "Land Tenure and Rural Development in Africa," *Agri-*

cultural Development in Africa: Issues of Public Policy, ed. R. Bates and M. Lofchie (New York: Praeger, 1980), p. 365.

32. John J. Okumu, "The Socio-Political Setting," in *Development Administration: The Kenyan Experience*, ed. G. Hyden, R. Jackson, and J. Okumu (Nairobi: Oxford University Press, 1970), pp. 37–39.

33. David Leonard, *Reaching the Peasant Farmer* (Chicago: University of Chicago Press, 1977), chap. 3.

34. For example, see Kenneth Meier and Lloyd Nigro, "Representative Bureaucracy and Political Preferences," *Public Administration Review* 36, no. 4 (July 1976): 458–69. See also Ezra Suleiman, *Politics, Power and Bureaucracy in France: The Administrative Elite* (Princeton: Princeton University Press, 1974), chap. 4.

35. For evidence from West Africa, see Robert Price, *Society and Bureaucracy in Contemporary Ghana* (Berkeley and Los Angeles: University of California Press, 1975).

36. Leys, *Underdevelopment in Kenya*, chap. 5.

37. Nicola Swainson, *The Development of Corporate Capitalism in Kenya: 1917–1977* (Berkeley and Los Angeles: University of California Press, 1980); Mugomorhagerwa Mushi, "The Promotion of Entrepreneurship for National Development: A Study of Public Policies in Kenya and the Ivory Coast" (Ph.D. diss., Department of Political Science, University of California, Berkeley, 1983).

38. *Financial Review* (Nairobi), 29 June 1987, p. 5.

39. Okumu, "Socio-Political Setting," pp. 33–34.

40. Colin Leys, "Politics in Kenya: The Development of a Peasant Society," *British Journal of Political Science* 1 (1971): 313–43.

41. Gertzel, *Politics of Independent Kenya*, p. 43.

42. Mr. Anyieni speaking in Parliament, in *Government and Politics in Kenya*, ed. C. Gertzel, M. Goldschmidt, and D. Rothchild (Nairobi: East African Publishing House, 1969), pp. 132–33; J. M. Kariuki, "Election Manifesto" (Nairobi, 1975), pp. 12–13.

CHAPTER 5

1. Aristide Zolberg, *Creating Political Order: The Party-States of West Africa* (Chicago: Rand McNally, 1966). See also Henry Bienen, *Kenya: The Politics of Participation and Control* (Princeton: Princeton University Press, 1974).

2. Cherry Gertzel, *The Politics of Independent Kenya: 1963–8* (Nairobi: East African Publishing House, 1970), pp. 12–13; David Goldsworthy, *Tom Mboya* (Nairobi: Heinemann, 1982), pp. 182, 191.

3. Gertzel, *Politics of Independent Kenya*, pp. 32–34.

4. Ibid., p. 83.

5. Ibid., p. 166.

6. Goldsworthy, *Tom Mboya*, pp. 267–71, 283–85.

7. Thomas Mulusa, "Central Government and Local Authorities," in *Development Administration: The Kenyan Experience*, ed. G. Hyden, R. Jackson, and J. Okumu (Nairobi: Oxford University Press, 1970), p. 251.

8. Kenya, National Assembly, *Report of the Select Committee on the Disappearance*

and Murder of the Late Member for Nyandarua North, the Hon. J. M. Kariuki, M.P. (Nairobi, 1975).

9. Joseph Karimi and Philip Ochieng, *The Kenyatta Succession* (Nairobi: Transafrica, 1980).

10. Gertzel, *Politics of Independent Kenya*, p. 167.

11. Constance Anthony, *Mechanization and Maize: Agriculture and the Politics of Technology Transfer in East Africa* (New York: Columbia University Press, 1987), pp. 55–57.

12. Frank Holmquist, "Implementing Rural Development Projects," in *Development Administration: The Kenyan Experience*, ed. Hyden, Jackson, and Okumu, pp. 201–32.

13. *Weekly Review* (Nairobi), 24 March 1975, p. 15.

14. Gertzel, *Politics of Independent Kenya*, p. 168. My own conversations with a former provincial commissioner in 1969 confirmed that he believed himself more capable than elected officials of representing the needs of the Kenyan people.

15. *Speech by His Excellency the President* at the Kenya Institute of Administration, 15 December 1965. Kenya News Agency Handout, no. 768, as cited in Gertzel, *The Politics of Independent Kenya*, p. 169.

16. See also Bienen, *Kenya*, pp. 59–60, and John Okumu, "The Socio-Political Setting," in *Development Administration: The Kenyan Experience*, ed. Hyden, Jackson, and Okumu, pp. 28–30.

17. Robert H. Jackson and Carl G. Rosberg, *Personal Rule in Black Africa: Prince, Autocrat, Prophet, Tyrant* (Berkeley and Los Angeles: University of California Press, 1982), p. 100; Richard Sandbrook, *The Politics of Africa's Economic Stagnation* (Cambridge: Cambridge University Press, 1985), pp. 89ff.

18. S. N. Eisenstadt, *The Political Systems of Empires* (London: Free Press of Glencoe, 1963); Leonard, "The Weberian Theory of Administration."

CHAPTER 6

1. The 28 percent social-benefit/cost figure must be taken as indicative only. The wide variety of assumptions that are necessary to such an analysis preclude a definitive number. Samuel Paul, *Managing Development: The Lessons of Success* (Boulder: Westview, 1982), pp. 60–62; International Tea Committee, *Annual Bulletin of Statistics, 1985*, p. 37; Denys Forrest, *The World Tea Trade* (Cambridge: Woodhead-Faulkner, 1985), p. 76; Geoffrey Lamb and Linda Muller, "Control, Accountability, and Incentives in a Successful Development Institution: The Kenya Tea Development Authority," Staff Working Paper, no. 550 (Washington: The World Bank, 1982), pp. 18–24.

2. Paul, *Managing Development Programs*, pp. 52–62. The following paragraphs on the history and early organization of the KTDA draw largely upon this source, except where otherwise indicated.

3. Lamb and Muller, "Control, Accountability, and Incentives," p. 6.

4. Ibid., pp. 34, 39.

5. Paul, *Managing Development Programs*, pp. 56–58; Lamb and Muller, "Control, Accountability, and Incentives," p. 6.

6. Torben Bager, *Marketing Cooperatives and Peasants in Kenya* (Uppsala: Scandinavian Institute of African Studies, 1980).

7. Arthur L. Stinchcombe, "Social Structure and Organizations," in *Handbook of Organizations*, ed. J. G. March (Chicago: Rand McNally, 1965), pp. 153–69.

8. *Standard* (Nairobi), 30 May 1968.

9. Arnold Meltsner in *Policy Analysts in the Bureaucracy* (Berkeley and Los Angeles: University of California Press, 1976) would argue that the successful policy analyst should have many of Karanja's attributes. Be that as it may, Moreithi did not.

10. L. H. Brown, *A National Cash Crops Policy for Kenya* (Nairobi: Ministry of Agriculture and Animal Husbandry, 1963).

11. Compare the provincial distribution of hectareages reported for 1970/71 and 1971/72 in the *KTDA Annual Report: 1971/72* with those in the *Annual Report* for 1979/80 and 1983/84.

12. Conversations with Jeffrey Steeves, author of "The Politics and Administration of Agricultural Development in Kenya: The KTDA" (Ph.D. diss., Department of Political Science, University of Toronto, 1975).

13. Lamb and Muller, "Control, Accountability, and Incentives," p. 59.

14. See the experience of Ghana as discussed in Tony Killick, "The Economics of Cocoa," in *A Study of Contemporary Ghana*, vol. 1, *The Economy of Ghana*, ed. W. Birmingham, I. Neustadt, and E. N. Omaboe (London: George Allen and Unwin, 1966), pp. 365–67.

15. Lamb and Muller, "Control, Accountability, and Incentives," p. 60.

16. For example, see David Dery, *Computers in Welfare: The MIS-match* (Beverly Hills: Sage, 1981).

17. Jon Moris, "Managerial Structures and Plan Implementation in Colonial and Modern Agricultural Extension," in *Rural Administration in Kenya*, ed. David K. Leonard (Nairobi: East African [Kenyan] Literature Bureau, 1973).

18. Lamb and Muller, "Control, Accountability, and Incentives," p. 6. See also Paul, *Managing Development Programs*, p. 215.

CHAPTER 7

1. *Standard* (Nairobi), 2 April 1964 and 20 November 1980; *Weekly Review* (Nairobi), 1 December 1978; *Nation* (Nairobi), 11 June 1981 and 11 April 1985. There were 332,000 grade cattle held by Europeans in 1963, plus a small number owned by Africans. By 1979 the national grade dairy herd was estimated to be 1.5 million. KCC intake in 1963 was 14 million gallons (63.6 million liters); in 1979 it was 51.5 million gal. (234.4 million liters).

2. For example, see Samuel Paul, *Managing Development Programs: The Lessons of Success* (Boulder: Westview, 1982).

3. *Standard*, 20 March and 10 October 1964; *Kenya Dairy Farmer* 12, no. 3 (March 1963): 5.

4. L. Winston Cone and J. F. Lipscomb, *The History of Kenya Agriculture* (Nairobi: University Press of Africa, 1972), pp. 38, 47.

5. George M. Ruigu, "An Economic Analysis of the Kenya Milk Subsystem" (Ph.D. diss., Department of Agricultural Economics, Michigan State University,

1978), pp. 26–34; L. D. Smith, "An Overview of Agricultural Development Policy," in *Agricultural Development in Kenya: An Economic Assessment*, ed. Judith Heyer, J. K. Maitha, and W. M. Senga (Nairobi: Oxford University Press, 1976), p. 133.

6. *Standard*, 21 September 1966.

7. Ruigu, "Kenya Milk Subsystem," p. 28.

8. *Standard*, 21 September 1966.

9. Gosta Oscarsson and Rune Israelsson, "The Kenya National Artificial Insemination Services (KNAIS): Review 1973–79: Planning 1981/82–1985/86" (Tryck: Sveriges lantbruksuniversitet, Uppsala, 1981), p. 7.

10. Ruigu, "Kenya Milk Subsystem," p. 77.

11. Ibid., p. 74.

12. Ibid., pp. 75–77.

13. Barbara Grosh, "Performance of Agricultural Public Enterprises in Kenya," *Eastern Africa Economic Review* 3, no. 1 (1987): 54–55.

14. *Daily Nation* (Nairobi), 11 December 1980.

15. These data come from a survey the author conducted for the Ministry of Livestock Development in 1983 and are based on a sample of 117 randomly selected farms in Murang'a.

16. *Standard*, 10 October 1964.

17. Peter N. Hopcraft, coordinator, "An Evaluation of the Kenya Dairy Production Improvement Programme (Artificial Insemination Service)," Occasional Paper, no. 20 (Nairobi: Institute for Development Studies, University of Nairobi, 1976), p. 53.

18. Hopcraft, "Kenya Dairy Production Improvement Programme," pp. 99–100; Oscarsson and Israelsson, "Artificial Insemination Services," pp. 16–17, 26.

19. E.g., Hopcraft, "Kenya Dairy Production Improvement Program," p. 104.

20. *Standard*, 28 August 1966.

21. Oscarsson and Israelsson, "Artificial Insemination Services," p. 12; Hultnas, Wicknertz, and Oscarsson, "Mid-Term Review of the Kenya Dairy Production Improvement Program" (Swedish International Development Assistance, 1973), p. 1.

22. Hultnas, Wicknertz, and Oscarsson, "Mid-Term Review," Appendix 2.

23. Hopcraft, "Kenya Dairy Production Improvement Programme," p. 196.

24. Ibid., pp. 56–57.

25. Oscarsson and Israelsson, "Artificial Insemination Service," pp. 13, 14, 48–49; Hultnas, Wicknertz, and Oscarsson, "Mid-Term Review," Appendix 2.

26. Oscarsson and Israelsson, "Artificial Insemination Services," pp. 15, 16, 18–21.

27. For more on this subject, see David K. Leonard, "The Supply of Veterinary Services: Kenyan Lessons," *Agricultural Administration and Extension* 26 (1987): 219–36.

28. C. Sere, "Towards an Economic Assessment of Veterinary Inputs in Tropical Africa," Working Document, no. 1 (Addis Ababa: International Livestock Center for Africa, 1979).

29. Frank Holmquist, "Implementing Rural Development Projects," *Devel-*

opment Administration: The Kenyan Experience, ed. G. Hyden, R. Jackson, and J. Okumu (Nairobi: Oxford University Press, 1970), pp. 201–29.

30. Government of Kenya, Directorate of Personnel Management, Kenyanization of Personnel tracking documents, 1972, 1980.

31. Stephen Sandford, *Management of Pastoral Development in the Third World* (Chichester, U.K.: John Wiley, 1983), p. 172.

32. File Note by I. Muriithi, VET/GEN/2- Centres-General, 27.4.71.

33. Hopcraft, "Kenya Dairy Production Improvement Programme," pp. 67–69.

34. Sandford, *Management of Pastoral Development*, pp. 195–97.

35. Paul, *Managing Development Programs*, chap. 2.

36. Israelsson and Oscarsson, "Artificial Insemination Services," p. 9.

37. Grosh, "Agricultural Public Enterprises in Kenya."

38. *Standard*, 7 and 12 January 1967.

39. John Cohen criticizes me for appearing to make an unqualified attack on integration in earlier articles and correctly argues that there are circumstances for which it is appropriate. John M. Cohen, *Integrated Rural Development: The Ethiopian Experience and the Debate* (Uppsala: The Scandinavian Institute of African Studies, 1987), pp. 227–58. See also, David K. Leonard, "Disintegrating Agricultural Development," *Food Research Institute Studies* 19, no. 2 (1984): 177–86; and David K. Leonard, "Putting the Farmer in Control: Building Agricultural Institutions," in *Strategies for African Development*, ed. R. J. Berg and J. S. Whitaker (Berkeley and Los Angeles: University of California Press, 1986), pp. 186–87.

CHAPTER 8

1. *Africa Confidential* (London) 23, no. 17 (25 August 1982); 24, no. 25 (December 1983).

2. Kenya Tea Development Authority, *Annual Report and Accounts: 1976–77* (Nairobi, 1978), pp. 38–39.

3. *Nation* (Nairobi), 5 December 1978.

4. *Nation*, 4 December 1978.

5. Letter to Charles Karanja from Stanley Oloitipitip dated 21 July 1978.

6. *Nation*, 5 December 1978.

7. *Nation*, 12 December 1978; *Weekly Review* (Nairobi), 9 February 1979, p. 31.

8. *Weekly Review*, 2 February 1978, p. 24; *Nairobi Times*, 21 and 28 January 1979.

9. *Weekly Review*, 2 February 1979, pp. 2, 24; *Standard* (Nairobi), 14 March 1979.

10. *Standard*, 21 February 1979.

11. *Weekly Review*, 1 July 1983, p. 3; 8 July 1983, p. 4.

12. *Weekly Review*, 26 February 1982, p. 5.

13. David K. Leonard, "The Supply of Veterinary Services: Kenyan Lessons," *Agricultural Administration and Extension* 26 (1987): 222–24.

14. David Leonard and David Kimenye, "Policies and Project Proposals for

the Strengthening of the Animal Production Extension Services: Report to the Ministry of Livestock Development" (Nairobi: United States Agency for International Development, 1982).

15. The magnitude of the drop in real government expenditure between the 1981–82 and the 1983–84 financial years depends on the index of inflation that one uses. If one uses the deflator that is implicit in the Government of Kenya calculations of real GDP per capita, the decrease in expenditure is 7.4 percent. If one uses instead the Consumer Price Index, which some economists consider to be more reliable, the drop is 20.2 percent. Government of Kenya, *Economic Survey* (Nairobi: Government Printer): *1984*, pp. 8, 17, 80; *1985*, pp. 8, 16, 76; *1986*, p. 69; *1987*, pp. xii, 9, 75.

16. For more on this budgetary practice, see Naomi Caiden and Aaron Wildavsky, *Planning and Budgeting in Poor Countries* (New York: John Wiley, 1974), pp. 73–75.

17. The author was management adviser to the Ministries of Agriculture and Livestock Development from 1980 to 1982 and acted as a budget officer for the latter in 1982. Most of his observations about the fiscal and managerial implications of the crisis derive from personal experience.

18. Aaron Wildavsky, *The New Politics of the Budgetary Process* (Glenview, Ill.: Scott, Foresman, 1988), pp. 82–84.

19. David K. Leonard, "African Practice and the Theory of User Fees," *Agricultural Administration* 18 (1985): 137–57.

20. J. B. Wykoff and K. W. Gitu, "Cost Sharing with Beneficiaries: The Case of Livestock Services" (Nairobi: Ministry of Livestock Development, May 1984).

21. Leonard, "Supply of Veterinary Services."

22. Bruce Johnston and William Clark, *Redesigning Rural Development: A Strategic Perspective* (Baltimore: Johns Hopkins University Press, 1982), p. 16.

CHAPTER 9

1. Ian Livingston, *Rural Development, Employment, and Incomes in Kenya* (Addis Ababa: International Labour Organization, 1981), p. 2:7.

2. Republic of Kenya, National Assembly, *Report of the Select Committee on Unemployment* (Nairobi: Government Printer, 1970), p. 24.

3. Eric S. Clayton, "Kenya's Agriculture and the ILO Employment Mission—Six Years After," *Journal of Modern African Studies* 16, no. 2 (1978): 314.

4. International Labor Office, *Employment, Incomes and Equality: A Strategy for Increasing Productive Employment in Kenya* (Geneva: ILO, 1972), pp. 9–30.

5. Colin Leys, *Underdevelopment in Kenya: The Political Economy of Neo-Colonialism* (Berkeley and Los Angeles: University of California Press, 1974), pp. 258–71.

6. Philip Ndegwa, chairman, *Report and Recommendations of the Working Party on Government Expenditures* (Nairobi: Government Printer, 1982), p. 15.

7. Republic of Kenya, *Sessional Paper No. 10 of 1973 on Unemployment* (Nairobi: Government of Kenya, 1973), p. i.

8. Republic of Kenya, National Assembly, *Sessional Paper No. 10 of 1965 on*

African Socialism and Its Application to Planning in Kenya (Nairobi: Government Printer, 1965).

9. David Goldsworthy, *Tom Mboya* (Nairobi: Heinemann, 1982), p. 251.

10. E.g., David Gould, *Bureaucratic Corruption and Underdevelopment in the Third World: The Case of Zaire* (New York: Pergamon, 1980).

11. Walter O. Oyugi, *Rural Development Administration: A Kenyan Experience* (New Delhi: Vikas, 1981), pp. 9–10; James R. Sheffield, ed., *Education, Employment and Rural Development: Report of the Kericho (Kenya) Conference* (Nairobi: East African Publishing House, 1967), p. 17.

12. Oyugi, *Rural Development Administration*, pp. 11–12.

13. Angelique Haugerud, "Development and Household Economy in Two Eco-Zones of Embu District," Institute for Development Studies Working Paper, no. 382 (Nairobi: University of Nairobi, 1981).

14. For a definitive evaluation of CADU, see John M. Cohen, *Integrated Rural Development: The Ethiopian Experience and the Debate* (Uppsala: The Scandinavian Institute of African Studies, 1987).

15. John M. Cohen, "Administration of Integrated Rural Development Projects," Harvard Institute of International Development Discussion Paper, no. 79 (Cambridge: Harvard University, 1979), p. 51.

16. For a more general discussion of the issues that the IADP case presents, including an argument for rural rather than agricultural credit, see David Leonard, "Putting the Farmer in Control: Building Agricultural Institutions," in *Strategies for African Development*, ed. R. J. Berg and J. S. Whitaker (Berkeley and Los Angeles: University of California Press, 1985).

17. This view is strongly supported by J. D. von Pischke, "The Political Economy of Farm Credit in Kenya" (Ph.D. diss., University of Glasgow, 1977), pp. 231–62.

18. Robert Bates, *Markets and States in Tropical Africa* (Berkeley and Los Angeles: University of California Press, 1981).

19. Judith Tendler, *Inside Foreign Aid* (Baltimore: Johns Hopkins University Press, 1975).

20. Uma Lele, *The Design of Rural Development: Lessons from Africa* (Baltimore: Johns Hopkins University Press, 1975), p. 144.

21. *Webster's Ninth New Collegiate Dictionary* (Springfield, Mass.: Merriam-Webster, 1984), p. 329; Martin Landau and Eva Eagle, "On the Concept of Decentralization," paper of the Project on Managing Decentralization (Berkeley: Institute of International Studies, University of California, 1981), pp. 1, 17.

22. For a more elaborate and comprehensive discussion of the types of decentralization, see David K. Leonard, "Analyzing the Organizational Requirement for Serving the Rural Poor," in *Institutions of Rural Development for the Poor: Decentralization and Organizational Linkages*, ed. David K. Leonard and Dale Rogers Marshall (Berkeley: Institute of International Studies, University of California, 1982), pp. 27–34.

23. Republic of Kenya, *Development Plan: 1974–1978* 1 (Nairobi: Government Printer, 1974) sec. 4.19–23; John M. Cohen and Richard M. Hook, "District Development Planning in Kenya," Development Discussion Paper, no. 229 (Cambridge: Harvard Institute of International Development, 1985), pp. 18–

23. This latter article provides a comprehensive and authoritative treatment of its subject.

24. Cohen and Hook, "District Planning in Kenya," pp. 22–40.

25. Ibid., pp. 26–29.

26. Peter Weisel, "Interim Evaluation of the Kitui Arid and Semi-Arid Lands Project, Phase II" (Nairobi: USAID, July 1985), pp. ii-vi; M. E. Adams, team leader, "Machakos Integrated Development Programme: Phase I Evaluation" (London: Overseas Development Institute, November 1982), pp. 1.4–1.6, 5.2–5.3, 5.13.

CHAPTER 10

1. S. N. Waruhiu, chairman, *Report of the Civil Service Review Committee, 1979–80* (Nairobi: Government Printer, 1980).

2. Philip Ndegwa, chairman, *Report and Recommendations of the Working Party on Government Expenditures* (Nairobi: Government Printer, 1982), pp. 53–54.

3. Republic of Kenya, Office of the President, *District Focus for Rural Development*, rev. (Nairobi: Government Printer, June 1984), p. 8.

4. H. K. Colebatch, "Government Services at the District Level in Kenya: Roads, Schools and Health Services," Discussion Paper, no. 38 (Brighton, U.K.: Institute of Development Studies, University of Sussex, 1974).

5. Kenya, *District Focus for Rural Development*, p. 1.

6. Joel D. Barkan and Michael Chege, "Final Evaluation: Rural Planning II" (Nairobi: USAID, 1987), pp. 34–35.

7. Fenno Ogutu, "District Planning in Kenya: A View from the Bottom" (Ph.D. diss., Department of City and Regional Planning, University of California, Berkeley, 1989), chaps. 5 and 7.

8. Kenya, *District Focus for Rural Development*, p. 6.

9. Garrett Hardin and John Baden, eds., *Managing the Commons* (San Francisco: W. H. Freeman, 1977).

10. Victoria E. Rodriguez, "The Politics of Decentralization in Mexico: Divergent Outcomes of Policy Implementation" (Ph.D. diss., Department of Political Science, University of California, Berkeley, 1987).

11. John M. Cohen and Richard M. Hook, "District Planning in Kenya," Development Discussion Paper, no. 229 (Cambridge: Harvard Institute of International Development, 1985), p. 59.

12. Ogutu, "District Planning in Kenya," chap. 5.

13. Ibid., chaps. 5 and 7.

14. Kevin Cleaver and Mike Westlake, "Pricing, Marketing and Agricultural Development in Kenya" (paper prepared as part of the Managing Agricultural Development in Africa studies [typescript], Washington: The World Bank, March 1987), pp. 3–7.

15. See the incident recounted in Appendix B.

16. Republic of Kenya, *Development Plan: 1970–1974* (Nairobi: Government Printer, 1969), pp. 197–98.

17. The accepted wisdom of the time is reflected in John C. de Wilde, "Case

Studies: Kenya, Tanzania and Ghana," *Agricultural Development in Africa: Issues of Public Policy*, ed. Robert Bates and Michael Lofchie (New York: Praeger, 1980), p. 127. It is interesting that de Wilde adopts the counterargument and presses for higher food prices in his conclusion to this same article (p. 165).

18. Cleaver and Westlake, "Pricing, Marketing and Agricultural Development," p. 25.

19. Robert H. Bates, *Beyond the "Miracle of the Market": The Political Economy of Agrarian Development in Kenya* (Cambridge University Press, 1989), chap. 4.

20. Cleaver and Westlake, "Pricing, Marketing and Agricultural Development," annex table 1.

21. Bates, *Beyond the "Miracle of the Market*," chap. 4.

22. Cathy L. Jabara, "Agricultural Pricing Policy in Kenya," *World Development* 13, no. 5 (May 1985): 611–26.

23. Cleaver and Westlake, "Pricing, Marketing and Agricultural Development," pp. 3, 26.

24. Republic of Kenya, *Sessional Paper No. 4 on National Food Policy* (Nairobi: Government Printer, 1981).

25. Cleaver and Westlake, "Pricing, Marketing and Agricultural Development," p. 26. This weighted average excludes sugar, which was priced *above* the world price.

26. Bates, *Beyond the "Miracle of the Market*," chap. 5.

27. Barbara Grosh, "Improving the Economic Performance of Public Enterprises in Kenya: Lessons from the First Two Decades of Independence" (Ph.D. diss., Department of Economics, University of California, Berkeley, 1988).

28. Michael Lofchie, *Policy Makes a Difference: Agricultural Performance in Kenya and Tanzania* (Boulder: L. Rienner, 1989), chap. 3. This indicator is somewhat different from, but consistent with, others developed in the literature on state autonomy. Theda Skocpol, "Bringing the State Back In: Strategies of Analysis in Current Research," in *Bringing the State Back In*, ed. P. B. Evans, D. Rueschemeyer, and T. Skocpol (Cambridge: Cambridge University Press, 1985).

CHAPTER 11

1. E.g., Robert M. Price, *Society and Bureaucracy in Contemporary Ghana* (Berkeley and Los Angeles: University of California Press, 1975); Goran Hyden, *No Shortcuts to Progress: African Development Management in Perspective* (Berkeley and Los Angeles: University of California Press, 1983).

2. Fritz Roethlisberger and William Dickson, *Management and the Worker* (Cambridge: Harvard University Press, 1939).

3. John D. Montgomery, "Probing Managerial Behavior: Image and Reality in Southern Africa," *World Development* 15, no. 7 (1987): 914.

4. Jon Moris, "The Transferability of Western Management Concepts and Programs, an East African Perspective," in *Education and Training for Public Sector Management in Developing Countries*, ed. L. D. Stifel, J. S. Coleman, and J. E. Black (New York: The Rockefeller Foundation, 1977), pp. 78–83.

5. David Gould, *Bureaucratic Corruption in the Third World: The Administration*

of Underdevelopment in Zaire (New York: Pergamon-Maxwell, 1980); David J. Gould and José A. Amaro-Reyes, "The Effects of Corruption on Administrative Performance: Illustrations from Developing Countries," Staff Working Paper, no. 580 (Washington, D.C.: The World Bank, 1983), pp. 8–12.

6. Joel Migdal, *Peasants, Politics and Revolution: Pressures Toward Political and Social Change in the Third World* (Princeton: Princeton University Press, 1974).

7. Robert Bates, *Beyond the "Miracle of the Market": The Political Economy of Agrarian Development in Kenya* (Cambridge University Press, 1989), chap. 5.

8. Michel Crozier, *The Bureaucratic Phenomenon* (Chicago: University of Chicago Press, 1964), p. 229.

9. See Barbara P. Thomas, *Politics, Participation, and Poverty: Development Through Self-Help in Kenya* (Boulder: Westview, 1985).

10. Frank Holmquist, "Class Structure, Peasant Participation, and Rural Self-Help," in *Politics and Public Policy in Kenya and Tanzania*, rev. ed., ed. Joel Barkan (New York: Praeger, 1984), p. 177.

11. *Daily Nation* (Nairobi), 4 February 1986, p. 12.

12. *Weekly Review* (Nairobi), 19 February 1988, pp. 10–11, and 11 March 1988, p. 19.

13. This and many other parts of this political dispute are recounted in a remarkable advertisement that Nyachae published in the Kenyan press. *Daily Nation*, 25 March 1988, pp. 12–13.

14. No reasons were ever given for Nyachae's candidacy's being barred. "When KANU's Secretary General . . . was asked why Nyachae had been barred, he said Nyachae should write to the head of state for the reasons behind the failure to clear him." *Weekly Review*, 19 March 1988, p. 11.

15. D. N. Ndegwa, chairman, *Report of the Commission of Inquiry: Public Service Structure and Remuneration Commission: 1970–71* (Nairobi: Government Printer, 1971), pp. 13–15; Colin Leys, *Underdevelopment in Kenya* (Berkeley and Los Angeles: University of California Press, 1974), p. 195.

16. David Leonard, "The Supply of Veterinary Services: Kenyan Lessons," *Agricultural Administration and Extension* 26, no. 4 (1987): 219–36.

17. E.g., *Weekly Review* (Nairobi), 10 April 1982, pp. 4–6; *Africa Confidential* (London) 27, no. 8 (9 April 1986): 3; 27, no. 18 (3 September 1986): 1; 27, no. 23 (12 November 1986): 4.

18. E.g., *Daily Nation* (Nairobi), 25 March 1988, pp. 12–13.

19. John A. Armstrong, *The European Administrative Elite* (Princeton: Princeton University Press, 1973), chap. 5.

CHAPTER 12

1. E.g., Goran Hyden, *No Shortcuts to Progress: African Development Management in Perspective* (Berkeley and Los Angeles: University of California Press, 1983); John D. Montgomery, "How African Managers Serve Developmental Goals," *Comparative Politics* (April 1987): 347–60; The World Bank, *Accelerated Development in Sub-Saharan Africa: An Agenda for Action* (Washington, D.C.: The World Bank, 1981).

2. Philip Ndegwa, chairman, *Report and Recommendations of the Working Party on Government Expenditures* (Nairobi: Government Printer, 1982), p. 42.

3. Barbara Ann Grosh, *Improving the Economic Performance of Public Enterprise in Kenya: Lessons from the First Two Decades of Independence* (Ph.D. diss., Department of Economics, University of California, Berkeley, 1988), p. 46.

4. United States Agency of International Development, "Africa Bureau Development Management Assistance Strategy Paper" (Washington, D.C.: USAID, 1984), p. 1.

5. The World Bank, *Accelerated Development in Sub-Saharan Africa*, pp. 40–80; The World Bank, *Africa's Adjustment and Growth in the 1980s* (Washington, D.C.: The World Bank, 1989).

6. David K. Leonard, "The Supply of Veterinary Services: Kenyan Lessons," *Agricultural Administration and Extension* 26, no. 4 (1987): 219–36.

7. Robert K. Merton, "Bureaucratic Structure and Personality," *Social Forces* 18 (1940): 560–68.

8. George Honadle, "Promoting Performance in Agricultural Projects: Management Lessons from Africa" (Washington, D.C.: Development Alternatives Inc., 1985).

9. Grosh, *Improving Economic Performance*, pp. 377–400.

10. Ibid.

11. Rwekaza Mukandala, *The Political Economy of Parastatal Enterprise in Tanzania and Botswana* (Ph.D. diss., Department of Political Science, University of California, Berkeley, 1988).

12. Philip Selznick, *Leadership in Administration* (New York: Harper and Row, 1957), pp. 7, 57, 59, 62, 66.

13. Chester Barnard, *The Functions of the Executive* (1958), p. 87.

14. In fact, they had *all* the attributes of effective chief executives found by Bennis and Vaill in the United States. See the footnote to this section.

15. Herbert Kaufman, *The Administrative Behavior of Federal Bureau Chiefs* (Washington: Brookings Institution, 1981), pp. 135, 174.

16. James C. and James G. March, "Almost Random Careers: The Wisconsin School Superintendency, 1940–1972," *Administrative Science Quarterly* 22 (1977): 405. See also James C. and James G. March, "Performance Sampling in Social Matches," *Administrative Science Quarterly* 23 (1978): 434–53.

17. James G. March, "How We Talk and How We Act: Administrative Theory and Administrative Life," in *Leadership and Organizational Culture*, ed. T. J. Sergiovanni and J. E. Corbally (Urbana: University of Illinois Press, 1984), pp. 27, 29.

18. Thomas J. Peters and Robert H. Waterman, Jr., *In Search of Excellence: Lessons from America's Best-Run Companies* (New York: Harper and Row, 1982), p. 26.

19. Albert Hirschman, *Development Projects Observed* (Washington: The Brookings Institution); Arturo Israel, *Institutional Development: Incentives to Performance* (Baltimore: Johns Hopkins University Press, 1987).

20. A. H. Hanson, *Public Enterprise and Economic Development* (London: Routledge and Kegan Paul, 1959).

21. Grosh, *Improving Economic Performance*; Mukandala, *Political Economy*.

22. John D. Montgomery, "Bureaucratic Politics in Southern Africa," *Public Administration Review* 46, no. 5 (1986): 411; J. D. Montgomery, "Life at the Apex: The Functions of Permanent Secretaries in Nine Southern African Countries," *Public Administration and Development* 6 (1986): 218–19.

23. I owe this observation to Emery Roe.

24. Montgomery, "Bureaucratic Politics in Southern Africa," p. 411; John D. Montgomery, "Probing Managerial Behavior: Image and Reality in Southern Africa," *World Development* 15, no. 7 (1987): 917, 920.

25. Robert Price, *Society and Bureaucracy in Contemporary Ghana* (Berkeley and Los Angeles: University of California Press, 1975).

26. The KTDA's access to World Bank funds was *aided by*, but was not *dependent on* Karanja's management. As Rwekaza Mukandala has pointed out to me, other, less well managed tea authorities were getting Bank monies at this time. The popularity of tea as a target of lending was due in large part to the KTDA's success, which in turn was influenced by Karanja.

27. Cherry Gertzel, *The Politics of Independent Kenya* (Nairobi: East African Publishing House, 1970).

28. David Leonard, *Reaching the Peasant Farmer* (Chicago: University of Chicago Press, 1977), pp. 62–63.

29. I owe this point to Norman Uphoff, who has observed the same phenomenon in Sri Lanka.

30. E.g., David Dery, *Computers in Welfare: The MIS-match* (Beverly Hills: Sage, 1981).

31. For more on the importance of creating surrogates for market competition, see Arturo Israel, *Institutional Development* (Baltimore: Johns Hopkins University Press, 1987).

32. Jon Moris, "Managerial Structure and Plan Implementation in Colonial and Modern Agricultural Extension," *Rural Administration in Kenya*, ed. David K. Leonard (Nairobi: East African [Kenyan] Literature Bureau, 1973), pp. 97–131. Montgomery, "Probing Managerial Behavior," p. 919.

33. Montgomery, "Bureaucratic Politics in Southern Africa," pp. 411–12.

34. As Emery Roe has pointed out to me, these observations indicate that the brain drain from the public to the private sector in Kenya has at least some compensating advantages.

35. Warren Bennis, "Transformative Power and Leadership," and Peter Vaill, "The Purposing of High-performing Systems," in *Leadership and Organizational Culture*, ed. Sergiovanni and Corbally.

36. Grosh, *Improving Economic Performance*, p. 33; Ndegwa, *Report and Recommendations of the Working Party on Government Expenditures*, pp. 46–49.

37. Martin Landau and Richard Stout, "To Manage Is Not to Control: The Danger of Type II Errors in Organizations," *Public Administration Review* 39, no. 2 (1979): 148–56; Michel Crozier, *The Bureaucratic Phenomenon* (Chicago: University of Chicago Press, 1964).

38. Hanson, *Public Enterprise and Economic Development*.

39. March, "How We Talk and How We Act"; Peters and Waterman, *In Search of Excellence*.

CHAPTER 13

1. The World Bank and the United Nations Development Programme, *Africa's Adjustment and Growth in the 1980s* (Washington, D.C.: The World Bank, 1989).
2. E.g., Michael F. Lofchie, *The Policy Factor: Agricultural Performance in Kenya and Tanzania* (Boulder: L. Rienner, 1989).
3. Max Weber, *Economy and Society*, ed. Guenther Roth and Claus Wittich, vol. 1 (Berkeley and Los Angeles: University of California Press, 1978), pp. 56, 65.
4. This conception of legitimacy as being the consent of other power holders, rather than of the governed, is derived from Arthur Stinchcombe, *Constructing Social Theories* (New York: Harcourt, Brace and World, 1968), pp. 150–51.
5. Theda Skocpol, *State and Social Revolutions* (Cambridge: Cambridge University Press, 1979), pp. 25–32.
6. The dictionary gives as one of the definitions of the state: "a politically organized body of people usually occupying a definite territory; especially one that is sovereign." *Webster's Ninth New Collegiate Dictionary* (Springfield, Mass.: Merriam-Webster, 1984). See also Robert H. Jackson and Carl G. Rosberg, "Why Africa's Weak States Persist: The Empirical and Juridical in Statehood," *World Politics* 35, no. 1 (October 1982): 1–24.
7. *Webster's Ninth New Collegiate Dictionary*, p. 529.
8. This is not to say that all contemporary users of the term "state" use it in the broad institutional sense that is generally accepted. For example, Nordlinger restricts it to authoritative decision makers and thereby makes it much closer to the narrower definition of government. Most of those currently writing about the state use it in the way that Skocpol does. Eric Nordlinger, *On the Autonomy of the Democratic State* (Cambridge: Harvard University Press, 1981), p. 11; Peter B. Evans, Dietrich Rueschemeyer, and Theda Skocpol, *Bringing the State Back In* (Cambridge: Cambridge University Press, 1985).
9. Alfred Stepan, *The State and Society: Peru in Comparative Perspective* (Princeton: Princeton University Press, 1978), pp. 3–21.
10. Stephen Krasner, "Approaches to the State: Alternative Conceptions and Historical Dynamics," *Comparative Politics* (January 1984): 223–45.
11. James G. March and Johan P. Olsen, "The New Institutionalism: Organizational Factors in Political Life," *American Political Science Review* 78, no. 3 (September 1984): 745.
12. Alan B. Amey and David K. Leonard, "Public Policy, Class and Inequality in Kenya and Tanzania," *Africa Today* 26, no. 4 (1979): 37–38.
13. Robert H. Bates, *Essays on the Political Economy of Rural Africa* (Berkeley and Los Angeles: University of California Press, 1983), p. 113; Rwekaza Mukandala, *The Political Economy of Parastatal Enterprise in Tanzania and Botswana* (Ph.D. diss., Department of Political Science, University of California, Berkeley, 1988); Guy C. Z. Mhone, "Agriculture and Food Policy in Malawi: A Review," in *The State and Agriculture in Africa*, ed. T. Mkandawire and N. Bourename (London: CODESRIA Book Series, 1987).
14. Mancur Olson, *The Logic of Collective Action* (Cambridge: Harvard University Press, 1965).

15. Dietrich Rueschemeyer and Peter B. Evans, "The State and Economic Transformation," in *Bringing the State Back In*, ed. Evans, Rueschemeyer, and Skocpol, p. 61.

16. Elinor Ostrom, "Issues of Definition and Theory: Some Conclusions and Hypotheses," in *Proceedings of the Conference on Common Property Resource Management*, prepared by the Panel on Common Property Resource Management, Board on Science and Technology for International Development, National Research Council (Washington, D.C.: National Academy Press, 1986), pp. 604–7.

17. David Gould, *Bureaucratic Corruption in the Third World: The Administration of Underdevelopment in Zaire* (New York: Pergamon-Maxwell, 1980).

18. Bates, *Political Economy of Rural Africa*, p. 129.

19. Crawford Young and Thomas Turner, *The Rise and Decline of the Zairian State* (Madison: University of Wisconsin Press, 1985), p. 45.

20. Richard A. Joseph, *Democracy and Prebendal Politics in Nigeria: The Rise and Fall of the Second Republic* (Cambridge: Cambridge University Press, 1987), pp. 57, 87.

21. Mancur Olson, *The Rise and Decline of Nations: Economic Growth, Stagflation and Social Rigidities* (New Haven: Yale University Press, 1982), p. 74.

22. Robert Jackson and Carl Rosberg, *Personal Rule in Black Africa: Prince, Autocrat, Prophet, Tyrant* (Berkeley and Los Angeles: University of California Press, 1982).

23. Robert Bates, *Markets and States in Tropical Africa* (Berkeley and Los Angeles: University of California Press, 1981); Joseph, *Democracy and Prebendal Politics in Nigeria*.

24. Rueschemeyer and Evans, "The State and Economic Transformation," p. 61.

25. Ibid., pp. 50–53.

26. Anthony Downs, *Inside Bureaucracy* (Boston: Little, Brown, 1967), pp. 84, 93–95.

27. Kenneth Meier and Lloyd Nigro, "Representative Bureaucracy and Political Preferences," *Public Administration Review* 36, no. 4 (1976): 458–69.

28. Joseph, *Democracy and Prebendal Politics in Nigeria*, p. 57.

29. James A. Armstrong, *The European Administrative Elite* (Princeton: Princeton University Press, 1973), chaps. 6 and 7; Rupert Wilkinson, *Gentlemanly Power: British Leadership and the Public School Tradition* (London: Oxford University Press, 1964).

30. David Leonard, *Reaching the Peasant Farmer* (Chicago: University of Chicago Press, 1977), pp. 200–202.

31. Silas Ita, "The Changing Role Expectations of the Chiefs in Mbere Division: 1900–1971," (B.A. diss., Department of Government, University of Nairobi, 1972).

32. Colin Leys, "Administrative Training and Development in Kenya," in *Administrative Training and Development*, ed. B. Schaffer (New York: Praeger, 1974), pp. 161–210.

33. Leonard White, *The Jacksonians: A Study in Administrative History: 1829–1861* (New York: Macmillan, 1954), pp. 16, 349, 352–53, 357.

34. Robert Daland, *Exploring Brazilian Bureaucracy: Performance and Pathology* (Washington, D.C.: University Press of America, 1981).

35. Wolfram Fischer and Peter Lundgreen, "The Recruitment and Training of Administrative and Technical Personnel," in *The Formation of National States in Western Europe*, ed. Charles Tilly (Princeton: Princeton University Press, 1975), pp. 527–43.

36. Armstrong, *European Administrative Elite*, chap. 5.

37. Leonard, *Reaching the Peasant Farmer*, chap. 12.

38. Arthur L. Stinchcombe, "Social Structure and Organizations," in *Handbook of Organizations*, ed. J. G. March (Chicago: Rand McNally, 1965), pp. 153–69.

39. Brian Chapman, *The Prefects and Provincial France* (London: George Allen and Unwin, 1955), pp. 32–43.

40. White, *The Jacksonians*, pp. 327–29, 348–49.

41. Gary Bonham, "Bureaucratic Modernizers and Traditional Constraints: Higher Officials and the Landed Nobility in Wilhelmine Germany, 1890–1914" (Ph.D. diss., Department of Political Science, University of California, Berkeley, 1985), pp. 371–99.

42. Arturo Israel, *Institutional Development* (Baltimore: Johns Hopkins University Press, 1987).

43. These observations owe much to Stephen Peterson.

44. Herbert Jacob, *German Administration Since Bismark: Central Authority Versus Local Autonomy* (New Haven: Yale University Press, 1963), pp. 108–51.

45. Jeremy R. Azrael, *Managerial Power and Soviet Politics* (Cambridge: Harvard University Press, 1966), pp. 28–64.

46. Franz Schurmann, *Ideology and Organization in Communist China*, 2d ed. (Berkeley and Los Angeles: University of California Press, 1968), pp. 220–365, 574–75, 582–92.

47. Richard L. Cole and David A. Caputo, "Presidential Control of the Senior Civil Service: Assessing the Strategies of the Nixon Years," *American Political Science Review* 73, no. 2 (June 1979): 399–413.

48. Peter Woll, *American Bureaucracy*, 2d ed. (New York: W. W. Norton, 1977).

49. Ezra N. Suleiman, *Politics, Power, and Bureaucracy in France: The Administrative Elite* (Princeton: Princeton University Press, 1974), pp. 361, 372.

50. Alfred A. Diamant, "The French Administrative System: The Republic Passes But the Administration Remains," in *Toward the Comparative Study of Public Administration*, ed. W. J. Siffin (Bloomington: Indiana University Press, 1957), and "Tradition and Innovation in French Administration," *Comparative Political Studies* 1, no. 2 (1968).

51. John D. Montgomery, "Bureaucratic Politics in Southern Africa," *Public Administration Review* 46, no. 5 (1986): 411–12.

52. Joel Aberbach, Robert Putnam, and Bert Rockman, *Bureaucrats and Politicians in Western Democracies* (Cambridge: Harvard University Press, 1981), pp. 9–16, 238–62.

53. Good examples can be found in the heritage of police operating procedures in Europe and the unanticipated manner in which the British rejection of

administrative law courts actually resulted in less judicial protection for English citizens against administrative abuse. David H. Bayley, "The Police and Political Development in Europe," in *The Formation of National States in Western Europe*, ed. Charles Tilly, pp. 328–79; Brian Chapman, *The Profession of Government* (London: Unwin University Books, 1959), pp. 192–96.

54. Joel S. Migdal, *Strong Societies and Weak States* (Princeton: Princeton University Press, 1988), p. 4.

55. Michael Lofchie, *Policy Makes a Difference*, chap. 3; Migdal, *Strong Societies and Weak States*, pp. 18–19, 264.

56. Goran Hyden, *No Shortcuts to Progress: African Development Management in Perspective* (Berkeley and Los Angeles: University of California Press, 1983), chaps. 1–3.

57. Migdal, *Strong Societies and Weak States*, pp. 264–65.

58. Frederick C. Mosher, *Democracy and the Public Service* (New York: Oxford University Press, 1968), pp. 209–16.

59. This factor is greatly stressed by John Powelson, *Institutions of Economic Growth* (Princeton: Princeton University Press, 1972).

60. Chalmers A. Johnson, *MITI and the Japanese Miracle: The Growth of Industrial Policy: 1925–1975* (Stanford: Stanford University Press, 1982).

61. Bruce Johnston and William Clark, *Redesigning Rural Development* (Baltimore: Johns Hopkins University Press, 1982).

62. I owe this hypothesis to Ernest Wilson of the University of Michigan.

63. White, *The Jacksonians*, pp. 16, 349, 352–53, 357; Daland, *Exploring Brazilian Bureaucracy*.

64. Fischer and Lundgreen, "Recruitment and Training," pp. 527–43.

APPENDIX B

1. Max Weber, *The Theory of Social and Economic Organization*, trans. A. M. Henderson and Talcott Parsons; ed. Talcott Parsons (London: Free Press of Glencoe, Collier-Macmillan, 1947), p. 384.

2. E.g., Graham T. Allison, *The Essence of Decision: Explaining the Cuban Missile Crisis* (Boston: Little, Brown, 1971); Francis E. Rourke, *Bureaucracy, Politics and Public Policy*, 2d ed. (Boston: Little, Brown, 1976); and Peter Woll, *American Bureaucracy*, 2d ed. (New York: W. W. Norton, 1977).

3. E.g., Ezra Suleiman, *Politics, Power and Bureaucracy in France: The Administrative Elite* (Princeton: Princeton University Press, 1974) v. Alfred A. Diamant, "The French Administrative System: The Republic Passes But the Administration Remains," in *Toward the Comparative Study of Public Administration*, ed. William Siffin (Bloomington: Indiana University Press, 1957), and "Tradition and Innovation in French Administration," *Comparative Political Studies* 1, no. 2 (1968).

4. Henry Bienen, *Kenya: The Politics of Participation and Control* (Princeton: Princeton University Press, 1974), pp. 58–65, 192–93; Cherry Gertzel, *The Politics of Independent Kenya* (Nairobi: East African Publishing House, 1970), pp. 166–70; Colin Leys, *Underdevelopment in Kenya* (Berkeley and Los Angeles: University of California Press, 1974), pp. 193–98; John Okumu, "The Socio-

Political Setting," in *Development Administration: The Kenyan Experience* (Nairobi: Oxford University Press, 1970).

5. Dorwin Cartwright, "Influence, Leadership, Control," in *Handbook of Organizations*, ed. James G. March (Chicago: Rand McNally, 1965); Robert A. Dahl, "The Concept of Power," *Behavioral Science* 2 (1957): 201–15, and "Power," in *International Encyclopedia for the Social Sciences* 12 (1968), pp. 405–15; James G. March, "An Introduction to the Theory and Measurement of Influence," *American Political Science Review* 49 (1955): 431–51, and "The Power of Power," in *Varieties of Political Theory*, ed. David Easton (Englewood Cliffs, N.J.: Prentice-Hall, 1966).

6. Dahl, "Power," p. 410.

7. On influence as a subset of cause and the need for multivariate analysis, see March, "Theory and Measurement of Influence."

8. Leys, *Underdevelopment in Kenya*, pp. 198–206.

9. Dahl, "Concept of Power," and "Power."

10. Dahl, "Concept of Power," pp. 212–14; Cartwright, "Influence, Leadership, Control," pp. 7–11.

11. For example, see Michel Crozier, *The Bureaucratic Phenomenon* (Chicago: University of Chicago Press, 1964), pp. 133–34.

12. Dahl, "Power," p. 410; March, "Theory and Measurement of Influence," p. 436; Arthur L. Stinchcombe, *Constructing Social Theories* (New York: Harcourt, Brace and World, 1968), pp. 32–33.

13. Weber, *Social and Economic Organization*, p. 100.

14. Otto Davis, M. A. H. Dempster, and Aaron Wildavsky, "A Theory of the Budgetary Process," *American Political Science Review* 60 (1966): 529–47.

15. Weber, *From Max Weber: Essays in Sociology*, trans. and ed. H. H. Gerth and C. Wright Mills (New York: Galaxy Books, Oxford University Press, 1946), p. 232.

16. John A. Armstrong, *The European Administrative Elite* (Princeton: Princeton University Press, 1974); Gertzel, *The Politics of Independent Kenya*, pp. 166–70; V. Subramaniam, "Representative Bureaucracy: A Reassessment," *American Political Science Review* 61 (1967): 1010–19; Rupert Wilkinson, *Gentlemanly Power: British Leadership and the Public School Tradition* (London: Oxford University Press, 1964).

17. Weber, *Social and Economic Organization*, p. 338.

INDEX OF PERSONS

INDEX OF SUBJECTS

Designer: Barbara Jellow
Compositor: Graphic Composition, Inc.
Text: 10/12 Baskerville
Display: Baskerville
Printer: Maple-Vail Book Manufacturing Group
Binder: Maple-Vail Book Manufacturing Group